D0999704

The Church Reform of Peter the Great

The Church Reform of Peter the Great

JAMES CRACRAFT

STANFORD UNIVERSITY PRESS
Stanford, California
1971

Stanford University Press
Stanford, California

Originating publisher: Macmillan and Co. Ltd, London, 1971

Printed in Great Britain

ISBN 0–8047–0747–2
LC 70–130823

Contents

Preface

The secularization of society is one of the larger themes of modern European history. It is, admittedly, a difficult term to use, implying as it does an archaic conception of the world as opposed to the church, of the city of man or of mammon as opposed to that of God. But with historians it is something of a technical term, and may be taken to connote the gradual turning of men's minds, in the course of the last few centuries, away from the things of God to those of the sensible and measurable world, and the corresponding shifts in our scale of values. It may be taken to mean, more specifically, the concentration on man in art and letters which began in the Renaissance; the rejection, beginning in the later Middle Ages, of established clerical authority, whether in politics or in social or moral questions; the confiscation, by the rising power of the state, of the often extensive wealth of popes, patriarchs, bishops, monasteries, and convents, and the conversion of what remained of the clergy into agents of the state; overall, the making of religion a private and peripheral or, in extreme cases, an illegal business: in short, all those features of that general revolt against Christian doctrine and ritual which forms an integral part of the historical process whereby European society was transformed, though not everywhere at the same time or at the same rate, from an essentially medieval into a typically modern condition. Underlying these changes in outlook and in the position and wealth of the clergy, it may be, were changes that took place in the everyday world of economics, where characteristically feudal ways of doing things gradually gave way to capitalism. At all events, the period in which these changes began seriously to affect the life of society, the very fabric of European civilization, was the seventeenth century. It was then, roughly speaking, that the lessons of the Reformation were digested, the wars of religion fought out (and the tools and methods of warfare revolutionized), overseas expansion undertaken in earnest, ever larger amounts of capital invested not just in adornment but increasingly in trade and eventually in industry, and the structure of society so severely strained that historians have recently been moved to describe the entire century as one of crisis or even of revolution.

In the seventeenth century high-minded puritanism was everywhere on the wane, degenerating into witch-hunting or other forms of fanaticism, into religious indifference, or into the moral code we should now call bourgeois. The churches of Europe became state churches, closely supporting and in turn closely supported by newly absolute governments, leaving the higher claims of Christianity to be defended by non-conformists or the papacy. Intellectuals had discovered the foundation of states and of society and morality no longer in revealed religion but in the laws of nature. And they had discovered science. By the end of the century the more enlightened spirits of the international republic of letters were advocating religious toleration and – another sure sign of the decline of religion – the union or reunion of the churches. More significantly, deists, sceptics, agnostics, even atheists appeared openly in European society for the first time since the age of St. Augustine. But such men were not of course numerous. Everywhere the people, awaiting enlightenment, still clung to the ancient beliefs, and so religion retained a political importance which insured the survival, in their progressively anachronistic forms, of the churches.

That Russian society, being in its way a part of European society, should in its way have undergone all or most of these changes, and participated in the wider movement of secularization, goes, I hope, without saying. What does require to be demonstrated, especially in English, is exactly how it all happened there. In this book is described an event or series of events which unmistakably set in motion the peculiar and somewhat belated secularization of Russian society: the church reform of Peter the Great. Under Peter the power of the Russian church was not destroyed nor simply neutralized but rather was put to secular uses. After Peter there was no returning to the quasi-theocracy of old Muscovy. Indeed, in historical retrospect what Tsar Peter did to and with the church appears the decisive step in the secularization of Russian society. And secularization, it may be stressed, is an essential element of that larger historical process of modernization about which we now hear so much.

If the church reform of Peter the Great can be dated to any one year, it is 1721. It was then that a curious and lengthy document, at once an academic treatise, a polemical tract, and a major legislative act, first appeared in the newly built city of St. Petersburg. In Russian the document is entitled *Dukhovnyi reglament*, which is best translated

Ecclesiastical Regulation; and it was, as suggested, the principal piece of legislation embodying Peter's reform. For in the first of its three main parts it provided for the abolition of the Russian patriarchate and for the establishment, in its place, of an Ecclesiastical College. And by the terms of the numerous provisions of Parts II and III of the *Regulation*, as well as by those of its so-called Supplement, the new Ecclesiastical College (at its official opening promptly renamed the Most Holy All-Ruling Synod) was empowered by Peter both to rule and to reform the church. The supreme administration of the Russian Orthodox church had been transformed, in other words, into an agency of the tsar's will, into a department of his government, into a major cog of the administrative machine of that absolute state the creation or rationalization of which was, his military conquests apart, Peter's greatest achievement and the most enduring monument to his genius. Such is the main conclusion of this book, which will not be new to students of modern Russian history. Yet it is to be hoped that the detailed review and reappraisal of Peter's church reform which are somewhat laboriously presented here will nonetheless be found useful.

For it must be said that the *Ecclesiastical Regulation* of 1721, and the establishment and initial operations of the Holy Synod, and indeed the whole problem of Peter's church reform, have been almost entirely neglected by Western (particularly English-language) and Soviet scholars, a neglect which is all the more surprising in view of the very substantial body of primary sources which are more or less readily available. These include, principally, the legislative acts of Peter's reign, which fill several large volumes; his letters and papers, eleven volumes of which have so far appeared covering the period up to mid-1711; the letters and other writings of the lesser protagonists in the reform drama; the memoirs and reports of diplomatic and other foreign observers; and the voluminous proceedings and acts of the Synod itself during the first few years of its existence.

But this is not to say that pre-Revolutionary Russian scholars have similarly neglected these matters, and I have drawn heavily on the work, in particular, of P. V. Verkhovskoi, who for his painstaking researches and editorial labours must still be ranked as the foremost authority on the church reform of Peter the Great. Verkhovskoi's critical edition of the *Ecclesiastical Regulation*, based on the author's rough draft of the document, which was read and amended by Peter himself, is the indispensable primary source for students of the reform, and is referred to extensively in the following pages. If my own work can be considered as in some ways complementary to that of Verkhovskoi, examining (as I do) aspects of the reform which he has ignored or quietly passed over, and reassessing those which he has in some fashion dealt with, it will have been worth the effort, and a contribution to historical scholarship will perhaps have been made.

I might add a word on the plan of this book, and another on one or two technical matters. The first two chapters are intended to set something of a background. In the first, the reader is reminded of the existence of a wider European world, and of the fact that the names Peter and Feofan Prokopovich, which appear so frequently in the later chapters, do not signify impersonal forces of historical change but rather creatures of flesh and blood. So as to place the reform in more dramatic historical relief, Peter's ecclesiastical policies before 1721 are studied, in the second chapter, in the context of those of his immediate predecessors. The heart of the book lies in Chapters 3 and 4. There, the sequence of events which began in 1700 and which led in the course of twenty years to the definitive reform of the church as it was embodied in the provisions of the *Ecclesiastical Regulation*, as well as the establishment, official opening, original membership, and initial administrative problems of the Holy Synod, are minutely described and analyzed. And if it is objected that in these chapters especially it is all politics and institutional or administrative history, I can only point out again that the essence of Peter's reform was a radical reorganization of the administration of the church, and that it was the result of a series of political decisions made by the responsible political authority for plainly political reasons and then imposed on the clergy with the more or less willing cooperation of a few of its leading members. That Peter intended that reforms in the beneficent or idealistic sense should flow from this crucial administrative reorganization, is not denied. Indeed that is the subject of the last two chapters, where the Synod's attempts under Peter to promote large-scale clerical and educational reform are discussed. The book concludes with the death of the dynamic tsar-reformer, with a brief summary of the content and immediate effects of his church reform, and with a few projections as to its long-term consequences, a much more detailed and precise account of which must await further research.

All dates in this book are given in the Old Style, which in the eighteenth century was eleven days behind the New Style calendar in use elsewhere in Europe (with the notable exception, until 1752, of England). Transliterations from the Russian have closely followed the system used by the British Museum, which seems to me to combine the advantages of simplicity and accuracy. I am guilty of a few arbitrary renderings of Russian words (e.g. 'ruble' instead of 'rouble', 'ikon' instead of 'icon'); in such cases my principle has been to follow as closely as possible the original Russian without obscuring the word's significance to an English reader. Similarly, in the matter of transliterating personal and geographical names I have acted somewhat arbitrarily; but in general I think I have used commonly accepted English equivalents whenever possible (e.g. 'Job', not 'Iov'; 'Joachim', not 'Ioakim'; 'Gabriel', not 'Gavriil'; 'Ignatius' rather than 'Ignatii'), or, in some cases, transliterations from the Russian that have become commonly accepted in English – or at least are readily intelligible (thus 'Aleksei' instead of 'Alexis', 'Stefan' rather than 'Stephen', 'Feofan' instead of 'Theophanus', 'Arkhangel'sk' rather than 'Archangel'). Also, for simplicity's sake, and at the risk of being accused of Great Russian chauvinism, I have preferred modern Russian to other spellings or versions of many place names ('Andrusovo', not 'Andruszowo'; 'Vil'no', not 'Wilno' or 'Vilnyus'; 'L'vov' rather than 'L'wow' or 'L'viv' or 'Lemberg').

This book began life as an Oxford D.Phil. thesis, an admission I hope will not unduly discourage the potential reader. And in the course of preparing the thesis, and then the book, I incurred many obligations, some of which ought to be explicitly acknowledged here. For material or moral support in the very earliest stages of my research I am indebted to Dr. Nicholas Zernov, to the late Warden of Keble, Dr. Farrer, to my uncle, Mr. J. E. Cracraft, and to Professor Robert W. Lowe, a former teacher and longtime friend. Dr. John Keep gave me very helpful advice at both the beginning and the end of my work (though he may not remember the former), while Mr. J. S. G. Simmons provided me, like so many others in the field, with timely and invaluable bibliographical suggestions. But I am indebted, above all, to the Warden and Fellows of St. Antony's College (and especially to Mr. H. T. Willetts), who provided me with the material means for three years of uninterrupted study, and to Professor Dimitri Obolensky, from whose own field of interest this work is somewhat removed but who nonetheless provided me with constant help and encouragement and with the model of his own elegant scholarship. Had it not seemed so inappropriately sentimental, I would have dedicated this book to my wife, to Caroline Pinder Cracraft, for reasons which any married scholar would have understood.

The Faculty Grants Committee of Mount Holyoke College gave me money to help prepare the manuscript for the publishers. It has been my pleasure to teach this year at Mount Holyoke, with some of whose remarkable and altogether charming students I was able again to wander the woods of European history after several years of searching up this one particular tree.

J. C.

South Hadley, Massachusetts
August 1969

Abbreviations used in the footnotes

AAE	*Akty sobrannye v bibliotekakh i arkhivakh rossiiskoi imperii arkheograficheskoyu ekspeditsieyu imp. Akademii Nauk.*
AAK	*Akty istoricheskie sobrannye i izdannye Arkheograficheskoyu Komissieyu.*
OAS	*Opisanie dokumentov i del khranyashchikhsya v arkhive Svyateishago Pravitel'stvuyushchago Sinoda.*
PiB	*Pis'ma i bumagi imperatora Petra Velikago.*
PRP	*Pamyatniki russkogo prava.*
PSP	*Polnoe sobranie postanovlenii i rasporyazhenii po vedomstvu pravoslavnago ispovedaniya rossiiskoi imperii.*
PSZ	*Polnoe sobranie zakonov rossiiskoi imperii s 1649 goda.*
SIRIO	*Sbornik imperatorskago russkago istoricheskago obshchestva.*
Verkhovskoi	P. V. Verkhovskoi, *Uchrezhdenie Dukhovnoi Kollegii i Dukhovnyi Reglament.*
ZAP	*Zakonodatel'nye akty Petra I.*

CHAPTER ONE

Peter, Prokopovich, and the wider European World

The figure of Peter the Great has inspired poets, philosophers, and humble historians, with the result that by now, nearly two and a half centuries after his death, the literature devoted to his life and times is vast. It would be excessive, in a book devoted solely to the problem of Peter's church reform, to attempt critically to review this literature, much less to provide a new or revised or definitive study of its subject.[1] Yet it will be seen in the following chapters that at every stage in the process of church reform under Peter the will of one man – Peter himself – was decisive. It will be seen that Peter himself helped to draft the major reform legislation of his reign and issued numerous personal decrees that deeply affected the church. Indeed in a way he was, as Feofan Prokopovich proclaimed at his funeral, addressing representatives of the clergy, 'both your David and your Constantine'.[2] And so it was thought worthwhile to begin the present work with a brief character-study of this imperious monarch to whom Stefan Yavorskii, for twenty years the unhappy head of the church, once said despairingly: 'Where shall I go from your spirit and how shall I flee from your face? . . . everywhere your sovereign power reigns over me; it is impossible to hide from it'.[3]

The next two sections of this chapter are devoted to two particularly well-documented episodes in Peter's life, namely, his meeting with the Anglican Bishop Burnet in the spring of 1698 and his visit to the Sorbonne in the spring of 1717. Each episode occurred, as it happened, on the eve of an important phase of Peter's church reform, and provides evidence of the state of his thinking on religious and ecclesiastical questions at those crucial times. Equally, in the course of both meetings Peter was exposed to what seemed, to a son of the Russian church,

[1] In any case, the leading German authority on Peter has recently published a work of such scope: R. Wittram, *Peter I, Czar und Kaiser: Zur Geschichte Peters des Grossen in seiner Zeit* (Göttingen, 1964), in 2 vols.

[2] I. P. Eremin (ed.), *Feofan Prokopovich: Sochineniya* (Moscow/Leningrad, 1961), p. 127.

[3] Quoted in I. Chistovich, *Feofan Prokopovich i ego vremya* (St. Petersburg, 1868), p. 68.

refreshingly new ideas about religion and the relation of church and state. For Bishop Burnet, with whom the young tsar spoke at great length, was an eloquent exponent of the principles of English Erastianism, while his hosts at the Sorbonne were leaders of a movement in France that rejected the more intrusive claims of the papacy and espoused the rights of the king. Peter came away from both encounters with direct, personal, and concrete knowledge of religion as it was practised abroad and, what interested him more, of alternatives to the system of church government that existed back in Russia. This is by no means to imply that Peter's church reform was purely imitative or a byproduct of his discovery of western Europe. But since Peter was remarkably open to western influences and was at the same time no intellectual (there is no evidence that he ever actually read any of the works that were altering the theoretical basis of church–state relations in Europe: that was Feofan Prokopovich's job), it can be argued that his personal experience in London helped to form, as his personal experience in Paris helped to fortify, views that he was later to express in legislative form; that these experiences were thus in their indirect way a factor in Peter's decision, taken in the latter part of 1718, radically to transform the administration of the Russian church and to set it (one of his favourite phrases) on the 'straight path of salvation'.

The fourth and final section of this chapter is concerned with Feofan Prokopovich. There was some doubt as to where, in the present work, Prokopovich should properly be dealt with. As the author of the *Ecclesiastical Regulation* and Peter's chief clerical collaborator in the latter and decisive years of the reign, he was judged too important to be relegated to those chapters in which are portrayed, in passing, the principal actors in the reform drama. On the other hand, his career is the subject of several scholarly studies, and there seemed to be no need to devote to him an entire chapter of this book. It was decided to set out the main facts of his life and to suggest the nature and extent of his influence in the chapter that otherwise is devoted to the life of his royal patron and to that wider European world to which in spirit they both belonged.

I

TSAR PETER: A CHARACTER-STUDY

It was said of Tsar Peter, by an Englishman who spent some fourteen years in his service, that he was, 'from the drummer to the general, a compleat soldier'.[1] This is, perhaps, the single most important fact in Peter's biography. His first toys were models of soldiers specially made for him by Kremlin craftsmen. When, at the age of seven, he passed from the care of women to the sterner tutelage of men, and began to learn his letters, little wooden instruments of war – sabres, broadswords, and pole-axes – were brought to his house. In 1682, when he was not yet ten, a miniature parade-ground was laid out for him in the Kremlin. There is evidence from the years 1682–1686 that the youthful Peter, who in the spring of 1682 had become co-tsar of Russia together with his elder half-brother Ivan, frequently ordered the Kremlin armoury to supply him with muskets, carabines, pistols, cannon, drums, uniforms, swords, shields, spears, pikes, and military standards, all to be used in the increasingly ambitious war games enacted by him and his comrades in the grounds of the royal residences at Preobrazhenskoe and Kolomenskoe, two villages not far from Moscow. At the age of eleven Peter retained a foreign tutor in explosives who inculcated in him a lifelong love of explosive devices that was to have fatal results for his enemies and occasionally for his friends. Several extracts from his exercise books of 1688 survive: one contains some primary arithmetical operations; a second, a simple geometrical maxim; a third, the rule for calculating the trajectory of a mortar.[2] Peter later recalled how at this time a Dutchman named Franz Timmermann 'came to our court and joined our company' and how from him 'I eagerly undertook to learn geometry and fortification'.[3] If in other respects Peter's primary education was deficient even by contemporary Muscovite standards, his grounding in what he would later learn to call the art of war was, by chance, remarkably solid. And it no doubt helped to instil in him that love of order, that regard for regulations, that sense of official responsibility which were to characterize the mature tsar.

For the child is the father of the man, and in due course Peter's youthful war games merged into preparations for his first real campaign, which culminated in the successful siege of the Turkish-held port of Azov, at the mouth of the river Don, in the summer of 1696. On 20 July 1696 he wrote to T. N. Streshnev, a former tutor, commanding

[1] John Perry, *The State of Russia under the Present Tsar* (London, 1716), p. 279. 'The most experienced general, officer, and soldier of his Empire' concluded another contemporary, a German diplomat who lived in Russia from 1714 to 1720 (F. C. Weber, *The Present State of Russia* [London, 1722–1723], i, p. 19).

[2] *PiB*, i, nos. 1–3 (pp. 1–10).

[3] Quoted in M. M. Bogoslovskii, *Petr I: Materialy dlya biografii* (Moscow, 1940–1948), i, p.62.

him to 'rejoice in the Lord, and again rejoice! Now our joy is complete, for the Lord in His mercy has rewarded our blood and sweat of two years. Yesterday Azov surrendered'.[1] By return of post the men of his intimate 'company [*kompaniya*]' – that band of foreign adventurers, former tutors, courtiers, officials, relatives, and ordinary soldiers who were in the habit of addressing him, the tsar, as 'Lord bombardier' or 'Lord commander', 'Great Skipper' or 'Most wise Lord captain' – showered congratulations on him. In Moscow triumphal celebrations were prepared: church bells were rung: the patriarch wept at Peter's news of the first Russian victory in a generation over these enemies of Christ. A great triumphal arch, the first ever seen in Russia, was raised; and under it passed, on the appointed day, a parade of soldiers and prisoners-of-war several miles long. And behind the splendid carriages of the princes and generals, to the dismay of his gaping subjects, marched Peter, wearing a plain German coat and a white feather in his cap. It was the garb of a simple soldier. He was never to discard such clothes. Subsequent portraits of the tsar show him, not in the ornate sacerdotal robes or more leisurely kaftans worn by his predecessors, but in the ceremonial armour favoured by contemporary European princes or in the rough linen and leather of an active field commander.[2]

The whole of Peter's adult life was dominated by military and related matters. In 1697–1698, in the course of his celebrated 'Grand Embassy', he spent sixteen months in western Europe. 'His humour', our English observer justly points out, 'did not lead him to the courts of princes to observe the politeness of government, or the pleasure and splendor there: he was . . . most strictly curious in making his inspections in the improvements of shipping and trade, and the arts and disciplines of war'.[3] And it was partly with the help of the officers and technicians whom he hired in the West in 1698 that Peter subsequently transformed old Muscovy into the chief military and naval power of eastern Europe. He personally participated in most of the numerous campaigns and naval engagements of the protracted war with Sweden,

[1] *PiB*, i, no. 113 (p. 95).

[2] I refer, in particular, to the splendid full-length portrait of Peter painted in England in 1698 by Godfrey Kneller, which now hangs in Kensington Palace, London; to the endlessly reproduced portrait executed in 1717 by the Dutch painter Karl Moor; and to the less familiar but extremely fine and realistic portrait done at Astrakhan in 1716 by the French artist Louis Caravaque – all of which were painted from life. See the twenty-eight excellent reproductions of Petrine portraits in *Gallereya Petra Velikago v imperatorskoi publichnoi biblioteke* (St. Petersburg, 1903).

[3] Perry, *op. cit.*, p. 159.

which began with the disastrous Russian defeat at Narva in the autumn of 1700, reached its turning point at the battle of Poltava in the summer of 1709, and was finally concluded, most favourably for the Russians, by the Peace of Nystadt in the summer of 1721. Indeed the official history of his reign, which was prepared under his personal direction in the last years of his life, is largely a history of the Swedish war,[1] which Peter thus clearly regarded as the major event of his time. The battle of Poltava, in which he personally led his troops and suffered his hat and saddle to be shot through, he seems to have regarded as the high point of his life. Apart from founding churches and monasteries to 'mark and eternally commemorate this glorious victory',[2] he later commissioned a French artist to design a tapestry portraying the battle.[3] Proposing the toast at a banquet in St. Petersburg in January 1719, some ten years after the event, Peter expressed the hope that this year would be 'as remarkable and fortunate' as 1709 had been, a year that was forever memorable for the victory of Poltava.[4] After 1721 the anniversaries of the Peace of Nystadt and of Poltava, together with those of three lesser victories over the Swedes, became, at Peter's command, national holidays, to be appropriately commemorated 'not only in Russian churches, but in the churches of foreign nations which are found in Russia'.[5]

Considering the major preoccupation of his life, it is no wonder that Peter not only dressed like a soldier, but thought of himself as one, and behaved accordingly. It was said of him that, in contrast to the venality of his senior officers and ministers, 'he allowes himself no more for the yearly charges of his family than what he defrays according to his military rank',[6] and that 'he has neither court, equipage, or other distinction from a private officer except when he appears on publick solemnities'.[7] To the Senate he once announced the birth of a son (who

[1] M. M. Shcherbatov (ed.), *Zhurnal ili podennaya zapiska . . . Gosudarya imperatora Petra Velikago, s 1698 goda dazhe do zaklyucheniya neishtatskago mira* (1st edn., St. Petersburg, 1770–1772), in 2 vols.; hereafter cited *Zhurnal*. For the history of the *Zhurnal*, see Shcherbatov's preface, I. P. Kondakov and others (eds.), *Svodnyi katalog russkoi knigi grazhdanskoi pechati XVIII veka* (Moscow, 1962–1967), i, no. 2282 (p. 352), and *ZAP*, nos, 140, 143, 147, 150, 183, 209.

[2] *Zhurnal*, i, pp. 234, 304.

[3] I. I. Golikov, *Deyaniya Petra Velikago* (2nd edn., Moscow, 1837–1843), vi, p. 601.

[4] French Foreign Ministry Archives (hereafter cited FMA), 'Correspondance politique: Russie', vol. 12, doc. 8: dispatch of H. LaVie, French commercial representative in St. Petersburg, dated 23 January 1719.

[5] *PSP*, iv, no. 1362 (pp. 205–206).

[6] *SIRIO*, lxi, p. 321: dispatch of G. Mackenzie, British resident in St. Petersburg, dated 29 November 1714.

[7] Baron C. Whitworth, *An Account of Russia as it was in the Year 1710* (Strawberry Hill, 1758), p. 60. See also the remarks in a similar vein in Weber, *op. cit.*, i, pp. 60–61.

soon died) with the words: 'another recruit has been given to me'.[1] To the learned doctors of the Sorbonne he described himself as 'only a simple soldier'; and on at least two other occasions during his six-week visit to France in 1717 he referred to himself in similar terms.[2] He invariably addressed the distinguished Prince Boris Kurakin, one of his senior diplomats, by his military rank ('Lord lieutenant-colonel . . .').[3]

In the following chapters the solicitude that Peter showed for his old and disabled soldiers (at the church's expense) will be seen. It will also be noted that in the later years of his reign he increasingly came to rely on his guardsmen to discharge the most sensitive and important commissions: to inspect the civil administration (the regime of procurators); to take the census and to collect the all-important soul tax; to seek out and register religious dissidents; etc. In 1724 he decreed that three members of the *Generalitet* – the body of nearly fifty general officers of the army – should sit in the Senate,[4] an institution which was, in theory, the supreme judicial, legislative, and executive organ (under the tsar) of the state. Indeed, by the end of his life the *Generalitet* had been raised by Peter to the status of as it were an estate of the realm equal in dignity to the body of senior civil administrators and to the hierarchy of the church. It was the *Generalitet*, acting together with the Senate and the Synod, that announced Peter's death and the accession of his wife Catherine.[5] And military terminology appeared in the most unlikely places, manifesting the creeping militarization of government and society. The administration of the church, as we shall see, came to be called the 'Synodal command'; and according to the *Ecclesiastical Regulation* seminarists were, at the sound of a bell, to proceed to the performance of their routine duties 'like soldiers at the beat of a drum'. In 1724 the Prussian ambassador remarked appropriately that Peter was attempting to establish 'an organised ecclesiastical militia [*eine geistliche regulirte Miliz*] on the model of the secular soldiers'.[6]

But Peter's most dramatic and moving testimonial to his faith in the

[1] *PSZ*, v, no. 3059 (p. 484).

[2] At Beauvais he by-passed an elaborate banquet prepared in his honour to dine instead with his officers at an ordinary country inn, saying, much to the chagrin of the bishop of Beauvais, who reported his words to Paris: 'I am a soldier. Provided I find bread and beer, I am content' (FMA, 'Correspondance politique: Russie', vol. 7, doc. 124). Later, during a tour of the Invalides in Paris, Peter took soup and drank wine with the inmates, calling them his 'comrades' (*Mémoires du Duc de Saint-Simon* [2nd edn., Paris, 1879–1904], xiv, p. 26).

[3] See Kurakin's *Bumagi, 1676–1727*, in M. I. Semevskii (ed.), *Arkhiv Kurakina*, i (St. Petersburg, 1890), pp. 1–38 *passim*.

[4] *SIRIO*, xi, pp. 440–441.

[5] *PSZ*, vii, no. 4643 (pp. 410–411).

[6] *SIRIO*, xv, pp. 245–248: Mardefeld to the king, Moscow, 9 June 1724.

profession of arms is contained in a letter that he wrote to his wayward son Aleksei in October 1715:

> I attribute your incapacity [Peter wrote] to your lack of inclination, for you cannot excuse yourself by any defect in your intelligence or strength, as though God had not favoured you with sufficient abilities.... You find military exercises burdensome, though it is thereby that we have emerged from our former obscurity and made ourselves known and esteemed by the nations around us.... All that I ask is that you apply yourself to learning the art of war. For it is impossible to govern well without knowing the rules of military discipline.... I could lay before your eyes a great number of examples to confirm the truth of what I say, but I shall only mention the Greeks, with whom we are united in the possession of the same faith. Whence came the fall of their empire if not from neglect of arms? It was idleness and indolence that weakened them, and made them prey to tyrants and subject to that slavery under which they have suffered so long.[1]

Aleksei's failure to learn the art of war was to cost him the throne and eventually even his life. For Peter the father was also tsar; he was the crowned soldier who brought to Russia what we should call the military revolution of the seventeenth century; and it was in the *Military Statute* of 1716, which regulated in great detail the affairs of the army, that Peter, typically, first gave public utterance to his stern and un-Orthodox conception of absolute monarchy. 'His Majesty', the *Statute* declared, 'is an autocratic monarch who need not account for his actions to anyone on earth, but as a Christian Sovereign has the power and authority to govern his realm and his territories according to his own will and at his own discretion'.[2] This theory, which can be attributed perhaps to the budding influence of Feofan Prokopovich, was subsequently invoked by Peter to justify not only his assumption of the right to deprive Aleksei of the throne and to name as heir whomever he pleased, but also his assumption of the power radically to reform the church.

Peter's passion for military things was one of the factors which led him, while still a boy, into close contact with western Europeans. The peculiar baroque culture of post-Renaissance, Counter-Reformation Poland, which had been seeping into Muscovy for half a century, to be

[1] Peter's letter of 11 October 1715 is printed in the official record of Tsarevich Aleksei's trial, which is cited below (p. 143, n. 3) in the course of my discussion of the trial Peter's explanation of the fall of Byzantium, as expounded in his letter to Aleksei, reappears in an entry in one of his notebooks dating from 1719: 'On the fall of the Greeks from contempt for war' (see *ZAP*, no. 78 [p. 78]).

[2] *PSZ*, v, no. 3006 (p. 325). See also *ZAP*, no. 33 (pp. 48–51) for the rough draft of the *Statute* amended by Peter himself.

discreetly promoted by Peter's father Tsar Aleksei, more openly by his eldest half-brother Tsar Fedor, and now somewhat aggressively by the Regent Sof'ya; a culture that was personified perhaps in the soft-spoken White Russian immigrant Simeon Polotskii (1629–1680), a former pupil of the Jesuits who after 1664 became a schoolmaster and royal tutor in Moscow, author of touching 'virshi' on, for instance, 'The Virgin',[1] and initiator in Moscow of what has been called the reign of the baroque sermon, characterized by its abundance of stylistic adornments:[2] this culture held no strong attraction for Peter, or for his increasingly conservative mother. Rather, he was drawn to the likes of Franz Timmermann, the practical Dutchman who could teach him geometry, the science of fortification, how to use an astrolabe and how to sail boats. His later mentors included the Scottish Jacobite exile, General Patrick Gordon, while a dashing soldier of fortune, the Genevan Franz Lefort, became the close and constant companion of his early manhood. As he was not on good terms with the Regent Sof'ya and was the junior of the two co-tsars, Peter largely escaped the tedious routine of Kremlin ceremonies and instead spent the years of the regency (1682–1689) pursuing his pleasures and personal interests at Preobrazhenskoe or in the district of Moscow reserved for western Europeans. This was the so-called 'German suburb', and was described in 1690 by a visiting Czech as 'tidier and more attractive than the other suburbs. Only Germans [i.e. western Europeans] live here, and there are many large and beautiful stone houses recently built by Germans and Dutchmen for their habitation.' Among the merchants, craftsmen, teachers, pastors, and military officers – a community of well over one thousand persons – were to be found, according to this same observer, 'various layabouts, men who have abandoned their wives and are given to duelling, vagabonds, and people who for various crimes hesitate to return to their own country'. In the German suburb 'even simple tradesmen ride about on horseback and in carriages', while 'the military officers live most freely': when not on campaign they 'spend their time calling on one another, smoking tobacco, and carousing'.[3] These were

[1] See N. K. Gudzii (ed.), *Khrestomatiya po drevnei russkoi literature* (7th edn., Moscow, 1962), p. 509.

[2] D. Čiževskij, *History of Russian Literature* (The Hague, 1960), pp. 348–350. See also, on Polotskii's career, K. V. Kharlampovich, *Malorossiiskoe vliyanie na velikorusskuyu tserkovnuyu zhizn'* (Kazan', 1914), pp. 379–394; and on the whole question of Polish-Ukrainian influences in Muscovy at this time, *ibid.*, pp. 250 ff.

[3] A. S. Myl'nikov (ed.), 'Svidetel'stvo inostrannogo nablyudatelya o zhizni Russkogo gosudarstva kontsa XVII veka', *Voprosy istorii*, 1968, no. 1 (p. 126).

the people with whom the young Tsar Peter mixed freely and often. It was in the German suburb that he experienced his first love affair – with the daughter of a German merchant.[1] Not surprisingly, he developed the tastes and habits and skills and even the general outlook of a soldier and artisan, and acquired a technical vocabulary of German, French, and English words as well as a speaking knowledge of Dutch.[2] Nor did he alter his way of life when, in 1689, he married a Muscovite maiden of his mother's choice and became tsar in his own right (his half-sister Sof'ya, following an abortive attempt on his life, was deposed as regent, while his feeble half-brother Ivan remained co-tsar only in name until his death in 1696). Peter continued to abhor the Kremlin and to consort with his company, and otherwise devoted his time to military exercises, to sailing, and to building warships to support the siege of Azov. He took to addressing his officials as 'Min Her' and to signing himself, also in Latin characters, as Petrus, Petru, Petros, or, most often, Piter.[3]

In other words, apart from a thoroughly practical, downright utilitarian cast of mind Peter acquired in early life a taste for foreign ways that was only confirmed by his prolonged stay in western Europe in 1697–1698. And this taste was to result in some of the most celebrated innovations of his reign. Thus, while he was still in Holland he sent a letter to the patriarch which was dated 'September on the 10th day 1697';[4] and when he returned to Moscow he decreed that in accordance with general European practice the calendar was to be calculated, not from the creation of the world, as was the Russian custom, but from the birth of Christ.[5] He not only dressed himself and his soldiers in European-style uniforms, but decreed that the inhabitants of towns, both men (except clerics) and women, should wear 'German' clothes and ride in 'German saddles' or pay a heavy fine.[6] At a reception to welcome him home from abroad in the autumn of 1698 he suddenly ordered the beards of his well-wishers clipped, sparing only the patriarch and two aged courtiers; 'all the rest had to conform to the

[1] Prince Boris Kurakin, *Gistoriya o tsare Petre Alekseeviche i blizhnikh k nemu lyudyakh, 1682–1694*, in M. I. Semevskii (ed.), *Arkhiv Kurakina* (St. Petersburg, 1890), i, p. 66.

[2] Ambassador Whitworth, who knew the language, records that Peter 'speaks High-Dutch pretty readily, which is now [1710] growing the Court language' (Whitworth, *op. cit.*, p. 60). Similarly, soon after he took up his post as French commercial representative in St. Petersburg (1715), H. LaVie attended a party at which he observed the tsar speaking to the Dutch resident 'en langue hollandoise' (*SIRIO*, xxxiv, p. 102).

[3] See *PiB*, i, *passim*.

[4] *PiB*, i, no. 186 (p. 194).

[5] *PSZ*, iii, no. 1735 (pp. 680–681); no. 1736 (pp. 681–682).

[6] *PSZ*, iv, no. 1887 (p. 182).

guise of foreign nations'.[1] Soon thereafter he imposed the notorious regulation whereby for the privilege of preserving their beards his subjects (excluding clergy and peasants) had to pay an annual tax.[2] It was said that he founded St. Petersburg – 'Sankt-Peterburkh' he called it – 'in hopes it might one day prove a second Amsterdam'[3] or 'another Venice'.[4] Doubtless Peter would have been pleased to hear a German diplomat remark, in 1720, that so long as one did not talk to Russians 'a stranger who comes into a polite assembly at Petersburg will hardly believe he is in Russia, but rather think himself in the midst of London or Paris'.[5] There can be no doubt, moreover, that his close and admiring acquaintance with westerners and western ways profoundly influenced his attitude towards the Russian church, and played an important part in his momentous decision to reform it.

Peter's prodigious capacity for drink and his gross sense of humour were the result of a youth largely spent in the genial company of foreign adventurers and ordinary Russian soldiers. In 1702 a resident English merchant in Archangel described a recent visit of 'His Majesty and the Court':

> He's no proud man, I assure you, for he'll eat or be merry with anybody. . . . He's a great admirer of such blunt fellows as saylors are. He invited all the nasty tars to dinner with him where he made 'em so drunk that some slop't, some danced, and others fought – he amongst 'em. And in such company he takes much pleasure. . . . He drove and lay about 30 or 40 of the top of his nobility, old and young, into a drop pond where he put two live sea horses to them and went in and swam and div'd after them himself. The company was sadly frighted but they hurt nobody. None of them can complain of his frolicks since himself is allways the first man.[6]

And with his company Peter found it especially agreeable to mock established authority. The fortification built at Preobrazhenskoe for the mock military exercises was designated the 'capital city of Pressburg' and was ruled by a middle-aged member of the company, Prince Romodanovskii, with the titles of 'Sovereign' and 'Caesar', 'Generalissimo' and 'Her Kenich'. Thus Romodanovskii was addressed by the

[1] As reported by J. G. Korb (who was there), *Diary of an Austrian Secretary of Legation at the Court of Czar Peter the Great*, trans. MacDonnell (London, 1863), i, p. 156.

[2] See N. G. Ustryalov, *Istoriya tsarstvovaniya Petra Velikago* (St. Petersburg, 1858–1863), iv, II, p. 552.

[3] Whitworth, *op. cit.*, p. 126. [4] Weber, *op. cit.*, p. 190. [5] *Ibid.*, p. 27.

[6] Brit. Mus. Addit. MSS. 33573, f. 178: Thomas Hale to his brother Bernard, 20 August 1702.

young tsar himself: 'My most illustrious and gracious sovereign.... Your most illustrious majesty's eternal servant, the bombardier Piter'.[1] Other members of the company were promoted admirals of the embryonic fleet and generals of the play regiments (the future Preobrazhenskii and Semenovskii regiments of guards). The city of Pressburg even had its own prelate. Peter's former tutor, Nikita Zotov, was referred to by the tsar as 'father the great lord and most holy Ianikita, archbishop of Pressburg and patriarch of all Yauza [a local river] and Kukui [a popular Russian name for the German suburb]'.[2] It was a deliberate play on the titles of the patriarch of Moscow and All Russia, whom Peter continued to address in appropriately respectful language.[3]

Indeed the established church was an obvious and favourite target of their mockery. There is evidence that as early as 1692 Peter and his intimate circle of friends and officials constituted themselves, for the purposes of jollification, the 'Most Drunken Council'[4] – a play, again, on the traditional 'Most Holy Council' of the Russian church. Prince Boris Kurakin, in his history of the early years of Peter's reign, records with evident distaste the activities of this group. He describes the first of the mock patriarchs, a maternal relation of Peter, as an 'elderly and stupid drunkard' whose

> costume was made in a facetious form, not the least bit like the [real] patriarch's: his mitre [*mitra*] was of tin, in the style of the mitres worn by Catholic bishops, and was engraved with the figure of Bacchus stuck in a cask, which was also sewn on the costumes of his retinue; similarly, in place of pectoral crosses they wore earthenware jugs trimmed with little bells. And in place of a Bible they made a book in which they carried several flasks of vodka. All this was used in the ceremonies enacted in honour of Bacchus.

Kurakin goes on to relate how on Palm Sunday, after the customary religious observances, 'they also held a procession at their pleasure palace [in the German suburb]. The mock patriarch was led on a camel around the garden and down to the wine cellar'. Moreover, 'ceremonies were also enacted at Pressburg by the mock patriarch and his

[1] *PiB*, i, no. 37 (p. 28) and *passim*.

[2] *PiB*, i, no. 40 (pp. 31–32): Peter to Romodanovskii, 10 June 1695. For the identification of Kukui with the German suburb, see Ustryalov, *op. cit.*, ii, p. 350, n. 24; Myl'nikov, *op. cit.*; and S. H. Baron (ed.), *The Travels of Olearius* (Stanford, 1967), p. 280. The name was doubtless derived from the stream called Kukui that flowed by the German suburb, which was situated between it and the river Yauza.

[3] See *PiB*, i, no. 50 (pp. 41–42); no. 111 (pp. 93–95); no. 186 (pp. 193–194); no. 189 (p. 196): Peter's letters of 1695–1697 to Patriarch Adrian.

[4] See Bogoslovskii, *op. cit.*, ii, pp. 136 f.

bishops . . .; we may say, briefly, that they involved drunkenness, lechery, and debauchery of every kind'. And Kurakin describes other festivities held by Peter and his company at Christmas and Epiphany in imitation of traditional religious rites – festivities that were halted only at the beginning of Lent, apparently out of respect for the season but also no doubt because of the resumption of military campaigning after the long winter in Moscow. Kurakin points out that members of some of the most distinguished families of Russia, many of whom also served in the government, took part in the revelry, the leading roles being played by the most dissolute persons available, who were often 'beaten, drenched with water, and otherwise abused' or even accidentally killed.[1]

And we know from other sources that members of Peter's company assumed mock ecclesiastical titles. Zotov, from 1701 the head of Peter's personal chancellery, was, as mentioned, archbishop of Pressburg and patriarch of Kukui or alternatively, according to Peter's mood, archbishop of Paris or Azov or Palestine or 'patriarch of all the down-river lands';[2] Tikhon Streshnev, another of the tsar's former tutors and a senior official of his household, was addressed as 'reverend bishop' or 'Min Her heilige Vader';[3] Boyar I. A. Musin-Pushkin, who was to become one of the most distinguished and influential members of the government and who for twenty years, as head of the Monastery Prikaz, was to be virtual minister of ecclesiastical affairs, was known as the 'metropolitan of Kiev and Galitsiya';[4] F. A. Golovin, the future chancellor of Russia, was only a 'priest',[5] while Peter himself, with characteristic self-effacement, remained a humble 'deacon'.[6] When Peter was away from Moscow, when he was on campaign or abroad on his Grand Embassy, 'Patriarch' Zotov would write to him, 'To our worthy servant of Nero the deacon P. A. [Peter Alekseevich]', conveying greetings from the Most Drunken Council. Zotov once requested his 'spiritual son' to send them the 'rules and other canons' without which the 'archdeacons and archbishops' could not get on with their revelries.[7]

What are we to make of it all? It was not mere youthful highjinks, for this mockery of ecclesiastical authority remained a conspicuous

[1] Kurakin, *Gistoriya*, pp. 71–74. [2] *PiB*, i, pp. 521, 533, 628.

[3] *PiB*, i, no. 55 (p. 46); no. 72 (p. 54); no. 113 (p. 95); etc.

[4] *PiB*, i, no. 32 (p. 26); no. 35 (p. 28); *PiB*, ii, p. 610. For the attribution of the title to Musin-Pushkin, see *ibid.*, p. 464.

[5] *PiB*, i, p. 788. [6] *PiB*, i, no. 35 (p. 28); pp. 730, 805.

[7] *PiB*, i, pp. 730–731, 759–760, 805–806. See also *PiB*, ii, no. 489 (pp. 126–127, 464–466).

feature of Peter's amusements until the end of his reign. In March 1721 the newly-arrived French ambassador described for his superiors a 'grande assemblée' which had recently taken place in St. Petersburg: at one table sat Peter with his sailors; at another sat Menshikov with the courtiers and foreign diplomats; at a third sat 'the patriarch and a dozen priests dressed as cardinals, whose only distinction was to imbibe much wine and vodka and to smoke tobacco'. 'The Patriarch to whom I refer', observed the ambassador, 'is a professional drunkard whom they call the Prince-Pope [*Knyaz-Papa*]'.[1] Later that month the ambassador attended another such party, where the 'Prince-Pope and his cardinals' sang horribly and smoked and drank incessantly: guards were posted at the doors so that no one could leave; 'never in my life', the ambassador complained, 'have I undergone such a terrible experience'.[2] In September 1723 Peter and his company buried their Prince-Pope 'with ceremonies appropriate to this dignity'; and arrangements were made, the ambassador reported, to elect a successor at a 'conclave' which was to be held, with the usual debaucheries, in a peasant's hut at Preobrazhenskoe.[3]

The French ambassador, seeking a reason for this outrageous behaviour, attributed it to Peter's desire to 'ridicule his clergy', and implied that it was somehow connected with his effort to reform the church.[4] He was neither the first nor the last foreign observer to detect some subtle political or educational purpose behind the mockery of ecclesiastical titles and rites. 'Who would believe', asked the Austrian secretary of legation in February 1699, after witnessing some particularly obscene and Bacchanalian rituals performed by the mock patriarch and his retinue, rituals which included the blessing of Lefort's new pleasure palace with a pair of crossed tobacco pipes – 'who would believe that the cross, the most precious symbol of our redemption, could be used this way in fun?'[5] The secretary would not believe it. But later historians, with the whole of Peter's reign before them, are aware (or should be aware) that the Most Drunken Council was instituted well before Peter perceived a need to reform the church, and that his drunken parodies of ecclesiastical rites continued, in one form or another, until well after the church had been reduced by him to impotence. So Professor Wittram speculates that the mockery originated

[1] *SIRIO*, xl, pp. 167–169: Campredon to Cardinal Dubois, 14 March 1721.
[2] *SIRIO*, xl, pp. 190–191: Campredon to Dubois, 28 March 1721.
[3] *SIRIO*, xlix, pp. 379–380: Campredon to Dubois, 10 September 1723.
[4] *Ibid.* [5] Korb, *op. cit.*, pp. 257–258.

in Peter's resentment of the fact that his mother's candidate, and not his own, had been elected to the patriarchal throne in 1690; and 'with the passage of time', Wittram speculates further, this resentment merged in Peter's mind with a 'rational political purpose: the discrediting of the patriarchal dignity and of all ecclesiastical titles'.[1] But Wittram's theory discounts the fact that Peter was wont also to mock his own authority (the 'Sovereign of Pressburg' parody) and that of the Roman church (in the presence of the French ambassador): did he mean thereby to discredit himself and deliberately to offend the principal Power of Europe?

To be sure, Peter's own candidate for the patriarchal throne in 1690 was not elected – a fact which is, no doubt, significant, if not perhaps in the way that Professor Wittram suggests. When Patriarch Joachim died in March of that year he left what was, from Peter's standpoint, an ambiguous legacy. On the one hand, he had on two occasions directly and favourably affected the young tsar's fortunes: in 1682, following the death of Tsar Fedor Alekseevich, it was Joachim who led the Moscow populace in proclaiming Peter, rather than his elder half-brother Ivan, tsar; and it was Joachim who, in August 1689, played a crucial part in thwarting the Regent Sof'ya's plot to deprive Tsar Peter of his throne.[2] Yet, on the debit side, Joachim had never concealed his profound animosity against the various foreigners living in Russia: against, in particular, General Patrick Gordon, Peter's mentor and trusted friend. In an entry in his diary for January 1688 Gordon noted that the patriarch was hostile towards him on the grounds that 'Muscovite arms could not hope to prosper so long as a heretic commanded the best troops of the empire'; and in February 1690, a month before Joachim died and the question of the patriarchal succession arose, Gordon was excluded from a banquet in the Kremlin because, as he noted in his diary, 'the Patriarch protested against the presence of a foreigner'.[3] Indeed, after Joachim's death it was found that his testament contained a lengthy diatribe against 'foreign heretics', under which epithet the patriarch had lumped 'Latins, Lutherans, Calvinists, and

[1] Wittram, *op. cit.*, i, pp. 106–111.

[2] For the events of 1682, see Ustryalov, *op. cit.*, i, pp. 17 ff. and E. Shmurlo, 'Kriticheskie zametki po istorii Petra Velikago. Ob uchastii patriarkha Ioakima v izbranii Petra Velikago na tsarstvo', *Zhurnal ministerstva narodnago prosveshcheniya* (May 1902), pp. 241–256; for those of 1689, Bogoslovskii, *op. cit.*, i, pp. 68 ff. For the latter, see also the interesting eye-witness accounts in F. de la Neuville, *Relation curieuse et nouvelle de Moscovie* (The Hague, 1699), pp. 109 ff. and Myl'nikov, *op. cit.*, no. 4, pp. 127–128.

[3] J. Robertson (ed.), *Passages from the Diary of General Patrick Gordon* (Aberdeen, 1859), pp. 164, 169.

godless Tatars': the co-tsars Peter and Ivan were enjoined to preserve their realm from all such foreigners, to forbid them to practise their religion or to build chapels or even to speak of their religious beliefs. In his testament, Joachim made it plain that he wished to see all foreigners banished from Russia or, at the least, excluded from positions of authority in the army and government; 'for how', he demanded, 'can heretics attached to an Orthodox army be of any benefit?'

> They do not share with us Christians the true Orthodox faith, are not in harmony with our national customs, and are strangers to our Mother the Orthodox Church. . . . When Orthodox Christians pray, the heretics sleep or do disgusting things and mock Christian prayer. Christians revere the most chaste Virgin Mary, Mother of God, and often seek her help and every blessing. But heretics at the head of a regiment revile this [custom]. . . .[1]

No doubt these sentiments were shared by the great majority of the tsar's subjects. But by the spring of 1690 Peter himself was too far advanced along his special path of development to be able readily to share them: he can only have resented Joachim's intemperate attacks on his teachers and friends and on, implicitly, the government's long-standing policy of hiring foreigners for the Russian army and of opening the country to foreign trade. It was for this reason, no doubt, that Peter attempted to frustrate the election to the patriarchal throne of Metropolitan Adrian of Kazan', a close friend and collaborator of the deceased Joachim who was equally suspicious of foreigners,[2] and to promote instead the candidacy of Metropolitan Markell of Pskov, a learned and openminded prelate of the type favoured by the recently-deposed Sof'ya. Thus that upright old veteran of Muscovite politics, General Gordon, tells it, and we have no reason to doubt his word:

> 15 July [1690]. Most of the Spirituality being convened, [they] began to advise in earnest on the choosing a Patriarch, the great ones being most for the choosing of Marcellus, the Metropolitan of Plesko [Pskov], a learned and civilized person, and the smaller ones against him. . . .
> 20 July. . . . on which day it was expected that the Patriarch, being chosen, should have been installed; but no agreement was made who it should be, nor no expedient found to reconcile the parties for the chief candidates, who were now Marcellus . . . and Adrian, the younger Tzar [Peter] with many of

[1] Joachim's testament is printed in Ustryalov, *op. cit.*, ii, pp. 467–477.

[2] He later expressed himself in print as greatly alarmed by those who 'have come to our All-Russian country like wolves in sheep's clothing and begun both openly and in secret to question our customs . . . asking what is the point of this and what use is that?' (quoted in N. S. Tikhonravov, 'Moskovskie vol'nodumtsy nachala XVIII veka', in Tikhonravov, *Sochineniya*, ii [Moscow, 1898], p. 158).

> the chief clergy standing for the first, the eldest Tzar [Ivan], the Queen Dowager [Peter's mother] with the abbots, priors, and inferior clergy standing for the last. The greatest fault they had to lay to Marcellus was that he had too much learning, and so they feared and said he would favour the Catholick and other religions. . . .[1]

On 22 August the co-tsars Ivan and Peter formally ratified Adrian's election[2] – 'notwithstanding', as Gordon observed in his diary, 'Peter's inclination for Marcellus . . . whom the old boyars and the generality of the clergy hated because of his learning and other great good qualities, and chose Adrian because of his ignorance and simplicity'. On 24 August Adrian was duly consecrated patriarch, an office he filled without distinction for the next ten years. Markell of Pskov was translated to Adrian's old see of Kazan', where he died in 1698, some two years before Adrian himself died and the patriarchal throne again became vacant.

It would seem, in other words, that in the patriarchal election of 1690 Peter's candidate had been rejected by a conservative majority in the electoral council, who in turn represented a majority of the Russian clergy and were led by a group of 'old boyars' headed, ultimately, by Peter's own mother. But this outcome of the struggle was, perhaps, inevitable. For Peter, who had lost his father at the age of four, was deeply attached to his mother:[3] the previous year he had married, at her behest, a woman who soon proved incompatible and in 1698 was confined by him to a convent – partly, no doubt, because she too disapproved of her husband's irregular ways and associated herself, as we shall see, with the conservative opposition to his regime. Moreover, in the summer of 1690 Peter was only eighteen years old; and his government, following the deposition of Sof'ya in the autumn of 1689, was, Muscovite-fashion, largely in the hands of his mother's family. And there is no way of knowing how vigorously, in fact, Peter had promoted Markell's candidacy – of knowing, that is, to what extent Markell's

[1] These passages from the complete MS. version of Gordon's diary, which has still not been published, are quoted in full in Ustryalov, *op. cit.*, pp. 350–351. For similar contemporary assessments of Markell and details of his career, see Kharlampovich, *op. cit.*, p. 259 and n. 1.

[2] *PSZ*, iii, no. 1381 (pp. 70–80).

[3] For Peter's apparently close and affectionate relationship with his mother, see their correspondence of 1689–1693 in the *PiB*, i, nos. 5–9 (pp. 11–12) and no. 14 (pp. 15–16, 490). In a letter to a friend of January 1694 Peter described his mother's recent death as 'my misfortune and latest sorrow, about which my hand and heart cannot write in detail . . .'. But mixed with such expressions of grief are expressions of resignation to the 'will of almighty God'; and the remainder of the letter is devoted to practical matters of shipbuilding (see *PiB*, *i*, no. 21 [pp. 18–19]).

defeat was a personal defeat for the young tsar. Still, the possible ramifications of the episode are considerable. After Adrian's death in October 1700 Tsar Peter, who was by now fully in charge of his government, declined to permit the election of a new patriarch, choosing instead to name a Ukrainian of Roman Catholic leanings, a man not unlike the sophisticated clerics favoured by Sof'ya, temporary head of the church.[1] Peter's memory of the patriarchal election of 1690 may have influenced this decision. It may even have influenced his momentous decision, taken some eighteen years later (in 1718), to abolish the patriarchal office itself.[2] In short, the clergy's demonstration in 1690 of opposition to Peter's partiality for westerners and western ways, as manifested both in his personal life and in his choice of a patriarchal candidate, may well have played a critical role in the formation of Peter's later policies. But it is unlikely that the origin of his practice of mocking the church lay, as Professor Wittram suggests, in the events of the summer of 1690.

Rather, that particular phenomenon of Peter's reign is best understood in the context of the often elaborate entertainments arranged by the tsar and his company, and is significant chiefly for the light it throws on Peter's character. Prince Kurakin, an observer of the earliest activities of the Most Drunken Council, regarded them as only another of Peter's 'amusements [*zabavy*]'.[3] Similarly, another contemporary, a German diplomat, records in the journal of his experiences in Russia a typical example of what he considered Peter's 'humour', when 'the Czar was pleased to add to the solemnities of the nuptials between his niece and the Duke of Courland [in 1710] the diversion of a wedding of a couple of dwarfs'. The latter event took place two days after the former, Peter himself giving away the bride on both occasions: 'it is easy to imagine', the diplomat assures us, 'how much the Czar and the rest of the Company were delighted at the comical capers, strange grimaces, and odd postures of that medley of pigmies'.[4] Elsewhere in his journal Weber graphically describes a 'great masquerade' held in St. Petersburg in January 1715 for which preparations had been made for three months. The occasion was the 'wedding' of the aged 'Prince-Pope', Nikita Zotov, with a buxom young widow; 'and the nuptials of this extraordinary couple were solemnized by the Court in masks or mock-shew'. No less than four hundred people of both sexes joined in the fun:

[1] See below, pp. 113 ff. [2] Below, pp. 147 ff. [3] Kurakin, *Gistoriya*, pp. 71 ff.
[4] Weber, *op. cit.*, pp. 285–289.

> The four persons appointed to invite the guests were the greatest stammerers that could be found. Old decrepit men who were not able to walk or stand had been picked to serve for bridesmen, stewards, and waiters. There were four running footmen who had been troubled with gout most of their lifetime, and were fat and bulky. . . . The Mock-Czar of Moscow [Prince Romodanovskii], who was dressed like King David, was carried on a sled, to the four corners of which were tied as many bears, which being prikt with goads by fellows purposefully appointed for it made such a frightful roaring as well suited the confused and horrible dinn raised by the disagreeing instruments of the rest of the Company.
>
> The Czar himself was dressed like a Boor [peasant] of Frizeland, and skilfully beat a drum in company with three generals. . . .

The happy couple were married by an ancient and blind priest and feted for several days on end at Peter's pleasure palace. 'Thus much may suffice to show', Weber concludes, 'that the Czar among all the cares of government knows how to set apart some days for the relaxation of his mind, and how ingenious he is in the contrivance of those diversions'.[1]

But was the cause of Peter's indulgence in these 'oppressive, exhausting festivities', which were 'indecent to the point of cynicism', merely his 'need for vulgar dissipation after a hard day's work? Or was it', the historian Klyuchevskii asks, 'his habit of not reflecting on his conduct?' Rejecting the attempts of some foreign observers to see an ulterior motive in these 'indecencies', Klyuchevskii reduces the matter to a question of temperament. Peter's father, he reminds us, displayed a taste for buffoonery. Similarly, 'with Peter and his company it was more a matter of playing the fool than of creating conscious parodies. They mocked at everything, sparing neither tradition nor popular sentiment nor their own dignity; they were like children who imitate the words, gestures, and even the facial expressions of adults without ever meaning to criticize or insult them'.[2] But Klyuchevskii, it must be said, has dealt no more profoundly with the problem than have the contemporary observers cited above. For if these 'oppressive festivities' were not inspired by any overt political or educational purpose and were not, in particular, directly related to Peter's ecclesiastical policies, they do tell us something of the man, and are not devoid of a darker significance. They speak, loudly and clearly, of a gross, even sadistic sense of humour; of a mocking distaste, amounting to contempt,

[1] Weber, *op. cit.*, pp. 89–91.
[2] V. O. Klyuchevskii, *Sochineniya* (Moscow, 1956–1959), iv, pp. 39–41.

for all forms of ritual; of a total indifference, moreover, to the sensibilities of those for whom the ritual of traditional Muscovite life remained meaningful and precious. Elements of scepticism, satire, irony, indeed of cynicism were never absent from Peter's entertainments – signs, it may be, of an awareness of the fragility or possible futility of all human institutions or enterprises; indications, perhaps, of a sense of disillusionment, of disgust, or even of despair. Above all, it is Peter's sense of alienation from the society in which he lived and over which he ruled that is revealed in these accounts of his amusements, a factor which no doubt did as much to create the character of the 'tsar-reformer' as it did to arouse the hostility, both active and passive, of his increasingly bewildered subjects.

We have only to consider the early testimony in this connection of Father (*Starets*) Avraamii, who was no fool. Nor was he a hide-bound traditionalist selfishly reacting to real or imagined threats to his personal security. For most of his life (since 1660) he had been a dedicated monk and then igumen (abbot) of the Andreevskii monastery outside Moscow, which was founded by a favourite of Tsar Aleksei, boasted a school for clergy, and had become a centre, owing to Avraamii's presence there, for mendicants and pilgrims of all ranks and classes, from members of the highest court circles – including the tsar's own family – to more humble tradesmen and artisans. Indeed, Avraamii was a patron of the new learning which had been seeping in from the west, as evidenced by the references in his writings to the 'natural laws' on which the tsar's authority rested and perhaps also by the distinction he drew between pious tsars, who must be followed, and unjust ones, who must be shunned. An interest in monetary reform had brought him into contact with that marvellous entrepreneur of peasant origins and self-taught economist, who was then a worker at the mint, Ivan Pososhkov. But in the later 1690's, reflecting on the first years of Peter's personal rule, Avraamii was a troubled man, and had the courage and the compassion for his equally troubled clients openly to say so. In January 1697 he submitted certain notes (*tetradi*) which he had written to Peter himself, whom he had first met as a child visitor to his monastery and whom only a few years before he had accompanied to Lake Pereyaslavl', where Peter had sailed while Avraamii talked of 'monetary matters'. And in his notes Avraamii said that people were unhappy with Peter's first independent measures, that instead of busying himself with state affairs he had given himself up to activities that were often 'displeasing to God', that everyone had hoped that when he married he would become 'like a mature man, whence all would be governed for the better', but that Peter had continued to devote himself to 'unseemly and unnecessary games' and instead of an auspicious, promising start to his reign had produced widespread sadness and grief by his 'ridiculous talk and jokes and actions displeasing to God'. According to Avraamii, there was serious doubt abroad as to whether any good could come of this reign, and so he was laying before the tsar this reminder of his heavy duties as judge and ruler, strongly implying that the delays and inefficiency and even corruption in the civil administration were due to Peter's neglect and personal conduct. And Avraamii did not confine himself to adverse criticisms but went on to express certain general wishes: that the tsar would behave as befit his high rank; that he would use his influence and power to improve the state of the clergy, so that only 'learned and intelligent' men were consecrated bishops and ordained priests; that he would appoint only 'able, intelligent, and just' men to the government; that he would cut back the expenditure of his household and lower taxes and take other measures to cope with the rising prices. Avraamii concluded by saying that many people felt as he did but were afraid to complain openly; that in his opinion 'the time has come and the hour drawn nigh when these evils must be shunned and good deeds begun'. For his pains he was promptly arrested and interrogated in the Preobrazhenskii Prikaz, the increasingly busy office of Peter's political police founded in the village of his boyhood games and headed by his jolly mock-tsar, Prince Romodanovskii. Avraamii was tortured until he revealed the names of everyone who had complained to him and then was incarcerated in a distant monastery. He was lucky. Only a few years later, when Peter's opponents had become more numerous and occasionally violent, he would have been executed without regard for his age or calling.[1]

Not everything Avraamii had said to him, for instance his suggestions regarding the clergy, was lost on Peter, who soon (March 1697) went off on his prolonged tour of western Europe. But to the end of his life Peter seems never to have grasped the essence of Avraamii's plea: that the tsar must pay heed to his subject's feelings, especially to their moral and religious scruples. Having little or no personal discipline, having a gargantuan capacity for drink and fun and games, and perhaps only dimly conscious of what he was doing, Peter continued

[1] For Avraamii's *tetradi* and the original record of his interrogation, see B. B. Kafengauz, *I. I. Pososhkov: zhizn' i deyatel'nost'* (Moscow, 1951), chap. iii and pp. 174–182.

with his motley company to indulge in their drunken parodies, and so to trample on the symbols of a whole way of life. And to the end of his reign Peter continued to regard those who were thereby offended as obstinate children who would not see that most things western or new were better than most things Russian or old, that in Russia radical reform had become urgently necessary. To preserve our perspective, and to understand more fully the psychological motor of his policies, it is worth remembering this darker side of Peter's character, this possibly tragic flaw in the founder of the Russian Empire. It was not appreciated by his friends and admirers, by his closest collaborators and immediate heirs and earliest historians, whose picture of the reign was deeply coloured by Peter's own views and shot through with the assumptions of the Early Enlightenment.[1]

It has been suggested that 'from a simple psychological point of view' Peter's 'celebrated masquerades . . . were not incompatible with a rough, elementary, sometimes incoherent, but sincere religious feeling'.[2] To be sure, this soldier-monarch, this royal artisan with his predilection for foreign ways and vulgar habit of mocking the church, remained to the day of his death a Russian Orthodox Christian. Peter was, in modern Soviet parlance, a 'believer'. But in contemporary Russia it would have been difficult to find a man who was not a believer; and as tsar of Russia Peter could hardly have professed to belong to other than the established church.

Yet Peter clearly did not possess that quality of faithful, devoted, ardently reverential, longwinded, churchgoing, even mystical piety (*blagochestie*) which characterized the religious life of perhaps a majority of his subjects, as it had that of his late and much lamented father, the 'most pious' Tsar Aleksei, a man 'strict in his devotions and a savourer of his religion'.[3] Tsar Peter, Captain Perry observed to his satisfaction,

[1] See for example J. Staehlin's *Original Anecdotes of Peter the Great, collected from the conversation of several persons of distinction at Petersburg* (London, 1787): some 110 anecdotes assiduously gathered from ten to twenty years after Peter's death which provide good evidence of the impression he had made on his contemporaries and of his reputation among the ruling circles of Russia in the first half of the eighteenth century. See also Voltaire's celebrated *Histoire de l'Empire de Russie sous Pierre le Grand* (n.p., 1765), which was commissioned by Peter's daughter, Empress Elizabeth; and Captain John Perry's memoir of fourteen years in Peter's service (Perry, *op. cit.*). All three works were widely read in the eighteenth century.

[2] S. Blanc, 'L'Église russe à l'aube du "Siècle des Lumières"', *Annales Économies Sociétés Civilisations*, xx (May–June 1965), p. 443.

[3] S. Collins (Tsar Aleksei's English physician), *The Present State of Russia. In a letter to a Friend at London* (London, 1671), p. 44. Aleksei's great piety was commented on by most

'has a more rational sense of God and religion'.[1] 'Reason', wrote Peter himself near the end of his life, 'is above all the virtues, for without reason virtue is nothing'.[2] 'His natural great genius', remarked Thomas Consett, chaplain to the British Factory in St. Petersburg in the latter years of Peter's reign, 'led him very early in his life to give himself satisfaction in the doctrines and discipline of the Greek church; and his travels afterwards gave him the opportunity of examining into the doctrines of foreign churches, and of comparing them with his own: by which inquiries he rub'd off the rust of that bigotry to his own religion which his people seem generally to have contracted; and as was seen in all his conversation, he was both an impartial and excellent judge of any controverted points in religion'.[3] Indeed, 'he was not ashamed, as some are, to take the greatest pleasure and delight in hearing and talking of religious matters. He made it his business frequently to inform erroneous and doubtful consciences, to free them from the bonds of superstition, and to lead them to knowledge of the truth . . .; and for this purpose he always carried with him a ready stock of theology, knew perfectly the doctrines of Scripture, and knew by heart, in particular, all the Epistles of St. Paul'. So said Feofan Prokopovich, who had reason to know.[4] We may conclude that if by the end of his life Peter had come to believe in the primacy of reason, he had not thereby abandoned religion.

We know that apart from the ability to read and write Peter's primary education had provided him with a knowledge of Scripture, the psalter, the book of hours, St. John Chryostom's commentaries on the Acts of the Apostles, as well as the usual smattering of history, geography, and pre-Copernician 'cosmography'.[5] And Peter's lifelong habit of quoting Scripture and of invoking God and the saints attests to the fact that this primary religious instruction had taken root in his mind and was never rejected by him. His simple soldier's faith – it was

contemporary observers from the more secularized parts of the world: for instance, by an Orthodox monk from the Middle East (Paul of Aleppo, *The Travels of Macarius*, trans. F. C. Belfour [London, 1829–1836], i, p. 391; ii, p. 252) and by a German scholar and diplomat (Baron, *op. cit.*, p. 175).

[1] Perry, *op. cit.*, p. 223.

[2] *ZAP*, no. 211 (pp. 151–152).

[3] T. Consett, *The Present State and Regulations of the Church of Russia* (London, 1729), p. xv.

[4] Quoted in *ibid.*, p. 325. I have somewhat modernized Consett's translation of this part of Prokopovich's sermon on Peter's nameday, 1725, on the basis of the Russian text in Eremin, *op. cit.*, pp. 129 ff. See also the British Museum's copy of same printed July 1725 at St. Petersburg (cat. no. 590.e.18[10]).

[5] Bogoslovskii, *op. cit.*, p. 56; I. Smolitsch, *Geschichte der Russischen Kirche* (Leiden, 1964), p. 67.

perhaps never anything more than that – is strikingly revealed in his early letters to close friends and officials, many of whom were, ironically, charter members of the Most Drunken Council: thus, 'Min Her heilege Vader [T. N. Streshnev]. Now with St. Paul rejoice in the Lord, and again I say rejoice . . . Azov has surrendered';[1] 'My friend [Menshikov, the favourite]. . . . Hope, it seems, is from God. God grant us more of it';[2] 'Min Her General Feltmarshzal [Sheremetev]. We are extremely pleased by your deeds, which the Lord has granted you for having rendered Him praise. . . . God grant that in future we hear such news [of victory over the Swedes] from you';[3] 'Her Bruder [Musin-Pushkin]. . . . This [the conquest of Nöteborg] has come about outside of all human determination; one must attribute this miracle to the glory of God alone'.[4] Reviewing, in the last year of his life, the achievements of his reign, Peter wrote: 'All other nations have a policy of maintaining a balance of power among their neighbours, but especially of preventing us from achieving enlightenment in all things, particularly military things; but in this [the latter] they have not succeeded. . . . This is truly a miracle from God; therein it can be seen that all human designs are as nothing before the will of God'.[5]

And like his tastes and sense of humour, Peter's religious habits and attitudes were no doubt influenced by his early and extensive contact with the citizens of the German suburb. Equally, it is doubtless significant that owing to circumstances largely beyond his control he was in his youth able to avoid the daily participation in religious rites that was normally expected of a tsar. Already in 1698–1699 the Austrian secretary of legation would notice that Peter on the one hand willingly stood as godfather to the son of the Danish envoy while on the other he summarily cancelled various of the religious ceremonies that traditionally took place in Moscow.[6] In fact, Peter's peripatetic and intensely active mode of living and ruling his country encouraged him to dispense with tedious ceremonial, while his taste for foreign ways developed in him that quality of religious tolerance which was praised above by the Reverend Consett. But if, for these and other reasons, his people tended to regard him as anti-religious (as early as 1700 extremists were calling him Antichrist), foreigners whom Peter met were prone to mistake his attitudes for a disposition to convert to their religion. In Novem-

[1] *PiB*, i, no. 113 (p. 95). [2] *PiB*, ii, no. 410 (p. 17). [3] *PiB*, ii, no. 445 (p. 79).
[4] *PiB*, ii, no. 451 (p. 91). [5] Quoted in Wittram, *op. cit.*, ii, pp. 193 f.
[6] Korb, *op. cit.*, pp. 182, 259.

ber 1697 the minister of the English Presbyterian church at Rotterdam, feeding on rumours arising from Peter's visit to Holland, informed a correspondent in London that 'the Muscovite Caesar or Czar 'tis said . . . is better verst in the points of religion than we should imagine, and inclines more to the Reformed than the Romish'.[1] The previous May a diplomat reported that Peter had remarked during a visit to the court of Brandenburg that he favoured the 'reformed religion on the question of predestination'.[2] On the basis of Peter's conversation during his stay in Vienna in the summer of 1698, however, the Spanish ambassador to the Imperial court advised the Vatican that a 'reunion' of the Russian and Roman churches was imminent.[3]

There can be no doubt that for Peter any talk of union with Rome was at best a diplomatic gambit employed to extract concessions from the Catholic powers: his personal dislike of Roman Catholicism will become clear in the following pages. It will also be seen subsequently that in practice Tsar Peter's religious tolerance had somewhat arbitrary and fixed limits. Yet there is a sense in which it could be said with justice that he inclined to the 'reformed religion' as opposed to the traditional teaching of the Russian Orthodox church. That is, Peter tended to stress the moral and educational role of the clergy at the expense of their liturgical or sacramental office, and to reduce the essentials of the Christian religion to an ill-defined set of moral precepts. It was a reflection both of his simple soldier's faith and of his political and utilitarian outlook on life.

By October 1700 he was informing Patriarch Adrian that the educational standards of the clergy must be improved: 'evangelical instruction and its light, that is man's knowledge of God, is more necessary than anything else even in this life. And from the seminary it would spread to the people, and satisfy their every need. . . . For just as faith without deeds and deeds without faith are equally dead', Peter insisted, 'so words without acts and improper and unnecessary labour are equally useless'.[4] He particularly deplored what he regarded as hypocrisy and an excessive attachment to ritual; an entry in one of his notebooks, dating from 1705, reads: 'From Matthew chapter 15 about

[1] J. R. Tanner (ed.), *Private Correspondence and Miscellaneous Papers of Samuel Pepys* (London, 1926), i, p. 144: Joseph Hill to Pepys, 11 November 1697.

[2] Quoted in Bogoslovskii, *op. cit.*, ii, p. 78.

[3] A. Theiner (ed.), *Monuments historiques relatifs aux règnes d'Alexis Michaélowitch, Féodor III et Pierre le Grand . . . Extraits des archives du Vatican et de Naples* (Rome, 1859), no. 299 (p. 375).

[4] *ZAP*, no. 4 (pp. 33–34).

what goes into the mouth'.[1] There is evidence, too, that Peter had conceived a certain regard for the figure of Martin Luther: an entry in his notebook of 1711 records that 'Luther was born in 1483 and died in 1546. He lived 63 years and has been dead for 165 years'.[2] However, the reason for this attention to Luther is suggested by a remark Peter is alleged to have made when recalling his visit to Wittenberg: 'The man really deserved [his monument]: he was of great use to many princes who were cleverer than the rest, and he courageously defied the pope and his army'.[3]

There are a number of documents illustrating Peter's religious views in the latter years of his reign, the years in which he embarked on his definitive reform of the church. The first of the 'Military articles' of the *Military Statute* of 1716, which Peter helped to draft, is entitled 'On the fear of God'. It provides an illuminating glimpse of the faith of the soldier-monarch:

> Although it is generally required of every Christian to lead a Christian and honourable life and not to maintain a hypocritical fear of God, it behooves soldiers and military persons to respect and heed this [precept] with special zeal; for God has called them to a station in life in which it often happens that not a single hour is safe, and in which their lives are constantly exposed to the utmost dangers in the service of their Sovereign. And since every blessing, victory, and good fortune proceeds from almighty God, the one true Source of all good things and the Giver of victories, to Him must we pray and in Him have hope for continued good fortune in all things and in all undertakings. Therefore all idolatry and superstition are absolutely forbidden and absolutely will not be permitted or tolerated in camp or anywhere else. . . .[4]

Equally, Peter's notion of the overriding importance of morality is exemplified in a speech he gave at a banquet held in November 1719 to mark the feast of St. Catherine. As reported by the French commercial representative in St. Petersburg,

[1] *PiB*, iii, no. 998 (p. 532). Cf. Matthew 15:1–11: 'Then the Pharisees and scribes came to Jesus from Jerusalem and said, "Why do your disciples transgress the tradition of the elders? For they do not wash their hands when they eat". He answered them, "And why do you transgress the commandment of God for the sake of your tradition? . . . You hypocrites!" . . . And he called the people to him and said to them, "Hear and understand: not what goes into the mouth defiles a man, but what comes out of the mouth defiles a man".'

[2] *ZAP*, no. 13 (p. 38).

[3] Quoted in Golikov, *op. cit.*, iv, p. 150; also Verkhovskoi, i, p. 81.

[4] *PSZ*, v, no. 3006 (pp. 320–322).

> The Tsar was seated at a large table with the archbishop [presumably Metropolitan Stefan Yavorskii, the temporary head of the church] and several other distinguished prelates and priests. He addressed a rather long speech to them on his sentiments concerning the primitive church, saying to them that he was persuaded that the great number of fasts and ceremonies they observed were less pleasing to God than a humble and contrite heart; he exhorted them to preach morality to the people above all else, so that little by little superstition should be banished from his country and both God and himself better served by his subjects.[1]

Some possible political implications of Tsar Peter's personal religious beliefs will by now be apparent. As will be seen in later chapters, beginning in 1720 his government made an intensified effort to improve the moral and religious standards of clergy and people. The readiness with which Peter granted complete religious toleration to the Lutheran inhabitants of the conquered Baltic provinces may also be attributed, perhaps, to a personal factor: to Peter's appreciation of the ritual simplicity and moral rectitude of evangelical Protestantism. Given the fact that Peter depreciated the monastic life – as may be seen (to cite only one example) in a preface he wrote in 1722 for a popular book on the Beatitudes:

> Many believe that the path of salvation and one's vocation consist merely in renouncing the vanity of this world and in observing the divine commandment, that is, the saying that whoever becomes a monk has served the earthly tsar but now will serve the heavenly tsar – a saying which hypocrites explain in various ways: some say that if you do not renounce the world and become a monk you will not be saved; others say that you must attend divine services all day every day, or two or three times a day; still others say that it it most important to chant the services with two or three or more voices, or to make numerous prostrations and to observe other rites. They place all their hope in such things, forgetting the work entrusted to them and their responsibilities.[2]

– given this attitude, it is not surprising that Peter's ecclesiastical legislation included numerous restrictions on the monasteries. Above all, Peter's belief that in essence religion consists of an acknowledgment of Divine Providence and of the duty to lead an upright life prepared him, psychologically, to view the church chiefly as an instrument for promoting the moral reform of his subjects. Of course objective economic and purely political factors influenced and largely determined

[1] *SIRIO*, xl, pp. 66–67.

[2] *ZAP*, no. 154 (p. 119).

Peter's ecclesiastical as well as his other policies. But it can be said that his religious beliefs, combined with his belief in the absolute nature of his power, provided him with that element of personal conviction, that personal sense of righteousness, that intellectual predisposition which was needed to transform the church (as he did) into a department of the state and to set it (so he earnestly believed) on the 'straight path of salvation'.

A contemporary Anglican observer conjectured that, had Peter lived longer, he might have 'further advanc'd reformation of doctrines in his country'.[1] With all due respect to the Reverend Consett, and in consideration of the abundant evidence concerning Peter's church reform that we have at our disposal, we may state with assurance that it was never Peter's intention to embark on a 'reformation of doctrines' in Russia. For Peter's reform, it will be seen, consisted essentially of a radical reorganization of the supreme administration of the church to which was coupled a campaign to banish superstitious practices and to raise the moral standards of clergy and people through improved standards of education. To be sure, in thus reforming the church Peter destroyed its administrative autonomy (which raised certain canonical problems) and abolished or sharply curtailed the clergy's economic and judicial privileges. He also made use of the church for propaganda purposes. He attempted to enlist the clergy's services in the suppression of opposition to his regime. At one point he even ordained that, in the interests of state security, the clergy should violate the secrecy of confession. But the dogmas or basic tenets of the Orthodox faith, as embodied in the doctrinal definitions of the ecumenical councils, in the teachings of the Fathers, and in the various doctrinal statements formulated up to Peter's time,[2] were never explicitly questioned or repudiated, in whole or in part, by Peter or his chief clerical and lay collaborators. Except for deleting the patriarchal commemoration, the services of the church were in no way altered. Communion with the Orthodox churches of the East was carefully preserved. In short, there is absolutely no evidence that Peter ever intended to forsake the faith of his fathers (however imperfectly he understood it); and the charges or claims to this effect advanced by Orthodox or Catholics or Protestants are the outcome either of misunderstanding or of wishful thinking or of both. So far as Peter was concerned he remained, as he himself declared in a

[1] Consett, *op. cit.*, p. xv.

[2] For which see T. Ware, *The Orthodox Church* (London, 1963), pp. 203 ff.

letter of September 1721 to the Eastern patriarchs, 'a devoted son of our Most Beloved Mother the Orthodox Church'.[1]

II

PETER AND A WISE OLD ANGLICAN

For students of Peter's church reform it is worth noting that during his Grand Embassy to western Europe in 1697–1698 he frequently encountered churchmen of various kinds and even went to their services.[2] In Holland he met Calvinists; in North Germany, Lutherans; in Vienna, Roman Catholics. The burgomaster of Amsterdam found him 'very zealous for religion, well educated in the articles of the faith, and versed in Holy Scripture, of which he has an ample acquaintance'.[3] Captain Perry relates that in England Peter 'went often to our churches and cathedrals to see the order of our established religion, and also had the curiosity to see the Quakers and other meeting-houses in the time of their service'.[4] But from the standpoint of the development of his attitude towards his own church, and in the light of his later church policies, Peter's most significant personal encounter during his visit to England, or indeed during his stay in western Europe, was undoubtedly that with Gilbert Burnet, bishop of Salisbury. Historians have not, however, hitherto fully related the facts of this encounter or stressed sufficiently its significance.[5]

Peter spent his first month in England seeing the sights of London. But early in February (1698) he prevailed on King William to let him live at nearby Deptford, which was the centre of important docks and building yards. There he remained for the next three months. And there, according to the journal kept by his entourage, Peter received, on 15 February, a delegation of English bishops.[6] The visit was formal, lasting half an hour, during which, according to another version of the same journal, 'they conversed about many things, but mostly about the

[1] Quoted in Verkhovskoi, i, p. 678.

[2] For Peter in western Europe, see esp. Bogoslovskii, *op. cit.*, ii, *passim.*

[3] W. Guerrier (ed.), *Leibniz in seinen Beziehungen zu Russland und Peter dem Grossen* (St. Petersburg/Leipzig, 1873), no. 32 (p. 37): Witsen to Leibniz, 22 May 1698.

[4] Perry, *op. cit.*, p. 166.

[5] Thus Verkhovskoi, i, p. 75; Bogoslovskii, *op. cit.*, pp. 321–329; A. I. Andreev, 'Petr I v Anglii v 1698g.', in Andreev (ed.), *Petr Velikii: Sbornik statei* (Moscow/Leningrad, 1947), pp. 65–66, 74; Wittram, *op. cit.*, i, p. 160; ii, p. 172.

[6] See Ustryalov, *op. cit.*, iii, p. 603.

Greek faith'.[1] We know from another source that Gilbert Burnet led this delegation, and that he himself had already met the tsar. On 18 February the unofficial representative in London of Duke Cosimo III of Tuscany, Thomas Platt, reported that 'a few days ago Dr. Burnet, bishop of Salisbury, went to see H. M. [Peter] again at Deptford, and was very well received'. 'These bishops', Platt remarked sardonically, 'are trying to convert him, but it is unlikely that he would wish to risk the loss of his kingdom'.[2]

The Austrian resident in London put it more judiciously. Late in February he reported to Vienna that the 'local clergy have taken it upon themselves to acquaint him [Peter] with local rites and worship, and to this end have sent him the celebrated Doctor Burnet, at present bishop of Salisbury'. Resident Hoffmann also reported that it was proposed to Peter that he might like to attend an Anglican service, 'to which he readily agreed, but stipulated that he could go nowhere where a crowd might gather, which is to him unbearable'.[3] By the end of the month the necessary arrangements had been made, presumably by Bishop Burnet; and Peter's insistence on privacy had been discreetly accommodated. On 27 February, again according to the Russian journal of the Grand Embassy, Peter 'went off to see the archbishop of Canterbury';[4] and on 1 March Hoffmann informed Vienna that the 'day before yesterday, Sunday [i.e. 27 February], he [Peter] was in attendance incognito at the chapel of the archbishop of Canterbury and then took breakfast with him'.[5] Burnet himself reported the visit to his friend Dr. Fall, precentor at York, in a letter dated 19 March: 'Since you went', Burnet wrote, 'the Czar came once to Lambeth, and saw both an Ordination and a Sacrament, and was much pleased with it'. And in this letter to Fall Burnet remarked that 'I have been oft with him. On Monday last [i.e. 14 March] I was four hours there. We went through many things'.[6]

We need not rely solely on Burnet's own testimony to establish that he enjoyed close contact with Tsar Peter. On 8 March, just over a week

[1] Quoted in Bogoslovskii, *op. cit.*, p. 325.

[2] A. M. Crino (ed.), *Fatti e Figure del Seicento Anglo-Toscano: Documenti inediti sui Rapporti litterari, diplomatici, e culturali fra Toscano e Inghilterra* (Florence, 1957), p. 304: Platt to Apollonio Bassetti (secretary to Duke Cosimo), 19 February 1698. Platt's thirteen letters (in Italian) to Bassetti of January–April 1698 (printed in *ibid.*, pp. 297–307) contain one of the best contemporary accounts available of Peter's visit to England.

[3] Quoted in Bogoslovskii, *op. cit.*

[4] Ustryalov, *op. cit.*

[5] Bogoslovskii, *op. cit.*, pp. 325–326. Perry also relates that Peter 'was once to see the Archbishop of Canterbury at his palace' (*op. cit.*).

[6] Bodl. MSS. Add. D. 23, f. 10: Burnet to Fall, 19 March 1698.

after Peter's visit to Lambeth Palace, Hoffmann noted in another dispatch to Vienna that on the basis of his several conversations with the tsar Burnet had been able to assure him, Hoffmann, that Peter intended to go from England directly to Vienna, thence to Venice and finally, the following October, to return home again.[1] Hoffmann was naturally anxious to send to his government the fullest possible particulars of Peter's activities in England, especially in view of his declared intention to visit Vienna next. It can be deduced from his report that already by 8 March Burnet had Peter's ear, that he was known in London as a good source of information about the tsar, a source that diplomats cultivated. Indeed in the first of his reports to Vienna referred to above Hoffmann remarked that Peter had shown 'a most singular deference' to Burnet; moreover, that the tsar had dealt so 'openly and favourably' with the English bishops generally that they had come to the agreeable conclusion that 'he must have great esteem for clerics'.[2] Burnet can be believed (and we can sympathize with him) when in mid-March he observed to Dr. Fall that the tsar 'grows so fond of me that I can hardly get from him'.[3] For in the past few weeks he had frequently met with Peter, their sessions sometimes lasting for as long as four hours; and Peter, it seems, showed signs of wishing yet more time with the bishop.

The venerable Gilbert Burnet could not have failed to impress the highly impressionable young tsar. A famous preacher and prolific publicist, Burnet had by 1698 already published some twenty-nine sermons and numerous letters, book reviews, tracts, and 'discourses'. He was, apparently, a genuinely pious man; for his times he certainly was exceptionally learned. Scots by birth and education, tolerant in outlook, a moderate in controversy, well-travelled, civilised, a believer in compromise, friend and biographer of statesmen, adviser to kings; scholar, ascetic, family man and man of affairs in the way of Thomas More (whose *Utopia* he translated); the first English historian of the Reformation: Gilbert Burnet was in 1698 England's most distinguished prelate, perhaps the most outstanding churchman of his age. And he was frankly Erastian. Throughout his long life (1643–1715) he evinced a deep loyalty to England and the Protestant Monarchy, though never in a wholly uncritical way. He had waited with William of Orange in Holland for the call to the English throne, and he would attend the king on his deathbed. He had preached the sermon at the coronation of

[1] See Bogoslovskii, *op. cit.*, p. 348. [2] *Ibid.*, p. 325.
[3] Bodl. MSS. Add. D. 23, f. 10: Burnet to Fall, 19 March 1698.

William and Mary in 1688, and had been given the see of Salisbury that same year. Because of his influence at court he enjoyed an authority in the church beyond his actual rank. He was the vigorous foe alike of Papists and Calvinists, of High Churchmen, Non-jurors, and Puritans. He was the model court bishop. In short, he well represented the Established Church of England, whose form he had helped so much to fix. Certainly Tsar Peter of All Russia had never before encountered a senior cleric of his quality, and certainly not one of his views.[1]

Burnet, for his part, had been apprised of Peter's presence in Europe and been told something of the man several months before they actually met. In August of the previous year Leibniz had written from Hanover to report on 'the Grand Embassy of this [Muscovite] Empire, in which the monarch himself travels incognito'. Leibniz had not in fact met Peter, though he had tried hard to do so when the Embassy passed through Minden (they finally met in October 1711, in Torgau, at Tsarevich Aleksei's wedding). His source of information was his pupil and patroness the Electress Sophie of Brandenburg, who with her husband had seen much of the tsar during his progress through North Germany. In July 1697 Electress Sophie had given an informal party for Peter which was attended only by her immediate family and the electresses of Brunswick and Hanover. 'It was only in the presence of the Electresses', Leibniz informed Burnet, 'that he was willing to pass for himself'. And on the basis of their impressions the philosopher reported that 'although this prince does not have our manners, he does not lack great intelligence. The Tsar, who speaks a little Dutch or German . . . thinks at present only about making the Turks uncomfortable. And his great pleasure is *la marine*, which he has studied and learns to perfection with a view to making himself master of the Black Sea'.[2]

Thus, Burnet was prepared to some extent to meet the tsar of Muscovy when he should come to England. On 2 December 1697 he referred to Peter's imminent arrival in a sermon preached before King William at Whitehall. Expanding on the text for the day, Burnet manage to draw this happy parallel: that just as the queen of Sheba came to Jerusalem to sit at Solomon's feet, and was amazed at his wisdom, so 'a mighty Northern Emperour, resolving to raise his nation and enlarge his empire, comes to learn the best methods of doing it' from the lips of the Stadtholder-king, 'and goes away full of

[1] See T. E. S. Clarke and H. C. Foxcroft, *A Life of Gilbert Burnet* (Cambridge, 1907).

[2] Guerrier, *op. cit.*, no. 17 (pp. 24–25): Leibniz to Burnet, 24 August 1697 (in French).

wonder, possessed with truer notions of government'.[1] In the event, Burnet's fulsome rhetoric was to prove not wholly inapposite.

On the strength, doubtless, of his wide learning, of his proficiency in languages (including Dutch) and of his leading position in the church, Burnet was 'sent' to Peter by the English hierarchy, as Resident Hoffmann reported, as part of their plan to instruct the distinguished visitor from outlandish Muscovy, this 'Caesar or Czar' who had shown himself so well disposed towards them. In his *History of My Own Times*, published posthumously by his sons,[2] Burnet himself tells us that he 'was ordered, both by the King and the Archbishop and bishops, to attend upon him, and to offer him such informations of our religion and constitution as he was willing to receive'. During the months that Peter stayed in England, Burnet recalls here, 'I waited often on him'. 'I had good interpreters', he points out, 'so I had much free discourse with him'.[3] It would seem conclusively established that for a period of several weeks at least, in February and March of 1698, Bishop Burnet met frequently with Tsar Peter, and that on these occasions they had long private talks together. It remains to discuss the topics of those conversations.

We know already, from the sources cited above, that when Peter first met with the English bishops they talked 'mostly about the Greek faith', that the bishops in turn were concerned to acquaint him with 'local rites and worship', but that when he met privately with Burnet they 'went through many things', that Burnet indeed had been told to inform the tsar generally about 'our religion and constitution'. Fortunately, in his letter to Dr. Fall and in his subsequent *History*, Burnet has left a more detailed account of his discussions with Peter.

In his letter to Fall, written in the midst of his period of close contact with the tsar, Burnet noted, with a suggestion of surprise and pleasure, that 'he has a degree of knowledge I did not think him capable of; he has read the Scriptures carefully'. On this basis, apparently, Burnet felt they might proceed to discuss the old theological differences between East and West: 'I convinced him that the question of the

[1] Gilbert Burnet, *A Sermon Preached before the King at Whitehall*... (London, 1698), p. 13.

[2] *Bishop Burnet's History of His Own Time*, vol. i (ed. G. Burnet): *From the Restoration of King Charles II to the Settlement of King William and Queen Mary*... (London, 1724); vol. ii (ed. T. Burnet): *From the Revolution [1688] to the Conclusion of the Treaty of Peace at Utrecht [1713]* (London, 1734). Hereafter cited *Burnet's History*.

[3] *Burnet's History*, ii, p. 221.

Procession of the Holy Ghost was a subtilty that ought not to make a schisme in the Church'. Encouraged by Burnet, Peter 'yielded that saints ought not to be praied to, and was only for keeping the picture of Christ, but that it ought only to be a remembrance and not an object of worship'. Encouraged on his part by Peter's pliancy, Burnet seized the chance to promote the cause of the reformed religion: 'I insisted much to shew him the great designs of Christianity in the reforming men's hearts and lives, which he assured me he would apply himself to'. The letter contains no further indications of the content of their discussions except for the highly significant remark that Peter 'hearkened to no part of what I told him more attentively than when I explained the authority that the Christian Emperours assumed in matters of religion and the supremacy of our Kings'.[1] Peter's interest in the theology of the Trinity, in right religious practice and in Protestantism, was evidently subordinate to his interest in Burnet's exposition of the English sovereign's supremacy in matters of religion and the historical precedents sanctioning such a position. It is also evident that during these sessions Burnet did most of the talking.

In addition to Dr. Fall, and at about the same time, Burnet seems also to have reported his meetings with Peter to Leibniz, for early in April Leibniz wrote to congratulate the English Church in general, and Burnet in particular, on the sympathetic attitude taken by the tsar, who might facilitate the introduction of the reformed religion into the neighbouring empire of China, hitherto abandoned to the missionary zeal of the Jesuits.[2] The project was dear to Leibniz, and exemplifies the hopes aroused in European intellectuals by Peter's visit. And his letter indicates that at the time Burnet wrote to him, he, Burnet, was well pleased with the direction his talks with Peter were taking. The impression of Bishop Burnet confidently expounding the principles of true religion to the intent, respectful young tsar, an impression gained from a reading of his letter to Fall, is thus confirmed.

For more purely theological discussions Burnet met with Peter's chaplain. Their meetings, if indeed they ever met more than once, were inconclusive. On 5 April Burnet wrote again to Dr. Fall, and mentioned in passing that 'the Czar's priest is come over, who is truly a holy man, and more learned than I could have imagined, but thinks it a great piece of religion to be no wiser than his fathers, and therefore cannot bear the thought of imagining that anything among them can want

[1] Bodl. MSS. Add. D. 23, f. 10: Burnet to Fall, 19 March 1698.

[2] Leibniz's letter is cited in Clarke and Foxcroft, *op. cit.*, p. 349.

amendment'.[1] The chaplain, Burnet had discovered, was not so amenable as his master. The gulf of misunderstanding between them was wide, and neither could suspend belief long enough to bridge it. On the one hand Peter's chaplain, by Burnet's account, would seem to have represented the best in Russian Orthodoxy. By Burnet's account he was a holy man; and he was 'learned' probably in the sense that he was seen to possess the instinctive wisdom which a highly developed consciousness of the worth of the past alone can bestow. For the Orthodox believed that dogma was immutable, that the traditional teaching of the church, as formulated in the decrees of the ecumenical councils and in the sermons of the Fathers, was eternally valid; that this was, theologically speaking, all there is to know, and all you need to know. Burnet, on the other hand, believed that in the revolution of the centuries the pristine purity of the Apostles' faith had been polluted by superstition and sinful practices, that therefore 'reform' was good and necessary, that Scripture must be restored to its primary place as the source of faith, that church organization was really a vital problem, because behind it lay an even more important one: whose was the supreme authority in the further development of dogma; who was finally to decide how to deal with problems not provided for or sufficiently developed in the writings of the Fathers and in the resolutions of the councils. Such problems were vital to both Catholics and Protestants; but they could never have been of serious concern to Orthodox churchmen, since for them the theological heritage of their church was amply sufficient, and it was necessary only to preserve it carefully. Moreover, for a Russian priest ritual had a transcendent significance; for him the Liturgy was the supreme act of faith and worship, the very centrepiece of the life of the Christian community: in the Liturgy, earth touched heaven and was transformed, and at moments of such ecstasy nothing else mattered. But for Burnet, as for most Protestants, the clergy's evangelical mission, aimed at the moral uplift of the people and best achieved by preaching and good example, was more important than its liturgical function.

We can find in Bishop Burnet's 'Conclusion' to his *History* a very useful digest of his views on 'matters of religion'.[2] He wrote the piece as a sort of last testament to the nation and intended it to be published

[1] Bodl. MSS. Add. D. 23, f. 12: Burnet to Fall, 5 April 1698.

[2] *Burnet's History*, ii, pp. 633–670. See also the 'Life' of Burnet by his son Thomas (*ibid.*, pp. 671–726); the sympathetic portrait drawn by his friend J. LeClerc in *The Life of Dr. Burnet, Late Lord Bishop of Sarum, with an Account of his Writings* (London, 1715); and Clarke and Foxcroft, *op. cit.*

posthumously (as indeed it was published, by his son Thomas, nearly twenty years after his death). In it he offers advice to everyone responsible for the moral and religious welfare of the country, everyone from the ordinary clergy to the monarch himself. He particularly urges that 'popery' should be seen 'in a true light, as a conspiracy to exalt the power of the clergy, even by subjecting the most sacred truths of religion to contrivances for raising their authority. . . . Popery is a mass of impostures'. His fellow bishops Burnet exhorts to 'think themselves obliged to preach as much as their health and age can admit of', though 'the discreet conduct of your clergy is to be your chief care'. Then follow long pages devoted to the evils of absentee bishops, of simony, of idle, luxurious living, and of involvement in politics: 'the more abstracted bishops live (from the world, from courts, from cabals, and from parties)', Burnet assures them, the more they will have 'quiet within themselves; their thoughts will be free and less intangled, and they will in conclusion be the more respected by all'. On the basis of 'much free discourse with five of our Sovereigns', and of his long experience of public affairs, Burnet went on to outline the rules for a successful reign:

> The first, the most essential, and most indispensable rule for a King is, to study the interest of the nation, to be ever in it, and to be always pursuing it; this will lay in for him such a degree of confidence that he will be ever safe with his people, when they feel safe in him. . . .
>
> Great care ought to be taken in the nomination of judges and bishops. I join these together; for law and religion, justice and piety, are the support of nations and give strength and security to governments: judges must be recommended by those in the high posts of the law; but a prince may, by his own taste and upon knowledge, choose his bishops. They ought to be men eminent for piety, learning, discretion and zeal; not broken with age, which will quickly render them incapable of serving the church to any good purpose.
>
> But . . . the great and comprehensive rule of all is, that a king should consider himself as exalted by Almighty God into that high dignity as into a capacity of doing much good and of being a great blessing to mankind, and in some sort a god on earth. . . .

And just as the king's ministers work 'to advance his service, his interests and his glory', so he 'whom God has raised to the greatest exaltation' should apply himself wholly to the execution of his supreme office, should become a paragon of all virtue to his people, etc., etc. It is no wonder that in their conversations Tsar Peter hearkened to no part of what Burnet told him more attentively than when he expounded his theory of kingship. After due study of this and other of Burnet's opinions, conveniently digested in the 'Conclusion' to his *History*, we can fill out considerably our picture of the content of those conversations. That is, we can imagine that in their many long talks together Burnet said much the same thing about the same sorts of subjects as he said at the end of his *History*. There is no reason whatever to suppose that in the last fifteen years or so of his life his basic thinking on these 'matters' underwent any significant change.[1]

The impasse Burnet had reached in his conversation with the tsar's chaplain, rather than the warmth, deference, and receptive attitude shown by Peter himself, more accurately reflected the theological distance which separated the churches of England and Russia. But the Reformation in England, as on the Continent, had been effected largely through the intervention of the state in what hitherto had been considered the exclusive province of the church. In the spring of 1698, when Burnet wrote to Leibniz and to Dr. Fall, when he thought things were going so well in his talks with Peter, he must have hoped that, however intractable the tsar's chaplain might be, the tsar himself would see the light, and carry it back with him to Muscovy. He evidently thought that Peter was genuinely interested in the doctrines of the reformed religion, in the 'great designs of Christianity in the reforming [of] men's hearts and lives'. Scepticism, and a truer appreciation of Peter's real interests, came later. To Fall he had remarked, rather ambiguously, that 'the Czar will either perish in the way or become a great man'.[2] But in his *History* he concluded for posterity that Peter seemed 'designed by nature rather to be a ship carpenter than a great prince'. And of the substance of their talks together Burnet noted there only that 'he was desirous to understand our doctrine, but he did not seem disposed to mend matters in Muscovy'.[3]

Peter had not been converted by Bishop Burnet. If in the midst of their talks together Burnet had succumbed to a hope that the tsar might institute a sort of Reformation on his return to Russia, he soon abandoned it. He was not the first western churchman to mistake Peter's willingness to talk freely and frankly about religious matters and to

[1] The narrative of *Burnet's History* concludes with the Peace of Utrecht (1713); he died in 1715. Therefore his 'Conclusion' must have been written between 1713 and 1715 at the latest, though possibly earlier. His meetings with Peter occurred in 1698.

[2] Bodl. MSS. Add. D. 23, f. 12: Burnet to Fall, 5 April 1698.

[3] *Burnet's History*, ii, pp. 221–222.

criticize Russian religious practices for a disposition to inaugurate what westerners, especially Protestants, would have considered a thoroughgoing reform of the Russian church. Yet in those conversations with Bishop Burnet Peter's ever alert and practical mind had hearkened most attentively to his exposition of the 'authority that the Christian Emperours assumed in matters of religion and the supremacy of our Kings'. Indeed, it is highly unlikely that Peter had ever before heard the notions of monarchical supremacy over the church, of the 'Rights of Princes in the disposing of Ecclesiastical Benefices and Church-lands',[1] of religion as the 'support of nations' and the 'strength and security of governments', of the sovereign's clear right to appoint bishops and to exact loyalty from them, of the bishops' duty to keep out of politics, and of the king's all-embracing and divinely-appointed commission to see to the good of his subjects, so cogently, confidently, and forcefully put to him. Peter had received from Burnet, in short, an intensive course in the political ideas of the Early Enlightenment – ideas which he was later to introduce into Russia with far-reaching, indeed revolutionary consequences. And Burnet himself had presented to Peter a living example of what a bishop ought to be: learned but practical, pious but worldly-wise, above all unquestionably loyal to his king. And that was quite enough for the young tsar. He had not been, and never was to be, interested in the nicer points of doctrine.

III

PETER AND THE DOCTORS OF THE SORBONNE

Near the end of his visit to Paris in the spring of 1717 a dramatic bid was made to enlist Peter's support for a projected union of the Russian and Roman churches. According to contemporary eye-witness accounts, the tsar and his suite were welcomed at the entrance to the Sorbonne on the morning of 14 June by the Abbé Boursier, a leading member of the Paris theological faculty. A number of his colleagues, attracted by the commotion, soon gathered, and the entire group, led by Boursier and the tsar, went first to the chapel, where they viewed the tomb of Richelieu, and then to the college library, where Peter moved about so quickly inspecting the library's curiosities that Boursier and the others had difficulty engaging him in conversation. Finally they succeeded in fixing his attention on some books in Slavonic, whereupon they drew him into an 'affable' discussion of

[1] The title of one of Burnet's many tracts, published London, 1682.

religion. Boursier broached the question of ecclesiastical union, hastening to point out that if Peter could 'reunite and reconcile' the Russian and Roman churches his glory would be complete, and that insuperable difficulties need not arise if the business were handled 'cautiously and in a spirit of charity'. Peter is said to have greeted this thrust with a smile, and to have remarked that he was only a soldier, 'which left one to understand' – Boursier recalled – 'that he did not wish to get mixed up in religion'. But 'you are a hero', Boursier objected, and 'in your capacity as prince you are the protector of religion'. No doubt flattered, Peter nonetheless replied that union was no easy thing, that there were three points which divided the eastern and western churches, namely the pope, the procession of the Holy Ghost, and. . . . 'And the azymes and the chalice', Boursier prompted. 'That's it', exclaimed Peter, adding that on this point there would be no trouble in reaching an agreement. To this Boursier and his colleagues swiftly assented, suggesting in turn that the age-old dispute over the procession of the Holy Ghost was only a 'dispute over words' and that in recognizing, 'in accordance with the principles of the Gallican church', only the 'primacy' of the pope, nothing need be changed in the present administration of the Russian church. 'Ah well', said Peter, 'draw up a memoir for me on this matter, and hurry, for I am leaving [Paris] soon. I promise that I will give it to the bishops of my country and will oblige them to reply to you'. The memoir, embodying the Sorbonne's proposal of union, was drawn up in twenty-four hours by an informal committee under Boursier's direction and signed the next evening by some eighteen doctors of theology. An official of the French government advised that a Latin translation should be made for the benefit of the Russian bishops. The translation was duly produced and copies of the two versions were notarized by the vicar-general of the archdiocese of Paris on 19 June. On 20 June, Peter having left Paris that morning, the memoir was dispatched to him en route to Spa.[1]

[1] The most detailed contemporary account of Peter's visit to the Sorbonne is contained in the posthumous collection of Boursier's papers edited by his friend the Abbé Coudrette: see *Histoire et analyse du livre* '*L'Action de Dieu*'. *Opuscules de M. Boursier relatifs à cet ouvrage. . . . Relation des démarches faites par les docteurs de Sorbonne pour la réunion de l'Église de Russie et l'Église Latine. Recueil des pièces qui concernent cette affaire* (Paris, 1753), iii, pp. 285–291; hereafter cited *Relation de M. Boursier*. The visit is also described in the opening paragraphs of the memoir itself, of which a French and two Latin copies are deposited in the French Foreign Ministry Archives: 'Correspondance politique: Russie', vol. 8, docs. 24, 26, 27. Peter's visit is also the subject of a contemporary memoir prepared by an anonymous official of the French Foreign Ministry (see FMA, 'Mémoires et documents: Russie', vol. 3, doc. 14); and a description of the visit was published in the August 1717 issue of the *Suite*

Apart from the problem of church union, we know of one other specific matter that was raised during Peter's visit to the Sorbonne. Boursier records that at the end of their meeting in the library the tsar turned to one of the doctors present, the Abbé LeMoine, and asked him about the '*Unigenitus* affair'. LeMoine replied, 'with candour', that 'if a majority of the bishops are for it, a majority of the doctors are against it'. Boursier noted that Peter was 'well informed' about the controversy over the papal bull, and that in a recent conversation with the regent (Philip, duke of Orleans) was reported to have expressed approval of the conduct of Cardinal Noailles, a leader of the opposition to accepting the bull. One could not condemn the cardinal, Peter was reported to have said, by supposing that the pope was infallible. Indeed, if the pope believed himself infallible, 'he is a fool'; and if not, 'he is a knave'; and in either case Peter professed to be unable to understand how 'a man could persuade himself that, being human, he has the gift of infallibility'.[1]

It is not surprising, therefore, that Peter rebuffed a concurrent attempt by the papal nuncio in Paris to discuss 'reunion' with him. His trip to Paris had excited great interest in the Curia. On 11 May Bentivoglio (the nuncio) had been authorized by the cardinal secretary of state, Paulucci, to make contact with the 'Zar di Moscovia' and when addressing him to use liberally, but only 'in voce', the title 'Maestà'. Peter, it was still thought in Rome, desired papal recognition of his royal dignity for the sake of his status in Europe; but formal attribution of the royal title by the Holy See to a 'schismatic' would be a considerable concession, requiring one of equal weight in return. In a lengthy 'istruzione' of 18 May Bentivoglio was given his terms for negotiating with the tsar: formal recognition of his royal status, as well as papal support for his candidate for the Polish throne and for an anti-Turkish alliance of the European powers, were to be exchanged for concessions for Catholics living in Russia and for Peter's support of the Vatican's long-cherished dream of 'reunion'. On 13 June, the day before Peter

de la Clef du Cabinet des Princes de l'Europe, ou Recueil Historique & Politique sur les matières du tems, pp. 111–112. The principal Russian account of the meeting appears in the official history of Peter's reign (*Zhurnal*, i, pp. 411–412); Peter's 'travel journal' of 1717 merely records that he visited the Sorbonne on 14 June (see M. Poludenskii, 'Petr Velikii v Parizhe', *Russkii arkhiv*, iii [1865], col. 76).

Most of these sources appear not to have been consulted by P. Pierling, S. J. when preparing his study *La Sorbonne et la Russie, 1717–1747* (Paris, 1882), which still contains the most complete secondary account of the visit. Apart from this technical deficiency, Pierling's book often descends into old-fashioned polemics.

[1] *Relation de M. Boursier*, pp. 288–289.

visited the Sorbonne, Bentivoglio finally obtained an audience. It was, as he reported to Paulucci next day, inconclusive: Peter had been non-committal; and on leaving Bentivoglio had been told by an official that the tsar had other matters to attend to at present, though the project of an anti-Turkish alliance might be put forward again at a more favourable moment. Bentivoglio also reported, suspiciously, that on the morning of the audience Peter had received a certain Jansenist priest who had brought him some sort of message (from the Sorbonne?). And Bentivoglio informed his superior that on that very day (14 June) the Sorbonne had proposed to Peter a union of the churches without reference to the pope. Obviously someone sympathetic to the papal cause had been present at the Sorbonne that morning and had immediately reported the result of Peter's visit to the nuncio.[1]

Papists, Gallicans, Jansenists; the nuncio, the cardinal, the regent; the '*Unigenitus* affair': Peter's six-week stay in Paris in the spring of 1717 had coincided with a critical phase in a prolonged controversy within the French church and state and he had become involved in it, however peripherally. As the Abbé Boursier recalls, 'he came suddenly, unexpectedly, to the Sorbonne on 14 June, precisely at that moment when the Court had forbidden the Faculty to hold their meetings because of their Appeal of 5 March',[2] an appeal which had demanded that the question of the papal bull *Unigenitus* should be referred to a general church council. At the risk of oversimplification, a brief discussion of the controversy may be included here, as a concrete illustration of church–state relations in that wider European world of which Peter – who was soon to alter radically the relations between church and state in Russia – had direct and personal knowledge. Equally, when placed in the context of the *Unigenitus* controversy, it will be seen that the Sorbonne's 'ecumenical' gesture to the Russian church, embodied in the memoir which it had presented to Peter, was probably not much more than a manoeuvre designed to embarrass the papacy or at best to obtain the approval and support of a non-Roman church as a way of consolidating its own position in France.

The bull *Unigenitus* was promulgated in Rome by the 'timorous and undecided' Clement XI, yielding to pressure from the French king, on

[1] For the relevant documents from the Vatican archives, see A. Tamborra, 'Russia e Santa Sede all'epoca di Pietro il Grande', *Archivio Storico Italiano*, cxix (1961), pp. 230–236. For Peter's reception of the papal nuncio on 13 June 1717, see also P. Pierling, *La Russie et le Saint-Siège* (Paris, 1906), iv, pp. 241–242.

[2] *Relation de M. Boursier*, p. 286.

8 September 1713.[1] In it a hundred and one propositions extracted by a papal commission from P. Quesnel's *Le Nouveau Testament, avec des réflexions morales* were anathematized. Most of the 'errors' condemned in Quesnel's book were deduced from his teaching on the nature of grace. Quesnel, it was asserted, propounded a form of the doctrine of predestination which had already been condemned (in 1653) in the *Augustinius* (published Louvain, 1640) of C. Jansen, bishop of Ypres – a doctrine which was taken by some to imply that in the economy of salvation the institutional church was unnecessary and the authority of its priests insignificant. Quesnel's doctrinal pessimism was expressed in the general harshness of tone and tendency to morbid rigorism in matters of morality which were characteristic of that peculiarly French form of puritanism known as 'Jansenism'. Some of Quesnel's 'réflexions' harked back to earlier notions of the conciliar nature of ecclesiastical authority. Elsewhere he maintained (according to the ninety-first proposition of *Unigenitus*) that fear of unjust punishment should be no deterrent to duty, a principle which seemed designed to serve the interests of the French king at the expense of those of the pope. His arguments were bolstered with scriptural and patristic references. It seemed, in sum, that both religious customs and established ecclesiastical authority were being impugned.[2]

Though the *Réflexions morales* were condemned in 1708 by a decree of Clement XI, the condemnation had not been received in France. Moreover, by hesitating to authorize publication of the decree, the cardinal-archbishop of Paris, Noailles, had left the question dangerously suspended, producing a division in the French hierarchy.[3] In 1711 King Louis XIV, impatient with the delay and resolved to suppress the Jansenist 'heresy', had revoked the royal privilege for printing Quesnel's book and demanded from Rome a formal bull condemning it once and for all. Thus the promulgation, in 1713, of *Unigenitus*, which was intended to put an end to the Jansenist controversy but served to open a new crisis in the history of the French church which was to endure beyond the middle of the eighteenth century. For though

[1] L. Pastor, *The History of the Popes*, Eng. ed. E. Graf (London, 1941), xxxiii, p. 534. See also H. C. Judge, 'Church and State under Louis XIV', *History*, xlv (October 1960), p. 231.

[2] On Quesnel (1634–1719) and 'quesnellisme', see A. Vacant and others (eds.), *Dictionnaire de théologie catholique* (Paris, 1903–1950), xiii, pt. 2, cols. 1460–1535.

[3] Noailles himself had once written a commendatory preface to the second edition of Quesnel's book. In the opinion of a contemporary French churchman, this approbation was 'la première cause de toutes les divisions qui ont agité l'Église de France' (quoted in *ibid.*, col. 1480). For Noailles, see *ibid.*, ix, pt. 1, cols. 678–681.

Unigenitus had been framed so as to avoid giving offence to Gallican susceptibilities, it was accepted in 1714 by an assembly of the French hierarchy and registered by the *parlement* of Paris only with serious reservations. A party led by Cardinal Noailles refused categorically to accept it: 'We ask only that the Court of Rome should not be given any reason for believing that we act simply as the executors of its decrees', they declared to the assembly, insisting that no point of doctrine divided them from the majority. From a lukewarm Jansenist Noailles had become an enthusiastic Gallican.[1]

'Gallicanism' (the term was first used only in the nineteenth century) had for our purposes been defined by the assembly of the French clergy early in 1682. Inspired by representatives of Louis XIV, the assembly produced the famous four Gallican articles: (i) kings are not subject to ecclesiastical authority in temporal matters; (ii) popes are supreme in spiritual matters, though the French church accepts the decrees of the Council of Constance (thus reviving, in a negative way, the theory of the superiority of general councils over the pope enunciated at Constance); (iii) the canons of the church and the rules and customs admitted by France and the Gallican church are to be the rules guiding the relations between the papacy and France; (iv) the pope's judgment in questions of doctrine is not irreformable unless backed by the approval of the church (a definite denial of the doctrine of papal infallibility, a doctrine on which Catholic opinion was still in any case divided). Clearly, the fourth article was the most important; its acceptance in France rendered nugatory all papal decrees of which the assembly of the French clergy – that is, Louis XIV – did not approve.[2]

Louis never formally repudiated the Gallican articles; but in 1693 he opportunistically reached an agreement with the pope whereby he may be said to have 'abandoned' them.[3] Yet despite the king strong or at least articulate opposition to the claims of the papacy persisted in France, and was brought to a head with the promulgation of *Unigenitus*. And the point of contact between the more purely religious phenomenon of Jansenism and the wider, more secular and political movement of Gallicanism lay in this: that if on important doctrinal questions (such as *Unigenitus* dealt with) the decision of the pope was not final until

[1] See E. Préclin and E. Jarry, *Les luttes politiques et doctrinales aux XVIIe et XVIIIe siècles* (Paris, 1955), pp. 220 ff.

[2] See the pithy summary and analysis of the Gallican articles of 1682 in D. Ogg, *Europe in the Seventeenth Century* (8th edn., London, 1961), pp. 298–299; also Judge, *op. cit.*, pp. 223–225.

[3] Préclin and Jarry, *op. cit.*, p. 220.

approved by a general or even a national church council, as the Gallicans maintained, then the successful application of this principle against *Unigenitus*, a group of 'political-Jansenists' now perceived, might save persecuted, declining Jansenism from total extinction. Thus began the second and last phase of the Jansenist controversy in France, the interminable politics of which filled the first half of the eighteenth century and made a profound impression on its history.[1]

Religion and politics had once more become inextricably confused, and the ageing Louis XIV – who hated Jansenism, but was the erstwhile champion and a chief beneficiary of Gallicanism – found himself, having failed to force unqualified acceptance of *Unigenitus* by the French clergy, in an extremely delicate position. His death on 1 September 1715, before any further action had been taken, led some to hope that the government of Philip of Orleans would adopt a more conciliatory church policy. Cardinal Noailles reappeared at court; J. B. Bossuet, an enemy of the Jesuits (the arch-opponents of the Jansenists) and nephew of the great Gallican bishop of Meaux, was nominated to the vacant see of Troyes. But Pope Clement attempted to delay his consecration, and that of several others, in order to force acceptance of the bull, and the regent made noises which smacked of schism. Then, on 5 March 1717, four bishops led the Sorbonne in publicly calling for a church council to decide the *Unigenitus* question, to which the regent (as noted above) retaliated by imposing a ban on the Sorbonne's meetings. It was in the midst of these developments that Tsar Peter arrived in Paris. In the contemporary journal of events kept by an obscure librarian in Paris we read under date of 25 April 1717 (for example): 'The regent held a long conference today on the subject of the appeal of the four bishops. . . . They have furnished the Hôtel Lesdiguières for the tsar. . . . Cardinal Noailles has received a brief letter from the pope, full of tender sentiments, attempting to persuade His Eminence to receive the Constitution [*Unigenitus*]'.[2]

In sum, at the time of Peter's arrival the French clergy, for lack of a clear lead from their government, remained divided for and against the bull into *acceptants* and *appelants*, the former retaining the court generally and most of the hierarchy behind them, while the latter were

[1] The extensive literature devoted to the various aspects of Jansenism is itself largely polemical. But for a detailed analysis of the subject together with full bibliography, see J. Carreyre's article in the *Dict. Théol. Cat.*, viii, pt. 1, cols. 318–529. See also Pastor, *op. cit.*, pp. 177 ff.

[2] J. Buvat, *Journal de la Régence, 1715–1723*, ed. E. Campardon (Paris, 1865), i, pp. 264–265.

strong in the *parlements* and in the theological faculties. Opposition to the bull was especially strong in the diocese of Paris and in the Sorbonne, which was a hotbed of political-Jansenism.[1] At its meeting on 1 February 1717 the faculty had resolved to publish a collection of its *Censures et conclusions . . . touchant la souveraineté des rois, la fidelité que leur doivent leurs sujets, la sureté de leurs personnes et la tranquillité de l'Estat.*[2] At various points in the collection and in speeches made by a deputation of the Sorbonne when presenting copies to the boy-king Louis XV, the regent, Cardinal Noailles, and others, the faculty insisted that the royal authority was 'independent of any other save that of God Himself', that it was independent of all 'foreign doctrines and powers'.

Prominent among the doctors of the Sorbonne at this very moment was the Abbé Boursier, a 'very influential Jansenist' and an articulate defender of the four appellant bishops.[3] It was Boursier, as we have seen, who greeted Tsar Peter when he visited the Sorbonne and who was chiefly responsible for the project of union proposed to him there. Of the eighteen doctors who signed the resultant memoir, only one was not an appellant. The doctrine of ecclesiastical authority contained in the memoir itself is explicitly Gallican: the pope, it is said, possesses a 'purely spiritual authority' and 'has received from Jesus Christ neither direct nor indirect power over the temporal authority of Kings'. Peter, probably knowingly, had entered the centre of opposition to the papal bull and had discussed religion and the rights of princes with some of its leading representatives.

And so it was out of sympathy, no doubt, for the Sorbonne's attitude to the question of royal versus papal power that Peter promised to convey their memoir on union to the bishops of his church, while at the same time rebuffing the papal nuncio's overtures. This curious project of union was to prove, of course, abortive. But we can assume, in view of the measures which he was shortly to introduce in Russia, that Peter had thoroughly digested at least one of the arguments put to him at the Sorbonne: that, as Boursier expressed it, 'in your capacity as prince you are the protector of religion'. Moreover, apart from the explicit approval he was reported to have expressed for the conduct of Cardinal Noailles in the controversy, there is evidence that Peter had

[1] See P. Feret, *La Faculté de théologie de Paris et ses docteurs les plus célèbres* (Paris, 1909), vi, pp. 123–126.

[2] Published in London, in an English translation, in 1718, and in Paris, in the original French, in 1720.

[3] *Dict. Théol. Cat.*, ii, col. 1116.

become curious about him as a churchman. Marshal de Tessé, who was deputed to look after the tsar during his stay in Paris, records in his memoirs that on 27 May Peter declared that he wished to see Noailles preside at a service in Notre Dame: 'I do not know who gave him the idea', Tessé writes, but the arrangements were promptly made.[1] Elsewhere Peter is said to have gone into the cathedral on this occasion and to have observed approvingly to one of his aides that the cardinal, whom he reckoned to be like a patriarch, celebrated mass alone and not with a cleric at either side, as was the custom in Russia.[2] Peter, perhaps, had come to respect Noailles for what he was reputed to be (there is no evidence that they ever actually met): an austere, learned, and pious cleric, a noted reformer, and a loyal servant of his king. In these respects he was not unlike that bishop of Salisbury, Gilbert Burnet, with whom Peter had been greatly impressed nearly twenty years previously.

The response of the Russian bishops to the Sorbonne's memoir, though negative, is nonetheless interesting. An entry in Peter's notebook dating from the early part of 1718 reads: 'About an answer to the Sorbonne's letter, since I promised'.[3] By June of 1718 an official Russian reply to the memoir had been drawn up by Bishop Feofan Prokopovich, approved by Peter, and signed by the temporary head of the church (Metropolitan Stefan Yavorskii), Prokopovich himself, and Archbishop Barnabas of Kholmogory. It was dispatched to Paris on 15 June, almost a year to the day since Peter had visited the Sorbonne. After assuring the doctors of their esteem, gratitude, and own constant fervour for church union, the Russian bishops stated in their reply that the project was not to be easily or quickly executed; that the Orthodox church was not co-extensive with the Russian state, vast though it was, but was composed of many other nations as well, without whose advice and consent the Russians could not act in the matter. In particular, the Sorbonne was informed, the four Eastern patriarchs had to be consulted, lest the Russians should risk breaking the ties of an ancient union in seeking to form a new one. It was from fear of such an eventuality, the Russian bishops maintained, that they had deferred their reply until now. The latter closes with a proposal that theologians from either side

[1] Quoted in A. Rambaud, 'La visite de Pierre le Grand à Paris: simple notes', *Revue politique et littéraire* (*Revue Bleue*), lii (1896), p. 501.

[2] Poludenskii, *op. cit.*, col. 73.

[3] *ZAP*, no. 43 (p. 55); also no. 44 (p. 56).

should discuss matters further, by letter, in a private exchange of views that would prepare the way for an eventual reconciliation without prejudicing the public position of either side.[1]

There was, however, a second reply to the Sorbonne's memoir which was never sent, having been rejected by Peter, apparently, as the less 'moderate' of the two.[2] This second reply is replete with the elaborate compliments and pompous Latin rhetoric typical of Stefan Yavorskii's style. On behalf of the Russian hierarchy, of whom he was nominally the head, Yavorskii stated that, however desirable reconciliation might be, canon law forbade them to act without their supreme head. For 'the throne of the Most Holy Russian Patriarchs is vacant and remains as it were in a state of widowhood, as is known abroad. And therefore should the bishops wish to undertake anything without their patriarch, it would be as if the members should wish to act without the head, or the stars to complete their course without the first principle of motion. This is the pressing limitation which in the present matter forbids us to say or do anything more'. Yavorskii concluded his reply by suggesting that their only recourse was to submit the matter to the Eastern patriarchs, on whom the whole splendid edifice of the church was built.[3]

In 1720 a modified German translation of this second Russian reply to the Sorbonne's memoir was published.[4] The translation contains this curious aside, which is absent from the Russian original just summarized:

> We should not neglect to point out that it is neither through fear nor through ignorance that we refrain from embarking with you on an examination of these matters of the faith. Those who are dejected in spirit could suffer such a reproach. For our part, we are not discouraged; the justice of the cause which we uphold and the remembrance of the words of the prince of the Apostles

[1] For the Russian original of the reply, see the *Zhurnal*, ii, pp. 436–438. A copy of the Latin translation of the reply which was sent to Paris is deposited in the FMA: 'Correspondance politique: Russie', vol. 9, doc. 53. French translations of the reply and of the Sorbonne's memoir, as well as the Latin texts of both documents, are printed in the 'Recueil des pièces' appended to the *Relation de M. Boursier* (pp. 369–424). Abridged French translations of both documents are reprinted in Feret, *op. cit.*, pp. 331–337.

[2] See Golikov, *op. cit.*, vii, pp. 131–140; Poludenskii, *op. cit.*, col. 77; *Zhurnal*, ii, p. *a*.

[3] Yavorskii's reply is printed in the *Zhurnal*, ii, pp. *a–e*.

[4] *Die Reussischen Clerisen Antwort auf das schreiben welches die doctores der Sorbonne, wegen Vereinigung der Reussischen und Franssosischen Kirchen*, n.p., 1720. (A copy of this pamphlet is deposited in the FMA: 'Correspondance politique: Russie', vol. 10, doc. 163). It was on the basis of a copy of this pamphlet, presumably, that the French translation of Yavorskii's reply which is appended to the *Relation de M. Boursier* (pp. 425–439) was made. An abridged version of this translation is printed in Feret, *op. cit.*, pp. 437–439.

> do not permit us to remain despondent. 'Do not fear', said St. Peter, 'the evils with which they wish to make you afraid, and do not be troubled.' . . . The silence we maintain is therefore not the result of fear; it is through humility and in order to observe exactly the apostolic canon cited above [Yavorskii refers to the prohibition against acting in the absence of a patriarch], that we desist from engaging in a disputation. Indeed it is better to obey the laws by keeping silence with humility than to violate them by discussing and conferring with others. . . .

At first glance the meaning of the aside is obscure. In both the German translation and the Russian original Yavorskii had previously explained that the delay in replying proceeded from a wish to reflect carefully on the matter as well as from the canonical inability of the Russian bishops to act in the continued absence of a patriarch (the patriarchal throne in Russia had in fact been vacant since October 1700, since when Yavorskii had served as temporary head of the church). Yavorskii's talk – in the German version of his reply – of a dejected spirit, of not being discouraged, of the justice of his cause, of the necessity for silence and humility, as well as his restatement of the illegality of discussing the matter further, would appear, in the light of the Sorbonne's memoir, excessive, if not superfluous. And it is not immediately apparent why his reply, considerably revised, should have been published in German in 1720.

The matter is further complicated by the fact that in 1719 a book in Latin appeared at Jena purporting to demonstrate, with reference to the Sorbonne's memoir, the utter irreconcilability of the Russian and Roman churches.[1] The work has been attributed to Feofan Prokopovich;[2] but it is virtually certain that Prokopovich only supplied the ostensible author, his friend Buddeus, with a copy of the memoir.[3] In the book Buddeus rigorously examines, from a rationalistic and Protestant point of view, the arguments for church union advanced by the Sorbonne doctors. Amidst the flattering references to Tsar Peter and the violent diatribes against the Roman church, one can detect the central thread of Buddeus's argument: Peter ought not to surrender his supremacy over the church to the pope of Rome. It was perhaps in an effort to deflate this basic assumption – that Peter had the right to decide the fate of the church – that Yavorskii was induced to publish his own reply to the Sorbonne's memoir. If this was in fact the case, the

[1] J. F. Buddeus, *Ecclesia Romana cum Ruthenica irreconciliabilis.*

[2] R. Mintslof, *Petr Velikii v inostrannoi literature* (St. Petersburg, 1872), p. 378.

[3] See Verkhovskoi, i, p. vii.

memoir had become the victim of a personal controversy between the two leading members of the Russian hierarchy: Stefan Yavorskii and Feofan Prokopovich.

As for the discrepancies between the original and published versions of Yavorskii's reply, these can be explained by his reaction to the course of events in Russia between June 1718, when the reply was submitted to Peter and rejected by him, and 1720, when the revised reply was published. For in the autumn of 1718, as will be seen in a following chapter, Peter relieved Yavorskii of his duties as temporary head of the church and informed him that he was thinking of establishing an 'Ecclesiastical College'; and in February 1720 the *Ecclesiastical Regulation*, which had been written by Feofan Prokopovich and amended by Peter without reference to Yavorskii, and which provided for the abolition of the Russian patriarchate and the establishment of the Ecclesiastical College, was submitted to the hierarchy for their formal ratification. In the context of these events, the differences between the two versions of Yavorskii's reply can be viewed as the differences between a draft composed before Peter had decided to reform the church and a final version revised for publication abroad when the definitive reform was well under way. In the former, his original reply, Yavorskii stated that in the continued absence of a patriarch the Russian hierarchy could not canonically consider the project of union. In the revised version, prudently published abroad, Yavorskii maintained his former position and now, in the light of events, made an appeal for sympathy to Catholic Europe: 'we are not discouraged; the justice of the cause which we uphold does not permit us to remain despondent. . . . It is better to obey the laws by keeping silence with humility'. For although he accepted the presidency of the new Ecclesiastical College; and although, in that capacity, he took an oath acknowledging the tsar as his 'Supreme Judge', Yavorskii opposed, as his revised reply makes plain, any resolution of ecclesiastical matters without a patriarch. Yavorskii utterly opposed, in other words, Peter's church reform, at the heart of which lay his abolition of the patriarchate. Thus, the publication in 1720 of Yavorskii's revised reply to the Sorbonne's memoir was not merely the fruit of a personal duel with Feofan Prokopovich; it was also a significant, if characteristically discreet and futile manoeuvre by Yavorskii in what we shall later refer to as the politics of church reform under Peter.

The polite but vague and unpromising reply to the Sorbonne's memoir that was sent to Paris in June 1718 with Peter's approval was written, as mentioned, by Feofan Prokopovich. That his reply should have been preferred by Peter to that of Yavorskii was yet another personal triumph for the newly-consecrated bishop of Pskov, a short account of whose life now follows.

IV

FEOFAN PROKOPOVICH, AUTHOR OF THE *Ecclesiastical Regulation*

From his earliest childhood Prokopovich seems to have been destined to pursue a career in the church. He was orphaned soon after his birth in Kiev in 1681 and was brought up by his uncle Feofan, a learned monk and sometime rector of the Kiev academy.[1] He completed the

[1] The educational institution usually referred to as the Kiev academy dates from 1631–1632, when the head of the Kiev Monastery of the Caves, Peter Mogila, merged his recently founded school with the existing school run (since 1615) by the Kiev branch of the Orthodox Brotherhood of the Ukraine. In 1637 Mogila was consecrated metropolitan of Kiev, and under his enlightened patronage (until his death in 1647) the school, which was closely modelled on the Jesuit colleges of the Polish state (one of which was in the immediate vicinity of Kiev), became the principal institution of higher education in the Slavonic-Orthodox world. Its curriculum was dominated by Latin studies and by the Jesuit version of medieval scholasticism, which caused the Greek church to view it with the greatest suspicion. However in 1667 the school, together with the Orthodox church of the Ukraine, was forced to leave the jurisdiction of the patriarch of Constantinople and to submit to that of the patriarch of Moscow; and so the school became a major factor in the spread of 'Latin' influences in the Russian church. In 1694 it introduced a theology course (though its most promising students continued to be sent abroad to the Jesuit colleges for further training); and in 1701 it was raised from the status of *kollegium* to that of *akademiya*, though Russians continued to call it, confusingly, the 'Kievan' or 'Mogilian school [*shkola* or *uchilische*]'. For the history of the academy, see M. Bulgakov (Metropolitan Makarii), *Istoriya Kievskoi akademii* (St. Petersburg, 1843) and L. R. Lewitter, 'Poland, Ukraine, and Russia in the Seventeenth Century', *Slavonic and East European Review*, xxvii (May 1949), pp. 414–418. For useful information from Ukrainian as well as Russian sources, see S. M. Horak, 'The Kiev Academy: A Bridge to Europe in the Seventeenth Century', an unpublished paper read at the 82nd annual meeting (December 1967) of the American Historical Association: I am grateful to Mr. Horak for supplying me with a copy of his paper.

It will be seen in the following chapters that Tsar Peter, following the example of his predecessors, appointed numerous graduates of the Kiev academy to important positions in the Russian church. Indeed, it would be difficult to exaggerate the influence of graduates of the Kiev academy in the ecclesiastical and cultural life of early modern Russia; not only did they occupy a high proportion of the episcopal sees but, as Pekarskii says, 'Kievans in the first half of the eighteenth century were the promoters of education in Russia; all translations from classical languages, all treatises on dogma, all manuals of religious instruction, the majority of literary works, theatrical pieces – all were written by Little Russian [Ukrainian] scholars or under their direct supervision' (P. Pekarskii, *Nauka i literatura v Rossii pri Petre Velikom* [St. Petersburg, 1862], ii, pp. 4–5. See also L. R. Lewitter's article, 'Peter the Great, Poland, and the Westernization of Russia', *Journal of the History of Ideas*, xix [October 1958], pp. 493–506, and esp. Kharlampovich, *op. cit.*, pp. 459 ff.).

academy's seven-year course at the precocious age of seventeen and was sent abroad to continue his studies at various of the Jesuit colleges in Polish territory. He became, as was necessary for one of his background, a Uniate, and then a monk of the special Basilian order. He so impressed his superiors that he was soon made a prefect and teacher of poetics and rhetoric at the Uniate school in Vladimir, Volyniya, and ordained deacon by the local Uniate bishop. Within a year or so he was sent to the College of St. Athanasius in Rome, a special school for Greek and Slav Uniates and a training centre, in fact, for the Counter-Reformation offensive in eastern Europe. There he perfected his command of the arts of rhetoric and poetry and improved his Aristotalian philosophy; he read in the classical authors as well as the fathers of the church and completed the full course of scholastic theology. He was in Rome for the election of Pope Clement XI (author of the *Unigenitus* controversy). One effect of this close contact with the Roman church was to instil in the young Prokopovich a lasting hatred of the papacy and all that it seemed to him to stand for. He was later to remark that nowhere was the truth of Christianity so much in doubt as in Italy. The Jesuits attempted to persuade the brilliant young scholar from Kiev to join their order. But in 1701 he went home.[1]

In other words, Prokopovich belonged by birth and upbringing to

[1] The principal authorities on Prokopovich include: I. Chistovich, *Feofan Prokopovich i ego vremya* (St. Petersburg, 1868) – a major work of some 700 pages; P. Morozov, 'Feofan Prokopovich kak pisatel'', *Zhurnal ministerstva narodnago prosveshcheniya*, 1880: vols. 207 (pp. 416–476), 208 (pp. 72–133), 209 (pp. 107–148, 251–311); 210 (pp. 1–49, 293–354), 211 (pp. 1–65); Yu. F. Samarin, *Stefan Yavorskii i Feofan Prokopovich* (Moscow, 1880); and B. Titlinov, 'Feofan Prokopovich', *Russkii biograficheskii slovar'*, xxv (St. Petersburg, 1913), pp. 399–448 – with complete bibliography. Four of Prokopovich's lesser known works are printed in Verkhovskoi, ii, III (pp. 3–81). For a recent edition of his major literary works, see I. P. Eremin (ed.), *Feofan Prokopovich: Sochineniya* (Moscow/Leningrad, 1961); and for an eighteenth-century translation (from the Latin) of four of his theological treatises, see M. Sokolov (trans.), *Feofan Prokopovich: Chetyre sochineniya* (Moscow, 1773). Unfortunately, the eighteenth-century edition of Prokopovich's letters (*Epistolae illustrissimi ac reverendissimi Theophanis Prokopovitsch, variis temporibus et ad varios amicos* [Moscow, 1776]) was not available to me, and I have had to rely on the Russian translations of the letters printed in the authorities cited above.

Recent western studies of Prokopovich's career include: R. Stupperich, 'Feofan Prokopovič in Rom', *Zeitschrift für Osteuropäische Geschichte*, v (1931), pp. 327–339; Stupperich, 'Feofan Prokopovičs theologische Bestrebungen', *Kyrios*, iv (1936), pp. 350–362; Stupperich, 'Feofan Prokopovič und Johann F. Buddeus', *Zeitschrift fur Osteuropäische Geschichte*, ix (1935), pp. 341–362; Stupperich, 'Feofan Prokopovič und seine akademische Wirksamkeit in Kiev', *Zeitschrift für Slavische Philologie*, xvii (1941), pp. 70–101; F. Venturi, 'Feofan Prokopovič', *Annali della facoltà di Lettere e Filosofia e di Magistero dell'Università di Cagliari*, xxi, pt. 1 (1953); and J. Šerech, 'On Theofan Prokopovič as Writer and Preacher in his Kiev Period', *Harvard Slavic Studies*, ii (1954), pp. 211–223.

that East Slavonic or 'Renaissance'[1] civilization which was centred in Kiev, was formed of Polish–Latin and native Russian (or Ruthenian or Ukrainian) elements, and though Greek Orthodox in religion was in its theology, religious art, architecture, and letters heavily influenced by the militant, baroque, Jesuit Roman Catholicism emanating from Poland. It had flourished throughout the seventeenth century among the upper classes of the territories under Polish suzerainty and, especially after 1667, when Kiev and the Ukraine east of the Dnieper were incorporated in the Muscovite tsardom by treaty with Poland, had increasingly influenced the upper levels of Muscovite society, thus beginning the process of secularization and westernization in the Russian heartland. But now it was entering its own baroque phase and in the rush of events had begun to decline, overshadowed by the growing Imperial or All-Russian civilization emanating from Moscow and, after 1704 or so, from St. Petersburg. Prokopovich was so far, at the age of twenty-one, a typical product of this culture – with one or two important differences. He was not, unlike so many of his later colleagues in the Russian hierarchy, of gentle or noble birth, but rather was vaguely middle class, an orphan as mentioned, poor, and thus wholly dependent on the church not only for his education but for his very livelihood. Owing to this element of insecurity and of social inferiority in his early life he was, perhaps, less than impregnated with this upper-class culture of his native land; or rather, he perhaps saw it less as a way of life than as a thing primarily of literature, a thing of the mind, and therefore mutable. Moreover, having proved a brilliant student, and having studied therefore in Rome itself, at the age of twenty-one Prokopovich was, as suggested, already antipathetic to Roman Catholicism and to, in particular, its papal and Jesuit aspects. Prokopovich was not fully satisfied with his cultural heritage. And these early differences between him and most of the members of his cultural community may help to explain his subsequent development.

On his return to Kiev in 1702 Prokopovich promptly reverted to Orthodoxy. He became a monk of the Pochaevskii monastery and took the name Samuel; in 1705, in memory of his uncle, he changed his name to Feofan. In 1704 he began to teach poetics at the Kiev academy, in 1706 a course in rhetoric, and in 1707 the course in philosophy. He wrote treatises in Latin on both poetics and rhetoric which manifest

[1] H. Birnbaum, 'Some Aspects of the Slavonic Renaissance', *Slavonic and East European Review*, xlvii (January 1969), pp. 37–56.

an attempt, on the basis of classical models, to purify the disciplines of scholastic and baroque accretions. As early as 1707 he tried to introduce arithmetic, geometry, and physics into the academy's curriculum by teaching the subjects in his own classes. A contemporary Danish visitor noted in his journal that Prokopovich exhibited an 'indescribable love' of mathematics.[1] Moreover, at this time the young academic (he was still in his twenties) expressed in his literary efforts a certain national consciousness that was tinged, inevitably, with politics. In the Jesuit tradition of academic drama he wrote a five-act tragicomedy in verse on the theme of the Christianization and enlightenment of the 'Slavonic–Russian lands' under the tenth-century prince, St. Vladimir. It was performed on 3 July 1705 at the Kiev academy in the presence of Ivan Mazepa, hetman (prince) of the Ukraine, a patron of the academy, and an ally (or rather satellite) of Tsar Peter. The play concluded with the chorus chanting these words:

> . . . Grant might and strength,
> Grant length of days and to every undertaking
> A happy conclusion; and in war, always victory!
> Grant health, power, peace, security!
> Grant this to Tsar Peter, crowned by Thee,
> And to his most loyal chieftain, Ivan![2]

In the summer of 1706 Peter himself came to Kiev to inspect the fortifications of the Monastery of the Caves and on 5 July attended services in the Sofiiskii cathedral, where he heard Prokopovich preach. No doubt the latter had already begun to develop the distinctive and powerful style that characterizes his later sermons; but there is no evidence that on this occasion the tsar did anything more than make a mental note of the preacher's existence. In the tense year of 1708, unlike most of the higher clergy of the Ukraine, Prokopovich swiftly took the side of Tsar Peter when Hetman Mazepa, in league with the Swedes, betrayed him. A year later, following the Russian defeat of the Swedes at Poltava, Peter came again to Kiev, and again was formally welcomed in the Sofiiskii cathedral by Prokopovich, now prefect of the academy, who preached a magnificant panegyric on the tsar's

[1] Quoted in Chistovich, *op. cit.*, pp. 627–628.

[2] The critical edition of 'Vladimir' is printed in Eremin, *op. cit.*, pp. 149–206. For a slightly different and abridged version, see A. V. Kokorev (ed.), *Khrestomatiya po russkoi literature XVIII veka* (Moscow, 1965), pp. 55–69; and for an analysis of the play, Tikhonravov, *op. cit.*, pp. 120–155.

victory which cannot have failed to please him. The occasion is mentioned in the official history of Peter's reign;[1] and the panegyric was published both in Slavonic and Polish and also in Latin, so that the 'whole of Europe should know of this triumph'.[2] In December of that year (1709) Peter's chief favourite, Alexander Menshikov, visited Kiev, and was treated to a welcoming oration by Feofan Prokopovich. Within a few months Menshikov was recommending this 'learned man' to the influential Metropolitan Job of Novgorod, who apparently was willing to find him a post. But before any such action could be taken Peter himself intervened. In June 1711 he summoned Prokopovich to military headquarters in Moldavia, where on the second anniversary of the Poltava victory he preached a rousing sermon. He remained to witness the Russian defeat by the Turks at the battle on the Pruth (July 1711), and recorded the event in a poem where he urged that an enlightened Christendom would yet be liberated from the 'power of paganism'.[3] His efforts continued to please the tsar. Later that year, only a few months after his thirtieth birthday, Prokopovich was appointed igumen (abbot) of the Kiev-Brotherhood monastery, rector of the Kiev academy, and professor of theology there.

It was to be four more years before the tsar called Prokopovich to St. Petersburg, where he began the second half of his remarkable career. Meanwhile, he devoted himself to the administration of the academy and to his theological lectures, in which, as might be expected, he showed himself strongly critical of his old masters and of the tendency to refute Protestant, rather than Roman Catholic, divines. His increasingly radical theological method has been aptly described as critical-historical, in the sense that he consistently argued that the exposition of dogma must be based on Scripture, the Fathers, and church history as opposed to the syllogistic exercises, the deductive reasonings, the spurious self-evidencies, the commentaries on commentaries of decadent Latin scholasticism. Whether for this reason, or simply because he was a good teacher, his lectures proved a great success with the students; at the same time, they aroused the hostility of his colleagues, some of whom were later to accuse him of un-Orthodoxy. But on the whole his term as rector passed uneventfully, owing partly no doubt to the fact that

[1] *Zhurnal*, i, p. 224.

[2] A copy of the Latin version of Prokopovich's *Panegyricus Petro Primo* . . . is preserved in the British Museum (cat. no. 590.i.23, doc. 2). For the Slavonic version, see Eremin, *op. cit.*, pp. 23–38.

[3] The poem is printed in full in Chistovich, *op. cit.*, p. 16; and in Eremin, *op. cit.*, pp. 214–215.

he enjoyed powerful political protection. And during these prosperous years Prokopovich formed a close and useful association with the sophisticated governor of Kiev, Prince D. M. Golitsyn, often retiring to his house or to that of an aristocratic former pupil, Ya. A. Markovich, where in comfort they discussed the classics as well as the new philosophies of Bacon, Descartes, Grotius, Hobbes, Pufendorf, and Locke with local and visiting intellectuals. One of the latter, a German named Bayer, has evoked the atmosphere of these 'attic gatherings' in the dedication to Prokopovich of one of his books:

> Everyone emerged a little wiser. It was enough that you began to speak for me immediately to believe that I was in Greece, in the schools of rhetoric, poetry, or philosophy.... Similarly, you transported me so to speak to Rome or some other city of Italy celebrated for its sacred or classical monuments: you resurrected for me the ages past.[1]

Prokopovich's tastes were becoming increasingly cosmopolitan, his theology increasingly 'Protestant', his interests increasingly secular and political, political in both the theoretical and practical sense. Given his background, youth, ability, connections, and his obvious ambition, it will not surprise us shortly to discover in him an ecclesiastical politician of the first rank, an All-Russian Imperialist, and, what is perhaps most important, the first authentic voice in Russia of the Early Enlightenment.

Late in 1715 Prokopovich received Peter's summons to St. Petersburg. The prospect of a bishopric, among other things, was being held out to him – or so he understood the summons. This and his somewhat ambiguous sentiments on leaving Kiev are reflected in his letter to Markovich of 9 August 1716:

> You have perhaps heard that I am being called to the episcopacy. This prospect both attracts and repels me.... I envy good men their mitres, copes, crosiers, and other paraphernalia; add to this still bigger and tastier fish. But if I become interested in it, if I answer the call, may God punish me in some even worse way. I like episcopal affairs and would like to be a bishop, were it not that to be a bishop one must indulge in histrionics; for that is a most corrupt profession if it is not guided by divine wisdom. For my part, I will make every effort to avoid this honour and return quickly to you. I have not yet finished my theological lectures; when I have finished, I would consider spending some time as a bishop – if not for the multitude, if not for another, then at least for my own sake![2]

[1] Quoted in Chistovich, *op. cit.*, pp. 619–620; also in Blanc, *op. cit.*, p. 451.
[2] Letter quoted in Chistovich, *op. cit.*, pp. 24–25.

He arrived in St. Petersburg in October 1716 and at the tsar's order immediately began writing a popular catechism. The work survives in a manuscript to which is attached a 'Notice', also in Prokopovich's own hand, which explains that 'wishing to serve his Majesty the Tsar and the needs of the people I have written, to the best of my ability, this little book of Christian instruction'; but that since the catechism had not fulfilled Peter's requirements for 'brief and simple instruction, suitable for study and memorization by youths', it had been abandoned and another begun: the 'Notice' is signed by the 'Rector of the Kiev school' and is dated 17 February 1717 at St. Petersburg.[1] At this time Prokopovich also compiled a regal table of the Russian grand princes and tsars which was plainly political in inspiration: a secular and All-Russian Imperialist history, however limited in scope, which recounted the glories of the Russian sovereigns from Vladimir to Peter, to whom it was presented by Menshikov and promptly published.[2] In June 1717 he preached at the customary commemoration of the Poltava victory in the Trinity cathedral in St. Petersburg; in October, he delivered an oration on behalf of the 'Russian people' to the tsar on his return from abroad; in November he preached a sermon, again in the Trinity cathedral, in honour of Peter's wife, Tsaritsa Catherine.[3] He had quickly become a figure in the new capital, Peter's collaborator, and the cynosure, no doubt, of malevolent eyes.

For Prokopovich did not conceal his contempt for his fellow clergy and especially for the so-called 'Latinizers', the graduates of the Kiev academy who had been called to serve in the Russian church. 'What can one say about the priests and monks and about our Latinizers?' he exclaimed in a letter to Markovich soon after his arrival in St. Petersburg. 'Their brains are full of bits and pieces of theology snatched sometime by some grand Jesuit from miscellaneous scholastic, patristic, and pagan authors'. More, 'our Latinizers so arm themselves with sophistries that nothing remains of their education . . . [they] think so highly of themselves that their sophistries could fill the ocean'. In recent years, Prokopovich reported to Markovich,

> These so-called oratorical exercises have become the fashion: what is the significance of the five letters in the name Maria? Why did Christ immerse himself in the Jordan by standing, and not by lying down or sitting? Why

[1] The 'Notice' is printed in Verkhovskoi, i, pp. 389–390.

[2] *Rodoslovnaya rospis' velikikh knyazei i tsarei rossiiskikh do gosudarya Petra I* (St. Petersburg, 1717).

[3] All three orations are printed in Eremin, *op. cit.*, pp. 48–59, 60–67, 68–76.

> were the fish not destroyed in the waters of the great flood, since they were not preserved in Noah's ark? And so on. And extremely weighty and complex answers are given to questions like these.... Now we are all, as you see, theologically sick. Oh, if only, following your splendid example, everyone were consumed by a thirst for knowledge and study, as opposed to the tyranny of the said opinions. Then there would be hope that from the darkness light might come. But this, as we see, is not the case. Everyone aspires to teach and almost no one wants to be taught....[1]

His contempt for the mass of the lower Muscovite clergy, for manifestations of the popular religion, and especially for the beliefs and practices of the Russian schismatics, was no less complete, and in its insensitivity and perhaps incomprehension reminds us of his royal master. 'I have begun a large treatise on hypocrites, having a great supply of material for this purpose', he informed Markovich in the spring of 1720.

> I am also writing a short treatise on martyrdom ... [which] the Emperor [*sic*] commanded me to write, feeling sorry for the blind fanatics who in order to win the name of martyr exhibit a mad zeal and with the greatest audacity assail not only the clergy but the Sovereign himself, because of the changes in dress, the wigs [*pariki*], the shaving of beards, and similar trifles. I heard a funny story. Some novice whom I don't know, having read the lives of the martyrs, became inflamed with a zeal for martyrdom, and not knowing how to manage it conceived this ploy: I will buy, he said, an Old-Russian saddle, which it is forbidden to use, and one fine day ride in it to Moscow, in defiance of the Tsar's edict; perhaps I will be put to death. Thus the ways of thought of these unfortunates. It is this evil that we wish to extirpate....[2]

Indeed Peter had found, after long searching, a senior cleric whose sympathies (or antipathies) closely corresponded to his own. And as Prokopovich's sense of the imperfections of his new surroundings grew, so too did his devotion to Peter, and his faith in the power of the tsar to put things right. They soon became, it seems, as close as a subject and his monarch, an intellectual and a practical man of affairs, a learned Kievan and a gross Muscovite, a cleric and Peter, could have become. Prokopovich was allowed to entertain the tsar and to visit him at his various retreats; and apart from high ecclesiastical office and important royal commissions, his efforts were rewarded more tangibly: with a gift of books, a pleasure boat, a house by the sea, additional

[1] Letter quoted in Chistovich, *op. cit.*, pp. 38–39.
[2] Quoted in *ibid.*, pp. 48–49.

estates, or hard cash. Prokopovich could not of course have been expected to join the Most Drunken Council, and so was excluded, perhaps, from Peter's innermost circle of friends. But he could and did join, as orator, the tsar's somewhat more serious club, the 'Neptune society', which was composed of the favourites and qualified foreigners who supposedly were devoted to the advancement of science.

On Palm Sunday (6 April) 1718 Prokopovich preached a remarkable sermon on the theme of the 'honour and power of the tsar'. As an example of his general intellectual outlook, method of argument, and evolving political philosophy, the sermon, which is not devoid of elements of opportunism and self-justification, cannot be surpassed. It was a time of acute unrest in Russia. Successive interrogations of Peter's hapless son, Tsarevich Aleksei, had revealed a loosely organized but widespread conspiracy against the tsar, and in his sermon Prokopovich combined condemnations of the conspirators and of all 'oppositionists' with lamentations on the general state of ignorance and salutary warnings against the snares of false theology. 'Do we not see here [in the story of Christ's triumphal entry into Jerusalem] what honour is paid to the King? Does this not require us *not* to remain silent about the duty of subjects to esteem the supreme authority, and about the great resistance to this duty that has been exposed in our country at the present time?' For we see, declared the preacher, 'that not a small part of the people abide in such ignorance that they do not know the Christian doctrine concerning the secular authorities. Nay more, they do not know that the supreme authority is established and armed with the sword by God, and that to oppose it is a sin against God Himself, a sin to be punished by death not temporal but eternal'. Warming to his theme, Prokopovich excoriated those who did not 'consider themselves ignorant' and yet were 'opponents of true doctrine' – those who, 'because of their boorishness, appear as babblers, understanding neither Scripture nor the power of God'. They cite 'the words of Christ Himself: "For what is exalted among men is an abomination in the sight of God" [Luke 16:15]; and from this they deduce that wisdom, power, glory, and all human authority are abominable in the sight of God'. Here, indeed,

> We behold the height of theology, oh listeners! And who cannot see how effective and forceful this is with the simple ignorant folk, especially when it is proclaimed with honeyed words and an affected countenance, with sighs and noddings of the head.

But this teaching of Christ, Prokopovich assured his audience, 'is not directed to the high authority of the state, for the lowliness that God loves may be found in the imperial purple, when a king confesses before God that he is a sinner and places his hope solely in His mercy, as did David, Constantine, Theodosius, and others'. And having thus disposed of the 'abominable words' of false teachers, Prokopovich proceeded to explain what 'nature herself and the word of God teach us concerning human authority'.

The student of the new philosophy – of the works especially of Grotius, Hobbes, and Pufendorf – pointed out to his Russian audience that 'laws like these are written in the heart of every man: to love and fear God, to preserve one's own life, to wish for a never-declining prosperity for the human race, not to do to others what one does not wish for oneself, and to honour one's father and mother. . . . And might there not also be among these natural laws this one: that there must be an authority holding supreme power in every nation? There is indeed! This is the supreme law. For because the ill-will of a depraved race does not hesitate to break the law to love ourselves and not to do to others what we do not wish for ourselves, always and everywhere a guardian has been desirable, a protector and a strong upholder of the law; and this is the authority of the state'. Therefore 'we hold it certain that the supreme authority receives its beginning and cause from nature herself'; and 'if from nature, then from God Himself, the creator of nature. . . . We cannot help but call God the cause of the authority of the state'. Prokopovich also assured his audience, with numerous quotations from Scripture, that the 'written word of God . . . seals the establishment of governments with His blessing and commands that they be obeyed'.

Finally, Prokopovich's relentless, hammering rhetoric brought him to the main point of his sermon: 'to show what honour we owe the authorities, what love and loyalty, what fear and obedience'. If biblical and patristic history demonstrated that 'Christians have to be subject even to perverse and unbelieving rulers, how much more must they be utterly devoted to an Orthodox and just sovereign'.

> For the former are masters, but the latter are also fathers. What am I saying? That our autocrat [Peter], and all autocrats, are fathers. And where else will you find this duty of ours, to honour the authorities sincerely and conscientiously, if not in the commandment: 'Honour thy father'! All the wise teachers affirm this; thus Moses the lawgiver himself instructs us. Moreover the authority of the state is the primary and ultimate degree of fatherhood,

> for on it depends not a single individual, not one household, but the life, the integrity, and the welfare of the whole great nation.

And Prokopovich did not neglect to deal with 'one doubt that remains like a thorn in the conscience', namely the belief that the clergy were exempt from the duties of service and loyalty to the sovereign. 'This thorn – or better say sting, for this is the sting of the serpent – is the papist spirit'. For,

> As there is one task for the army, another for civil administrators, another for doctors, another for the various artisans, so also pastors and teachers and all those concerned with ecclesiastical affairs have their particular task; and they, too, are subject to the authority of the state, in order that they should remain steadfast in their vocation . . . and fulfil the obligations they have in common with the rest of the people. . . . The clergy is another order or rank of the people, and not a separate state.

Nor did Prokopovich neglect fulsomely and feelingly to praise Tsar Peter,

> the Orthodox monarch who has so benefited Russia that from the beginning of the All-Russian state historians cannot point to one equal to him. . . . He has given Russia a new birth; but what is his reward from us?
>
> Terrible to his enemies, forced to fear his own subjects! Glorious among foreigners, dishonoured among his own people! . . . Let us beware that this saying does not arise about us: the sovereign is worthy of such a country, but the people are not worthy of such a sovereign.[1]

If Peter had need of any further proof that Prokopovich was his man and was willing and able to assist him in the radical reform of the church (on which the tsar had about made up his mind), this sermon surely provided it. And Prokopovich's sermon of 6 April 1718 marked his public *début* as the chief ideologist of the Petrine state and the original propagator of the Petrine legend. It was a role that he was to play with distinction in the remaining years of his life. In his sermons, orations, and poems he did not overlook an opportunity to extol Peter's genius and to praise his achievements, however mundane.[2] He helped to prepare the official history of Peter's reign and by himself wrote an

[1] 'Slovo o vlasti i chesti tsarskoi . . .', printed in Eremin, *op. cit.*, pp. 76–93. The sermon was published in St. Petersburg in August 1718 (see T. A. Bykova and M. M. Gurevich, *Opisanie izdanii napechatannykh kirillitsei, 1689–1725* [Moscow/Leningrad, 1958], no. 117 [pp. 205–206]).

[2] See Eremin, *op. cit.*, pp. 103–112 and 219–220 for, respectively, a sermon 'In Praise of the Russian Fleet' and a poem 'On the Ladoga Canal'. One is reminded of the excesses of socialist realism.

account of the years up to the Poltava victory.[1] He also wrote a popular catechism in which, it will be seen in a subsequent chapter, he expounded in a greatly simplified form the doctrine of authority contained in the sermon. In 1722 he published a treatise on the 'justice of the monarch's will' in which he justified, on the basis of natural law and historical precedent, Peter's assumption of the right to name his own successor, explaining that his acts were 'independent of any superior power, in that they cannot be annulled by any other human will'.[2] Moreover in July 1721 he published an essay expressing the view that since Constantine's time the Christian emperors had exercised the powers of a bishop, 'in the sense that they appointed the bishops, who ruled the clergy'. This was, in short, a justification of Peter's assumption of complete jurisdiction over the government of the church; for a 'Christian sovereign', Prokopovich concluded in a celebrated definition of the term, is empowered to nominate not only bishops, 'but the bishop of bishops, because the Sovereign is the supreme authority, the perfect, ultimate, and authentic supervisor; that is, he holds supreme judicial and executive power over all the ranks and authorities subject to him, whether secular or ecclesiastical'. 'Patriarchalism [*patriarshestvo*]' – the belief that a patriarch should rule the autocephalous Russian church – Prokopovich equated with 'papalism', and dismissed it accordingly.[3]

But the *Ecclesiastical Regulation*, which he was commissioned by Peter to write in the latter part of 1718 and which was first published in the autumn of 1721, is Prokopovich's greatest literary achievement and the most enduring monument to his genius. The numerous provisions of this revolutionary document, which touch on virtually every aspect of the life of the church, will be referred to or quoted in the following chapters. Yet it may be noted here that although the *Regulation* was the principal piece of legislation embodying Peter's church

[1] *Istoriya imp. Petra Velikago, ot rozhdeniya ego do Poltavskoi batalii*, ed. M. M. Shcherbatov (St. Petersburg, 1773). I follow Chistovich (*op. cit.*, p. 122) in attributing this work to Prokopovich, though there is some doubt.

[2] *Pravda voli monarshei vo opredelenii naslednika derzhavy svoei* (Moscow, 1722). The treatise was also published in Latin at Leipzig in 1723, and in German at Berlin in 1724 (Pekarskii, *op. cit.*, ii, pp. 571–575). In Russia it was regarded as an official document and appended to the succession law (*PSZ*, vii, no. 4870 [pp. 602–643]); and either independently, or together with the law, it was frequently reprinted. For a legal analysis of the treatise and its sources (works of Grotius, Hobbes, and Pufendorf), see G. Gurvich, '*Pravda voli monarshei*' *Feofana Prokopovicha* (Yur'ev, 1915).

[3] See his essay 'Rozysk istoricheskii o pontifikse . . .', printed in Verkhovskoi, ii, III, pp. 5–20.

reform, it retained the character of an academic treatise and the personal stamp of its extraordinary author. It is not accidental, for instance, that the necessity of education is an insistent theme of the *Regulation*, and that fully a fifth of its text is devoted to a discussion of the projected ecclesiastical schools. Similarly, to students of Prokopovich's earlier career the *Regulation*'s denunciations of 'ill-grounded sophists' and florid preachers and ignorant schismatics have a familiar ring. We are not surprised to find in the document, knowing its author, a defence of 'secular learning' or a provision recommending that the 'ancient and modern philosophers, astronomers, rhetoricians, historians, etc.', as well as the church fathers, should be read by seminarists. Nor are we surprised to discover, in a passage justifying the suppression of the Russian patriarchate, a quite irrelevant aside concerning the 'mischief' done at other times and places by the popes of Rome. Only Prokopovich, among contemporary Russian churchmen, would have adduced specific examples of the 'nonsense' practised in Italy with respect to relics as a guide to the reformers of the Russian church. In short, Prokopovich's own background and outlook and personal prejudices were obviously of great importance in determining the shape and scope and emphases of Peter's church reform.

And it was not only a question of his intellectual or literary influence. Prokopovich was also an extremely active churchman. He managed to overcome his initial scruples about the episcopacy and to accept Peter's offer of the see of Pskov, to which he was consecrated, after an abortive attempt by his enemies to prevent it, on 1 June 1718. On 31 December 1720 he was promoted to the rank of archbishop on Peter's personal orders; and in January 1721 Peter appointed him second vice-president of the new Ecclesiastical College (renamed the Most Holy All-Ruling Synod in February), which had replaced the patriarchate as the supreme administrative organ of the Russian church. It was symbolic that Prokopovich, and not the president or first vice-president of the Synod, should have preached the sermon on the occasion of the Synod's official opening (14 February 1721). For in the years that followed he dominated the Synod's proceedings, frequently serving as Peter's channel for communicating his wishes to that body and often personally writing many of the admonitions, pronouncements, and decrees that were issued in its name. And after Peter's death, in January 1725, Prokopovich became a principal custodian of the great tsar's legacy. He was instrumental in ensuring that Empress Catherine should succeed to the throne, as Peter apparently had intended. In 1730 he helped to persuade Empress Anna, Peter's niece, to renounce the 'constitution' imposed on her by a cabal of magnates and so to preserve, intact, the rights of the autocrat. In the midst of the political infighting he found time to befriend or patronize the poet Antiokh Kantemir, Tatishchev the historian, and Lomonosov. And he consistently resisted attempts to restore the patriarchate – to undo, as though it were possible, the church reform of Peter the Great. Whatever else may be said of him, he was devoted to Peter and to his memory, and until his death in 1736 remained a champion of what came to be called enlightened absolutism.

CHAPTER TWO

Government, Church, and Society in Russia, 1649–1721

If the *Ecclesiastical Regulation* of 1721 was the principal piece of legislation embodying the church reform of Peter the Great, it should not be thought that its provisions were in every respect unprecedented, whether in the legislation of the previous twenty or so years of Peter's own reign or in that of his immediate predecessors. Indeed, a systematic study of the laws of the Russian state promulgated between 1649 and 1721 – between the publication of the *Ulozhenie* (law code) of Tsar Aleksei and the first appearance of the *Ecclesiastical Regulation* – reveals that, with certain outstanding exceptions, Peter's legislation relating to the ecclesiastical institutions of Russia or to the religious profession of his subjects was solidly based on precedent. It suggests that, in this field anyway, the modifications of traditional policies that were introduced under Peter prior to 1721 may be termed innovations, rather than radical or revolutionary reforms. This is not simply a question of terminology. For a just appreciation of the nature of Peter's definitive reform of the church, it is essential that the *Ecclesiastical Regulation* and related measures should be situated squarely in the context of their legislative precedents.

For this purpose, the policies pursued by successive Russian governments in the religious and ecclesiastical field between 1649 and 1721 are discussed, in the pages that follow, under six headings: (I) religious minorities; (II) economic matters; (III) education and social welfare; (IV) the clergy; (V) judicial matters; and (VI) the patriarchal domain. The discussion will, it is hoped, show that Peter's religious and ecclesiastical legislation, as compared with that of his immediate predecessors, contained much that was new; but that no single one of his innovations enacted before 1721, nor all of them together, constituted that church reform which we associate with his name. Had Peter died in 1720, he would have left the church in disarray; but it could not have been said that he had reformed it. The task of permanently reforming the church, it will be seen in the following chapters, was accomplished between the promulgation of the *Ecclesiastical Regulation* in 1721 and Peter's death in 1725.

I

OFFICIAL PERSECUTION OF RELIGIOUS MINORITIES

Peter's legislation affecting his Muslim or 'pagan' subjects is a minor but telling example of the extent to which his policies were based on those of his immediate predecessors. In the *Ulozhenie* of 1649, for instance, it was prescribed that Muslims who, 'by force or by fraud, should convert a Russian to their Muslim religion', were liable to death by burning, while their Russian converts were to be handed over to the patriarch or to the local bishop for trial according to ecclesiastical law – presumably for apostasy.[1] In 1675 Tsar Aleksei decreed that service and hereditary estates held by Tatars and 'other tribesmen [*inozemtsy*]' were to be confiscated and distributed to Russians and those 'newly-baptized in the Orthodox faith': 'vacant estates' were to be found for Tatars willing in future to accept baptism.[2] Archdeacon Paul of Aleppo, who visited Russia during Aleksei's reign and was full of admiration for the tsar, described the history of the numerous Tatar menials whom he had met in the service of Muscovites: 'continually carried into captivity by the tsar's armies . . . their lands are conquered, their houses burnt, and their women and children taken and sold at the meanest prices. . . . [And] as soon as they are purchased they are instantly baptized and made Christians'.[3]

Aleksei's policy of discrimination against the indigenous peoples of the south and east in favour of land-hungry Orthodox Russians was only partially modified during the reign of his son and successor, Fedor (1676–1682). Now, very temporal rewards were dangled before Tatars and others who (in the words of a relevant edict), 'having discovered the true religion of the Greek rite, and wishing in good faith to live piously, have petitioned [the tsar], that he should deign to order them to be baptized'. The said petitioners were duly received into the church, whereupon their leaders were honoured with Russian titles and given estates and money for division among their 'newly-baptized brethren', all of whom were granted a three-year exemption from military service.[4] Similar decrees of the following year provided rewards for Tatar Muslims who 'perceive the light of Orthodoxy'; but those in possession of estates who remained in darkness were to suffer

[1] *PRP*, vi, p. 434; also *PSZ*, i, no. 1 (p. 156).
[2] *PSZ*, i, no. 616 (p. 1029).
[3] Paul of Aleppo, *op. cit.*, i, p. 275.
[4] *PSZ*, ii, no. 823 (p. 267): edict of 21 May 1680.

confiscation of their property.[1] Clearly, the burden of such legislation was to make retention of estates by the tsar's non-Christian subjects conditional on their acceptance of baptism, a policy which was no doubt inspired as much by the government's continuous need for service estates as it was by the missionary zeal of the Russian church.

During the regency of Aleksei's daughter Sof'ya (1682–1689) an attempt apparently was made to separate the political and religious aspects of the question and to reject, not the policy of encouraging genuine conversions to Orthodoxy, but that of requiring conversion as a condition of state service, with the associated privilege of land-owning.[2] Sof'ya's intentions are clearly indicated in a lengthy edict to Metropolitan Paul of Tobol'sk and Siberia which was dispatched in April 1685 in response to complaints from local Tatars and others that had been forwarded to Moscow by the local Russian *voevoda* (governor): the metropolitan was commanded to baptize only persons who desired it 'of their own free will'; he was to question them carefully on this point both before and at baptism; only then was it promised that those who freely submitted would be rewarded from the state treasury; and nothing whatever was said of persons not inclined to conversion, or of their property.[3] For the rest, Sof'ya confirmed, under pain of death, the disciplinary measures enacted by previous governments: *inozemtsy* residing in Tobol'sk, 'in their old places', were to live peacefully; in particular, they were not to 'shriek nor to commit any impropriety' during the time of Orthodox services or to entice their erstwhile co-religionists, the local *novokreshchentsy*, back to the old faith. They were to stand 'fearfully, politely, to doff their caps and to commit no facetiousness or impropriety' when the holy processions with ikons passed by their houses.[4]

Tsar Peter, on the other hand, appears to have been an enthusiast of the church's evangelical mission in the south and east. In an interview with the dying Patriarch Adrian in October 1700 he made known his concern that Tatars, Mordvinians, the Cheremiss and other non-Christian peoples should be brought to the 'love and knowledge of God' by missionaries specially trained at the Kiev academy.[5] Nor was

[1] *PSZ*, ii, no. 867 (pp. 312–313): no. 870 (p. 315).
[2] See, for example, *PSZ*, ii, no. 923 (p. 403); no. 944 (p. 456).
[3] *PSZ*, ii, no. 1117 (pp. 662–663). [4] *Ibid.*
[5] See *ZAP*, no. 4 (pp. 33–34), which is, evidently, a secretary's notes of the meeting. For edited versions of the same text, see S. M. Solov'ev, *Istoriya Rossii* (Moscow, 1962–1966), viii, p. 89; Ustryalov, *op. cit.*, iii, p. 512; S. G. Runkevich, *Uchrezhdenie sinoda* (St. Petersburg, 1900), pp. 22–23.

this the first occasion on which the young tsar had discussed the matter with the head of the church. The previous June, in an edict concerning trade in Siberia and with China, Peter had inserted a passage declaring that

> for the strengthening and augmenting of the Christian Orthodox faith, and for the propagation of the Holy Gospels among these idolatrous peoples, and for the conversion to the Christian faith and to holy baptism of the heathen tribes who live near Tobol'sk and the other Siberian towns, the Great Sovereign [Peter], in speaking of this with the Most Holy Patriarch, commanded him to write to the metropolitan of Kiev: that he [the metropolitan], pursuant to this holy and God-pleasing work, should search among the heads of monasteries in his province for a good, educated, pious, and chaste man to be metropolitan of Tobol'sk. [The latter] should be able, with God's help, to convert people in China and in Siberia from the blindness of idolatry and other irreligious practices to the knowledge and service and worship of the true, living God. He should bring with him two or three good, educated and young monks who could learn the Chinese and Mongolian languages; and having perceived their superstitions, they would be able by solid arguments drawn from Scripture to lead many souls from the realm of Satanic darkness into the light of knowledge of Christ our Lord. . . .

Peter had gone on to express the somewhat extravagant hope that eventually even the 'Chinese Khan and his courtiers, and his whole nation, might be brought to this Holy matter'.[1] On a more practical level, the see of Tobol'sk, which had been raised to the rank of a metropolitanate by the church council of 1667,[2] was designated by Peter the centre of a renewed Siberian mission; and on 23 March 1701 Dimitrii Tuptalo, archimandrite of the Novgorod-Severskii monastery in the Ukraine, was consecrated metropolitan.[3] Similarly, Peter at this time envisaged collaborating with Patriarch Dositheus of Jerusalem in establishing in the newly-conquered town of Azov Orthodox clergy

[1] *PSZ*, iv, no. 1800 (pp. 59–61). Similar sentiments were voiced by the tsar to the metropolitan of Ryazan' on his appointment, in December 1700, as temporary head of the church (see Runkevich, *op. cit.*, p. 34).

[2] *PSZ*, i, no. 412 (pp. 707–708). The see was founded in 1620.

[3] Though he never took up his post. In April 1701 an official wrote to Peter at Voronezh, informing him that 'the bishop of Siberia, Sovereign, awaits your sovereign edict: shall he leave Moscow on his journey before your Majesty's arrival, or shall he wait, as he himself would wish' (*PiB*, i, p. 853). Peter replied, on 14 May: 'let the bishop wait' (*ibid.*, no. 374 [p. 449]). Later he accepted the ailing Dimitrii's objections to the rigours of the Tobol'sk see, and in January 1702 nominated him metropolitan of Rostov (*ibid.*, p. 855; see also I. A. Shylapkin, *Sv. Dimitrii Rostovskii i ego vremya* [St. Petersburg, 1891], pp. 276–283).

who should be able 'not only to guide the local Christians to salvation, but also the border peoples to the Holy Orthodox Catholic faith'.[1]

It has been suggested that Peter regarded his 'China mission' as a politically awkward competitor of the Roman Catholic effort in this field, an effort which he had himself facilitated, while in Vienna in 1698, by consenting to the passage of Jesuit missionaries through his territories.[2] Indeed, from Vienna Peter had written to one of his officials in Moscow: 'you report that in Peking they have built a Christian church of our rite, and that many Christians have been baptized. The business has gone well enough; only for God's sake act in this matter with extreme caution, lest the Chinese lords become spiteful and also the Jesuits, who have had their nest there already for some time'.[3] Obviously, the existence in China of a Jesuit mission with Imperial patronage acted as a brake on Peter's own ambitions in this direction. Thus in February 1721, among the first of the questions submitted to him by the newly-created Synod, was one concerning 'the monk Innokentii Kunchitskii, who has been nominated Bishop of Irkutsk and Nerchinsk: is he to be consecrated for the territories adjoining the Chinese State? and would this most conveniently be managed by dividing the Siberian diocese?' Peter replied: 'Consecrate the bishop; but it would be better [to do so] without [conferring on him] any titles of towns, since these towns border on China – lest the Jesuits misinterpret anything and become upset'.[4] On 17 March the Synod announced that 'for the Chinese mission, for the propagation of the Word of God and for the spread of the Holy Orthodox Eastern faith, the monk Innokentii . . . has been consecrated bishop of Pereyaslavl''[5] – a see safely within Russian borders. On 12 May the Synod and Senate jointly dispatched Innokentii to China with instructions to conceal his episcopal rank, lest 'obstacles' be put in his way 'by the enemies of our Christian faith, especially by our chief enemies, the Jesuits'. Innokentii was to appear there merely as a sort of chaplain to the resident Orthodox merchants.[6]

To be sure, in the last year of his life Peter did show signs of having remained true to the enlightened missionary spirit of his lengthy

[1] *PiB*, i, no. 394 (pp. 472–473): Peter to Dositheus, 10 September 1701.

[2] Wittram, *op. cit.*, ii, pp. 180; 479–480.

[3] *PiB*, i, no. 241 (pp. 253–254): Peter to A. A. Vinius, 12 June 1698. For Vinius's report, see *ibid.*, pp. 694–695.

[4] *PSZ*, vi, no. 3734 (pp. 355–356); also *PSP*, i, no. 3 (pp. 33–34).

[5] *PSP*, i, no. 40 (pp. 53–54).

[6] *PSP*, i, no. 93 (pp. 121–122).

declaration of June 1700, as quoted above.[1] Yet the main burden of his policy towards the non-Christian peoples of the southern and eastern regions – so far as his legislative record is any guide – remained basically that of his predecessors. During Peter's reign these peoples were, at one time or another, subjected to the same old disciplinary measures,[2] to economic pressures (in the form of material rewards for conversion),[3] or to economic discrimination (deprivation of property for non-conversion);[4] or their fate was decided by purely diplomatic considerations.[5] There was also an element of straightforward religious persecution in Peter's policy: late in 1714 an edict was sent to Metropolitan Fedor of Tobol'sk authorizing him to destroy the pagan idols he found in his vast diocese (as well as to offer on the tsar's behalf to Tatars and other *inozemtsy* whom he encountered on his pastoral rounds the gift of a linen shirt for baptism and exemption from the payment of tribute).[6]

[1] Thus, in an edict of 20 January 1724 Peter evinced concern that his projected academy of sciences should translate the 'necessary books' into the Kalmyk language in order to 'win them over to Christianity' (*PSZ*, vii, no. 4422 [p. 207]). Later that year the Synod was told that 'His Imperial Majesty has commanded that teachers be found who could convert persons of the Kalmyk nation to the true religion, and that when they are found, H.I.M. is to be informed' (*PSZ*, vii, no. 4492 [p. 278]; also *PSP*, iv, no. 1245 [p. 145]). The Synod's implementing decree was sent to the relevant bishops on 15 June (*PSP*, iv, no. 1321 [pp. 149–150]).

[2] Edict of the Siberian Prikaz of 11 October 1703 to the *voevoda* at Tobol'sk (*PSZ*, iv, no. 1946 [pp. 226–227]), for example.

[3] See, for example, the Senate's decrees of 1720 to the governor of Siberia, providing that for 'payments to the newly-baptized for baptism', and for the building and maintenance of churches for them, the metropolitan of Siberia was to be supplied with 1000R a year from the governor's revenues, and that all converted *inozemtsy* were to be exempt from all state taxes (*PSZ*, vi, no. 3636 [p. 234]; no. 3637 [pp. 234–235]). The itemized accounts of government expenditure printed in P. N. Milyukov, *Gosudarstvennoe khozyaistvo Rossii . . . i reforma Petra Velikago* (2nd edn., St. Petersburg, 1905), pp. 614–668, contain previously unnoticed information of interest in this connection: under 'miscellaneous expenditure' for the year 1701, for instance, is found the entry 'To pagan peoples as gifts . . . 230R' (p. 619); under expenditure for 1702 marked 'Church and good works' is entered the sum of 283R paid to various tribesmen 'for reception of Orthodoxy' (p. 625); also, that year, 'To the Metropolitan of Siberia and his monks . . . 341R' (*ibid.*); under the same heading in the budget for 1703: 'For the reception of the Christian faith by Tatars and others of the down-river towns . . . 137R' (p. 683); in that for 1704: 'To Tatars for baptism . . . 152R' (p. 637); in 1706: 'To Mordvinians and Kalmyks for baptism . . . 146R' (p. 653).

[4] *PSZ*, v, no. 2734 (pp. 66–67); no. 2920 (p. 163).

[5] Fugitive subjects of the Kalmyk khan, unless they submitted to baptism, were not to be settled in Russia; and baptized Kalmyks were forbidden to induce their compatriots to follow them into Russian territory and were to settle well away from their former homes 'so as not to displease Ayuk Khan' or to violate the tsar's agreements with Turkey (see Senate decrees of 1716–1717 in *PSZ*, v, no. 3001 [pp. 201–202]; no. 3062 [pp. 485–487]).

[6] *PSZ*, v, no. 2863 (p. 153).

In 1720 Metropolitan Fedor reported to the Senate that he had spent the greater part of the preceding year in the mission fields of Siberia, baptizing *inozemtsy*.[1] Based on his reports, the *St. Petersburg Gazette* for 30 September 1720 claimed that 30,000 of the 'infidel peoples' of Siberia had been baptized; moreover, that in the Kazan' diocese more than 4000 such persons had become Christians.[2] In January 1721 the *Gazette* reported that the total number of pagans baptized in Siberia had reached 40,000, that twenty churches had been built for their use, and that, 'with God's help, the pagan houses of prayer have been destroyed and their idols burned'.[3] Soon thereafter the zealous Fedor retired. But in a letter to the Synod sent sometime late in 1721 he complained that the 40,000 *novokreshchentsy* of his former diocese were being subjected to much 'harassment, abuse, injury, and depredation without regard to age, disability, or poverty', and that, since the secular authorities showed them no mercy, they had no one to protect them.[4] One is disposed to accept at face value the report of the English ambassador in Moscow, who observed that of the 'oppresions' lately inflicted on the Tatars of the Kazan' province by agents of the central government 'the most material has been the forceable baptizing near twelve thousand of them into the moscovite religion'.[5] Forcible baptism was no doubt one of the reasons why the various Tatar tribes living within Russian borders continued to rise, spasmodically and hopelessly, against the tsar's government.[6]

During Peter's reign, in other words, a certain increase in the number of pagan converts to Russian Orthodoxy was no doubt achieved. But in the means employed to this end traditional policies had been reaffirmed. Conversion to Orthodoxy, technically administered by the church, continued to be regarded by the government as the appropriate method for transforming semi-free tribute-paying *inozemtsy* into fully-obligated Russian subjects. The habits of government and people had proved impervious to Peter's intermittent bouts of high-minded iconoclasm and to his commands (for instance in July 1719) that Tatars and other 'infidels' should not be baptized 'against their will'.[7] The absence of any reference to the tsar's non-Christian subjects in the *Ecclesiastical Regulation* of 1721 tends to confirm that until the end of

[1] Cited in Runkevich, *op. cit.*, p. 35.
[2] Pekarskii, *op. cit.*, ii, p. 498.
[3] *Ibid.*, p. 535.
[4] *PSP*, ii, no. 388 (pp. 43–45).
[5] *SIRIO*, xxxix, p. 466: Whitworth to Mr. Secretary Harley, 10 March 1708.
[6] Akademiya Nauk SSSR, *Materialy po istorii Bashkirskoi ASSR*, i: *Bashkirskie vosstaniya v XVII–XVIII vv* (Moscow/Leningrad, 1936), *passim*.
[7] *PSZ*, v, no. 3410 (pp. 726–727).

his reign Peter considered the religious profession of such persons as in essence a political matter lying within the competence of the ordinary civil authorities.[1] This did not prevent the Synod, after 1721, from somewhat reluctantly assuming the role of protector of the *novokreshchentsy* from the depredations of their Russian co-religionists. But the Synod played this role well within the limits devised during the previous years of Peter's reign, during the reigns of his immediate predecessors – indeed, as they were first laid down under Tsar Aleksei.[2]

In view of the evidence cited above, it would appear that Peter's propagandistic claim, in his open letter to the Ukrainian people of February 1709 – that 'in Kazan', Astrakhan, Siberia, and in our other lands it has long been permitted that Muslims should have their mosques and the Kalmyks and other heathens their places of prayer'[3] – was quite untrue. But there were other groups of his subjects professing alien religious beliefs whom Peter made no pretence of tolerating. He is quoted by a contemporary as having once said: 'I want to see the lot of the Muslims and pagans improved, but not that of the Jews. They are liars and cheats. I shall root out the evil, not spread it. There will be for them in Russia neither places to live nor goods to trade, however much they strive for them and bribe those closest to me'.[4] At the time (spring 1702) the Moscow government had been receiving reports from its representatives in the Chernigov district of certain outrages perpetrated by the local Jews; it was alleged, for instance, that under interrogation 'the Jew David confessed without torture that he and his brother-in-law Jacob have married Christians'; that 'many Jews have gathered in the village of Zhukovets to celebrate their feastdays. . . . forty and more persons'; that for one such occasion the said David had been asked to procure the blood of a Christian, 'which he did'.[5]

A petition submitted to the Synod in November 1722 tells perhaps the whole dismal story. Two merchants of Smolensk, Gerasim Shilo and Semen Paskin, wrote that after the Muscovite government had taken the town and province (in 1654) from the Polish king 'the one

[1] Thus the relevant Senate decrees of the post-1721 period (*PSZ*, vi, no. 3884 [p. 483]; *PSZ*, vii, no. 4254 [p. 85]; no. 4335 [pp. 139–141]; no. 4556 [pp. 342–343]).

[2] See *PSP*, i, no. 123 (pp. 171–175); no. 222 (pp. 275–278); *PSP*, ii, no. 388 (pp. 43–45); no. 581 (pp. 224–225); *PSP*, iv, no. 1382 (pp. 230–232); no. 1393 (pp. 251–252); no. 1407 (p. 275).

[3] *PiB*, ix, no. 3029 (p. 65); also *PSZ*, iv, no. 2224 (pp. 444–448).

[4] Quoted in Solov'ev, *op. cit.*, viii, p. 76, citing L. N. Maikov (ed.), *Rasskazy Nartova o Petre Velikom* (St. Petersburg, 1891), no. 33 (pp. 30–31).

[5] See Solov'ev, *op. cit.*, p. 76 and nn. 51, 18, 19, 20 (p. 304).

holy Christian faith was established and the infidel Jewish religion rooted out without trace'.[1] But, they complained, a former vice-governor of Smolensk, Prince Vasilii Gagarin, had

> permitted Jews from across the Lithuanian border to keep taverns and to collect customs and to engage in every kind of trade in the province; and they with their wives and children have increased among the Christian folk, and living in Smolensk and in the districts of this province have caused disturbance and temptation to the simple folk with their religion of the old dispensation, praising it as the true religion. They revile the Christian faith and set it at nought, boasting to the common folk of their own religion. They keep their Sabbath strictly, according to their religion, and on Saturdays do not engage in trade or do any kind of work; but our Sundays and other feastdays they violate, and trade in everything with the simple folk of the Christian faith, and do every kind of work. And many Christians, following their accursed example, work not only on Sundays but on all the feastdays of the Christian rite; and they [the Jews] thereby subvert the simple folk away from God's churches at the times of divine service. And of the cattle these Jews slaughter, those with contaminated meat they pack in mice-ridden casks as though edible, and sell them to Orthodox Christians; and simple folk buy them and defile themselves in ignorance of their perfidy. Even more scandalous, a most intolerable affront to Orthodox Christians has been perpetrated by the Jew Borakh Leibov, a tax-collector of the village of Zverovich. . . .

The merchants Shilo and Paskin retailed how the said Leibov had built a school in his village where 'they practise their infidel religion'. The local priest, in his zeal to preserve the Orthodox, had opposed the building of the school and had reproached Leibov and his associates 'for their outlandish faith, for which the Jew Borakh viciously beat the said priest, cracked his skull, and having dared to put him in irons, released him; and from the torments inflicted by this Jew the priest never recovered, but died, whence his widow has lodged a suit in Smolensk against this Jew'. The merchants concluded:

[1] Stopping in Smolensk very soon after the event, Paul of Aleppo was told that 'on taking possession of the city, the Muscovites found in it a great number of Jews. . . . By command of [Tsar Aleksei] they were all collected together; and he required of them that if they wished to save their lives they should be baptized. Those who believed, and afterwards received baptism, he permitted to live; the recusants he ordered placed in houses of wood, which were set fire to, and they all burnt to death' (Paul of Aleppo, *op. cit.*, i, p. 336). Indeed, it has been estimated that in the mid-seventeenth-century massacre of the Jews by the Russian authorities about 200,000 people, or more than a third of the Jewish population of eastern Europe, were killed (J. Billington, *The Icon and the Axe* [London, 1966], p. 674, n. 2).

> And the Jew Borakh, as well as the other Jews, have come to the Smolensk province not only to trade their wares but more, that they might spread their Jewry in the Russian Empire. And of their other Jews' tricks and of all the damage they have done to the people in their simplicity, we do not know. But we trust in the resolution of the Most Holy All-Ruling Synod, and we pray that these Jew enemies of the Christian faith should be banished from the Smolensk province across the Lithuanian border, and that their tax-collecting concessions and trading concerns should be abolished, for the strengthening of the Orthodox Christian faith.[1]

This document was accepted by the Synod at face value and even embellished by it ('and because of the many injuries done to the clergy . . .'). On 5 December 1722, evidently confident that the matter fell within its jurisdiction, the Synod resolved that Leibov's school should be 'razed to the ground' and 'any books or other things of their wicked religion found in it, burnt without trace'. With reference to the action of Prince Gagarin 'in allowing these Jews to collect taxes', and concerning the unfortunate Leibov and other matters requiring 'satisfaction', and 'concerning the expulsion from the Smolensk province of all the Jews to be found there', the Synod resolved to send a memorandum to the Senate coupled with a request that Jews be forbidden to engage in trade or industry not only in Russia, but 'in those countries where Orthodox Christians live' as well.[2]

There is no evidence to suggest what action the Senate and the civil authorities may have taken in response to the Synod's request. The absence of any further reference to the matter in the printed legislation of Peter's reign tempts one to hope that the request was ignored for political reasons, this despite Peter's own attitude to the Jews of Little Russia as quoted above. 'One cannot pain a Russian more than by calling him a Jew', observed a German visitor in the mid-seventeenth century.[3] Neither in his personal outlook nor in his public policy did Peter do anything to solve the 'Jewish problem' which he had inherited.

In a manifesto promulgated in April 1702 relating the conditions of service in Russia for foreigners, Peter promised that 'whereas here in Our Capital freedom of worship has already been introduced for all faiths *except the Christian sects separated from our church* [italics mine], nonetheless we adopt this means to confirm once again that by the authority given to Us by the Most High we do not wish to constrain

[1] *PSP*, ii, no. 922 (pp. 649–650). [2] *Ibid.* [3] Baron, *op. cit.*, p. 277.

men's consciences, and readily leave to every Christian the responsibility of caring for the well-being of his own soul'. The manifesto was of course drafted for European consumption by a German in the Russian service who was concerned at the time with plans for reorganising the tsar's army; and its express purpose was to aid in recruiting foreign officers, who naturally would not have been discouraged by the exemption of Russians from the religious toleration guaranteed to them.[1] Equally, it was for practical reasons of state that Peter agreed to concede complete freedom of worship for Lutherans and the autonomy of their church in the several accords and instruments of capitulation concluded in 1710 with the governor of Riga, the nobility of Livonia, and representatives of the cities of Revel and Pernau and of the principality of Estonia – just as he had simultaneously consented to leave the civil administration of these places in the hands of Germans 'because the inhabitants are of the German nation'.[2] It is clear that the drafters of these documents thought the tsar had replaced the vanquished Swedish king not only as overlord of the petty Baltic states, but as protector of their dominant Lutheran religion as well. The Russian realm (it was not yet formally an 'Empire') had become, in terms of the religious profession of its Christian inhabitants alone, what today we should call a pluralistic state. But neither this fact, nor considerations of political expediency, nor any personal conviction induced Tsar Peter to tolerate Russian religious dissidents – the 'Christian sects separated from our church'. To judge simply from the amount of legislation devoted to

[1] Both the original German text of the manifesto and a contemporary Russian translation are printed in the *PiB*, ii, no. 421 (pp. 39–50). The Russian translation in the *PSZ*, iv, no. 1910 (pp. 192–195) is not a contemporary one and, as compared with the original German text printed in the *PiB*, is not entirely accurate. The German original was published in 1702 in the form of a brochure and distributed in Europe (see the copies of the printed German and French translations of the April manifesto preserved in the FMA, 'Correspondance politique: Russie', vol. 2, docs. 36, 38); its author appears to have been Johann Patkul (see *PiB*, ii, p. 337), who by a decree of the tsar issued together with the manifesto was given full powers to recruit for the Russian service abroad (*ibid.*, no. 422 [p. 45]). See also Wittram's discussion of the manifesto in the context of the *de facto* toleration of foreign faiths in Moscow since the sixteenth century. Wittram is impressed by the 'new, astonishingly modern reasoning' apparent in the manifesto and suggests that Peter 'brought back with him from his journeys abroad an awareness of the legitimacy of the claims of the separate Christian confessions'. He concludes, somewhat laboriously, that 'if Peter could adopt the far-reaching principle [of religious toleration], still one must add that neither did he overlook the practical political consequences of it; nor was he always prepared to draw the conclusions' (Wittram, *op. cit.*, ii, pp. 176–177).

[2] *PSZ*, iv, no. 2277 (pp. 501–514); no. 2279 (pp. 519–526); no. 2286 (pp. 537–538); no. 2287 (pp. 544–545); no. 2297 (p. 557); no. 2298 (pp. 560–561). See also *Zhurnal*, ii, pp. 236–264.

them, they constituted a much greater problem for Peter's regime than did either his pagan or Jewish subjects.

It was during the regency of Tsarevna Sof'ya that the Russian government formally declared war on the luckless adherents of the dissident minority in the great church schism of the 1660's, adding heresy and schism to its list of crimes punishable by death. But its hand had been forced by the church council of 1666–1667, at which the schism itself had been brought into the open and formally condemned. There, in the presence of two of the Eastern patriarchs, and after opposing speeches by Simeon Polotskii, the 'Latinizer' and royal tutor, and by Archpriest Avvakum, a zealous puritan and leading defender of the old Muscovite faith, the purity of which was (so he and his followers believed) seriously threatened by the liturgical and doctrinal reforms recently introduced by the learned savants of the official church led, at first, by the overbearing Patriarch Nikon (active 1652–1658): after speeches by them and by others, after inquisitions and deliberations, the council, composed almost entirely of senior monastic clergy (Avvakum and many of his followers were married, secular clergy), condemned those who would not conform and excommunicated their leaders.[1] And at the council the question whether 'heretics and schismatics should be punished by civil law or only by the church' was resolved by the assembled clergy on the basis of certain Byzantine precedents, 'from which we perceive that heretics and schismatics are to be punished not only by the church, but by the Tsar, that is by civil law and punishment'.[2] In the following years the civil and ecclesiastical authorities cooperated in a notably unsuccessful attempt to contain and exterminate religious dissent, where necessary by violence.[3] Indeed, so adverse did the situation appear by late 1684 that the government felt compelled to take further, draconian measures for which the way had been prepared, again, by a church council: in November 1681 the patriarch and higher clergy had requested that all unrepentant 'dissidents and apostates', 'oppositionists and schismatics' should be turned over to the civil courts for condemnation and execution;[4] and three years later Sof'ya's government, after an initial, expedient show of sympathy for the 'Old Believers', decreed that

[1] See esp. P. Pascal, *Avvakum et les débuts du Raskol* (2nd edn., Paris, 1963), pp. 373 ff.
[2] *PSZ*, i, no. 412 (pp. 705–706).
[3] See again Pascal, *op. cit.*, esp. pp. 439 ff.
[4] *AAK*, iv, no. 75 (pp. 111–112).

those who appear to be heretics or schismatics, by some pernicious teaching or by opposition and schism and every filthiness against the holy church; and do not go to church or hear the entreaties of the clergy in their houses; and do not confess to a priest and receive the Holy Sacrament, and among Christians cause scandal and sedition: such persons are to be severely interrogated, under torture, concerning their activities and their friends and adherents. . . .

Moreover those who, while still under torture, 'remain obstinate, and will not submit to the holy church', even after repeated threats of execution, were to be burnt to death, while those who on the point of being executed signalled their conversion were to be remanded to the ecclesiastical authorities 'for the correction of a true confession'; and after publicly receiving communion they were to be freed of the indictment of schism. (However, those who repented falsely and, once freed, returned to their evil ways, were to be rearrested and executed 'without trial'.) The edict contained further detailed provisions against self-confessed or suspected schismatics and their sympathizers: for example, persons who submitted to rebaptism by schismatics, even if they were guilty of no other 'act of opposition', were to be flogged and handed over to their bishop 'for correction'; local officials, ecclesiastical and civil, were to ensure that 'no opposition to the church and no schism' occurred within the areas under their control; etc.[1] Certainly the barbarity of the judicial processes described – the liberal use of torture, the knout, and execution by fire – if not the spirit of intolerance which inspired the edict, distinguish it from similar legislation enacted elsewhere in contemporary Europe.[2] It was use of these devices, especially of the death penalty, that Tsar Peter largely forsook, thus bringing to an end the 'heroic age' of the schism. But in dealing with the schismatics Peter relinquished the use of torture and violence only in favour of more commonsensical – more profitable – methods of persecution. For like his predecessors he steadfastly regarded all schismatics as in opposition to the official church, rather than merely separated from it, as their name implies; and as 'oppositionists' Peter considered them the responsibility of the government just as

[1] *PSZ*, ii, no. 1102 (pp. 647–650).

[2] Most notably, the revocation of the Edict of Nantes in October 1685 by Louis XIV of France. It is an irony perhaps typical of the times that Sof'ya's government should have invited the victims of Louis's edict to Russia, as witness the circular published in Moscow in January 1689 entitled (in the English version printed at London in April), *A Declaration of the Czars of Muscovy against the French King in favour of the poor Protestants distress in their present persecution. . . .*

'blasphemers and church rioters' had always been.[1] Moreover for Peter's government, with its disposition to radical reform, there was this additional problem: that many if not most schismatics were, as the Prussian ambassador reported near the end of the reign, 'sworn enemies of everything new, whether in religion or politics'.[2]

Peter's chief innovation with regard to the schismatics was to grant them a species of legal existence, though at a considerable price. The new policy was inaugurated on 8 February 1716. On that day the tsar ordered the Senate to command all bishops and provincial governors to announce to all classes of men and women that once a year they were to confess to their 'spiritual fathers' in church: those who did not comply were to be brought by their parish priest before the diocesan court, or in the country districts to the senior priest (*starosta popovskii*), to be registered; and the lists of their names were to be forwarded to the civil authorities, who should impose special fines on the delinquents. 'And where there are schismatics', the edict continued, 'there the governors shall register them, women as well as men'; and having registered them, the governors were to double their present taxes and to send the lists of names and taxes levied to the Senate chancellery.[3]

Obviously the efficacy of the whole system thus inaugurated depended entirely on the ordinary parish priests and confessors, who appear to have been remiss in fulfilling their duties.[4] An edict issued by the Monastery Prikaz on 16 March 1718 indicated grave official displeasure with the lists submitted in the past two years of those who had not made their annual confession and of 'opponents of the church (or

[1] That is, for nearly half a century before the period of Peter's active rule. In Chapter 1 of the *Ulozhenie* of 1649 – entitled 'O Bogokhul'nikakh i o tserkovnykh myatezhnikakh' – penalties ranging from death by fire to floggings and prison terms were prescribed for persons guilty of blasphemy or of disturbing the order of church services in a variety of specified ways (*PRP*, vi, pp. 22–23; also *PSZ*, i, no. 1 [p. 3]). It is worth repeating that the *Ulozhenie* is thus the earliest secular Russian legislative document to specify and prohibit offences against religion; that it contains, moreover, the earliest prescription in Muscovite legislation of the penalty of death by fire, which appears to have been used in Pskov in the sixteenth and even fifteenth centuries to punish church thieves and incendiaries; that, finally, the notion of blasphemy employed in it derives probably from west Russian, rather than Muscovite or Kievan-Byzantine, sources – from, that is, the region of Novgorod, where western European influences were strong (see editor's 'Kommentari', *PRP*, vi, pp. 24–25).

[2] *SIRIO*, xv, pp. 219–220: Mardefeld to the king, 26 February 1723.

[3] *PSZ*, v, no. 2991 (p. 196).

[4] Wittram suggests that the clergy accepted bribes from schismatics not wishing to be registered as such in the lists (*op. cit.*, ii, p. 179); but he cites no evidence in support of the suggestion.

schismatics)'. The edict was drafted on the basis of suggestions put forward by a certain Archimandrite Pitirim (later bishop of Nizhnii-Novgorod) and was amended by Peter personally:[1] it provided that severe penalties were to be imposed on priests whose lists were inaccurate or 'secretive' – 'that is, if those who have not confessed are registered as if they had, or opponents of the church are not so registered'. Not only parish priests but archpriests and other clergy and even confessors to convents were now to compile such lists, under pain of unfrocking, confiscation of all property, and condemnation by the civil courts to terms of hard labour. When collecting the lists, Archimandrite Antonii of the Zlatoustovskii monastery, who had been put in charge of the business, was to warn the clergy that should their consciences reproach them about 'concealments' in the lists they would be given three months' grace to set them right; 'and after this period, whoever does not confess his fault will not be forgiven, but dealt with as indicated'. It was even stipulated that should Antonii himself 'show too much indulgence to an [offending] cleric, and not prosecute him, in order to conceal the affair – not only shall he be deprived of his rank, but he will be severely punished'.[2] Such was the importance that Peter attached to the matter.

Nor was this to be the end of it. The measures described appear to have been part of a wider campaign to impose uniform religious discipline both on those who regarded the rites of the official church as invalid, and on those who were merely sluggish in their observance of them. On 17 February 1718 the head of the Monastery Prikaz announced that.

> It has been reported to the [tsar] that many of the common people, townsfolk, and former peasants live idly, and not only on Sundays but on major feastdays do not go to church to divine services or confess their sins.... Wherefore it has been decreed, by edict of His Majesty Himself, that printed notices are to be posted in the towns and villages to the effect that on major feastdays and Sundays all of the above-mentioned persons are to go to church, to vespers, to matins, but especially to the holy liturgy (excepting those who are ill or otherwise unable to go), and to confession once a year.

The edict was to be enforced, once again, by the parish clergy assisted by the stewards or overseers responsible for the persons mentioned. Annual registers were to be kept indicating those who had and had not

[1] For the drafts of the edict, see Verkhovskoi, ii, II, pp. 114 ff.
[2] *PSZ*, v, no. 3183 (pp. 554–555).

confessed, and were to be sent to the diocesan courts. Fines were specified for 'non-confessors', to be exacted by the clergy according to the class of offender and the frequency of his offence, as 'from the commoners and townsfolk, for the first [offence], a ruble; for the second, two rubles; for the third, three rubles'; but 'from the country-folk, for the first, two den'gi [i.e. five copecks]'; etc. Those who remained unreformed were to be sent to the local government officials for punishment, and then made to confess to selected priests. If some still refused to confess, the priests were not to denounce them but to exact from them still further fixed fines. Moreover, the privilege of state service, at any level, 'in Moscow and in the towns, and everywhere else', was to be denied to anyone 'who has not made his annual confession and has no testimonial from his confessor or parish priest that he has done so'.[1]

The decrees of 8 February 1716, and of 17 February and 16 March 1718, it will be seen, remained the legal basis of Peter's policy towards the non-conformists – whether 'schismatics', 'oppositionists', or 'non-confessors' – until the end of his reign. The problem of how they were in fact to be enforced, and some of the effects of enforcing them, will be discussed in a subsequent chapter. But some of the difficulties in the way of implementing this legislation were publicized in 1720, and may be mentioned here. In March of that year an edict issued by the Prikaz of Ecclesiastical Affairs (*Tserkovnykh del*) complained that

> many schismatics, not wishing to make known their schism and to pay the double tax, secretly continue to live under the appearance of Orthodoxy, and to make fraudulent confessions and to repent insincerely, because they fear the civil punishment for schism. Therefore let those schismatics wishing to return from schism to union with the holy church make themselves known to the Prikaz of Ecclesiastical Affairs and be received into the holy church without an interrogation; and let those not wishing to return to the holy church, but instead to persist in their schismatic delusions, present themselves at the Prikaz and register to pay the double tax without fear or worry about receiving empty advice.

Peter's government, having in 1718 conceded the administration of schismatic affairs to an ecclesiastical office (an office hitherto responsible chiefly for the discipline and conduct of the clergy of the Moscow diocese), did not fail to anticipate that there would be schismatics unwilling to do either of the alternatives presented to them by this

[1] *PSZ*, v, no. 3169 (pp. 544–545).

edict: 'they will be detected; and these transgressors will be subjected to severe civil punishment and made to pay, in addition to the double tax, a double fine'.[1]

The problem of the schismatics was to be touched on in several of the provisions of the *Ecclesiastical Regulation* of 1721. It was to preoccupy the Synod during much of the first four years of its existence. And in a later chapter it will be seen that in keeping with its duty to reform the church the Synod introduced a new element into Peter's policy towards the schismatics: that of attempting to persuade them, in free and open discussion, of the error of their ways.

II

GOVERNMENT AND CHURCH: THE ECONOMIC SQUEEZE

Viewed from another perspective, Tsar Peter's policy of taxing schismatics at double the rate imposed on loyal church-going subjects, and in general of exacting exorbitant fines as the penalty for religious nonconformity, was only an element of his overall fiscal policy. Indeed, on the evidence of the legislative record of his reign, it was fiscal matters – especially taxation – that attracted Peter's most continuous attention, and with good reason: financing the development of native industries, the construction of canals, roads, fortresses, whole towns, a merchant marine and a navy – all this required, as compared with the expenditure of previous governments, an enormous outlay of funds. Above all, it was to defray the cost of his protracted wars – with Turkey (1695–1700; 1711), Sweden (1700–1721), and Persia (1722–1723) – that Peter was compelled to levy new and heavier taxes on his not always patient subjects. In 1701 an estimated 82 percent of state expenditure was consumed by military requirements; in 1705, 96 percent; from 1706 to 1709, 80 to 83 percent; in 1724, 63 percent. On the other hand, if during the years 1703 to 1708 total state expenditure annually exceeded revenue by as much as 25 percent, thereafter revenue exceeded expenditure (at least on paper); and between 1701 and 1724 total state revenue had more than tripled.[2] The Swedish war was won without contracting

[1] *PSZ*, vi, no. 3547 (p. 169). Additional legislation of the period 1718–1720 relating to particular groups of schismatics may be found in the *PSZ*, v, no. 3232 (p. 590); no. 3161 (pp. 542–543); no. 3340 (p. 687). A decree in October 1720 foreshadowed a subsequent development: by it all provincial administrators were informed that a certain Sergeant Zinov'ev of the Life Guards, responsible to the new College of State Revenue, was to supervise the registration and collection of taxes from schismatics (*PSZ*, vi, no. 3662 [pp. 248–249]).

[2] Figures from Milyukov, *op. cit.*, pp. 175–176; 490–491; 494–495. Also B. Kafengauz,

foreign debts and without the aid of the substantial foreign (French) subsidies received by the Swedish king. In short, the figures suggest an economy strained to the breaking-point by the continual effort of waging war yet saved from collapse by the stringent fiscality of a hard-pressed government. The tsar's oft-quoted instructions to the Senate in 1711: 'Collect as much money as possible, for money is the artery of war'; 'See that all unnecessary and, in particular, useless state expenditure is eliminated',[1] were, as has been remarked, the 'motto of Peter's government throughout the whole of his reign'.[2] And such, very briefly, is the general background against which Peter's legislation affecting the church as an economic institution must be viewed.

For it was by the exercise of his powers to tax and to 'regulate' that Peter largely succeeded in bringing the economic life of the church under the more or less direct control of his government. This radically new situation, it should be noted, was created by Peter without resorting to the large-scale secularization of ecclesiastical property and the dissolution of the monasteries which are the familiar features of the much earlier church reform of Henry VIII of England. Rather, it was created by him essentially through a stricter, more energetic, and more comprehensive application of the policies of his predecessors. And in this respect Peter's legislation falls into two distinct categories.

(A) On the one hand, during the years 1701 to 1720 the ecclesiastical institutions of Russia, in common with the rest of society, were subjected by Peter's government to a steady barrage of monetary taxes, troop levies, and supply requisitions, numerous instances of which can

'Finansovaya reforma i gosudarstvennyi byudzhet', in Kafengauz and N. I. Pavlenko (eds.), *Rossiya v pervoi chetverti XVIII veka. Preobrazovaniya Petra I* (Moscow, 1954), pp. 383; 392–393: Kafengauz in some instances gives slightly different figures than Milyukov. Devaluations in 1698 and 1718 had by the latter part of Peter's reign decreased the purchasing power of the ruble almost by half: thus in terms of real money total state revenue between 1701 and 1724 may be said to have doubled – still a very sizable increase.

[1] *PSZ*, iv, no. 2330 (p. 643); also *PiB*, xi, nos. 4288, 4289, 4290 (pp. 100–103).

[2] E. Spiridonova, *Ekonomicheskaya politika i ekonomicheskie vzglyady Petra I* (Moscow, 1952), p. 250. Of course Peter's fiscal successes cannot be judged separately from the results, good and bad, of his economic policies generally – in particular, of his promotion of trade and industry, on the one hand, and of his neglect of agriculture and the peasantry, on the other. To some extent Peter's measures must have been responsible for increasing the economy's ability to pay the more numerous and heavier taxes imposed on it. Yet society was so organized that the main weight of all taxation fell squarely on the peasantry, especially by means of the 'soul tax' introduced late in Peter's reign. Levied on the basis of a census which reduced almost all peasants to the level of tax-paying serfs, and from which the serving classes – nobility and clergy – were exempt, the soul tax alone accounted for 54 percent of total state revenue in 1724, the first year in which it was collected (see Milyukov, *op. cit.*, p. 490).

be adduced from the surviving legislation of the period.[1] This aspect of Peter's policy culminated in the inclusion in the general census cf male 'souls' first taken in 1718 (on which the new universal 'soul tax' was to be based) of all classes of male peasants of whatever age living on the estates of 'patriarchal, episcopal, monastic, and [other] ecclesiastical landowners'.[2] The soul tax, first collected in 1724 on the basis of the 'revised' census of 1722–1723, replaced all other forms of direct taxation imposed by the central government. Yet the principle of taxing peasants living on church lands at the same rate as those living on private (service or hereditary) and crown estates, was not new. The census of peasant households of 1678 (which continued to be used for assessing direct taxes until it was replaced by Peter's census of souls) included those found on all types of church lands;[3] equally, patriarchal,

[1] *PSZ*, iii, no. 1711 (pp. 656–665); *PSZ*, iv, no. 1757 (p. 11); no. 1803 (pp. 64–66) – measures enacted 1699–1700 relating to the introduction of a stamp tax to be paid by clergy and laity alike 'without exception, beginning with the Most Holy Patriarch'. See also *PSZ*, iv, no. 2372 (pp. 691–695) and *PSP*, iv, no. 1395 (pp. 212–221), which contain reports of the results of a special tax levied annually between 1707 and 1722 on the secular clergy for the purchase of horses for the cavalry. See also *PSZ*, v, no. 2888 (p. 149): from the proceeds of the sale of surplus salt the Solovetskii and Kargopol' monasteries were to pay an annual 2000R to the Admiralty Prikaz. From roughly 1698 to 1702 the wealthy Trinity-Sergiev monastery was required to contribute large sums to the tasr's shipbuilding programme (see *PSZ*, iii, no. 661 [p. 528]; *PiB*, ii [p. 360]). See also *PSZ*, v, no. 3026 (pp. 472–473), whereby all bishops were ordered to contribute to the costs of maintaining hospitals (*lazarety*) for army veterans from the proceeds of the parochial 'wedding fees'; again, in 1719–1720 orders to collect special taxes from peasant households for new construction on the Vasil'evskii Island in St. Petersburg, and for the building of the Ladoga–Schlissel'burg canal, expressly included those located on ecclesiastical estates (*PSZ*, v, no. 3305 [665–666]; no. 3501 [pp. 123–124]); etc. Simultaneously, and in addition to paying the usual taxes and dues to their landlords, peasants and others – excluding clergy – living on ecclesiastical lands were explicitly included in the recurrent troop levies and conscriptions of workers for the tsar's various building projects (*PSZ*, iv, no. 2036 [pp. 291–295]; no. 2078 [p. 326]; no. 2082 [pp. 329–330]; no. 2108 [p. 351]; no. 2421 [p. 732]; *PSZ*, v, no. 2362 [pp. 5–6]; no. 2650 [pp. 18–19]; no. 3240 [p. 595]; no. 3419 [pp. 731–732]; etc.). Sometimes, during the darkest years of the Swedish war, lesser church people – 'episcopal judicial and administrative staff, monastic servitors, sons of priests, cantors, sextons, and other clergy' – were drafted into the army or, if over age, were registered to pay a special tax in return for exemption from military service (*PSZ*, iv, no. 2130 [pp. 360–362]). Sometimes churchmen were quite arbitrarily taxed, without the normal legal niceties; but usually in such cases the tsar was motivated by the need to meet a sudden emergency, as in the following example: on 4 June 1703 General Sheremetev reported that 'there is no lead in Pskov', and that a large quantity was needed for the present campaign: 'but the Metropolitan [Joseph Rimskii-Korsakov, metropolitan of Pskov] has much lead, which he sends secretly to Moscow to sell and does not declare'. Peter's order, minuted on the report, was to 'seize it forcibly, and pay [for it] in money later' (*PiB*, ii, no. 538 [p. 175]).

[2] *PSZ*, v, no. 3245 (p. 597); no. 3287 (pp. 618–620); *PSZ*, vi, no. 3481 (p. 1).

[3] For the 1678 census (the enabling legislation is not printed in the *PSZ*), see H. L.

episcopal, and monastic peasants were expressly included in a supplementary census of households ordered by Tsarevna Sof'ya in 1682.[1] And at least once during Sof'ya's regency (in 1686) a special tax was levied on the patriarch, bishops, and monasteries (as well as on the service nobility) to pay for an imminent campaign against the Turks: the enabling decree is prefaced by a report citing various precedents from 1677 onwards and itemizing the sums of money collected 'during time of war . . . for the army' from ecclesiastical as well as other sources.[2] Dr. Collins, Tsar Aleksei's physician for nine years, quite correctly observed that the tsar 'makes bold with the Church Treasury upon loan in time of war, and pays it back *ad Graecas Calendas* [i.e. never]'.[3] And Olearius noticed, when in Moscow in the 1630's, that in time of war 'the monasteries, too, must furnish and maintain a given number of soldiers, depending upon the number of villages and peasants they possess'.[4] The difference was that, unlike his immediate predecessors, Tsar Peter was continuously at war, a fundamental fact of his reign which is clearly reflected in his taxation policies.

(B) Simultaneously, Peter acted to suppress the financial privileges that were traditionally enjoyed by the clergy in Russia. With few exceptions, he refused to renew the charters granting such privileges to individual monasteries or bishops or churches, and declined to issue new ones: often he simply announced that a privilege had been suspended.[5] He also legislated new and stricter prohibitions against the acquisition of any further estates by the clergy.[6] Occasionally he confiscated outright certain church lands – sometimes with, but often without, compensation to their previous owners.[7] And if the increase in the number and weight of his taxes, as compared with those of his predecessors, can be attributed to the relatively greater cost of his wars, so this other, complementary policy pursued by Peter was the outgrowth of tendencies at work for more than a century. In their capacity as landowners and industrial entrepreneurs of very considerable size,

Eaton, 'Cadasters and Censuses of Muscovy', *Slavic Review*, xxvi (March 1967), pp. 54–69; also Milyukov, *op. cit.*, pp. 638 ff.

[1] *PSZ*, ii, no. 973 (p. 483).

[2] *PSZ*, iii, no. 1210 (pp. 817–820).

[3] Collins, *op. cit.*, pp. 123–124.

[4] Baron, *op. cit.*, p. 265.

[5] *PSZ*, iii, no. 1711 (pp. 656–665); no. 1721 (p. 671); no. 1725 (p. 672); *PSZ*, iv, no. 1762 (p. 13); no. 1839 (pp. 159–160); etc.

[6] *PSZ*, iii, no. 1541 (pp. 234–235); no. 1661 (p. 528); *PSZ*, iv, no. 1828 (p. 132); no. 1839 (pp. 159–160); *PSZ*, v, no. 2662 (p. 22); etc.

[7] *PSZ*, iv, no. 1926 (pp. 210–214); no. 2462 (p. 775); no. 2514 (p. 824); *PSZ*, v, no. 2662 (p. 22); no. 2888 (p. 149); *PSZ*, vii, no. 5207 (p. 904); etc. Also, *OAS*, i, no. 34 (cols. 24–25); no. 81 (cols. 55–56).

the ecclesiastical institutions of Russia had been subject to regulation by the tsar's government and to recurrent attempts to limit their growth since long before Peter's reign.[1]

In this respect, the most important legislation enacted under Peter's immediate predecessors were certain provisions of the *Ulozhenie* of Peter's father, Tsar Aleksei (1649). In the chapter devoted to the question of hereditary estates, the right of lesser nobles (*deti boyarskie* and *dvoryane*) in the service of the senior clergy to retain such properties was confirmed, but that of patriarchal, monastic or episcopal 'serving people [*sluzhilye lyudi*]' who were not of the nobility – not *prirodnye deti boyarskie*, but only *nesluzhilykh ottsov deti* – was abolished; and the latter category of persons was required either to transfer to the tsar's service or to forfeit their lands.[2] The tendency evident in this provision is more fully expressed in a later article of the same chapter. There, citing precedents from *his* father's time, Tsar Aleksei decreed that henceforth the patriarch, the bishops, and the monasteries were not to buy any more land, nor to hold land in mortgage, nor to accept estates for the remembrance of souls. The Moscow Pomestnyi (Estates) Prikaz was no longer to register any such deeds, an action which in effect would have rendered them nugatory. Nor was any holder of an hereditary estate to give it, or to bequeath it, to a monastery; and any estate made over to the patriarch, a bishop, or to a monastery, by sale, bequest, or as a gift, was to be seized by the tsar without compensation 'and given to whomever should petition for it'.[3] Elsewhere in the *Ulozhenie* exchanges involving monastic estates were prohibited.[4] Childless widows were forbidden to leave their property to monasteries or to parish churches.[5]

[1] The whole question of the origins and growth of ecclesiastical landownership in Russia until the end of the eighteenth century has been thoroughly examined in V. Milyutin, 'O nedvizhimykh imushchestvakh dukhovenstva v Rossii', *Chteniya v imperatorskom obshchestve istorii i drevnostei rossiiskikh pri Moskovskom universitete*: October–December 1859 (pp. 1–118); July–September 1860 (pp. 119–272); January–March 1861 (pp. 273–414); April–June 1861 (pp. 415–571). Milyutin points out that in theory the clergy's *votchinnye prava* were based, not on traditional Russian law, but on Byzantine canon and secular law (p. 16); that the greatest increase in the extent of church property occurred during the period of the Mongol yoke (pp. 17–42); that soon thereafter (ca. 1500) a demand for the 'return' of ecclesiastical lands to the state arose and was pursued as a policy by successive Muscovite governments wishing to deprive the church of its excess landed wealth and to limit and eventually to suppress the clergy's right to acquire and even to own land (pp. 391 ff.).

[2] *PRP*, vi, p. 255. [3] *Ibid.*, pp. 256–257. [4] *Ibid.*, p. 203.

[5] *Ibid.*, p. 246. See also pp. 258–259 for repetitions of various of these provisions.

The *Ulozhenie*'s restrictions on the further acquisition of land by the church would seem to have been absolute. Yet most of them had been imposed before, by previous governments, and apparently without effect.[1] For with the surplus revenue derived from their estates the clergy continued to buy land, as can be seen in various charters dating from the second half of the seventeenth century as well as from earlier periods.[2] And Aleksei himself, like his predecessors, was only the most conspicuous violator of his own prohibitions: in 1672–1673, for instance, he assigned large tracts of land in the Ukraine to the patriarch, the bishops and to some fifty monasteries (as well as to the members of various ranks of the service nobility) 'for the supply of grain'.[3] Similarly, during the brief reign of his son Tsar Fedor and the regency of his daughter Sof'ya the government with one hand continued to grant lands, money, grain, water rights, tax concessions, and judicial privileges to the clergy,[4] while with the other it confirmed the *Ulozhenie*'s prohibitions against further acquisitions of land by the church.[5] It was partly to limit the expansion of ecclesiastical landownership that the government conducted its regular fiscal surveys of the country, the records of which survive in the various cadastral and census books of this and earlier periods.[6] But – to cite one further instance – by a decree of 1681 Tsar Fedor assigned large numbers of peasant households to both newly-created and existing episcopal households for their maintenance.[7] Indeed, it was estimated in 1718 that since 1653–1654 the number of peasant households on patriarchal and episcopal estates had increased by 37 percent; on monastic estates, by 36 percent.[8] On the whole, therefore, the efforts of Peter's predecessors to limit the church's landed wealth would seem not to have succeeded.

Peter's legislation in this field, however, constituted a largely

[1] Milyutin, *op. cit.*, pp. 42–118; 391 ff.

[2] *AAK*, iv, no. 71 (pp. 191–194); no. 73 (pp. 195–198); no. 200 (pp. 371–373); etc. For the earlier periods, see Milyutin, *op. cit.*, pp. 94–96 and nn. 187, 190.

[3] *PSZ*, i, no. 521 (p. 899); no. 549 (pp. 932–933).

[4] *PSZ*, ii, no. 625 (p. 7); no. 676 (pp. 88–89); no. 681 (pp. 92–94); no. 698 (pp. 108–109); no. 703 (pp. 141–143); no. 705 (pp. 143–145); no. 716 (pp. 150–151); no. 720 (p. 153); no. 769 (pp. 211–215); nos. 807–811 (pp. 240–253); no. 947 (pp. 458–9); no. 993 (p. 500); no. 994 (pp. 500–501); no. 1007 (pp. 518–519); no. 1012 (p. 522); no. 1016 (pp. 536–538); no. 1041 (p. 561); no. 1090 (p. 639); no. 1160 (pp. 753–757); no. 1242 (pp. 852–857).

[5] *PSZ*, ii, no. 633 (p. 21); no. 697 (pp. 107–108); no. 731 (pp. 175–178); no. 1025 (pp. 543–548); no. 1035 (pp. 556–557).

[6] See Eaton, *op. cit.*

[7] *PSZ*, ii, no. 898 (pp. 362–366).

[8] Kafengauz and Pavlenko, *op. cit.*, p. 372.

successful effort to enforce the long-standing provisions of the law.[1] Yet, for all that, it did contain novel elements. Apart from forbidding the clergy to acquire additional land, and apart from confiscating outright certain ecclesiastical properties, as mentioned above, Peter decreed that in a certain district of Siberia no new monasteries were to be built nor land provided for them without his government's permission: 'for the number of monasteries and convents in Siberia, wherein all ranks of Orthodox Christians take vows and save their souls, is sufficient'.[2] Moreover, as early as December 1696 he ordered that no more buildings were to be erected within monastic precincts without the prior consent of his government; requests for such permission were to be accompanied by an estimate of the expenses involved and, ostensibly to give effect to this regulation, it was ordered that henceforth all monasteries as well as all bishops were to send their account books each year to the tsar's Prikaz of the Great Court (which was responsible chiefly for collecting the revenues from the crown estates), whence they were to obtain permission for *any* 'extraordinary' expenditure.[3] Again, a decree promulgated by the Prikaz of the Great Court in 1697 informed the hierarchy and all monastic superiors that no 'superfluous' buildings could be raised by them without an edict of the sovereign; also, that their money and grain revenues and all their expenditures were to be entered in books to be sent to Moscow.[4] Finally, by a decree dated 11 March 1701 the patriarchal household was forbidden to purchase land and monastic superiors to exchange estates with private landlords or to erect new buildings in stone (or even to repair old structures) without the approval of agents of the newly-formed Monastery Prikaz.[5] If carried out, these and related measures[6] would have ended the practice of investing surplus revenue in 'superfluous' church buildings or in the purchase of more lands, thus freeing

[1] Compare a recent estimate – that at the beginning of the eighteenth century the number of peasant households on patriarchal, episcopal, monastic, and parish lands totalled 154,196 – with the estimate of the College of State Revenue in 1721 – that the number of households on ecclesiastical lands totalled 153,254 (Kafengauz and Pavlenko, *op. cit.*, p. 372). The figures indicate both that Peter had successfully resisted any further growth in ecclesiastical landownership and that his outright confiscations of church property had been minimal.

[2] *PSZ*, iii, no. 1629 (p. 450).

[3] See the extended reference to an edict of 6 December 1696 to this effect in a *gramota* sent by Archbishop Athanasius of Kholmogory to the abbot of the Arkhangel'skii monastery: *AAE*, iv, no. 315 (pp. 466–467).

[4] *PSZ*, iii, no. 1613 (p. 425).

[5] *PSZ*, iv, no. 1839 (pp. 159–160).

[6] *PSZ*, iii, no. 1664 (pp. 529–530); *PSZ*, iv, no. 1897 (pp. 188–189); *PSZ*, v, no. 2662 (p. 22).

it for the tsar's use. At the same time, by requiring that all episcopal and monastic account books should be submitted to it annually, Peter's government had taken a large step towards assuming direct control of the church's economic life.[1]

With regard to the monasteries in particular, Peter's policy was made plain in an edict promulgated by the Monastery Prikaz in December 1701:

> Monks and nuns living in monasteries and convents are to be granted a fixed sum of money and grain for their maintenance and are not to own estates or any immovable property, [this] not for the sake of ruining the monasteries but for the better fulfilling of the monastic vocation. For the monks of old were wont to work with their own hands to produce food and the other necessities of life; and many poor people were fed by their hands. Monks today are not only fed by the labours of their poor peasants, but themselves are engaged in alien pursuits: the senior monks have fallen into luxury, while their hungry subordinates have been brought to quarrelling and murder and other lawlessness for the sake of a piece of land. And for these reasons the [tsar] has decreed that various measures be taken.

Accordingly, all monks, regardless of rank, were to receive an annual stipend of ten rubles in cash and a certain quantity of grain and firewood, while all other revenues collected by their monasteries were to be turned over to the Monastery Prikaz in Moscow and then disbursed 'for the care of the poor in [urban] almshouses and for the poor on monastic estates'. (Actually, after 1701 an increasing proportion of the Monastery Prikaz's revenue was diverted to military expenditure, as will be seen presently.) Those monasteries whose revenues were insufficient to support their monks at the fixed rate were to receive allowances from the government; they were also instructed to retain only the smallest possible number of domestic servants. No actual provision was made, it should be noted, for the outright confiscation or 'secularization' of monastic property.[2]

The practical effect of these measures in succeeding years is difficult

[1] Runkevich (*op. cit.*, p. 25) states that the decree of 1697 forbidding the hierarchy and monasteries to erect superfluous buildings and requiring them to send their account books to Moscow – in effect, laying it down that the bishops and monasteries could not spend their income except with the tsar's permission – contained 'nothing new'. He does not explain the remark, however. Nor does he place the decree in the context of earlier legislation (how else to judge whether it was 'new' or not?). To be sure, Runkevich does consider two decrees of this period – that forbidding the founding of new monasteries in Siberia (above, p. 85) and that suspending the annual stipends to the landed clergy of the Verkhoturskii district (see *PSZ*, iii, no. 1664 [pp. 529–530]) – 'as heralds of the impending reforms' (p. 25).

[2] *PSZ*, iv, no. 1886 (pp. 181–182).

to estimate. If the figures compiled by some authorities are roughly accurate, it seems that by 1710 the monks of perhaps 10 percent of the monasteries in Russia subsisted on fixed stipends paid by the state out of the revenues of these or other monasteries.[1] After this date, instances of the application of the 1701 edict to particular monasteries can be found in the legislative record of the reign.[2] But in October 1720 it was decreed that 'estates which were taken from the monasteries and for all tax purposes subjected to the Monastery Prikaz, excluding those which have been given in perpetuity to private persons by edicts of His Sovereign Majesty, are to be returned to the monasteries and to the supervision of their archimandrites and igumens, as formerly'; and all monastic revenues lately collected by the Monastery Prikaz were to be returned forthwith.[3] This action has been judged Peter's 'most important retreat from the principle enunciated by him in 1701'.[4] In fact, it probably signified no more than a belated return to normalcy (following the successful conclusion of the Swedish war) which was motivated by purely practical considerations. For Peter did not, thereby, relinquish his government's overall supervision of monastic finances. Indeed, it will be seen that by the terms of the *Ecclesiastical Regulation* of 1721 and related legislation the principle of an at least indirect control of the church's economic life by organs of the tsar's government, a principle first implemented as early as 1696, remained in force. It is true, nonetheless, that sometime between 1701 and 1720 Peter abandoned the attempt to place all monks and nuns in Russia on state-determined allowances, and that this most radical of his policies towards the monasteries thus languished.

Similarly, there is evidence that during the middle years of Peter's

[1] M. I. Gorchakov, *Monastyrskii Prikaz, 1649–1725* (St. Petersburg, 1868), estimates (p. 175) that by 1710 approximately 2500 monks in some 80 monasteries were supported in this way. On the other hand, Smolitsch (*op. cit.*, p. 713) calculates that in 1701 there were 965 monasteries in Russia and 236 convents; moreover, that in 1724 there were 14,534 monks and 10,673 nuns living in an unspecified number of monasteries and convents. Allowing for a certain decrease in the monastic population due to Peter's policies, the figure of 10 percent adduced above would seem reasonable. But estimates do vary widely: Ustryalov (*op. cit.*, iv, I, p. 539) says that in 1700 there were 'not less than 557' monasteries and convents in Russia, while a contemporary, the Dutch resident in Moscow, claiming to quote official government statistics, reported a total of 663 *cloîtres* (H. Van-der Hulst to the States-General, Moscow, 15 March 1701: printed in Ustryalov, *op. cit.*, iv, II, p. 669). Verkhovskoi (i, p. 113) states that the regulations in question affected 'hardly 58 of an overall total of more than 700 monasteries'.

[2] *PSZ*, iv, no. 2462 (p. 775); no. 2482 (p. 804), for example. See also *OAS*, i, no. 40 (cols. 31–33); no. 49 (cols. 37–38); no. 77 (cols. 53–54).

[3] *PSZ*, vi, no. 3659 (p. 248).

[4] Milyutin, *op. cit.*, p. 520.

reign his government actually assumed an unprecedented degree of control over episcopal finances. Thus, between 1709 and 1716 various members of the hierarchy were required to hand over their revenues to the Monastery Prikaz or to the local governments, whence fixed sums were to be paid to them for the upkeep of their households. In August 1711, for example, the Senate allowed the metropolitan of Krutitsy an annual stipend of 1000R – determined, it was said, by comparison with the incomes permitted to the other bishops – which was to be paid to him by the Monastery Prikaz from the revenues of his own diocese.[1] In 1712, 1500R of the archbishop of Smolensk's annual income were set aside by the Senate for his own use, while the surplus was to be given to the provincial governor.[2] A Senate decree of 29 December 1712 confirmed the tsar's charter of 1709 granting the archbishop of Tver 1200R a year for his own needs from the income of his diocese.[3] The metropolitan of Ryazan' himself, who in 1701 was named temporary head of the church, suffered his revenues to be made over that year to the Admiralty Prikaz, while he was given the income of the vacant see of Tambov.[4] (In 1711 the metropolitan's own revenues were restored to him 'so that he might live [could afford to live] in Moscow'.)[5] And indeed the power to collect all state taxes and peasant dues from the estates of the church, as well as such purely ecclesiastical emoluments as the parochial wedding fees, had been assigned by Peter to the Monastery Prikaz at its founding in 1701 and confirmed by edict in 1702.[6]

The authority thus granted to the Monastery Prikaz appears to have been exercised primarily with the aim of raising as much money as possible from the estates of the church for the purpose of defraying an ever larger proportion of the government's annual expenditure. Evidence of this may be found in the annual budgets of the Monastery Prikaz for the years 1701 to 1709. Thus, for the year 1701 the Prikaz reported receipts of approximately 50,500R from the bishops and monasteries (patriarchal revenues, totalling approximately 33,000R for that year, were accounted separately); and until 1705 the Prikaz's annual income averaged about 55,000R. In 1705, however, the Prikaz reported revenues of more than 130,000R. Although in the following year its income fell to approximately 77,000R, for the remaining years

[1] *PSZ*, iv, no. 2415 (pp. 727–728). [2] *PSZ*, iv, no. 2597 (p. 871).

[3] *PSZ*, iv, no. 2615 (pp. 879–880). See also *PSZ*, v, no. 2686 (p. 36); no. 3038 (pp. 476–477); *OAS*, i, no. 44 (cols. 34–35); no. 48 (col. 37), for similar governmental acts.

[4] *PSZ*, iv, no. 2346 (pp. 658–659). [5] *Ibid.* [6] *PSZ*, iv, no. 1829 (p. 133).

for which figures are available its revenues totalled: 224,502R (1707); 156,570R (1708); 143,965R (1709).[1] In other words, in the space of less than a decade the Prikaz's average annual income had tripled: at one point (1707) it had, as compared with previous years, more than quadrupled. When these figures are compared with the 50,000R collected in 1701; when it is remembered that during the period 1703–1708 total state expenditure annually exceeded revenue by as much as 25 percent; and when it is recalled that between 1701 and 1709 from 82 to 96 percent of this expenditure was devoted to military purposes, it is impossible not to connect the institution and operations of the Monastery Prikaz with the exigencies of Peter's war effort.[2]

We may also consider the following figures, which provide further evidence of the uses that were made of the Monastery Prikaz's revenue: in 1702 a sum equal to one-fourth of 'total receipts' (the term to include, after 1701, the actual receipts of a given year *plus* the balance of unused income left over from the previous year) was designated in its budgetary report 'remittances to other *prikazy*'; in 1703 a sum equal to four-fifths was so designated; in 1707 the proportion was more than one-third; in 1709 more than one-half. Expressed as percentages of the total annual expenditure reported by the Prikaz for these years, the figures would be: 80 percent (1702); 90 percent (1703); 50 percent (1707); and 64 percent (1709).[3]

So it seems that beginning as early as 1711 Peter gradually restored to the bishops, and eventually to the monasteries (by the decree of 1720), most of the immediate administrative and tax-collecting

[1] Figures from the records of the tsar's Privy Chancellery, as reproduced in Milyukov, *op. cit.*, appendix iii (pp. 578–613).

[2] Compare, too, individual entries in the itemized accounts of all government income and expenditure prepared from the budgetary reports to the Privy Chancellery of the various *prikazy*: thus, under 'indirect revenue' collected in 1707 'for military needs' are listed: 36,911R 'from patriarchal, monastic and other peasants'; 3,016R 'from the priests of the Moscow district for horses for the dragoons'; 5,999R 'from monastic servitors not wishing to serve in the dragoons'; and 2,345R for the purchase of military provisions 'from patriarchal and monastic estates' (Milyukov, *op. cit.*, p. 655). Similar entries can be found in the accounts for 1708 (*ibid.*, p. 664). It may also be noted that in February 1705 a government official reported to the tsar that he had taken 10,000R from the Monastery Prikaz and given it to the Artillery Prikaz (*PiB*, iii, p. 743); moreover, acting on a special order from the tsar the Privy Chancellery in March 1705 directed that a further 5000R be transferred from the Monastery Prikaz to the Artillery Prikaz (*ibid.*, pp. 779, 798); in early April, by order of Peter from Voronezh, a similar transfer of 10,000R was executed (*ibid*, pp. 799, 813); and in May yet another transfer of 10,000R was ordered (*ibid.*, p. 814). In 1705, therefore, at least 35,000R of the Monastery Prikaz's total reported expenditure of 126,000R, or 28 percent, was spent on guns and ammunition.

[3] Calculations based on figures printed in Milyukov, *op. cit.*, pp. 578 ff.

authority that they had formerly enjoyed in their respective domains.[1] He had in practice abandoned the notion of directly managing episcopal and monastic finances. In short, it can be said that in 1701 his government, sorely tried by the early disasters of the Swedish war, had assumed an unprecedented degree of control over both episcopal and monastic revenues which it later, on the verge of promulgating the *Ecclesiastical Regulation*, relinquished – most probably in anticipation of that event and of the new administrative order that it was to introduce.

And therefore it cannot be said that during the period 1701–1720 (or at any other time) Peter simply 'secularized' either episcopal or monastic lands, as might be hastily concluded.[2] For it is clear from the evidence cited above that at no time was the greater part of such property given over to private persons or joined to the estates of the tsar. The church was never dispossessed under Peter. Nor is it permissible, in the light of available evidence, to imply[3] that Peter set about completely to suppress the clergy's *votchinnye prava*, their very rights to own land. The complete suppression of those rights, that is a genuine secularization of all church lands, occurred only under Catherine II, approximately forty years after Peter's death – and then in such a way as to render much of its effect nugatory. For Catherine (to suggest only one reason), like Peter, proved unwilling completely to disband the monasteries, which had, therefore, to be permitted to retain a measure of land to ensure their subsistence.[4]

III

THE CHURCH IN EDUCATION AND SOCIAL WELFARE

The principle of using 'surplus' ecclesiastical revenue for general social, as distinct from either military or properly ecclesiastical, purposes, remained a feature of Peter's legislation until the end of his reign. As early as 1701, as we have seen, he expressed his belief that such revenue was not to be spent by ecclesiastical landlords in acquiring additional estates or in erecting or repairing superfluous buildings. Rather, it was to be invested, at the government's direction, in the care of the sick and the poor (when it was not to be used to buy guns,

[1] Verkhovskoi (i, p. 113) states that in any case only 12 of 28 episcopal households had been affected by the measures referred to above (p. 88).

[2] Cf. J. Mavor, *An Economic History of Russia* (2nd edn., London, 1925), i, pp. 134, 233.

[3] As does Milyutin, *op. cit.*, pp. 505–506.

[4] See J. Blum, *Lord and Peasant* (New York, 1964), pp. 362–366. But the question needs to be gone into much more thoroughly.

horses for the cavalry, ammunition, naval stores, etc.). Thus, in July 1701 the treasury of the patriarchal household was ordered to maintain almshouses (*bogadel'ni*) and to provide doctors and medicines for them.[1] Later that year, a special section of the Monastery Prikaz (all of whose income derived from ecclesiastical sources) assumed the principal responsibility for supporting the almshouses; and under its direction many new houses were built. In 1709 the administration of the almshouses was transferred to the patriarchal Palace Prikaz, which was, in practice, another subsidiary of the Monastery Prikaz. By 1721 there were 31 male and 62 female almshouses in Russia, mostly in Moscow, with a total of 4411 inmates in receipt of annual subsistence grants totalling 13,852R and derived entirely from the income of the patriarchal (now Synodal) household.[2] The figures contrast markedly with the 420 inmates of the one pre-Petrine almshouse in Moscow, which had been maintained by a special annual tax on all the dioceses first levied by Patriarch Joachim in 1678.[3]

The Monastery Prikaz also maintained the Moscow surgical hospital and school which were founded on Peter's orders in 1706. In 1712 the head of the hospital, the Dutch Dr. Bidlo, submitted a report to the tsar summarizing his progress since, 'with God's blessing and the care of his excellency Count Musin-Pushkin [head of the Monastery Prikaz]', it had opened its doors in November 1707:

> In this hospital Your Majesty was pleased that I should teach surgery based on anatomy to several young men of this nation who were skilled in Latin and Dutch, that I should minister to the sick and maimed sent to me, and, finally, that I should talk with all the people who were sent to see me. . . .

Bidlo submitted that he had fulfilled his commission; that over the years he had enrolled some fifty students, of whom thirty-two remained (six had died, eight had 'fled', and three had been taken away on the tsar's orders); that from 1708 to 1712, 1996 patients had been treated, of whom 1026 were cured; and that he had at present 142 patients.[4] Thereafter, until 1720, Bidlo's surgical school continued to support between thirty-five and forty students drawing total annual subsidies of from 175R to 370R.[5] By 1720 the Monastery Prikaz's annual 'hospital'

[1] *PSZ*, iv, no. 1856 (p. 168).
[2] See the lengthy report on the almshouses submitted to the Synod on 7 October 1721 by the Monastery Prikaz (*PSP*, i, no. 309 [pp. 361–363]).
[3] *PSZ*, ii, no. 956 (p. 468).
[4] Bidlo's report quoted in full in Pekarskii, *op. cit.*, i, pp. 132–133.
[5] See the Monastery Prikaz's report to the Synod of 10 April 1722 (*PSP*, ii, no. 539 [pp. 184–188]).

budget exceeded 5000R.[1] In 1721, as we shall see, the Synod inherited ultimate responsibility both for the almshouses and for Bidlo's hospital, thus becoming, in a sense, Peter's ministry for social welfare.

Apart from paying for rudimentary medical services for the army,[2] ecclesiastical funds were also employed to provide for old and disabled soldiers. Not surprisingly, such persons were the object of Tsar Peter's special concern. By an edict of 1710 he required that veterans unfit even for routine training duties were to be turned over to the care of the Moscow almshouses.[3] Later, in 1714–1715, Peter decreed that the proceeds of the wedding fees collected in the patriarchal domain and in the dioceses should be sent directly to the Senate, whence they would be consigned to the maintenance of special military hospitals (called *lazarety*).[4] And in 1719–1720 there appeared the first of those orders whereby retired soldiers were to be lodged in certain monasteries and given money and food allowances from the monasteries' revenues equivalent to the pay and allowances of the local garrison troops.[5] After 1721 this policy was to be the subject of somewhat acrimonious exchanges between the Synod and the Senate. But the policy was not in essence invented by Peter. According to the former *prikazchik* G. Kotoshikhin, writing in 1666–1667, it was the practice in Muscovite Russia that soldiers badly wounded in service could retire to a monastery, where they would be cared for (or at least fed) for the rest of their lives.[6]

Under Peter, the principal educational institution of Muscovite Russia continued, quite naturally, to be supported by ecclesiastical funds. The

[1] *PSZ*, ii, no. 901 (p. 619).

[2] It seems that many, if not most, of Bidlo's graduates were seconded to the army (see *PiB*, x, p. 605, for a list of 39 such persons thus disposed of between 1712 and 1719). The Monastery Prikaz also paid for medicines for the army (see *PiB*, vii, no. 2402 [p. 186]).

[3] *PSZ*, iv, no. 2249 (p. 476).

[4] *PSZ*, v, no. 2821 (p. 114); no. 2844 (pp. 123–124); no. 3026 (pp. 472–473). It should be noted that the *lazarety* were not maintained exclusively by ecclesiastical funds. Peter's government devised quite ingenious methods of raising ever more money for the 'fund for the military hospitals'. For example, by a decree of 1715 any *prikazchik* who petitioned for promotion to *d'yak* (the senior, non-noble rank in the bureaucracy) was required to contribute 100R 'of his own money' to the fund on obtaining his promotion (*PSZ*, v, no. 2911 [p. 158]; no. 3026 [pp. 472–473]). Again, the Military and Naval Statutes of 1716 and 1720 provided that for such breaches of discipline as cursing and being absent from church services fixed contributions were to be made to the fund (*PSZ*, v, no. 3006 [pp. 322–323]; *PSZ*, vi, no. 3485 [p. 50]).

[5] *PSZ*, v, no. 3409 (p. 726); *PSZ*, vi, no. 3576 (pp. 188–189).

[6] G. K. Kotoshikhin, *O Rossii v tsarstvovanie Alekseya Mikhailovicha* (2nd edn., St. Petersburg, 1859), p. 114.

so-called Slavonic–Greek–Latin academy in Moscow, which was founded about 1685 by immigrant Greeks and in 1700 was entrusted by Peter to the new temporary head of the church, the 'Latinizer' Stefan Yavorskii (thus inaugurating, in the school, a 'cultural revolution' from Greek to 'Latin learning [*latinskoe uchenie*]'), had always drawn its sustenance from patriarchal revenues.[1] But jurisdiction over its teachers and students 'in all things except robbery and murder' was taken from the temporary head of the church by an edict of 1718 and given to the Monastery Prikaz, whose officials were specifically charged with enforcing discipline in the academy.[2] Apart from it and the Kiev academy, which continued to be managed by the local ecclesiastical authorities under the vague supervision of the temporary head of the church in Moscow; and apart from a small school of translators attached to the patriarchal press in Moscow, there were in Russia in the early years of Peter's reign only a scattering of elementary schools located in the major monasteries and episcopal towns. Founded for the most part in the previous century, the church schools of Muscovy seem not to have thrived (they fared somewhat better in the Ukraine), the victims of tight-fisted officialdom but also, doubtless, of the increasingly bitter split between the Old Believers and the official clergy on the one hand, and, on the other, between those of the latter who favoured the Greek and those the Latin learning. The situation was such that at the end of the seventeenth century a Czech Catholic priest who had lived in Moscow for three years could observe simply: 'among the Russians there is no education', a situation which he himself attributed, with some reason, to the fact that 'they adhered to the Greek schism'.[3]

There were some highlights in the generally dark picture, however. Between 1702 and his death in 1709 the episcopal school of Rostov flourished under the enlightened patronage of Metropolitan Dimitrii Tuptalo; during those years some 200 students, mostly sons of clergy, were taught Slavonic and Latin grammar, religion, some Greek, rhetoric, and even a bit of scholastic philosophy by three teachers, two of whom were Ukrainians like Dimitrii himself.[4] Similarly, in the early years of the eighteenth century the admirable Metropolitan Job established in his wealthy and large Novgorod diocese

[1] On the origins and early history of the Moscow academy, see S. K. Smirnov, *Istoriya moskovskoi Slavyano-greko-latinskoi akademii* (Moscow, 1855), pp. 18–77.

[2] *PSZ*, v, no. 3182 (p. 554).

[3] Myl'nikov, 'Svidetel'stvo inostrannogo nablyudatelya', *Voprosy istorii*, 1968, no. 4, p. 142.

[4] Shlyapkin, *op. cit.*, pp. 327–353.

two higher schools of Greek and Latin studies and some fourteen grammar schools.[1] And then, by a series of decrees in 1714–1716 Peter introduced his celebrated system of 'cipher schools', which were to be established in or near episcopal palaces or monasteries and to draw their students from all classes except the nobility. The students, including sons of clergy, were to study not Slavonic grammar and religion, but arithmetic and geometry; and they were to be taught by graduates not of the Moscow or Kiev academies, but of the Admiralty's School of Mathematics and Navigation, which had been founded by Peter in 1701.[2] The cipher schools were not a great success, at least in terms of the number of students enrolled in them or of the number of graduates they produced. After 1721 they were merged with, or rather submerged by, the episcopal schools established under provisions of the *Ecclesiastical Regulation*. Indeed, the *Ecclesiastical Regulation* itself contains the most important provisions of Peter's reign relating to the church's role in education, and the whole question is further discussed in Chapter 6.

The institution of new almshouses in Moscow, as well as the formulation of schemes for provincial asylums,[3] were related to another of Peter's innovations in what today we should call very broadly the field of social welfare: his attempt to eliminate the time-honoured custom of public begging. The problem had received some attention before Peter's reign, for instance in the vague resolution of the church council of 1666–1667 that certain pseudo-clerics, 'hypocrites and tempters, who live in the midst of towns and villages in the guise of hermits and holy men, wearing long hair and monks' habit and even chains', should be discouraged from begging, for 'they live not under God nor in justice nor even prudently'.[4] But a determined effort to abolish the custom seems not to have been made until Peter's time.

By an edict of 1710 persons living in the almshouses were made to undergo a monthly examination to determine who were really fit, had

[1] Kafengauz, *Pososhkov*, p. 61; I. Chistovich, *Istoriya S. Peterburgskoi dukhovnoi akademii* (St. Petersburg, 1857), p. 3.

[2] *PSZ*, v, no. 2778 (p. 86); no. 2971 (p. 187); no. 2979 (p. 189). In 1715 the navigation section of the School was transferred from Moscow to St. Petersburg and renamed the Naval Academy, while the preparatory section of the School remained in the Sukharev Tower of the Kremlin, now forming, as it were, the cipher school of Moscow (see N. Hans, 'The Moscow School of Mathematics and Navigation', *Slavonic and East European Review*, xxix [June 1951], pp. 532–536).

[3] *PSZ*, iv, no. 2467 (p. 779); no. 2477 (p. 791).

[4] *PSZ*, i, no. 412 (pp. 700–701).

wives and children, or knew a trade, for any of which reasons they were to be immediately expelled.[1] A personal decree of the tsar promulgated in 1712 forbade begging anywhere in Moscow by persons of either sex or of any age: offenders were to be arrested and brought to the Monastery Prikaz, where they were to be thoroughly inspected, 'punished', and sent to an almshouse or to a monastery or, if they were fugitive serfs, back to their former villages.[2] In 1718 the head of the Monastery Prikaz announced that

> Mad monks and male and female beggars who appear in Moscow and wander about the markets and streets and sit at crossroads, and beg alms and gifts from the almshouses and from door to door and at windows, are to be sent, as formerly, to the Monastery Prikaz. Moreover those who stand at the exits of churches, singing and praying 'for the love of God', are on no account to be given alms. . . . and those who give alms, heedless of the Tsar's personal edict, shall, on detection, also be sent to the Monastery Prikaz and shall pay five rubles for the first [offence] and ten for the second.[3]

Even stricter measures were introduced some months later. Beggars violating the earlier decrees were now liable to flogging, banishment to the galleys, or to work in a textile mill or other factory, while their masters (if the culprits were peasants) were to be fined five rubles for negligence.[4]

The practice of begging was to be criticized at length in a passage of the *Ecclesiastical Regulation* of 1721. And there, as well as in the preceding legislation, the problem was inevitably linked with that of the 'excess' clergy, the elimination of whom had been an express aim of Peter's government since the early days of his reign.

But first, one or two of Peter's other innovations in the welfare field should be mentioned. It was unprecedented that the wives of serving soldiers should be supported as a matter of law by the monastery or episcopal household in which their husbands had formerly served, as was required on Peter's orders throughout the whole of the period 1707–1721.[5] More significant still of the new approach to social problems was Peter's decree of 1704 to the clergy of the Moscow district, ordaining that midwives should be forbidden under pain of death to destroy or 'hide away' malformed infants; rather, they were to bring such children to the parish priest, who should report the fact to the

[1] *PSZ*, iv, no. 2249 (p. 476).
[2] *PSZ*, iv, no. 2470 (p. 782).
[3] *PSZ*, v, no. 3172 (p. 546).
[4] *PSZ*, v, no. 3213 (pp. 578–579).
[5] *PSP*, i, no. 243 (pp. 292–293).

Monastery Prikaz.[1] Ten years later the concern for the fate of unfortunate children was broadened to include bastards. By a personal edict of the tsar, who was inspired by the example of Metropolitan Job of Novgorod, orphanages for infants born of unwed mothers were to be built in Moscow and in the other towns near the parish churches, 'as is seemly'; competent women were to be found to look after the children and were to be given fixed allowances from 'surplus' parish revenue.[2] These two edicts provide evidence that child-abandonment or worse, infanticide, were practised to a noticeable extent in contemporary Russia, a deduction which is sustained by a Senate resolution of November 1715 conferring Peter's 1714 edict. Orphanages were to be built and staffed, the Senate reiterated, for the care of illegitimate infants whose mothers, 'because of shame, cast away the unfortunate little ones, whence they die or are murdered; ... infants shall not be put away in unsuitable places but brought to the orphanages and secretly laid in a window, which shall be shuttered, so that the persons bringing them shall not be seen. And if illegitimate infants are murdered, those guilty of such an evil shall themselves be put to death'.[3] But it appears that Peter's scheme was never implemented: a Senate decree in 1720 once again ordered that the said orphanages should be built 'according to the edict promulgated in 1715'.[4] And the matter is not referred to again in the printed legislation of the reign.

Yet the intentions of Peter's government in this respect are clear, and contrast sharply with the attitude of the official church expressed as late as 1697 by Patriarch Adrian. In a lengthy Instruction to the clergy Adrian devoted four extended passages to sex offences: unwed mothers, repenting of their sin, were to be interrogated by patriarchal courts, 'mercilessly beaten by slapping', and sent in irons to a convent, where for a month they were to follow the rule, attend all the offices, 'and after the Liturgy each day do a hundred prostrations'. Equally, the (much lighter) punishments for the men by whom such women had illegitimately conceived were spelt out. The child itself of such a union was mentioned once, almost casually, when it was directed that at birth the repentant mother should give the infant to the attending midwife.[5] In short, the patriarch was concerned with punishing the sin of the parents; Tsar Peter, with saving the life of the child.[6]

[1] *PSZ*, iv, no. 1964 (p. 243).
[2] *PSZ*, v, no. 2856 (p. 128).
[3] *PSZ*, v, no. 2953 (p. 181).
[4] *PSZ*, vi, no. 3502 (p. 124).
[5] *PSZ*, iii, no. 1612 (pp. 413–425; see p. 418).
[6] Cf. the halfway house of article 26, chapter xxii of the *Ulozhenie* of 1649, which prescribed that 'should a woman leading a wanton and abominable life in her lechery

IV

GOVERNMENT CONTROL OF THE CLERGY

Peter was not the first authority to act on the premise that there were too many 'ecclesiastical persons' in the country. The church council of 1666–1667, for instance, had recommended certain restrictions on the admission of novices to monasteries and convents; a reduction in the traffic between monasteries of novices and wandering holy men; the concentration of monastic industry on the task of providing for the needs of the brethren; and the elimination (as mentioned above) of some forms of begging.[1] Equally, the council had obligingly resolved that, upon detection, fugitive serfs who had entered holy orders were to be unfrocked by an ecclesiastical court and returned to their masters, for the genuineness of their vocation (the council felt) was open to doubt. Moreover, the sons of peasants who had legally (i.e. with their masters' leave) become priests and deacons were to be considered serfs, and returned to their fathers' former masters, unless it could be shown that they were born after their fathers' ordination, in which case they were 'eternally free'.[2] But all such mesaures only peripherally touched on what came to be a consistent policy of Peter's government: an absolute prohibition of any increase in the numbers of clergy of all kinds coupled with a radical diminution of certain categories of ecclesiastical dependants.

Already in 1694 an order was issued requiring that 'homeless monks and nuns' and priests and deacons leading 'useless and scandalous lives', as well as 'idlers with an arm or leg trussed up, as though crippled, or others who blink and cover their eyes, as though blind, and with a disarming guile beg alms in the name of Christ, though on inspection they prove to be in good health' – that all such persons were to be brought to officers of the Moscow garrison for interrogation and the genuine clerics among them referred to the patriarchal Ecclesiastical Prikaz, 'so that on no account may they wander about the streets and haunt the taverns'.[3] In 1701, the year in which the poorer monasteries

beget children, and [then] herself destroy these children or order someone else to do so . . . such a lawless woman, as well as whoever on her orders destroyed her children, are to be put to death without mercy, so that such lawlessness and abominations should not be perpetrated and that lechery should be restrained' (*PRP*, vi, p. 434).

[1] *PSZ*, i, no. 412 (pp. 700–701). [2] *PSZ*, i, no. 412 (p. 704).

[3] *PSZ*, iii, no. 1489 (pp. 176–177). This order refers to a decree of 1692 to the same effect.

were instructed to retain only the smallest possible number of servants,[1] Peter decreed, in rapid succession: that monks and nuns were forbidden to leave their monasteries without the written permission of their superiors; that henceforth no lay persons could remain in the monasteries, whether as cantors or lectors or clerks; that foreign monks – Greeks, Armenians, and Indians (*Indeitsy*) – could no longer stay in Russian monasteries; and that the numerous relations of nuns living in convents were either to leave and to marry or, if at least forty years of age, to take the veil.[2] Then, in 1702, peasants and others living on ecclesiastical estates were ordered not to undertake working arrangements binding them to their landlords for more than five years; nor were they or their sons to marry women 'from outside' unless they registered with the Monastery Prikaz and paid a (prohibitive) tax.[3] The injunction against lay persons living in monasteries was repeated in 1703, with the addition that those who did not leave promptly and return to their former homes would be exiled for life to the monasteries of the far north.[4]

Thus, from measures designed to clear the streets of unattached, impoverished, or fraudulent clerics, Tsar Peter's government had proceeded in the space of a few years to enact others which imposed unprecedented restrictions on ecclesiastical persons. More was to come. In 1706 various categories of ecclesiastical persons, hitherto exempt, were drafted into the army.[5] The following year Peter instructed his recruiting officer in central Russia thoroughly to investigate the ranks of the clergy there and to conscript all but properly ordained and functioning priests and deacons.[6] Finally, in April 1711, in an effort expressly designed to limit the number of persons who could claim exemption from military service, a list of regulations governing the selection of priests and deacons was sent to all the bishops. 'Enacted by the Holy Council and the All-Ruling Senate',[7] the regulations in effect froze the numbers of such clergy at current levels and severely restricted the ordination of new priests and deacons: the lower age limit for

[1] As mentioned above, p. 86.

[2] *PSZ*, iv, no. 1834 (pp. 139–140); no. 1839 (pp. 159–160); no. 1856 (p. 168).

[3] *PSZ*, iv, no. 1920 (p. 200).

[4] *PSZ*, iv, no. 1948 (pp. 227–228).

[5] *PSZ*, iv, no. 2108 (p. 351); no. 2130 (pp. 360–362).

[6] *PiB*, v, p. 35.

[7] '. . . pursuant to an edict of the Great Sovereign': the formula was a cliché of Muscovite legislation, except that now the term 'All-Ruling Senate' had replaced the traditional 'Boyars' Council'. There is no reason to suppose that on this occasion a 'Holy Council' of the senior clergy had been convened to deliberate on and to ratify the new regulations, however. On this point see also Verkhovskoi, i, p. 151.

deacons was set at twenty-five, that for priests at thirty;[1] deacons could no longer be ordained priests for parishes that were poor by the government's reckoning; priests and deacons could not be transferred from parish to parish; 'ignorant and lazy' deacons were to be absolutely rejected as candidates for the priesthood; etc. And dire punishments were prescribed for any bishop who should ignore the regulations.[2]

Motivated evidently by a desire both to eliminate begging and to maximize the number of potential recruits for the army, Peter's government now showed itself increasingly disposed to assume control of the selection and discipline of the church's ministers. Other measures manifesting this tendency prior to 1721 include the several-times reiterated order that only sons of the clergy who had successfully passed through the appropriate schools were to be ordained to their fathers' places.[3] The concession in 1718 to officials of the Monastery Prikaz of disciplinary powers over the students and faculties of the Moscow academy, the training ground for the higher clergy, has been mentioned.[4] Mention may also be made in passing of the imposition in 1719–1720 of a form of government censorship over the printing of ecclesiastical writings; the question will be discussed in the concluding chapter. Moreover, as early as 1701 it was laid down that monks should have neither ink nor paper in their cells, but should do their writing in the refectory, 'openly, and not secretly', in the presence of their superiors.[5] And the activities of monks attached to the army and navy as chaplains were closely regulated by the Military and Naval Statutes, whereby unfrocking was prescribed for such offences as 'incontinence, lawlessness, and the giving of scandal', or for drunkenness (third offence) during the time of services.[6]

Control of the parish clergy was further intensified by the propensity of Peter's government to make them its agents in various invidious ways. The role assigned to parish priests and confessors in the campaign to impose uniform religious discipline on all subjects was described above. In addition, the priests were made to play an important part in an intensified effort to 'root out thieves, rebels, bandits, fugitive soldiers, and similar people'. Notices concerning the detection

[1] These were, in fact, the canonical ages for ordination: see A. Pavlov (ed.), *Nomokanon pri Bol'shom Trebnike* (Moscow, 1897), p. 343.

[2] *PSZ*, iv, no. 2352 (p. 668).

[3] *PSZ*, iv, no. 2186 (p. 401); no. 2308 (p. 581); no. 2352 (p. 668); *PSZ*, v, no. 3175 (p. 548).

[4] Above, p. 93.

[5] *PSZ*, iv, no. 1834 (pp. 139–140).

[6] *PSZ*, v, no. 3006 (p. 240, 322–324); *PSZ*, vi, no. 3485 (pp. 42–43).

and punishment of such persons were to be posted in all the parish churches; on Sundays, feastdays, and market-days the priests were to read the relevant decrees and to preach to their congregations on 'the fear of God'; and thus, hearing the former 'in this place, where the Word of God and the Monarch's decrees are read', the people would learn what 'is forbidden by Divine and earthly law'.[1] Similarly, by a decree of the Senate in October 1720 the clergy and their churches were to be used to publicize the tsar's new tax regulations.[2]

The tendency of Peter's government to assume control of the clergy was to culminate in the promulgation of the *Ecclesiastical Regulation* and related legislation.

V

RESTRICTION OF THE CHURCH'S JUDICIAL PRIVILEGES

What was to be left to the church? During the years prior to the appearance of the *Ecclesiastical Regulation* Peter also acted to suppress the judicial privileges traditionally enjoyed by the clergy, a policy which naturally complemented his efforts (described above) to eliminate the financial privileges enjoyed by ecclesiastical landlords and was, like those efforts, solidly based on precedent. The judicial privileges in question were of two kinds: those (A) that were exercised by the clergy as landowners; and those (B) that were derived from their status as clerics.

(A) As part of their *votchinnye prava* (literally, 'hereditary estate rights') all bishops, most monasteries, and some parish clergy enjoyed more or less complete jurisdiction over persons living on their estates. This situation was, in part, simply the result of applying the law of bonded servitude (*krepostnoe pravo*), as it was finally formulated in the *Ulozhenie* of 1649, to ecclesiastical landowners who, like any others, were thereby assured of extensive judicial rights over their peasants or 'bondsmen'.[3] More importantly, by a long series of charters dating from Mongol times the church had been guaranteed, in addition to complete administrative autonomy, complete jurisdiction over both the clergy and their dependants – over, that is, everyone who lived in or served a monastery, an episcopal household, or a parish church, as well as over those who lived on an estate or urban property belonging to a bishop or a monas-

[1] *PSZ*, v, no. 3223 (p. 585); no. 3334 (pp. 681–684); no. 3445 (pp. 748–750); no. 3477 (pp. 773–775).

[2] *PSZ*, vi. no. 3684 (pp. 241–243).

[3] *PRP*, vi, esp. pp. 165 ff.

tery. Yet there is evidence in the legislative documents dating from the time of Ivan IV (1533–1584), if not earlier, of a countervailing tendency under successive governments to limit not only the material growth of the church (as discussed above), but the scope of its judicial authority as well.[1]

The *Ulozhenie* of 1649 explicitly included within the orbit of the tsar's justice brigands, robbers, thieves, rebels, fugitive serfs, and the accomplices of all such persons living on patriarchal, episcopal, and monastic estates.[2] Also, under the *Ulozhenie*, murder in its various forms was a crime reserved exclusively to the tsar's jurisdiction,[3] as were personal injury cases involving clerics (except in those cases where a member of the service nobility caused injury to the patriarch or to a bishop, when jurisdiction was shared by the tsar with the patriarch or the bishop).[4] Above all, the *Ulozhenie* provided for the institution of a 'Monastery Prikaz' with jurisdiction over all civil (in the modern sense of the word) actions involving clerics or their dependants,[5] though the dependants – clerical and lay – of the patriarch remained subject to the central patriarchal courts in all but criminal matters.[6] While the legal distinction between ecclesiastical and other persons had been scrupulously maintained, in sum, the exclusive jurisdiction of the (non-patriarchal) ecclesiastical authorities over their dependants had been formally suppressed; and something very tentatively like a unitary judicial system, centred in the royal and patriarchal *prikazy* in Moscow and having ultimate jurisdiction over all the tsar's subjects in all civil and criminal cases, had been created.

It was left to Tsar Peter, in fact, resolutely to enforce the *Ulozhenie*'s provisions by abrogating, one after another, those numerous charters granted to individual bishops or monasteries or churches whereby they had continued to enjoy, throughout the latter half of the seventeenth century, extensive judicial as well as financial privileges in their respective domains.[7] But Peter, it must be stressed, never tampered with the law of serfdom as it applied to ecclesiastical peasants – except for the decree, early in his reign, and probably never enforced,

[1] Milyutin, *op. cit.*, pp. 243 ff; 415 ff.

[2] *PRP*, vi, pp. 400–401.

[3] *PRP*, vi, pp. 22, 92–93, 102–104, 107, 123, 140, 187, 399.

[4] *PRP*, vi, pp. 84–89.

[5] *PRP*, vi, pp. 185–187. It was also provided that litigation involving an ecclesiastical person with someone of another 'order', for example in a dispute with a private landlord, could be tried in another *prikaz*, for example in that concerned with service-estate matters (the Pomestnyi Prikaz). In such cases, however, the ecclesiastical person was entitled to initiate a countersuit in the Monastery Prikaz.

[6] *PRP*, vi, p. 183.

[7] See the legislation cited above, p. 82 and n. 5.

restricting labour contracts between such persons and their landlords to periods of no more than five years.[1] Peter's legislation in this respect only served to reinforce the trend to judicial centralization, leaving ecclesiastical landlords with the same judicial authority over their peasants as was exercised by private landlords or by the administrators of the estates of the crown.

(B) The second type of judicial privilege traditionally enjoyed by the clergy in Russia – their own immunity from the jurisdiction of the civil courts – has been touched upon. From the preceding discussion it is clear that after the promulgation of the *Ulozhenie* and the establishment of the Monastery Prikaz criminal and civil cases involving clerics were subject to adjudication by the tsar or his agencies. Yet it had been the tradition in Muscovite Russia, embodied in the series of charters referred to above, that the clergy should be liable only to the judgment of their bishops; and despite developments to the contrary, the clergy continued to regard the tradition as sacrosanct. As recently as 1667 the same church council that had deposed the theocratic Patriarch Nikon had gone on record as opposed to the judging of clergy by laymen, a practice (the council said) which was forbidden by certain canons of both the ecumenical and local church councils and by certain laws of the Byzantine emperors. The council explained that

> there are two tribunals in the world, one ecclesiastical, which judges souls, and the other secular, which has jurisdiction only over the body; and there are two kinds of death, one which is eternal and one in this world. And therefore one judge cannot punish both the body and the soul, for it is not given that one should hold the secular and ecclesiastical powers jointly. . . .

It was a reassertion of the Byzantine theory of the parallel powers, from which the council proceeded to argue that separate and exclusive jurisdictions must be preserved, so that a cleric who should 'lose himself in unseemly affairs, contrary to the Tsar's law', was to be punished first by the church, 'according to the ecclesiastical canons', and then, for a second offence, by a civil court. And lest any doubt remained in the matter, the council roundly declared that 'bishops, archimandrites and igumens, priests, deacons and monks, and all other members of the ecclesiastical order and their dependants, are not to be judged by laymen in any matter whatever: they are to be judged in all things by the bishop of their diocese, or by someone appointed not from the laity but from the ecclesiastical order'.[2] Indeed, apart from cases of schism

[1] *PSZ*, iv, no. 1920 (p. 200).

[2] *PSZ*, i, no. 412 (pp. 699; 702–703).

and heresy (the prosecution of which, as we have seen, the council enthusiastically conceded to the government), only acts of sacrilege, that is the stealing or despoiling of church property, appear to have been recognized by the council as a matter belonging to the jurisdiction of the civil courts.[1]

Goaded perhaps by the council's attitude, Tsar Aleksei less than two years later promulgated a fourteen-point code governing the prosecution of clerics accused of crimes ranging from theft and counterfeiting to murder. The code was expressly designed to supplement the bare provisions of the *Ulozhenie*. It required that the apprehension, interrogation, and punishment of ecclesiastical criminals were to be done by specially appointed officials assisted by the tsar's police (*strel'tsy*): the bishops were to cooperate in the judicial process but were to have no voice in deciding its outcome; no mention was made of the distinction between first and second offences, a distinction which was drawn by the council of 1667.[2] Still, the principle that the clergy should receive special treatment before the law (*viz.* the appointment of special officials and the drafting of a special code) had been reaffirmed. Moreover, the tsar in 1672 confirmed that in all but criminal matters patriarchal dependants were to remain subject to patriarchal jurisdiction only.[3] On the patriarch's petition he even designated a certain official to adjudicate all land disputes between patriarchal dependants and 'outsiders', thus saving the former the bother of litigating in the numerous courts to which ordinary subjects had to bring their grievances.[4] And the closing of the Monastery Prikaz in 1677 must have represented something of a concession to the clergy in the matter of their judicial immunities, though that office appears to have been more concerned with its tax-collecting than with its judicial functions.[5]

Tsar Peter proved less placable. From the earliest years of his reign his legislation served to reverse the recent tendency to conciliate the clergy in respect of their judicial immunities. In 1692 he ordered that the jurisdiction of the patriarch's courts over litigation involving clerics with laymen was to be shared in some cases with certain secular courts in Moscow.[6] In 1697 ecclesiastical jurisdiction over all clergy and laymen in 'ecclesiastical matters' (matters of church discipline, marriage

[1] *PSZ*, i, no. 412 (p. 703). Sacrilege had already been prohibited by the *Ulozhenie* (*PRP*, vi, p. 385).

[2] *PSZ*, i, no 442 (pp. 800–802). [3] *PSZ*, i, no. 505 (pp. 869–870). [4] *Ibid.*

[5] *PSZ*, ii, no. 711 (p. 148); *PRP*, vii, p. 365 and editor's note, p. 381. See also Kotoshikhin's description of the Monastery Prikaz, *op. cit.*, p. 90.

[6] *PSZ*, iii, no. 1452 (p. 145).

and divorce cases, sex offences, etc.) was guaranteed by the tsar, with ultimate appellate jurisdiction assured to the patriarch.[1] In sum, the deeper trend to judicial centralization had reasserted itself and, for the first time, patriarchal dependants had become liable to secular jurisdiction in other than criminal matters. And already in the 1690's a juridical distinction between purely 'ecclesiastical' and other matters had clearly emerged. All these developments were to receive dramatic confirmation in Peter's subsequent legislation.

In December 1700 it was decreed that all cases formerly heard in the patriarchal Razryadnyi Prikaz – including, specifically, those brought by clerics but excluding cases of 'schism, heresy, and opposition to God's church' – were henceforth to be subject to whichever of the civil *prikazy* was appropriate to the plaintiff's rank and the nature of his suit: the 'ecclesiastical' cases mentioned were to fall under the jurisdiction of the metropolitan of Ryazan', who was given charge of the patriarch's Ecclesiastical Prikaz (*Dukhovnyi prikaz*), with which was promptly merged (for the space of ten years) the patriarch's formerly autonomous Prikaz of Ecclesiastical Affairs (*Tserkovnykh del*), the organ of control of the Moscow clergy.[2] Very soon thereafter, in two decrees promulgated at the end of January 1701, it was announced that a new Monastery Prikaz had been formed which was to be located in the place formerly occupied by the patriarchal Razryadnyi Prikaz. The patriarchal and episcopal households, all ecclesiastical property and dependants, and 'all monastic affairs' were for administrative, judicial, and taxation purposes to be subject to this office; and suits from all classes of ecclesiastical persons, lay and clerical, were to be brought to it or to another prikaz, 'as the Tsar shall direct'.[3] Lastly, in November 1701 Peter confirmed that the jurisdiction over all clergy involved in civil cases with laymen once exercised exclusively by the patriarchal courts was now to be shared with a secular office (the Moscow *Sudnyi* or Court Prikaz), and that in all cases clearly belonging to the jurisdiction of other secular *prikazy*, suits by ecclesiastical persons were to be lodged there[4] – in effect, in most cases, in the newly formed Monastery Prikaz.

[1] See the Sovereign's edict appended to the patriarchal Instruction to the clergy of 26 December 1697 (*PSZ*, iii, no. 1612 [pp. 413–425]).

[2] *PSZ*, iv, no. 1818 (pp. 87–88); *PSZ*, iv, no. 2415 (pp. 759–761). See also below, p. 136.

[3] *PSZ*, iv, no. 1829 (p. 133); no. 1834 (pp. 139–140). During as it were the interim between the closing of the Monastery Prikaz in 1677 and its reopening in 1701, its functions had reverted to the Prikaz of the Great Court, where they atrophied.

[4] *PSZ*, iv, no. 1876 (p. 176), confirming edict of 1692 (*PSZ*, iii, no. 1452 [p. 145]).

Thus, at a stroke, one of the principal agencies of the patriarchal administration, its Razryadnyi Prikaz, had been abolished and two others (the Ecclesiastical Prikaz and that of Ecclesiastical Affairs), which had been merged under the nominal (as it turned out) jurisdiction of the metropolitan of Ryazan', were required to share their authority in all but purely ecclesiastical matters with certain organs of the tsar's government. Moreover if in some respects the Monastery Prikaz thus founded by Peter resembled the earlier institution of the same name, in other respects it was radically different. Like its predecessor, Peter's Prikaz proved to be primarily concerned with collecting taxes; and so with regard to its judicial function it is not surprising that the majority of cases adjudicated by it between 1701 and 1720 concerned disputes over property.[1] Yet the weight and number of taxes imposed on the church and the degree of control assumed by the Monastery Prikaz over the church's economy in pursuit of more money, troops, labourers, and provisions, as well as to finance a greatly expanded welfare programme, were, it was suggested above, quite unprecedented. And the assumption by Peter's Monastery Prikaz of jurisdiction over the vast domain of the patriarchal household represented a decisive break with previous practices.

In theory, the division of jurisdiction over the ecclesiastical and secular affairs of the church (as defined by the relevant decrees) between, respectively, the chief patriarchal court and the Monastery Prikaz remained in force until January 1721. In 1706 the latter's jurisdiction was formally reaffirmed,[2] as was that of the former in 1711.[3] But in practice no such clear-cut distinction obtained. It is true that the majority of cases decided by the Monastery Prikaz involved property disputes, and that ecclesiastical persons accused of murder, robbery, or treason were remanded, as before 1701, to the appropriate civil court.[4] But after 1716, for instance, cases of 'schism, heresy, and opposition to God's church' became subject to the new regulations of the tsar's government. And from as early as 1701, as we have also seen, the government assumed direct responsibility for the discipline of the monastic and secular clergy, going so far as to require unfrocking as the statutory penalty for certain infringements of state law.

[1] Gorchakov, *op. cit.*, pp. 199–200.

[2] *PSZ*, iv, no. 2108 (p. 351).

[3] *PSZ*, iv, no. 2451 (pp. 759–761).

[4] Gorchakov, *op. cit.*, p. 200. Also, after 1720, in addition to the crimes enumerated, clergy guilty of extortion or usury were to be tried only by the civil courts (*PSZ*, vi, no. 3586 [p. 194]).

The jurisdictional confusion engendered or exacerbated by Peter's legislation in the period 1700–1720 was to be partly resolved by the institution of the Most Holy Synod as, among other things, the supreme ecclesiastical court of Russia. But it should be noted that this confusion was not due solely to Peter's legislation affecting the offices responsible for ecclesiastical property and persons. It was due also to the changes he made in the whole administrative structure of the state. There was, firstly, the sweeping decentralization (1708) of the government, formerly concentrated in a bewildering welter of *prikazy* in Moscow, into eight (later ten) vast provincial administrations, to which were allotted very wide powers, especially as regards revenue and the other 'arteries of war'.[1] In 1711 the Senate was instituted partly to fill a resultant void at the centre. By the terms of its founding statutes, Peter decreed that 'because of Our perpetual absence due to war' all subjects, 'whether ecclesiastical or lay', were henceforward to submit to this body 'as to Us Ourselves, in all things', under pain of death; and thereby, Peter hoped, the 'interests of the Sovereign and of the State', especially in the matter of raising money, recruits, and provisions, would be better served.[2] Among the first nine senators appointed by Peter was Count Musin-Pushkin, head of the Monastery Prikaz, which was now, together with several other important offices, subordinated to the Senate's 'prikaz committee'.[3] With regard to the church, the effect of these measures was to interpose yet further layers of officials between the clergy and their dependants on the one hand, and the tsar, the source of all judicial as well as executive and legislative authority, on the other.

The shortcomings of this system, especially in its vital financial tasks, drove Peter to return the administration of ecclesiastical properties to their owners (as mentioned above) and, more importantly, to contemplate yet another overhaul of his whole government. So between 1718 and 1722 the central administration was transformed by the refashioning of the Senate and the creation of the procuratorship and the nine colleges, including one of justice. This final reorganization of the central government was accompanied by changes at the local level (1719), the most fundamental of which attempted to separate justice

[1] *PSZ*, iv, no. 2218 (pp. 436–438).

[2] *PSZ*, iv, no. 2321 (p. 627); no. 2328 (pp. 642–643); no. 2329 (p. 643); no. 2330 (p. 643); no. 2342 (pp. 652–654); no. 2349 (pp. 662–666); no. 2414 (pp. 726–727). For the original versions of the most important of these documents, written or corrected by Peter himself, see *PiB*, xi, 1, nos. 4286–4292 (pp. 98–104, 408–419).

[3] *PSZ*, iv, no. 2342 (pp. 652–654).

and administration. Eleven judicial districts were set up and were placed under the control of the Justice College in St. Petersburg, and not of the local governors.[1] But the attempted separation (if such it was) ran counter to the ingrained Muscovite habit of considering justice as part of administration, and did not succeed.[2] Indeed, each mention of either ecclesiastical or civil courts in the preceding pages was only a convenient way of referring to the organs of the ecclesiastical or secular administrations in their judicial aspect; and this fundamental confusion was never resolved during Peter's reign. A real separation of justice and administration was not effected until late in the nineteenth century.

VI

GOVERNMENT CONTROL OF THE PATRIARCHAL DOMAIN

The 'patriarchal domain' has been alluded to at various points in this chapter. It may be helpful to explain what in fact this was. For the suppression of the independent administration of the patriarchal domain, coupled with the eventual abolition (in 1721) of the patriarchal office itself, constituted Peter's most decisive break with the past, and lay at the very heart of his church reform.

Prior to Peter's reign, it was noted above, the hierarchy in Russia had owned and administered their estates and had enjoyed their financial and judicial privileges according to the terms of individual charters granted by the tsars and their predecessors to every bishop. But since the founding of the Moscow patriarchate in 1589 the incumbent of that office, as head of the church, had enjoyed both greater rights and immunities with regard to his own estates – most commonly referred to in the documents as, collectively, the 'patriarchal domain [*patriarshaya oblast'*]' – as well as ultimate judicial and administrative authority over all the lands of the church. To collect the dues owed to the patriarch in his dual capacity, two special *prikazy* were founded in 1620–1625 in imitation of the corresponding departments of the tsar's government: one, the patriarchal Palace Prikaz, was responsible for the revenues of the domain itself, while the other, the patriarchal Treasury Prikaz, was charged with collecting the taxes and tithes from churches and ecclesiastical estates throughout Russia.[3] The combined income of

[1] *PSZ*, v, no. 3269 (p. 607); no. 3380 (pp. 701–710); *PSZ*, vi, no. 3935 (pp. 524–525).

[2] For instructive commentaries, see M. M. Bogoslovskii, *Oblastnaya reforma Petra Velikago* (Moscow, 1902), pp. 246–256; and Klyuchevskii, *Sochineniya*, iv, pp. 185–186.

[3] See M. Gorchakov, *O zemel'nykh vladeniyakh vserossiiskikh mitropolitov, patriarkhov i sv. sinoda* (St. Petersburg, 1871), pp. 345 ff; also Milyukov, *op. cit.*, pp. 77, 114.

the two *prikazy*, averaging 40,000R to 50,000R a year, was a very small sum when compared with the total annual revenue of the tsar, even at pre-Petrine levels (approximately 1,500,000R in 1680). Yet the extent of the patriarchal domain, estimated to contain about 8700 peasant households at the end of the seventeenth century,[1] made the patriarch one of the largest landlords in Russia, while the scope of his overall administrative and judicial authority as head of the church (in 1680 perhaps 110,000 peasant households lived on episcopal and monastic estates)[2] was second only to that of the tsar himself. Clearly, when Tsar Peter came to the throne the Moscow patriarchate was an economic and social institution of the greatest importance.

And if in the latter part of the seventeenth century, as mentioned above, the episcopal and monastic estates came increasingly under the control of the tsar's government, especially during the years 1649 to 1677 (the period of Tsar Aleksei's Monastery Prikaz), the patriarchal domain remained free of such interference.[3] A separate chapter of the *Ulozhenie* of 1649 had guaranteed to the patriarch exclusive jurisdiction over his dependants, both clerical and lay, in all but criminal matters.[4] Despite the restrictions imposed by successive governments on the further acquisition of land by the church, there is evidence that from 1650 until well into Peter's reign the patriarchal domain continued to expand – from the roughly 6400 peasant households counted in 1646–1647 to the patriarchal Palace Prikaz's own estimate of 9300 households in 1714.[5] Not unexpectedly, one of Peter's earliest measures affecting the

[1] M. I. Gorchakov, *O zemel'nykh vladeniyakh vserossiiskikh mitropolitov, patriarkhov i sv. sinoda* (St. Petersburg, 1871), p. 345. Kotoshikhin estimated the total number of patriarchal peasants at 'more than 7000 households' (*op. cit.*, p. 117).

[2] Kotoshikhin's estimates total 111,000 (*op. cit.*, pp. 117–118); according to the census of 1678, the figure was 107,694 (Milyukov, *op. cit.*, p. 114). It may be noted that the total of peasant households counted in 1678 was approximately 790,000. Thus in, say, 1680, approximately 15 percent of the population of Muscovite Russia (i.e. a total of 118,700 patriarchal, monastic, and episcopal peasant households) lived on ecclesiastical lands. And so most contemporary foreign observers held grossly exaggerated notions of the extent of the church's landed wealth: see for example Dr. Collins, who reckoned that 'the church holds almost two-third parts of the Czardom' (*op. cit.*, p. 124); or the estimate of the French king's agent in Russia in 1689, F. de la Neuville, that 'la moitié des terres de Moscovie appartiennent aux moines' (*op. cit.*, p. 203).

[3] See Milyutin, *op. cit.*, pp. 274–284.

[4] *PRP*, vi, p. 183.

[5] Gorchakov, *O zemel'nykh vladeniyakh vserossiiksikh mitropolitov, patriarkhov i sv. sinoda*, pp. 343–345 and appendix, pp. 88, 93, 95, 97–99, 117, 158, 247, 250, 254; also pp. 219–224. Of course to a certain extent the increase in patriarchal peasant households was due to natural causes (see Eaton, *op. cit.*, p. 65). But for a documented history of how in this period the patriarchal domain was augmented through land-grants from the tsars, through purchase and foreclosure, and (after 1667) through the attachment of several new monasteries and their estates, see Gorchakov, *op. cit.*, pp. 329 ff.

patriarchal domain was absolutely to prohibit the patriarchal household from acquiring any more estates.[1]

In January 1701 the Monastery Prikaz was founded, the practical effect of which, with respect to the patriarchal domain, was to place patriarchal dependants under civil jurisdiction and patriarchal revenues at the disposal of the tsar, who did not hesitate to use them for military and other purposes. From 1701 to 1709 the patriarchal Palace and Treasury Prikazy, like all the civil *prikazy*, submitted annual budgets to the Privy Chancellery in which the same trend observed above with regard to the Monastery Prikaz's finances is noticeable. Thus, while the revenues of the two patriarchal offices remained relatively constant (such fluctuations as are indicated betray no discernible pattern, suggesting that they were due rather to circumstances than to any changes of policy), the proportion of their expenditure designated 'remittances to other *prikazy*' remained consistently high. In 1701, three-fourths of their combined expenditure was so classified; in 1703, two-thirds; in 1705, three-fourths; in 1707, one-half; in 1709, two-thirds.[2] Moreover in 1705 (for instance) at least 19,000R, or 44 percent of the combined expenditure of the two *prikazy* that year, were consigned on Peter's direct orders to the Artillery Prikaz.[3] Again, it was reported to Peter in July 1703 that 30,000R collected from six of the Moscow *prikazy* had been sent to the army in Lithuania: of this sum 3000R had been taken from the patriarchal revenues.[4] On 20 January 1710 Peter ordered that 'for the hiring of transport for artillery and other military supplies, to be taken this winter from Moscow to Voronezh', 12,000R were to be given to the relevant agency by the patriarchal Palace and Treasury Prikazy.[5] Such figures speak for themselves. Indeed, it will be suggested in the following chapter that it was precisely to gain control of the patriarchal revenues, rather than as a first step in the suppression of the patriarchate itself, that Peter in 1701 separated the ecclesiastical and secular authorities of the recently deceased patriarch, entrusting the one to the metropolitan of Ryazan' and the other to the head of the Monastery Prikaz.

As a separate administrative and territorial unit of the state, the patriarchal domain survived until 1721 – though in a greatly truncated form: it has been estimated that between 1700 and 1714 the estates subject to the patriarchal Palace Prikaz, measured in peasant households,

[1] *PSZ*, iv, no. 1839 (pp. 159–160): decree of 11 March 1701.

[2] See Milyukov, *op. cit.*, pp. 578–613.

[3] *PiB*, iii, pp. 779, 798, 799, 813, 814.

[4] *PiB*, ii, pp. 570–571.

[5] *SIRIO*, xi, p. 172.

had, by legislative action and by the 'natural' attrition of the times (the decline and steady impoverishment of the population of central Russia), decreased by half.[1] Ironically enough, the remaining patriarchal estates were destined to survive the final demise of the patriarchate itself, for in 1721 they were assigned to the support of the new supreme administrative authority of the Russian church, the Holy Synod.

It has been the chief aim of this chapter to show that most of the provisions of the *Ecclesiastical Regulation* of 1721 were anticipated – in principle if not in every detail – in the legislation enacted during the previous twenty or so years of Peter's reign; further, that Peter's policies affecting the religious profession of his subjects or the ecclesiastical institutions of Russia were solidly based on precedent. But this was not to deny that before 1721 Peter's legislation in this respect contained important innovations. If the religious profession of his Muslim and pagan subjects continued to be treated as in essence a political matter, and if the Jews of Little Russia, unlike the Lutherans of the Baltic states, were not tolerated, the persecution of Russian religious dissidents had become relatively more enlightened. A quantitative and qualitative improvement in the welfare services, financed from ecclesiastical funds, was achieved at this time (1701–1720). The diversion of large portions of ecclesiastical income – including much of the patriarchal revenue – to military purposes, coupled with the increased taxation and the greatly enhanced authority of the Monastery Prikaz over the church's economic life, were quite unprecedented. And if the policy of suppressing the judicial and financial privileges of the clergy and of prohibiting further acquisitions of land by the church belonged in origin to Peter's predecessors, it was he who finally enforced it. There were, moreover, the new regulations governing the selection, training, discipline, and judicial liability of the clergy and severely limiting the construction and repairing of ecclesiastical buildings.

To be sure, certain of Peter's potentially far-reaching innovations were abandoned before 1720: his assumption of direct control of episcopal and monastic finances, for instance; or his attempt to place all monks and nuns, as well as the bishops, on state-determined stipends. Indeed, the evidence strongly suggests that in general Peter's legislation affecting the church between 1700 and 1720 was conceived and

[1] Gorchakov, *O zemel'nykh vladeniyakh vserossiiskikh mitropolitiv, patriarkhov i sv. sinoda*, pp. 457–461. See his pp. 448–509 for a detailed discussion of the administration of the patriarchal domain in the years 1701–1720.

implemented (or abandoned) far more in response to the need for money and manpower to wage his wars and to develop the economic infrastructure of his country than from any disinterested desire to reform the church. Had he died in 1720, leaving the recently composed *Ecclesiastical Regulation* to rot in the archives, he would be remembered, with regard to his policies towards the church, as a remarkably domineering, active, yet vacillating, opportunistic, and perhaps ultimately ineffectual monarch not unlike Louis XIV of France.

CHAPTER THREE

The Politics of Church Reform under Peter, 1700–1721

In this chapter an attempt is made to analyze the sequence of events which led, not inevitably, to the definitive reform of the Russian church that was embodied in the provisions of the *Ecclesiastical Regulation* of 1721. More precisely, in the following pages an attempt is made, on the basis of available evidence, to isolate the decisive moments in the process; to suggest some of the factors which influenced Peter at those moments; to clarify his intentions; to examine his relations with the leading ecclesiastics of the day, above all with Stefan Yavorskii, who was for twenty years the temporary head of the church: to provide, in short, some account of the manoeuvres, of the moves and counter-moves, of the clash of personalities, of the 'politics' of church reform in the years 1700 to 1721. And for these purposes the chapter is divided into three main sections corresponding to what are called, quite prosaically, the initial, intermediary, and final phases of the politics of church reform under Peter.

The first section, which is devoted to a discussion of the initial phase, concentrates on Peter's decisions, taken in 1700–1701 after the death of Patriarch Adrian, to leave vacant the patriarchal throne, to appoint Yavorskii temporary head of the church, and to re-establish, with greatly expanded powers, the Monastery Prikaz. The second section is concerned with the long intermediary phase – in essence, with Yavorskii's role as head of the church, with the deterioration of his relations with Peter, and with his fall, in the spring of 1718, from Peter's grace. In the third section the final phase is studied, a period which began with Peter's decision of 1718 to abolish the patriarchate and ended (for the purposes of this chapter) with his proclamation on 25 January 1721 of the establishment of an Ecclesiastical College 'which shall have, in accordance with the *Regulation* which follows, the authority to administer all ecclesiastical affairs in the All-Russian Church'. A few concluding remarks, relating mostly to Yavorskii's obituary, form a fourth and final section of the chapter. Yavorskii had served as head of the church, if in very changed circumstances, for longer than any previous primate – patriarch or metropolitan – in Muscovite history; and his passing from the scene could not go unnoticed.

I
THE INITIAL PHASE, 1700–1701

Peter was at the front with his army, laying siege to the Swedish-held port of Narva, when he received word that Patriarch Adrian was dead. On 18 October 1700 three of his intimates in Moscow – Prince 'Fetka' Romodanovskii, Boyar 'Tishka' Streshnev, and 'Pronka' Voznitsyn – sent him reports of Adrian's last agony on the night of 15–16 October. In addition, Streshnev briefly summarized the contents of the patriarchal treasury: 'thirty thousand rubles in cash . . . gold, silver, and jewelled crosses, pearls and other things . . .'. The patriarch had left a will, as was customary, but Streshnev wished to know Peter's pleasure in the matter. He also requested that the tsar should indicate whom he intended to name temporary custodian of the 'Cathedral church [i.e. the *Uspenskii sobor*, the principal church of Moscow normally controlled by the patriarch]': the bishops of Smolensk, Krutitsy, and Vyatka were at present in Moscow; 'but formerly it was your wish to nominate his reverence of Kholmogory, only he has not been sent for. Do you wish to send for him? . . . To whom do you wish to entrust the affairs of the patriarchal household?' In anticipation of the tsar's orders, Streshnev wrote, the patriarchal sacristy had been sealed up.[1]

Streshnev's actions, as a senior official of the tsar's government, were perfectly in order – in the sense that they followed precedent. Traditionally, it was on the tsar's initiative that a council was convened to elect a successor to a deceased patriarch, just as it was his right to confirm the council's choice of a new patriarch.[2] Moreover, gradually during the seventeenth century the patriarchal domain had come to be

[1] The original letters are printed in Verkhovskoi, i, pp. 109–112; for Streshnev's letter in particular, see p. 109. Abridged versions of all three letters are printed in Ustryalov, *op. cit.*, iv, II, pp. 161–165.

[2] Thus the announcement of 5 July 1672 concerning the election of Patriarch Pitirim: 'By the will of Almighty God . . . and at the command of the great Sovereign, Tsar, and Great Prince Aleksei Mikhailovich . . . the Most Reverend Pitirim, Metropolitan of Great Novgorod, has been elected to the Moscow Patriarchal throne by the Most Reverend Metropolitans, Archbishops, Bishops, and the entire Holy Council. . . . in the presence of the Great Sovereign' (*PSZ*, i, no. 524 [pp. 905–906]). See also the similar document announcing the election of Pitirim's successor Joachim on 23 July 1674 (*PSZ*, i, no. 584 [pp. 985–986]). And for the patriarchal election of 1690, see above, pp. 14–17.

regarded by the tsar's government as but another unit of the realm, the administration and revenues of which were granted to successive patriarchs for their term of office. Although normally the tsar named the incumbent metropolitan of Krutitsy 'guardian of the patriarchal throne' for the duration of the *mezhdupatriarshestvo* – the interval between the death of one patriarch and the election of his successor – the patriarchal domain was always governed in the tsar's name.[1] And so on 18 October 1700 the officials of the patriarchal Palace Prikaz were informed by their colleagues of the Razryadnyi Prikaz that 'by command of His Majesty' their business was to be transacted 'in the name of the Great Sovereign'; on the original of the order one of the secretaries of the Palace Prikaz has noted: 'Done by his Sovereign Majesty's decree and entered in the register'.[2] But Peter himself cannot have issued the decree: he was not in Moscow at the time: he had not even heard, as yet, that Patriarch Adrian was dead. The order appears to have been issued in his name as a matter of course. In short, by 1700 it was in effect left to the tsar both to provide for the patriarchal succession and to endow the new patriarch with his worldly goods and powers. Now Peter declined to do either.

A week after the news of Adrian's death had been sent to him another of Peter's officials, A. A. Kurbatov, wrote recommending that he should 'choose from among the bishops, for the temporary administration of ecclesiastical affairs, someone who is efficient'. Kurbatov also advised that 'for the supervision of the finances and all other affairs of the [patriarchal] household and treasury, it seems best, Sovereign, to choose someone from among those zealously devoted to you'. Kurbatov even proceeded to suggest names: for the former position '[the bishop of] Kholmogory is thought by many to be a good man', while 'from the laity, for the inspection and collection of taxes' – indeed to head a special prikaz charged with inventorying and supervising not only episcopal and monastic properties, but the patriarchal domain as well – Kurbatov recommended 'Boyar Ivan Alekseevich Musin-Pushkin, or the Stol'nik [courtier] Dimitrii Petrovich Protas'ev, who is, Sovereign, a very good man'. In conclusion, Kurbatov advised that 'concerning the election of a patriarch, Sovereign, it seems to me best to wait for a time, that in all these matters your autocratic will may be done'.[3]

[1] Gorchakov, *O zemel'nykh vladeniyakh vserossiiskikh mitropolitov, patriarkhov i sv. sinoda*, pp. 444, 328–329.

[2] *Ibid.*, p. 443; the order is printed in the appendix, no. 44 (p. 125).

[3] For the original text of Kurbatov's letter, see Verkhovskoi, i, pp. 111–112; also Runkevich, *op. cit.*, pp. 27–28.

Kurbatov's recommendations coincided remarkably with the measures that Peter was soon in fact to adopt. But then it was Kurbatov's purpose in life to anticipate the tsar's wishes and to seek his interest in all things. He was an upstart, by birth a serf, a former bailiff who was now a careerist in the tsar's service, having been recently recruited from the suite of General Sheremetev. 'I walk in the midst of snares', he complained to Peter in the letter in question: 'I have only my hope and trust in your sovereign favour'. It was on the basis of an unofficial memoir submitted by Kurbatov (while still in Sheremetev's service) that the stamp tax had been imposed in 1699–1700 on clergy and laity alike 'without exception, beginning with the Most Holy Patriarch'.[1] For his efforts he had been appointed *pribyl'shchik* (official 'profit-maker', i.e. deviser of new taxes or seeker of new sources of revenue). Now, in October 1700, Kurbatov chose to view Patriarch Adrian's death as a sign (so he wrote to Peter) that 'God wishes you to assume responsibility for the better administration of ecclesiastical affairs', for 'in all these matters, Sovereign, there is much slackness and disorder. ... In truth, Sovereign, much money will thus be raised which is now wasted by capricious landlords'. As disaster closed around him (the siege of Narva was raised and the Russian army routed on 19 November), Peter naturally read with the greatest interest these latest suggestions from his new and promising, 'zealously devoted' servant.[2]

And soon after his return to Moscow he abolished the patriarchal Razryadnyi Prikaz: all matters formerly administered by it were to be referred to the appropriate civil prikaz while cases of 'schism, heresy, and opposition to God's church' were to fall under the jurisdiction, not of the archbishop of Kholmogory (who had been proposed by both Streshnev and Kurbatov), but of Stefan Yavorskii, the metropolitan of Ryazan' and Murom.[3] Late in January 1701 it was announced that Musin-Pushkin, a former governor of Astrakhan and a member of Peter's intimate company, a member, indeed, of the Most Drunken

[1] *PSZ*, iii, no. 1711 (pp. 656–665); *PSZ*, iv, no. 1757 (p. 11); *PSZ*, iv, no. 1803 (pp. 64–66).

[2] On Kurbatov, see Kafengauz, *Pososhkov*, pp. 37–38.

[3] *PSZ*, iv, no. 1818 (pp. 87–88): edict of 16 December 1700. In this and all subsequent official documents Yavorskii is never referred to as 'Guardian, Exarch, and Administrator of the Patriarchal Throne', titles conferred on him by later authorities (see Solov'ev, *op. cit.*, viii, p. 91; Runkevich, *op. cit.*, p. 28; Verkhovskoi, i, p. 112; Smolitsch, *op. cit.*, pp. 65, 81, etc.; Wittram, *op. cit.*, i, p. 173). In the official documents of the time Yavorskii is always referred to simply as the metropolitan of Ryazan', or in terms appropriate to that dignity.

Council, but withal a relatively civilised man[1] – that Musin-Pushkin had been appointed head of a new Monastery Prikaz which was to have jurisdiction over both the episcopal and the patriarchal households, over all ecclesiastical persons and property, and over 'all monastic affairs'.[2] Finally, by an edict of 7 November 1701 Peter confirmed that while (civil) cases involving monks, priests, and deacons as defendants would remain subject to the patriarch's Ecclesiastical Prikaz (which now was nominally under the control of the metropolitan of Ryazan'), clerics could nonetheless be called as witnesses in the Moscow Court Prikaz; moreover, that suits brought by ecclesiastical persons against laymen, particularly those concerning disputes over property, were to be subject to the civil courts only[3] – in practice, as we have seen, to the new Monastery Prikaz.

The immediate effect of these and related measures was discussed in the preceding chapter. The ecclesiastical and secular powers of the deceased patriarch had been divided between, respectively, the metropolitan of Ryazan' and the head of the Monastery Prikaz. The principal organ of the patriarchal administration (the Razryadnyi Prikaz) had been suppressed, while the jurisdiction of the patriarchal Ecclesiastical Prikaz had been sharply curtailed, leaving it effective authority only over 'ecclesiastical' matters (infringements of clerical discipline, marriage and divorce cases, sexual offences, as well as cases of schism and heresy). The Monastery Prikaz had assumed control, not only of episcopal and monastic estates and their inhabitants, but of the patriarchal domain as well – a sharp break with previous practices. Above all, Peter's measures betokened a determination to leave vacant, for an indefinite period of time, the patriarchal throne, since no provision had been made for the summoning of an electoral council. It was a fateful decision. For the ensuing *mezhdupatriarshestvo* was to last (who could have foreseen it then?) for twenty years, and was to be followed by the abolition of the patriarchal office itself.

Contemporary western observers were moved to speculate on the nature and significance of Peter's measures of 1700–1701 affecting the

[1] Cf. the Austrian ambassador's assessment: 'a very discreet, older man . . . a lover of philosophy and theology, as he has learned from Jesuits who have been here [in Moscow] and other clerical travellers not only Latin, as much as he could, but the fundamentals of other disciplines, and is therefore a lover of foreign and educated people' (Ustryalov, *op. cit.*, iv, II, pp. 553–4: Pleyer to Vienna, 2 February 1701).

[2] *PSZ*, iv, no. 1829 (p. 133); no. 1834 (pp. 139–140).

[3] *PSZ*, iv, no. 187 (p. 176).

church. The Austrian ambassador in Moscow reported to Vienna on 2 February 1701 that 'all the property and estates of the clergy are being inventoried', which was true;[1] that 'it is said the Tsar will assign to each monastery, as to the metropolitans, abbots, and ecclesiastical persons of similar rank, a certain stipend on which they shall live' – a policy which was indeed implemented after December 1701 (and later abandoned);[2] and that, 'since a few weeks ago the Patriarch died, the Tsar will not allow another to replace him, but instead has set over the *Consistorium* [the traditional "Holy Council" of the higher clergy?] and all the clergy a secular lord'. This statement we know to be mistaken, for Peter had entrusted overall responsibility for maintaining clerical discipline, and ultimate jurisdiction over all 'ecclesiastical' matters, not to a 'secular lord', but to the metropolitan of Ryazan'. In practice Musin-Pushkin's power, as head of the Monastery Prikaz, was exercised chiefly over the economic life of the church[3] – admittedly a broad commission, but not so broad as the Austrian ambassador implied. On the basis of his report the Imperial government might have concluded, erroneously, that a policy of secularization along familiar western lines had been introduced by Peter into Russia.[4]

At the same time, the Dutch resident in Moscow informed the States-General that the tsar 'has been pleased to appropriate all monastic lands and to allow to the monks no more than is necessary to prevent starvation and misery, so that they should constantly fast, do penance, and pass the whole day in prayer. This confiscation [*sic*] will procur incalculable riches for His Majesty and will also ensure that henceforth one will no longer encounter in this country so many idle monks'.[5] Thus the economic motive of Peter's measures, as well as his intention to reform monastic life, were stressed. But the Dutchman confused an appropriation of monastic lands with the appropriation of monastic *revenues* that was actually prescribed in the relevant legislation. He confused, moreover, decrees which were already in force (by March 1701, when he wrote) with others that were yet officially to appear,[6] though he does thereby furnish evidence that rumours of the latter were rife in Moscow early in 1701 and were considered by Peter's government as part of the same 'new deal' for the church.

[1] See *PSZ*, iv, no. 1834 (p. 139). [2] See above, pp. 85 ff. [3] *Ibid.*

[4] Ambassador Pleyer's report is printed in Ustryalov, *op. cit.*, iv, II, pp. 553–554.

[5] Dispatch of H. Van-der Hulst, dated 15 March 1701, in *ibid.*, p. 669.

[6] I refer principally to the edict on the monasteries promulgated in December 1701, which contained the provisions Van-der Hulst somewhat inaccurately summarized (for the edict, see *PSZ*, iv, no. 1886 [pp. 181–182]; it was discussed above, p. 85).

The economic and purely political motives of Peter's actions were emphasized by the English envoy Charles Whitworth, who records in his memoir that 'this [patriarchal] power has been so dangerous that the present Czar, on the death of the late Patriarch, sequestrated the office, committing the spiritual administration to the Archbishop of Rezan and the management of the temporal affairs to a lay commission, who have likewise the disposal of abbey lands and revenues. . . . which besides the annual advantage of one hundred and fifty thousand pounds sterling to his treasury, has quite broke their interest in the country, where they have no more free-hold left'.[1] But if Whitworth had grasped the principle of Peter's legislation of 1701, he was mistaken about its effects. He overestimated considerably the 'annual advantage' to Peter's treasury from monastic lands.[2] And like the Dutch resident and other foreign observers, Whitworth mistook the tsar's measures to mean that church lands had been 'confiscated' or 'secularized' or, on the English model, that the Russian clergy had 'no more free-hold left'.

Yet Whitworth did suggest, interestingly, that the 'dangerous power' of the patriarch was a factor determining Peter's decisions. Similarly, an emissary of the French king reported to his master in 1703 that 'the Czar has not nominated a patriarch since the last one died because of the great power which is attached to that dignity'.[3] It was in essence the interpretation which most foreigners favoured. 'This may be said of the Patriarch of Mosco', wrote Captain Perry: 'he was in very high esteem with the people, and indeed might be said to bear a kind of share in the Sovereignty of the Empire'; and therefore, on Adrian's death, 'the Czar refused to have any other patriarch elected, and took upon himself to be the sole head and governor of his church; only he appointed the present metropolitan of Razan . . . to take upon him the administration of ecclesiastical affairs'.[4]

Still another of Whitworth's compatriots, the Reverend Thomas

[1] Whitworth, *op. cit.*, pp. 46–48.

[2] On Whitworth's own testimony the ruble was officially valued at 10 English shillings; but because of measures introduced since the beginning of the Swedish war (1701), the ruble was 'suddenly reduced to half value', and '110 copecks now hardly weigh a crown' (see his report to Mr. Secretary Harley, dated Moscow 31 January 1707, in Brit. Mus. Addit. MSS. 37355, f. 304). Thus Whitworth's figure of £150,000, when converted at the official rate, was equivalent to 300,000R; or in terms of real money, it was equivalent to 600,000R. But the *maximum* annual revenue reported by the Monastery and two patriarchal *prikazy* between 1701 and 1709 was approximately 260,000R (Milyukov, *op. cit.*, appendix iii, pp. 578–613).

[3] Dispatch of M. de Baluze, dated Moscow 3 October 1703, in *SIRIO*, xxxix, pp. 23–33 (see p. 30).

[4] Perry, *op. cit.*, pp. 207–208.

Consett, explained in the introduction to his translation of the *Ecclesiastical Regulation* that 'in order to carry on his present scheme of regulations, [Peter] removed one great obstacle, or rather prevented the succession of patriarchs on the death of Adrian; their power being unlimited [*sic*!], he apprehended [that it] would always obstruct and interfere with his designs, and would by no means suffer itself to be controul'd by the regal power in ecclesiastical matters'. A section of Part 1 of the *Regulation* itself, Consett rightly pointed out, was 'particularly leveled against patriarchal power'.[1] But Consett wrote in the 1720's, following the promulgation of the *Regulation*, and apparently assumed that the provisions of that document had been consciously anticipated by Peter as long ago as December 1700.

The Russians themselves appear not to have regarded the measures of 1700–1701 as portents of Peter's resolve eventually to abolish the patriarchate. In July 1705 (to cite only one instance) General I. A. Repnin sent an eloquent appeal to Patriarch Dositheus of Jerusalem requesting permission to marry a fourth time, 'since [as Repnin wrote] we are at present without a patriarch [*u nas mezhdupatriarshestvo*], and except by your leave our pastor is unable to grant the permission'.[2] As late as 1718 Peter himself recorded in one of his notebooks that he was thinking 'about a *patriarchal* [italics mine] order whereby the bishops should assign subordinates to the army, so that in the army and navy there should be chaplains'.[3] Peter sent a decree to this effect to the Senate with instructions that it be forwarded to the metropolitan of Ryazan' for formal validation.[4]

It clearly is wrong to assert that in December 1700 Peter foresaw that some twenty years later he would formally abolish the patriarchate, and that in 1700 he acted in conformity with a long-range plan.[5] On the other hand, it is doubtless true that in 1700–1701 the economic factor was the decisive one for Peter.[6] His advisers had impressed upon

[1] Consett, *op. cit.*, p. xv. [2] *PiB*, iii, p. 983. [3] *ZAP*, no. 62 (p. 67).

[4] *ZAP*, no. 63 (p. 68); see also Verkhovskoi, i, p. 152.

[5] Cf. Solov'ev, *op. cit.*, viii, p. 90: 'We do not think it right to say that the notion of completely suppressing the patriarchate had matured in Peter's mind already in 1700; most probably it matured with the passage of time. . . .'

[6] When analyzing the relevant legislation of 1700–1701, historians have tended to stress its provisional and practical aspects: see Verkhovskoi, i, pp. 112–113; Wittram, *op. cit.*, ii, pp. 173–175; Runkevich, *op. cit.*, p. 31 (Runkevich, if anything, overemphasizes the 'economic character' of this legislation); Smolitsch, *op. cit.*, pp. 59–65. To be sure, there is also evidence that as early as 1701 Peter hoped to promote, by legislative action, monastic reform as such: the relevant decree (cited above, p. 85) invoked the 'better fulfilling of the monastic vocation' as one reason for imposing the new regulations on monastic finances.

him the advantages, especially financial, of delaying for a time the election of a new patriarch; and Kurbatov, in particular, had indicated that his views were shared by others in Moscow – no doubt by the champions or beneficiaries of the general trend, which was described in the previous chapter, towards limiting ecclesiastical landownership and suppressing the financial and other privileges traditionally enjoyed by the clergy. And in the circumstances, Peter was disposed to accept their advice.

What those circumstances were has been neatly summarized for us in the official history of the reign which was composed under Peter's personal direction. The siege of Narva and the resultant Russian losses are described in detail and the causes of the defeat are assessed: 'and after this terrible check we were obliged to redouble our industry, and to make the utmost effort to compensate for our lack of experience'. On his return to Moscow, the official history continues, 'the Sovereign issued a decree that some of the bells of the churches and monasteries of the principal towns were to be collected for making canons and mortars. It was done throughout that winter [1700–1701]. . . . and in the spring this artillery was sent to Novgorod'[1] – to, that is, the front. In other words, Peter's decisions of 1700–1701 affecting the church were taken in the midst of a grave emergency, and are clearly related to his attempts to cope with it. It was to gain control of the *patriarchal* as well as the episcopal and monastic revenues, rather than as a first step in the suppression of the patriarchate itself, that Peter separated the ecclesiastical and secular powers of the recently deceased patriarch, entrusting the one to Yavorskii and the other to the head of the Monastery Prikaz.[2]

But why Yavorskii? It is not difficult to see why Peter declined to promote Archbishop Athanasius of Kholmogory, even though he was recommended by Kurbatov on behalf of 'many' persons in Moscow and had, apparently, at one time been Peter's own choice for the post. The archbishop was elderly (60) and probably ill; he died less than two years later. But he remained in Peter's favour until his death and enjoyed the esteem of the tsar's entourage and of his own clergy.[3] In

[1] *Zhurnal*, i, pp. 24–26.

[2] See above, pp. 88–89 and 109 for facts and figures which support this conclusion.

[3] See the appreciation of Athanasius included in a contemporary memoir by an official of the cathedral church at Kholmogory (in A. Golubtsov [ed.]), 'Chinovniki Kholmogorskago preobrazhenskago sobora', *Chteniya v imperatorskom obshchestve istorii i drevnostei rossiiskikh pri Moskovskom universitete*, 1903 [iv], esp. pp. 246–252). There the author mentions numerous visits paid by Peter to Athanasius between 1692 and 1701, in

February 1707 Musin-Pushkin advised Yavorskii that 'for the Kholmogory diocese learned and cultivated clergy should be chosen, since the diocese surrounds a seaport [Arkhangelsk] where numerous and various foreigners come, with whom the local bishop must treat in a way that redounds to the honour and glory of the Russian realm, in the same way that the late Archbishop Athanasius conducted himself there'.[1] His good behaviour in the presence of the German, Dutch, and English Protestant merchants of Arkhangelsk, as well as his active interest in science and technical gadgets, no doubt strongly recommended Athanasius to Peter.[2] But late in 1700, when a temporary head of the church had to be found, Athanasius's age must have told against him.

Indeed, the previous year Peter had resisted Patriarch Adrian's attempt to transfer Athanasius to Moscow, as can be seen from Adrian's letter of July 1699 urging that Athanasius and not, as the tsar had commanded, Trifilii of Nizhnii-Novgorod, be nominated metropolitan of Krutitsy so that, 'because of my [Adrian's] illness . . . he might assist with the administration of affairs'. Adrian had reminded Peter, through this letter to Streshnev, that Trifilii was too old and ill and otherwise unsuitable for the see of Krutitsy, and that 'he himself, the Sovereign, when in my cell', had agreed that Athanasius was the man for the job.[3] Peter appears to have changed his mind. Probably he had simply wished that Athanasius should remain in the north, in the diocese which he had built from nothing, where he had served for twenty years, which Peter himself had frequently visited in the course of his sailing holidays, and where numerous foreigners lived; it was, in fact, a far more important position than the largely honorific post of metropolitan of Krutitsy. But whatever their merits or deficiencies, it is apparent that late in 1700 both Metropolitan Trifilii of Krutitsy and the archbishop of Kholmogory were disqualified, at least by reason of advanced age, from assuming the role of temporary head of the church envisaged by Peter. In any case, by then Stefan Yavorskii had come on

the course of his sailing holidays on the White sea. On the last of these visits, in May 1701 (five months after Yavorskii's promotion), Peter personally conferred on Athanasius a new episcopal cope.

[1] Musin-Pushkin to Yavorskii, 28 February 1707, in Chistovich, *Feofan Prokopovich*, p. 58, n. 2.

[2] In his spare time Athanasius wrote a handbook of medical advice (1696) and a *Hexaēmeron* or study of the natural world. He also collected western European calendars, globes, compasses, and telescopes, most of which came to him in Kholmogory by way of Arkhangel'sk. For Athanasius, see the anon. article in *Russkii biograficheskii slovar'*, ii (St. Petersburg, 1897), pp. 371–372.

[3] Adrian's letter to Streshnev is printed in Ustryalov, *op. cit.*, iii, pp. 500–501.

the scene, and through a demonstration of his skill in rhetoric had become the recipient of the tsar's irresistible favour.

Yavorskii had spent his youth and early manhood on the border of the Catholic and Orthodox worlds, and figuratively as well as physically had several times crossed over it. Born in 1658 and christened Semen, he was the son of Ivan surnamed Yavorskii (after the family seat), a member of the lesser nobility of that part of the Ukraine which remained under Polish suzerainty following the Peace of Andrusovo. Thereupon (1667) his family moved eastwards, across the Dnieper, to escape religious persecution, and settled not far from the town of Nezhin. Nothing definite is known of his primary education. But sometime not before 1673 he became a student of the Kiev academy, where he attracted the attention of the rector, Varlaam Yasinskii. Yasinskii, like so many of his compatriots, had once been a pupil of the Jesuits, and it was probably owing to his influence that in 1684 Yavorskii was sent abroad to complete his studies under their direction. He pursued the philosophy course at the colleges of L'vov and Lublin and read theology at those of Vil'no and Poznan'. As was customary for persons of his background, he became a Uniate, assuming the name Stanislav-Simeon. It was of course a 'conversion of convenience': as a contemporary in the same situation said of himself, it was 'not with the heart, but only with the lips'.[1] When in 1689 Yavorskii returned to Kiev bearing the degree 'artium liberalium et philosophiae magister, consummatus theologus', he promptly reverted to Orthodoxy.[2]

He became a monk of the Monastery of the Caves and took the name Stefan. His formal profession of monastic vows was attended by Hetman Mazepa, to whom Yavorskii dedicated a fashionably flowery panegyric.[3] In 1690 his patron Varlaam, who since 1684 had been head of the Monastery of the Caves, was elected metropolitan of Kiev and Yavorskii named teacher of rhetoric and oratory at the academy. In 1691 he became a prefect and professor of philosophy and, within a few years, professor of theology. Later his enemies were to claim that under

[1] Palladius Rogovskii, Ukrainian by birth and a former student (and later rector) of the Moscow academy who in the 1690's studied in Rome, as quoted in I. Morev (ed.), '*Kamen' Very' Mitropolita Stefana Yavorskago* (St. Petersburg, 1904), p. iii.

[2] For Yavorskii's biography see esp. A. Korolev's article in the *Russkii biograficheskii slovar'*, xix (St. Petersburg, 1909), pp. 413–422, with full bibliography; Kharlampovich, *op. cit.*, pp. 466–472 and *passim*; and Samarin, *op. cit.* A largely hostile portrait may be found in Runkevich, *op. cit.*, pp. 62–91 and esp. pp. 166–177.

[3] Published at Kiev in 1690 (see Bykova and Gurevich, *Opisanie izdanii napechatannyhk kirillitsei*, appendix II, no. 11 [p. 310]).

Yavorskii the academy became a hotbed of 'papist teaching'; and indeed on one theological point, the doctrine of the consecration, over which a fierce dispute had broken out in Moscow late in the 1680's, Yavorskii was not on the side of the Orthodox. The dispute was symptomatic of Muscovite resistance to the increasing penetration of their church by Ukrainians of Yavorskii's type, and had been ended, in a momentary triumph for the resisters, by the Regent Sof'ya's fall from power (1689), by Patriarch Adrian's election (1690), and by the execution (1691) of the 'Latinizer' Silvester Medvedev for having allegedly conspired to deprive Tsar Peter of his throne. In the dispute Medvedev, a clerical protégé of Sof'ya, had defended the Roman Catholic teaching that in the Liturgy the changing of the bread and wine into Christ's body and blood is effected by the so-called Words of Institution alone, and not on completion of the *Epiclesis*, or invocation of the Holy Spirit, as the Muscovite traditionalists (we should now say, the Orthodox) maintained.[1] The latter had condemned Medvedev and his followers as 'bread-worshippers'. Judging from his surviving theological lectures, Yavorskii had professed Medvedev's view; and although in the controversy he had tried to steer a middle course, he too had been branded a 'Latinizer' – a contemporary Muscovite expression of xenophobia only somewhat less heated, but much less precise, than the epithet 'bread-worshipper'.

In January 1700 Metropolitan Varlaam sent Yavorskii, who since 1697 had occupied the post of igumen (abbot) of the Monastery of St. Nicholas of the Desert, to Patriarch Adrian in Moscow with a request that either he or his companion (another igumen from Kiev) should be consecrated bishop of the vacant Ukrainian see of Pereyaslavl'.[2] Adrian promised to discuss the matter with the tsar. But while waiting in Moscow, Yavorskii was asked to preach at the funeral of one of Peter's lieutenants, the Boyar A. S. Shein, who had died on 2 February; and Peter was so impressed by Yavorskii's performance that he instructed Adrian to find a suitable see for him 'here in Great Russia, not far from Moscow'.[3] On 1 March Metropolitan Avraam of Ryazan' obliging-

[1] For the purely theological aspect of the question, see Ware, *op. cit.*, pp. 289–290. On the controversy as a whole, see Shlyapkin, *op. cit.*, pp. 111–266.

[2] Ustryalov, *op. cit.*, iii, p. 531.

[3] See Patriarch Adrian's letter to Peter of 17 March 1700, printed in Ustryalov, *op. cit.*, pp. 534–536. See also *PiB*, i, no. 296 (pp. 337, 798–799): a report of late February 1700 from the head of the Prikaz of Foreign Affairs to Peter at Voronezh, stating that 'the igumen of the St. Nicholas [monastery] from Kiev, whom you, Sovereign, have ordered to be consecreated bishop, requests a maintenance allowance . . .'.

ly retired to a monastery. But when the patriarch summoned Yavorskii to tell him that 'by the Tsar's edict and with our blessing' he was to succeed to that see, Yavorskii balked; as Adrian reported to Peter a fortnight later, 'he pleaded to be allowed to return to Kiev', and on 16 March had resisted an attempt to proceed with his consecration: should it proceed, the tsar was asked, or should Yavorskii be given his leave?[1] On 1 April Yavorskii himself submitted to one of Peter's officials a paper entitled 'The Reasons for which I fled from episcopal consecration. . . .'[2] It was to no avail. 'By the Tsar's edict' he was consecrated metropolitan of Ryazan' and Murom on 7 April, as Adrian later informed both Peter and Varlaam of Kiev, Yavorskii's erstwhile superior.[3] But the incident did not bode well for Yavorskii's future in Moscow.

By July 1700 he was actively engaged in the affairs of his new diocese. On 16 December he was entrusted by edict of the sovereign with the ecclesiastical affairs of the patriarchate. He had become temporary head of the church, or rather Peter's deputy for ecclesiastical affairs; or perhaps most accurately, he had become the chief priest of the Russian state.

It should be remarked that that redoubtable Greek, Patriarch Dositheus of Jerusalem, protested strongly to Peter about Yavorskii's promotion. In 1701 Peter had written to Dositheus, asking his consent to the establishment of a metropolitan see in the newly-conquered town of Azov, which Dositheus (since the Russian church was now without a patriarch) had granted.[4] In a further letter Peter had written to say that he should be grateful if Dositheus would choose from among his clergy two or three persons 'versed in the liberal arts, able to speak Slavonic, and worthy of the episcopacy', who would then be sent to Moscow for nomination 'to the said metropolitan see of Azov and to other Russian sees'.[5] Perhaps Dositheus's faithful emissary, Archimandrite Hyacinth, who brought this latest letter from Peter, had informed the patriarch of recent developments in Moscow. At any rate, in June 1702 Dositheus dispatched to Peter a long, somewhat rambling, passionate, and altogether extraordinary reply.

[1] Ustryalov, *op. cit.*, 534–536. [2] Solov'ev, *op. cit.*, viii, p. 92.

[3] The patriarch's two letters are printed in Ustryalov, *op. cit.*, pp. 539–540.

[4] See Peter's *gramota* to Patriarch Dositheus of 10 September 1701, acknowledging receipt of Dositheus's letter granting the request, in *PiB*, i, no. 394 (pp. 472–473).

[5] *Ibid.* See also *PiB*, ii, no. 613 (p. 313): an entry in Peter's notebook of the time which reads: 'about the *gramota* of Patriarch Dasitheus [*sic*] concerning bishops'.

Dositheus suggested, with regard to the request for clergy, that the tsar on the contrary should send several young Russians to him, to be trained as teachers for the Russian schools. 'We say, secondly, that if Serbs or Greeks or others should come there [to Russia], and even if by chance they should be the wisest and most pious of men, still Your Majesty is never to make a Greek, a Serb, or a Ukrainian [*Rusyanin*] metropolitan or patriarch, but only Muscovites; and not any Muscovites, but true-born Muscovites, however many faults they may have, however uneducated they may be'. Dositheus argued that 'a patriarch or metropolitan should be wise and virtuous', but that if they lacked these qualities 'they may be sustained by virtuous and wise subordinates'. For 'a Greek or a Serb or a Ukrainian would not have a similar position in Muscovy, since however good he might be, all would be opposed to him'. Moreover, 'foreigners, wherever they may be from, would introduce innovations into the church, instead of guarding it well. . . . It is important, most pious Lord, that a foreigner should not be brought to your great episcopal throne, and that Your Majesty should not send a Greek to Azov'. And Dositheus, after referring to the usurpatious Patriarch Nikon, who had been deposed in 1667, offered Peter further unsolicited advice on the choosing of another patriarch: 'It is fitting that [he] should have the virtue of humility; for he will be patriarch, not tsar-autocrat, and have power over the bishops and clergy under him, but not so as to behave like a beast towards them, lest the bishops, his brothers, fear him like slaves; and he will not praise other religions nor mix in civil affairs and try to dominate. . . . It is important, blessed Lord, not to give power to a man of a proud, tyrannical, and forceful character'.[1]

Unfortunately, there is no evidence to show what was Peter's immediate reaction to Dositheus's letter. Doubtless he had never heard, nor ever was to hear, such forcible language from any of his own ecclesiastics, least of all from Yavorskii. But concerning the importing of 'foreigners' and the choosing of a patriarch, Dositheus need not have wasted his breath. Though Peter sought and accepted Dositheus's

[1] Dositheus's letter to Peter of 2 June 1702 is printed in *PiB*, ii, pp. 715–721. In it he also chastizes Peter for planning to give his son Aleksei a 'German' education ('Your Majesty's ever memorable fathers and grandfathers and Your God-fearing Majesty did not learn to be strong, majestic, awesome, and indomitable from those Franks') and for forming an alliance with the Austrian emperor ('that false, pope-crowned Caesar. . . . a worse persecuter of the Orthodox than Diocletian'), who had, Dositheus reminded Peter, already 'betrayed' him by concluding a separate peace with the Turks.

advice in other matters,[1] events were to show that on these points he simply ignored it. Yet Dositheus's letter is significant in at least two other respects. He clearly assumed that Peter intended sometime to nominate a patriarch of Moscow, and he clearly disapproved of Yavorskii as a 'foreigner' likely to introduce innovations and to 'praise other religions'.[2] And Yavorskii took the implied rebuke to heart. For Dositheus had earlier criticized his running of the Kiev academy along 'Latin' lines, for which reason the students had learned from him 'much that is not Orthodox'; and now, when Dositheus seemed to renew the attack, Yavorskii sent him a detailed rebuttal. But the old patriarch remained adamant. On 15 November 1703 he wrote a long letter to the metropolitan of Ryazan', the temporary head of the Russian church, in which he accused him of not being 'fully Orthodox'.[3] It was left to Dositheus's successor Hyacinth, who became patriarch of Jerusalem in 1707, finally to make peace with Yavorskii. Owing to his frequent journeys to Moscow as Dositheus's emissary, Patriarch Hyacinth was perhaps more keenly aware of realities in Russia.

II
THE INTERMEDIARY PHASE, 1701–1718

When Yavorskii received his new commission in December 1700 he perhaps assumed that he should function as had previous temporary administrators of the patriarchal office. He at once issued several directives to the patriarchal Palace Prikaz concerning the current business of the domain.[4] But within little more than a month one patriarchal prikaz was abolished, as we have seen, and two others were amalgamated; and ultimate responsibility for the management of the patriarchal household and its domain was given to the head of the new Monastery Prikaz. Yavorskii was not allowed to use any of the patriarchal revenues (indeed the revenue of his own diocese of Ryazan' was made over in 1701 to the Admiralty Prikaz, while he was given the

[1] See N. F. Kapterev, 'Ierusalimskii patriarkh Dosithei v ego snosheniyakh s Russkim pravitel'stvom (1669–1707)', *Chteniya v imperatorskom obshchestve istorii i drevnostei rossiiskikh pri Moskovskom universitete*, 1891 (ii), pp. 52–57.

[2] Dositheus's criticisms find an echo in the work of a later Russian student of the times, who describes Yavorskii as 'the chief representative of Catholic rationalism in our church' (Samarin, *op. cit.*, p. 34).

[3] For the exchanges between Dositheus and Yavorskii, see Morev, *op. cit.*, p. xi.

[4] Gorchakov, *O Zemel'nykh vladeniyakh vserossiiskikh mitropolitov, patriarkhov i sv. sinoda*, p. 444.

income of the vacant Tambov see).[1] It was only by a special decree that he was allowed to travel to patriarchal villages near Moscow and to fish in their rivers for his domestic needs; a few weeks later (April 1702), by another decree of the Monastery Prikaz, he was permitted to draw an annual five *vedra* of wine from patriarchal properties near Astrakhan.[2] Exactly what, contemporary observers might well have asked, was Yavorskii's role to be? The history of the following years suggests, in reply, that Peter intended Yavorskii to act primarily as the chief priest and preacher of Russia, and secondarily as the tsar's adviser on ecclesiastical education and appointments; but that otherwise the metropolitan of Ryazan' should confine himself to administering the routine ecclesiastical affairs of his own and the Moscow (patriarchal) dioceses.

In Peter's published correspondence any number of instances can be found in which he informs Yavorskii, like Patriarch Adrian before him, of Russian military victories and then orders him, either directly or through subordinates, to conduct services of thanksgiving.[3] At all official and religious celebrations of major victories Yavorskii presided and preached the sermon.[4] Equally, Peter seems automatically to have informed Yavorskii, alone among the hierarchy, of the births, deaths, and marriages of members of his family, requesting at the same time that appropriate prayers should be said in all the churches of Russia.[5] On 31 October 1708 Peter wrote to him from army headquarters on the river Lesna condemning Hetman Mazepa for having 'abandoned Orthodoxy and fled to the heretic Swede' and for having joined in

[1] *PSZ*, iv, no. 2346 (pp. 658–659).

[2] Both decrees are printed in Gorchakov, *O Zemel'nykh vladeniyakh vserossiiskikh mitropolitov, patriarkhov i sv. sinoda*, appendix, pp. 139–140.

[3] *PiB*, ii, no. 497 (pp. 134–135, 482–483); no. 517 (p. 158). *PiB*, iii, no. 696 (p. 120); no. 1011 (p. 544). *PiB*, x, no. 3623 (pp. 61–62); no. 3862 (p. 325); no. 4083 (pp. 365–733). Also *OAS*, i, appendix I, nos. 1, 2, 4, 9 (cols. I–V). For similar letters to Adrian, see *PiB*, i, no. 50 (pp. 41–42; 524–526); no. 103 (pp. 80–82; 586–587); no. 111 (pp. 93–95); no. 186 (pp. 193–194; 648); no. 189 (p. 196; pp. 650–651); no. 202 (pp. 214–215; 666).

[4] See *PSP*, ii, no. 937 (p. 660): a Synodal resolution of December 1722 ordering the compilation of a book of the sermons preached by Yavorskii and others on the occasion of military victories 'from the beginning of the Swedish war and throughout its entire twenty-one years' duration'. Also *PSP*, iv, no. 1380 (p. 227): a resolution of September 1724 implementing instructions from Peter's personal cabinet that 'all the salutations and welcoming speeches by the late Most Reverend Stefan . . . on the occasion of His Imperial Majesty's triumphal entries into Moscow' were to be sent 'for inclusion in the history of the recent Swedish war'.

[5] *PiB*, x, no. 3987 (p. 334); *ZAP*, no. 217 (p. 162); *PSZ*, v, no. 3028 (p. 473); *OAS*, i, appendix I, nos. 7, 13, 14 (cols. IV, VII, IX).

Swedish depredations of Orthodox churches ('in one church not far from Novgorod the Swedes stabled their horses!'). Yavorskii was ordered 'publicly to issue, in the Cathedral church, an anathema against . . . this second Judas'.[1] The ceremony was duly performed on 12 November in the Uspenskii cathedral in Moscow. The metropolitan of Ryazan' led the clergy as they 'cursed and eternally anathematized this enemy of the cross of Christ, [a punishment] which he has merited for his treason'.[2] In the history of Peter's reign this is perhaps the extreme case of his use of the most solemn rites of the church for purely political ends; and Yavorskii, the chief priest of Russia, was his instrument.

In one of those little books in which Peter habitually jotted down notes there appears the entry, dating from late 1700 or early 1701: 'to Yevorskii [*sic*] about the schools'.[3] Twice in the second half of 1700, once in June and again on 4 October, Peter had discussed with Patriarch Adrian the need for better trained clergy.[4] 'The priests are almost illiterate,' he had declared on the latter occasion: 'they should be taught to administer the sacraments before being ordained'. For this purpose, Peter opined, 'more than one person' was required, as well as a specific place where students could be taught. 'Thanks be to God there is a school here [the Moscow academy], where this might be done; but little is learned there, for there is no one to supervise it, as is necessary'. Peter concluded that a person was needed who was 'distinguished in rank and name and sufficiently qualified to provide for the wants of teachers and students. . . . Can such a person be found?' The patriarch, owing to his state of health, cannot have responded with much interest to the tsar's proposals: within less than a fortnight he was dead. Indeed, among the 'many disorders' in ecclesiastical affairs mentioned by Kurbatov in his letter to Peter reporting Adrian's death was the sorry condition of the Moscow academy, 'which was under the care of the Patriarch': 'to teach or to study in it is impossible'; its ceilings were falling down; in sum, Kurbatov had submitted, it was in need of the tsar's attention.[5] In December 1700, when he entrusted certain of the patriarchal prerogatives to Yavorskii, Peter clearly intended that the latter should assume responsibility for reviving the Moscow academy. As a former professor of the esteemed Kiev academy, Yavorskii must have appeared eminently suited to the task, and his qualifications in this

[1] *OAS*, i, appendix I, no. 5 (cols. III–IV).

[2] *PSZ*, iv, no. 2213 (pp. 431–432).

[3] *PiB*, ii, no. 612 (p. 310). An identical entry appears in a notebook dated 'sometime before 1706' (see *ZAP*, no. 5 [p. 34]).

[4] See above, pp. 65–66.

[5] Letter quoted in Verkhovskoi, i, pp. 111–112.

respect were doubtless an important factor in Peter's decision to name him temporary head of the church.

Yavorskii was instrumental in securing the services of several graduates of the Kiev academy, most notably Gabriel Buzhinskii and Theophylact Lopatinskii. The latter served in the Moscow academy first as a teacher of philosophy and prefect (1704–1706) and then as teacher of theology and rector (1706–1722). He was a moderately good scholar and struggled to improve the school, though with little success: the responsible officials of the patriarchal administration and, after 1718, of the Monastery Prikaz were not forthcoming with the necessary funds.[1] But Lopatinskii himself, as an educated cleric, attracted Peter's attention and was entrusted by him with various commissions. In 1710 he was summoned to St. Petersburg to assist the tsar in the preparation of a special church service to commemorate the battle of Poltava.[2] That same year Peter wrote a letter to Musin-Pushkin which concluded with the words: 'Please speak to the bishop of Rezan [*sic*] about the morning and evening prayers that I requested from him for the army; and if he doesn't have time, Lapatinskii [*sic*] could be asked'.[3] Despite his later criticism of Feofan Prokopovich (which is discussed below), Lopatinskii eventually was raised to the episcopacy and made a member of the Synod.[4]

Buzhinskii, too, eventually became a bishop. He was moreover an original member of the Synod and for a time archimandrite of the Trinity-Sergiev monastery near Moscow. But unlike Lopatinskii, he became a firm supporter of Feofan Prokopovich. Like Prokopovich, he hated Roman Catholicism; like Prokopovich, he was an implacable enemy of superstition and a devotee of the secular learning that was seeping in from the West (he translated for Peter a work of Samuel Pufendorf); like Prokopovich, he acquired a reputation for high living and a certain number of enemies. And like Prokopovich and also Yavorskii, it was his eloquence that first attracted the attention of the tsar, who in 1714 appointed him the first priest-monk of the Alexander-Nevskii monastery in St. Petersburg and in 1718 chief chaplain to the

[1] Smirnov, *Istoriya moskovskoi Slavyano-greko-latinskoi akademii*, pp. 77 ff. 'A Latin school kept by a Popish priest; the scholars are few and not diligent' – thus Ambassador Whitworth described the academy in a 'Private Relation' to Mr. Secretary Harley dated Moscow 8 July 1705 (Brit. Mus. Addit. MSS. 37353, f. 628).

[2] *PiB*, x, p. 521.

[3] *PiB*, x, no. 3623 (pp. 61–62).

[4] See B. Titlinov, 'Feofilakt Lopatinskii', *Russkii biograficheskii slovar'*, xxv (St. Petersburg, 1913), pp. 457–466; also I. Ya. Moroshkin, 'Feofilakt Lopatinskii', *Russkaya starina*, January 1886, pp. 1–38 and February 1886, pp. 265–292.

fleet. Born in Polish Ukraine, a former student (as mentioned) of the Kiev academy, he was called to Moscow in 1706 by Stefan Yavorskii and appointed a teacher in the Moscow academy, where in 1709 he became prefect.[1]

It was in his capacity as chief priest, preacher, and theologian of Russia that Yavorskii was obliged soon after his promotion publicly to admonish one 'Grishka' Talitskii, who had been convicted of distributing leaflets in which the imminent end of the world was predicted, Moscow called Babylon, Peter himself denounced as Antichrist, and the people forbidden to serve the tsar or to pay his taxes. The erudite Kievan scholar failed to persuade the Muscovite *nachëtchik* (popular religious teacher) to abandon his views.[2] However, he was inspired to write a book on 'The signs of the Coming of the Antichrist and of the End of the World' which appeared in 1703 and was largely lifted from the work of a Roman Catholic theologian.[3] In his sermons Yavorskii often dwelled on this theme – the admonition of heretics. His Jesuit training had left its mark not only in his characteristic preference for logical and dialectical modes of expression, but in his deep antagonism towards the enemies of the Roman Catholic church. And it is to the same cycle of works that Yavorskii's chief theological treatise, *The Rock of the Faith* (*Kamen' Very*), a defence of Orthodox doctrine against Protestant enemies at home and abroad, belongs.

Exactly when *The Rock of the Faith* was written is not known. But the evidence points to 1713, for on 17 January 1714 Peter wrote to Yavorskii, saying: 'your letter of 27 November has reached us [in St. Petersburg], together with the book you have written against the enemies of the church'; and on the original of Peter's letter Yavorskii has noted: 'the Sovereign's gracious words about the book on the faith'.[4] Indeed, Peter had suggested in his letter that to the book 'should be added the reasons why it was written; secondly, [there should be added] moral instruction for the simple folk concerning holy ikons, so

[1] V. Sheremetevskii, 'Gavriil Buzhinskii', *Russkii biograficheskii slovar'*, iv (Moscow, 1914), pp. 28–32.

[2] For the Talitskii affair, see Solov'ev, *op. cit.*, viii, pp. 100–102 and N. B. Golikova, *Politicheskie protsessy pri Petre I* (Moscow, 1957), pp. 135–145. Talitskii and five of his associates (including two priests) were executed; and the bishop of Tambov, who had been charged with aiding the heretics, was deposed and banished to the Solovetskii monastery.

[3] Korolev, *op. cit.*, p. 416; Pekarskii, *op. cit.*, ii, p. 79; and esp. Bykova and Gurevich, *op. cit.*, no. 29 (pp. 92–94).

[4] *OAS*, i, appendix I, no. 8 (cols. IV–V); also *ZAP*, no. 16 (p. 39). See also Morev, *op. cit.*, p. 287.

that they should know what is against the teaching of the church (as it is written down in this book) and so that others may read it and the humiliation caused us by our enemies might be done away with'. Peter's sensitivity to Protestant opinion on the traditional Orthodox practice of venerating ikons was long-standing: his remark recalls his conversations with the Anglican Bishop Burnet fifteen years previously. Yet it is clear that Peter intended that Yavorskii's book, suitably revised, should be published. For in September 1714 Musin-Pushkin, the head of the Monastery Prikaz, wrote to his 'merciful father in the spirit' about 'the book you were pleased to compose against the iconoclasts', and requested that Yavorskii should 'correct it', whereupon he, Musin-Pushkin, would order it to be printed. Musin-Pushkin referred to 'Luther, Calvin, and other enemies' against whom it was 'not forbidden to write'; nevertheless one should oppose them, Musin-Pushkin observed, 'with arguments drawn from Holy Scripture, the holy councils, and the Fathers'. Yavorskii was also told that the tsar himself was willing to 'declare under his own name, in a preface or wherever appropriate, that this book was written by your labours'.[1]

Musin-Pushkin concluded his letter to Yavorskii by exclaiming: 'Do not be angry, merciful Father, that I so boldly presume to write to you' – words which suggest that at least he himself, if not Peter, saw some impropriety in advising the temporary head of the church to redraft his theology. Perhaps Yavorskii saw it that way too. It was three years before he sent the manuscript to Archbishop Antonii of Chernigov, at the latter's request, for printing at the Chernigov press. Antonii was instructed to edit the text, which he, Yavorskii, was too ill to do (so he wrote): 'wherever severe vexation against the enemy [protestantism] is found, remove it or soften it, as is appropriate; about this the Great Sovereign himself was pleased to speak to me. . . . For it is written, "Do not return evil for evil"'.[2] But *The Rock of the Faith* was finally published only after Yavorskii's death. By decree of the Synod, at Lopatinskii's urging, it was printed, and then reprinted, in 1727 and in 1729[3] – events which belong to the history of the political

[1] Musin-Pushkin's letter to Yavorskii of 15 September 1714 (printed in *OAS*, i, appendix III [cols. x–xi]) should dispose of the theory that 'although, at first sight, this book [*The Rock of the Faith*] seems to be directed against protestantism, it was in reality directed against Peter' (J. Šerech, 'Stefan Yavorsky and the Conflict of Ideologies in the Age of Peter I', *Slavonic and East European Review*, xxx [1951], p. 57). Neither Peter nor his subordinate, nor Yavorskii himself, appear to have taken this view.

[2] Quoted in Morev, *op. cit.*, p. 289.

[3] *PSP*, vi, no. 2073 (p. 108); no. 2228 (p. 339).

and ideological conflicts of post-Petrine Russia[1] and as such lie outside the purview of this book.

Yet for our purposes here it should be noted again that *The Rock of the Faith* is in essence a heated polemic against protestantism,[2] which by the time it was written had become a live issue in Russian church circles. Already in 1713 the celebrated case of Dimitrii Tveritinov, a Muscovite man of science, doctor, habitué of the German suburb, Latinist, student of the Bible and of Luther's catechism, had arisen. Tveritinov was denounced for propagating 'free-thinking' or 'Protestant' ideas at the trial of a student of the Moscow academy, who was alleged to be one of his hundreds of disciples. After an inquisition at the patriarchal Ecclesiastical Prikaz and a torture session at the Preobrazhenskii Prikaz, Tveritinov and another of his adherents, a government tax official, fled to St. Petersburg, where, claiming to have been falsely accused, they placed themselves under the protection of several senators and of Theodosius Yanovskii, archimandrite (abbot) of the new Alexander-Nevskii monastery. A compromise was worked out, they were pronounced Orthodox, and on 14 June 1714 the Senate ordered Yavorskii to issue a proclamation to that effect. Yavorskii, whose sights had long been fixed on this 'heretic', decided to resist the move, and on 28 October sent a long letter to the tsar detailing the history of the case and objecting that it did not come within the Senate's jurisdiction. Evidently displeased with the Senate's action, Peter ordered (15 December) that the metropolitan of Ryazan' was to bring the original documents of the case – the depositions of witnesses (mostly learned Latinizers), etc. – to St. Petersburg, where the case was to be retried. Yavorskii received Peter's order, signed by Musin-Pushkin and Streshnev, on 21 December. Two days later he again wrote to the tsar, this time to say that Senator Ya. F. Dolgorukii (Tveritinov's protector and Yavorskii's old enemy) had been sent copies of all the documents and that he, Yavorskii, ill and dispirited, would now like to avail himself of the permission previously granted him by Peter to go home to Nezhin to consecrate a church. Peter replied on 5 January 1715, acknowledging Yavorskii's letter 'submitted

[1] See Morev, *op. cit.*, pp. 289 ff.

[2] Cf. Samarin's assessment of the work: 'his [Yavorskii's] Catholic element entered [*The Rock of the Faith*] in the form of the argumentation. Striving to vindicate logically the dogmas of our church, he borrowed from the system of the Catholics its principal forms, into which he inserted Orthodox dogmas' (*op. cit.*, p. 51). Thus Yavorskii 'does not renounce Protestant rationalism, but combats it with Catholic rationalism' (p. 52) – 'a great error', since 'Orthodoxy has no system [*sistema*] and should not have one' (p. 163).

to us as protector of the church'. 'It is indeed necessary', Peter wrote, 'for you to come here [St. Petersburg] with the depositions to complete the case, in compliance with the first order sent to you . . . for without you it is impossible to administer and decide these things'.[1]

Yavorskii did his duty. He lent his presence to the retrial of Tveritinov and his adherents which opened on 21 March 1715 in the Senate chancellery. A special *konsilium* of senators (including Menshikov, Streshnev, Musin-Pushkin, and the learned governor of Kiev, D. M. Golitsyn) had been convened at which Yavorskii was the sole representative of the church. He presented his evidence – as it were the case for the prosecution – and thereafter was effectively excluded from the tribunal's further proceedings, perhaps because some of the senators were annoyed that he should have appealed over their heads directly to the tsar. Witnesses on Tveritinov's behalf, including Archimandrite Yanovskii, were heard, and the trial dragged on for months. Yavorskii asked Peter's leave to return to Moscow, which was finally granted in August.[2]

Yet Yavorskii may have derived some belated satisfaction from the dénouement of the whole affair. In January 1716 Peter ordered that the trial was to be brought to a prompt conclusion;[3] in February, that Tveritinov and his associates were either to confess their radical, free-thinking, rationalist errors, in which case they were to be turned over to their bishop and kept under strict watch 'so that they should remain firm in the faith'; or, if they would not confess, that they were to be executed forthwith.[4] In the event only one of the accused chose openly and defiantly not to repent, and was executed. For by opposing the veneration of ikons and other traditional practices, by advocating complete religious toleration, and by rejecting all religious authority other than Scripture, Tveritinov had overstepped the very limited bounds of Peter's tolerance of *Russian* religious dissent. Poor Tveritinov, with so many of whose views we know Peter actually sympathized. In the German suburb he had misread the tsar's manifesto of April 1702 to mean that its provision concerning religious freedom would apply to him.[5]

And it was as a function of his resistance to Protestant influences that

[1] Peter's letter is printed in *OAS*, i, appendix I, no. 10 (col. VI).

[2] *OAS*, i, appendix I, no. 11 (cols. VI–VII): Peter to Yavorskii, 14 August 1715.

[3] *SIRIO*, xi, p. 301: edict to the Senate of 22 January 1716.

[4] Solov'ev, *op. cit.*, viii, p. 567.

[5] For the Tveritinov affair, see the documents printed in *OAS*, i, appendix IV (cols.

Yavorskii opposed the nomination of Feofan Prokopovich to the vacant see of Pskov. In May 1718 Peter invited Yavorskii, through Musin-Pushkin, to come to St. Petersburg to preside at the consecration of several episcopal nominees, one of whom was Prokopovich: if Yavorskii were unwell and could not attend, he was to send in his stead the metropolitan of Krutitsy.[1] Yavorskii sent Aleksei of Krutitsy, having warned him by letter that the tsar must be informed of an impediment to Prokopovich's consecration, namely, that 'his doctrine is not in agreement with [that of] our holy, apostolic, Orthodox-Catholic church'. Aleksei was to ensure either that Prokopovich renounced certain of his teachings and made a public confession of his errors, or that with the tsar's permission the judgment of the Eastern patriarchs was sought in the matter. If Prokopovich recognized his doctrine for what it was, 'innovatory and opposed to our holy apostolic church', and renounced it in the prescribed manner, Aleksei was to 'consecrate him in compliance with the tsar's will'. 'Should it not be done in this way', Yavorskii added, 'I am not at fault, as you see'. Attached to his letter to Metropolitan Aleksei was a list of 'Conclusiones' in Latin and Russian deduced from Prokopovich's writings to illustrate seventeen points of doctrine which Yavorskii considered un-Orthodox.[2] Theophylact Lopatinskii and his colleague at the Moscow academy, Gideon Vishnevskii (another product of the Kiev academy and of the Jesuits), also wrote to Peter, objecting to Prokopovich's consecration on similar grounds.[3]

Prokopovich was outraged (his contempt for the 'Latinizers' was noted in a previous chapter). To a correspondent he retailed the ensuing scene of Yavorskii's humiliation with obvious pleasure. Prokopovich claimed that his 'enemies' had not read his theological works, and at the tsar's order a personal confrontation was arranged in St. Petersburg. Yavorskii was presented with Prokopovich's written rebuttal of the 'Conclusiones', whereupon, 'after prolonged reflection

XI–XVII); Tikhonravov, 'Moskovskie vol'nodumtsy nachala XVIII veka i Stefan Yavorskii', in Tikhonravov, *op. cit.*, pp. 156–304; and Solov'ev, *op. cit.*, pp. 560–567. Peter, somewhat maliciously it seems, ordered that Tveritinov himself should become a physician in Yavorskii's household, where he could satisfy his doubts about Orthodoxy. But Yavorskii clapped him in goal and otherwise hounded him until his, Yavorskii's, death (1722).

[1] See Chistovich, *Feofan Prokopovich*, pp. 39–40.

[2] Letter and 'Conclusiones' printed in I. Chistovich, *Feofan Prokopovich i Feofilakt Lopatinskii* (St. Petersburg, 1861), appendix I (pp. 1–4).

[3] See Titlinov, 'Feofilakt Lopatinskii', p. 458.

[as Prokopovich tells it], the archbishop of Ryazan' recognized the dogmas, exactly as I had formulated them, as Orthodox, and said that he himself thought exactly the same but had taken my words in another sense. Finally, he openly admitted he had not read my works. . . . After this conversation, the said bishop arose and humbly begged my forgiveness, which he received, with mutual embraces'. Musin-Pushkin and Archimandrite Theodosius Yanovskii had witnessed the scene. And as if to gloat over his victory, Prokopovich records that 'one week later, on 8 June, the Most Sacred Monarch, as a sign of his good will towards us, had lunch at my house and remained until 6 o'clock.'[1] Indeed, according to the journal of Prince Menshikov Peter himself had attended Prokopovich's consecration as bishop of Pskov in the St. Petersburg Trinity cathedral on 1 June.[2]

The confrontation of Yavorskii and Prokopovich on 1 June 1718, resulting in the former's abject surrender and followed by Prokopovich's consecration in the tsar's presence, is the decisive turning-point in the history of Peter's church reform. For coupled with the revelations of his semi-treasonous involvement with Tsarevich Aleksei (whose trial was scheduled to begin in a fortnight's time), Yavorskii's attempted obstruction of Prokopovich's consecration thoroughly discredited him in Peter's eyes. What is more, his displeasure with Yavorskii's conduct was doubtless an important factor in Peter's decision, taken later that year, that as a matter of principle no one man was capable of administering ecclesiastical affairs in a way that was consistent with the good of the state. However, it remains to account more fully for Yavorskii's fall from grace and so to conclude this discussion of the long, intermediary stage of what has been called the politics of church reform under Peter.

As early as 1707 Yavorskii complained in a letter to his friend Metropolitan Dimitrii of Rostov of his 'innumerable cares' and of this 'unbearable time', referring to Moscow (as had Gregory Talitskii!) as a second Babylon.[3] By 1710 his relations with Peter had come to a critical pass. In September of that year the tsar ordered him to come to St. Petersburg for the marriage of his niece Anna Ivanovna with the Lutheran duke of Courland, and Yavorskii, in a fulsome letter, refused

[1] Prokopovich's account of the meeting, in an undated letter to an unspecified person, is printed in Chistovich, *Feofan Prokopovich*, pp. 42–43. The lunch party of 8 June is also mentioned in the journal of Prince Menshikov, except that there it is recorded that the tsar remained 'until 8 o'clock in the evening' (quoted in Golikov, *op. cit.*, vii, p. 365).

[2] Quoted in Golikov, *op. cit.*, p. 364.

[3] Korolev, *op. cit.*, p. 417.

– because, he said, of his 'great illness'.[1] Theodosius Yanovskii presided instead at the wedding. Then in November Musin-Pushkin informed the tsar that he had received a letter from Yavorskii stating that 'he wishes to retire from the administrative affairs entrusted to him, and to leave Moscow. . . . he writes about his monastic *skhima* [the garment symbolizing profession of the strictest monastic vows]'.[2] Peter replied, half-jocularly, that he was 'very much shocked' to read that Musin-Pushkin apparently intended to give Yavorskii leave to become 'an idler and a grumbler' (such was Peter's opinion of the monastic life).[3] But Musin-Pushkin further reported that

> On my arrival in Moscow the metropolitan of Ryazan' went to Ryazan'. I wrote to him three times, asking him to come to Moscow, since many matters required his attention. To my third letter he replied stiffly that he was not obliged to come to Moscow and that such ecclesiastical affairs as he had charge of could be managed by somebody else. . . . And it is rumoured that he will take the *skhima*. I wrote to him and sent a secretary to say that without an edict from Your Majesty he could not do this; and I ordered [the secretary] to tell all the archimandrites and priests that no one was to invest the metropolitan with the *skhima* under pain of severe punishment. About this bishop: is he to be replaced by somebody else? or what is Your Majesty's will in the matter?[4]

It was Peter's will that Yavorskii should come to Preobrazhenskoe (near Moscow) for urgent discussion;[5] and there it was decided that he should remain at his post. Perhaps by way of concessions from the tsar, a certain large house in Moscow was to be 'returned' to Yavorskii 'for his Moscow residence',[6] the revenues of the Ryazan' diocese restored to him,[7] and the Prikaz of Ecclesiastical Affairs (with jurisdiction over the clergy of the Moscow or patriarchal diocese) re-established under the direction of his own nominee.[8]

But apart from his concern for his health, by 1710 Yavorskii had obviously become disenchanted with Peter's regime. His reasons are not difficult to imagine. Much of the legislation affecting the church

[1] *PiB*, x, no. 3987 (pp. 334, 716–717).
[2] *PiB*, x, p. 732.
[3] *PiB*, x, no. 4116 (p. 417).
[4] *PiB*, x, p. 755.
[5] *OAS*, i, appendix I, no. 6 (col. VI): Peter to Yavorskii, 28 January 1711.
[6] *SIRIO*, xi, p. 186: edict to the Senate of 6 March 1711.
[7] *PSZ*, iv, no. 2346 (pp. 658–659): Senate resolution of 11 April 1711).
[8] *PSZ*, iv, no. 2451 (pp. 759–761): Senate decree of 20 November 1711, from which it is clear that by an edict of the tsar of 1701 this patriarchal prikaz had been merged with the so-called (confusingly) Ecclesiastical Prikaz, which enjoyed ultimate jurisdiction over ecclesiastical matters in the entire Russian church and, though nominally under Yavorskii's supervision, had actually been run by a cleric of Peter's choosing.

enacted until then (and discussed in the preceding chapter) must have disturbed him. Thus, for the feast of St. John Chrysostom (13 November) in 1708 he prepared a sermon, which he never preached, criticizing the tsar for alienating church property and for holding riotous 'assemblies'.[1] Yavorskii cannot have enjoyed his part in the excommunication of his compatriot and former patron Hetman Mazepa, which was mentioned above. Moreover, it is possible that when he took the job of temporary head of the church in December 1700 he had been promised better things. He may even have been promised that in due course he would succeed to the patriarchate.[2]

In the years following his abortive resignation of 1710 the situation, from Yavorskii's point of view, hardly improved. In 1711 the Senate was founded and given complete authority, as we have seen, over all subjects, 'whether ecclesiastical or lay'.[3] Thereafter the Senate on occasion assumed jurisdiction in matters which previously had been the exclusive domain of the ecclesiastical authorities. The Senate's role in the heresy trial of Dimitri Tveritinov was mentioned above; and it will be recalled that much of the post-1710 legislation affecting the church, for instance the regulations governing the selection of priests and deacons, was promulgated by the Senate.[4] In 1716 it was the Senate that arranged for the temporary administration of the Novgorod diocese following the death of Metropolitan Job; by the same Senate decree Yavorskii was instructed to conduct Job's funeral.[5] Again, it was the Senate that sent Yavorskii the tsar's decree of 18 January 1719, ordering that the enclosed *gramota* from Patriarch Jeremiah of Constantinople concerning the rebaptism of Protestant converts to Orthodoxy (Jeremiah ruled that rebaptism was not necessary) should be observed.[6] Jeremiah's ruling in the matter had been sought, received, and distributed to the hierarchy by Peter, through the Senate, without reference to Yavorskii.[7] And it was the Senate which decreed on

[1] Korolev, *op. cit.* [2] Cf. Verkhovskoi, i, p. 152. [3] Above, p. 106.

[4] Chapter 2, *passim*; for the regulations referred to, see pp. 98–99.

[5] *OAS*, i, appendix 1, no. 29 (cols. XI–XIV).

[6] See the tsar's decree of 7 February 1719 to Archbishop Barnabas of Kholmogory, the preamble of which reads: 'On 18 January of the present year 1719 an edict [was sent] to Our Father the Most Reverend Stefan, Metropolitan of Ryazan' and Murom, from the Chancellery of the All-Ruling Senate in St. Petersburg . . . according to which translated copies of the enclosed *gramota* from Patriarch Jeremiah were to be sent to all the bishops, that they might do as provided in the *gramota*; and a copy of this *gramota* . . . is herewith sent to you under cover of Our Great Sovereign edict, that you Our Father should order it to be observed in your diocese . . .' (*PSZ*, v, no. 3300 [pp. 650–651]).

[7] Jeremiah's *gramota*, dated 31 August 1718 (*PSZ*, v, no. 3225 [p. 586]), refers to the

3 July 1719 that, 'pursuant to the report of the Armenian Bishop Minas, concerning the baptism and marriage of Armenians by Russian priests: this is to be done in accordance with ecclesiastical law, and on no account may anyone act contrary to it'. The metropolitan of Krutitsy – and not, significantly, the metropolitan of Ryazan' – was appointed by the Senate 'to look into this matter'.[1]

The Senate's actions can only have further distressed Yavorskii, a fact which this naturally timorous man found it increasingly difficult to conceal. One of his few public acts of defiance occurred on the occasion of Tsarevich Aleksei's nameday (17 March) in 1712, when he preached a sermon denouncing the interference of the 'fiscals' (tax-collectors and inspectors of revenue directly responsible to the Senate) in ecclesiastical affairs.[2] For this he was censured by the Senate, though Peter, on receipt of Yavorskii's long apologetic letter of 21 March, let him off with a strict warning.[3] Thereafter Yavorskii's spasmodic and fruitless efforts to have *The Rock of the Faith* printed, and his reluctant and restricted participation in the Tveritinov trial, reveal the increasing weakness of his position. Moreover, from the evidence already cited it will be apparent that after 1710 Musin-Pushkin, the head of the Monastery Prikaz, increasingly assumed the role of Peter's deputy in important ecclesiastical matters. It may be significant in this connection that while in 1708 the English ambassador referred to Musin-Pushkin as having the 'direction of all ecclesiastical revenues and [judicial] causes',[4] in 1710 he described him as a 'chief officer of state' having the 'inspection of *all ecclesiastical affairs* [italics mine] and revenues'.[5] Peter's tendency to subordinate him either to Musin-Pushkin or to the Senate (of which Musin-Pushkin was a leading member) perhaps galled Yavorskii most of all.

Potentially the most important of Yavorskii's functions as temporary head of the church was that of the tsar's adviser on senior ecclesiastical appointments. To be sure, certain important sees were filled by Yavorskii's candidates, all learned Kievans like himself: Dimitrii

tsar's 'recent *gramota*, in which You ask and require from [us] a ruling on Lutherans and Calvinists converted to our faith. . . .'.

[1] *PSZ*, v, no. 3400 (p. 721).

[2] Peter had expressly granted the fiscals the power to inspect the finances of the 'patriarchal and episcopal *prikazy* in Moscow and in the provinces' (*PSZ*, iv, no. 2414 [pp. 726–727]).

[3] See Chistovich, *Feofan Prokopovich*, pp. 61–64, for the whole episode.

[4] Brit. Mus. Addit. MSS. 31128, f. 132: Whitworth to Harley, 24 March 1708.

[5] Brit. Mus. Stowe MSS. 223, ff. 304–305: Whitworth to Harley, 7 February 1710.

Tuptalo, metropolitan of Rostov (nominated 1702); Filofei Leshchinskii, metropolitan of Tobol'sk (1702); Joseph Krokovskii, metropolitan of Kiev (1708); Dositheus Glebov, metropolitan of Rostov (1710); and Theophylact Lopatinskii and Gabriel Buzhinskii, who at Yavorskii's behest were appointed to the Moscow academy and later consecrated bishops. But if Yavorskii proposed, the tsar and his officials disposed. The case of Dimitrii Tuptalo has been mentioned already; originally consecrated for the Tobol'sk see (1701), he dallied in Moscow with Peter's permission until, on Peter's orders, he was transferred to Rostov.[1] The case of Joseph Krokovskii is particularly well-documented. He and an appropriate suite (he was archimandrite of the Kiev Monastery of the Caves) arrived in Moscow in March 1708 for his consecration as the new metropolitan of Kiev, in succession to Yavorskii's old patron Varlaam Yasinskii.[2] On 15 April Musin-Pushkin reported their arrival to Peter, asking: 'Who is to consecreate [Krokovskii]? Or does Your Majesty command him to go to St. Petersburg for consecration, so that this ecclesiastic, whom I believe worthy to be consecrated, should appear before Your Majesty?'[3] In reply Peter wrote: 'Order Krakovskii to remain in Moscow for consecration and to wait for [the metropolitan of] Rezan'.[4] There were further exchanges between Musin-Pushkin and the head of the Prikaz of Foreign Affairs, and between them and Peter, concerning the size of the customary payment of cash, furs, silver plate, and vestments to be given to the metropolitan-elect; and Krokovskii was finally consecrated on 15 August.[5] He died on his way to St. Petersburg in 1718 while under arrest for his part in the conspiracy surrounding Tsarevich Aleksei.[6] As for Yavorskii's other protégés, Metropolitan Dositheus of Rostov was executed for his part in the Aleksei conspiracy;[7] while Theophylact Lopatinskii and Gabriel Buzhinskii were made bishops only after Yavorskii's death.

From the tsar's point of view the record of Yavorskii's candidates was not an entirely good one. It is not surprising, therefore, that as well as nominating Prokopovich to the see of Pskov Peter frequently acted on his own initiative, without reference to Yavorskii, in the matter of ecclesiastical appointments. In a report to the tsar of 3 September 1701 the governor of Pskov asked: 'who is to be head of the [Pskov] Monastery of the Caves?' Peter's reply to the governor's query, issued at Preobrazenskoe on 9 February 1702, stated simply:

[1] See above, p. 66 and n.3. [2] See *PiB*, vii (2), p. 732. [3] *Ibid.*, p. 731.
[4] *PiB*, vii (2), no. 2371 (pp. 158–159). [5] *Ibid.*; also p. 526.
[6] See below, p. 146. [7] Also below, p. 146.

'you are to choose'.[1] In October 1710 Musin-Pushkin was directed by Peter to transfer Gregory Dashkov, archimandrite of the Trinity monastery in Astrakhan, to the Trinity-Sergiev monastery near Moscow, of which Dashkov became archimandrite in 1711.[2] Yavorskii's own report to Peter of 12 July 1711 indicates the contemporary state of affairs with regard to episcopal appointments:

> Now, as is already known to Your Most Illustrious Majesty, Bishop Kallistos of Tver has died [Yavorskii wrote]. . . . and now this throne is widowed and the people of this household petition me to give them a bishop. But without Your Majesty's edict I would not presume to do anything in this matter, except to advise that Bishop Varlaam of Irkutsk still lives in Moscow and without an edict will not go to Siberia. And I reported this to the Senate, and the Senate provided me with an edict; but I, Sovereign, cannot decide matters with which I am unfamiliar. . . . [this] can be settled only by your monarchical decree. And if Irkutsk will not go to Siberia, may it please the Great Sovereign to transfer him to Tver to replace the deceased bishop.[3]

On 21 January 1714 Peter ordered the bishop of Irkutsk transferred to Tver, as Yavorskii had once advised, and the new bishop of Tver transferred to the see of Krutitsy.[4]

That Peter intended that his control of ecclesiastical appointments should be complete is evident from two decrees promulgated in the autumn of 1715. By the first, which he directed to the governor of Kiev, he commanded that 'since good monks are needed in the new Trinity monastery [in St. Petersburg] select 20 or 25 persons of whom you do not have very great need there, but who will be most useful here – namely: the superior of the Monastery of the Caves, who shall be archpriest at Voronezh, and so on. Send them here at the first opportunity and they shall be made parish priests'.[5] At the same time, by an edict promulgated on 29 November it was provided that henceforth archimandrites for all the monasteries of Russia were to be chosen from among the monks of the Trinity Alexander-Nevskii monastery in St. Petersburg, and consecrated there, 'since monks in the provinces are not known to His Majesty the Tsar'.[6] It will be remembered that traditionally Russian candidates for the episcopacy came exclusively from the ranks of the monastic clergy. Accordingly, in November 1718 (in the wake of the Aleksei trial) Peter commanded that in order to fill

[1] *PiB*, ii, no. 408 (pp. 7–13).
[2] *PiB*, x, no. 4073 (pp. 390, 745).
[3] The letter is printed in Chistovich, *Feofan Prokopovich*, p. 91, n. 2.
[4] *OAS*, i, appendix III, no. 22 (col. 7).
[5] *SIRIO*, xi, p. 103.
[6] *PSZ*, v, no. 2959 (p. 184).

various episcopal vacancies Yavorskii was to draw up a list of candidates from among the 'good monks' who had been 'brought here to the Nevskii monastery to live, that they should become known [to us]'. Indeed, it was on this occasion that Peter intimated that for the 'better management' of episcopal appointments he was thinking of founding an Ecclesiastical College.[1]

Control over both present and future bishops was further ensured by the introduction in 1716 of a new episcopal oath. Before 1701 bishops taking office had made only a simple promise to obey the patriarch, to pay his taxes, and to attend church councils;[2] after 1701, in the absence of a patriarch, newly-consecrated bishops made a general promise to preserve the 'ecclesiastical canons', as will be seen shortly. But in January 1716 the bishops-elect of Vologda and Astrakhan, and Yavorskii himself (who had been summoned to St. Petersburg by the Senate for their consecration),[3] were presented with what Peter described as 'supplementary points to the pre-consecration oath of the bishops'.[4] Peter explained that 'although according to the present oath the bishops swear to preserve the ecclesisatical canons, yet for the sake of certain neglected matters of ours this special explanation [the "supplementary points"] has been drawn up, which is to be added to the present oath'.[5] That same day (22 January) the Senate sent copies of the new oath to all the bishops and to the provincial governors, stating that by command of the tsar the former were to take the new oath and 'without fail fulfil everything therein'.[6]

The seven points of the new oath embodied the essentials of much of Peter's legislation affecting the church enacted by 1716. Under points 1 and 2 the bishops undertook to exercise restraint, 'prudence, and meekness' in their dealings with heretics and other 'oppositionists'; to ensure (point 3) that the monks of their dioceses did not travel about without their written permission, 'given only for the most urgent reasons'; not to build 'superfluous' churches (point 4) nor to increase the number of clergy 'for the sake of squalid profits' beyond what was strictly necessary (point 5); to make annual visitations of their dioceses 'if at all possible, or at least once in every two or three years' – not 'out of avarice and for the sake of honours', but to ensure that their flocks remained faithful and the clergy zealous in admonishing 'schismatics,

[1] *PSZ*, v, no. 3239 (p. 595). [2] See Verkhovskoi, i, p. 519.

[3] *OAS*, i, appendix I, no. 28 (col. x).

[4] The original draft of the new oath is in Peter's own hand (see Verkhovskoi, ii, pp. 109–113). [5] *ZAP*, no. 36 (p. 51). [6] *PSZ*, v, no. 2985 (p. 193).

the superstitious, and the enemies of God' (point 6); finally (point 7), the bishops swore 'not to interfere in secular affairs and legal proceedings, unless some plain injustice is evident, whereupon I will first admonish and then write to His Majesty the tsar'.[1] Several of the points – not, it should be noted, the last – included references to the decrees of various church councils, indicating once again Peter's perpetual concern that his innovations should appear to have the sanction of traditional authority.

The new oath was to be confirmed under provisions of the *Ecclesiastical Regulation*. But it may be mentioned here that it was imposed on the bishops by Peter with only the formal participation of the metropolitan of Ryazan'. And Peter's measures of 1715–1718 regarding the selection and appointment of senior clergy should be borne in mind when we come to consider the apparent readiness with which, one after another, the hierarchy of Russia signed the *Ecclesiastical Regulation* in 1720.

Yavorskii's opposition to Peter's policies and to the latter's interference in what Yavorskii must have regarded as purely ecclesiastical matters, took various, usually indirect, and always ineffectual forms. Sometimes, as we have seen, he attempted simply to avoid difficult problems. At least once, in 1710, he attempted to resign. Later, he preached against the activities of the Senate's fiscals; and the significance in this respect of his response to the Sorbonne's proposal of church union was discussed at length in a previous chapter. But Yavorskii's attempted obstruction of Prokopovich's consecration is the outstanding case in point. Together with the contemporaneous revelations of his involvement in the Aleksei affair, his opposition to Prokopovich (it was suggested above) precipitated Yavorskii's fall from Peter's grace. It was also suggested that Yavorskii's opposition was an important element in Peter's momentous decision to abolish the patriarchate and to overhaul the supreme administration of the church.

The mere fact that after 1700 Peter continued to delay the election of a successor to Patriarch Adrian until late in 1718, when his decision to abolish the patriarchate obviated the question, is evidence enough that during the prolonged interval Yavorskii did nothing to dissuade the tsar from this course of action. To put the point more positively, Peter's decision to abolish the patriarchate must have been influenced

[1] *Ibid.*, pp. 193–194; also Verkhovskoi, ii, pp. 110–112. A rough contemporary English translation of the oath is printed in Weber, *op. cit.*, i, pp. 174–177.

by his increasing dissatisfaction, culminating in May–June 1718, with Yavorskii's conduct. But before proceeding further, the role of the Aleksei affair, both in Yavorskii's fall from grace and in Peter's decision to abolish the patriarchate, must be briefly shown.

The details of the case must not detain us. The question of whether Aleksei was guilty, as charged, of conspiring to commit treason and rebellion against his father, and the problem of Aleksei's sudden death (was it a 'natural' death, the result of repeated tortures? or was he in fact secretly executed, pursuant to his public condemnation? and if the latter, was it with Peter's concurrence, by his direct order, or indeed by his own hand, in a fit of rage?) are not of direct relevance here.[1] But judging from the high-level gossip circulating in St. Petersburg at the time,[2] and from the official documents published immediately after Aleksei's trial,[3] it seems that he was the somewhat unwitting dupe of reactionary circles who plotted to seize power on Peter's death, perhaps to hasten that event, and, once in power, to reverse many of Peter's policies. The aims of the conspirators, as described by them in their confessions, were vague: they were somehow to undo Peter's innovations and to return to the 'ancient customs and to live after the old ways'. It was rumoured, more specifically, that Aleksei's self-appointed champions intended to burn St. Petersburg, to destroy the Russian fleet, and to kill or banish all foreigners. Viewed retrospectively, the conspiracy can be seen as another manifestation of 'feudal' reaction to the increasing centralization and absolutism of Peter's regime; or of 'conservative' reaction to the new political and social forms and to the presence of numerous foreigners in favoured positions; or, finally, of

[1] See Ustryalov, *op. cit.*, vi, pp. 280–294, for nine more or less contemporary versions of the death of Aleksei. Ustryalov himself concludes that Aleksei died as a result of the repeated tortures which were an inevitable part of Russian justice.

[2] As recorded especially in the dispatches of Henry LaVie, French commercial representative (printed in *SIRIO*, xxxix, pp. 304 ff.), and in the journal of the German diplomat, F. C. Weber (*op. cit.*, i, pp. 201–203, 206, 208–220, 225–230, 243–245).

[3] See the *Manifeste du procez criminel du Czarevitch Aleksei Petrovitch, jugé et publié à Saint Petersbourg le 25 de juin 1718. Traduit sur l'original Russien, et imprimé par ordre de Sa Majesté Czarienne* (The Hague, 1718). I have made use of the English translation of the preceding (published in London, 1725; hereafter cited *Trial*) in conjunction with the Russian (or German) originals of these and related documents printed in Ustryalov, *op. cit.*, vi, appendices (esp. pp. 346 ff.; see also pp. 142 ff. for Ustryalov's authoritative account of the interrogation and trial of Aleksei and his accomplices) and with the numerous letters of the figures involved in the conspiracy and other documents edited by M. P. Pogodin, 'Tsarevich Aleksei Petrovich, po svidel'stvam vnov' otkrytym', *Chteniya v imperatorskom obshchestve istorii i drevnostei rossiiskikh pri Moskovskom universitete*, 1861 (iii), pp. 1–374.

popular discontent with the burdens imposed by Peter's government. For while relatively few persons were denounced in the course of the trial, the circle of Aleksei's tacit or potential supporters against his father, to judge from the evidence and also from the importance that Peter attached to the trial, was wide. Aleksei's trial was perhaps the first large-scale 'show-trial' in modern Russian history. But what is more relevant to the present discussion is the fact that the conspiracy centring on Tsarevich Aleksei enjoyed the backing of elements within the clergy, including the metropolitan of Ryazan' himself. In a final, completely self-abasing and self-incriminating confession, extracted at Peter's direct order on 22 June, Aleksei condemned the 'idle and bigoted priests and monks' who allegedly had led him astray.[1]

The proximate causes of Aleksei's trial were, firstly, his flight to the West early in 1717 and his placing himself under the Austrian emperor's protection, ostensibly to escape the dilemma imposed on him by Peter of having to choose either to accept the obligations of heir to the throne or to renounce the succession and enter a monastery; and, secondly, the revelations of the wider conspiracy contained in Aleksei's successive confessions to Peter after his return under escort to Russia early in 1718. In the first of those confessions (8 February) Aleksei stated that a principal confidant had once advised him to tell his confessor that he was being forced to enter a monastery, in the hope that the confessor would inform Yavorskii – although he, Aleksei, had later forbidden this: 'I do not know what intention [the confidant] had in advising me to act thus; but the confessor knew nothing of the plots, nor did I ever enter into any deliberations with him'. On this occasion Aleksei also revealed that under pressure from his Austrian protectors he had written to the metropolitans of Rostov and Krutitsy, proclaiming that he had been badly treated, was being forced to enter a monastery, and had therefore fled 'until the time it shall please God to recall me'; that meanwhile the metropolitans were 'not to forget me' nor to credit any rumour of his death 'or any other injurious rumour'.[2] It later transpired that Aleksei had written a similar letter to the metropolitan of Kiev, and that he had written all three letters on his own initiative and according to a pre-arranged plan.[3] On 14 May (in the interval his mistress and other accomplices had been examined by the tsar's officials) Aleksei further confessed that before his flight Yavorskii 'used to write to me sometimes, and I to him, but not often: only when I had urgent business'; and that when, shortly before his flight, Yavorskii

[1] *Trial*, pp. 94–98. [2] *Ibid.*, pp. 20–37, 43. [3] *Ibid.*, pp. 57, 65.

had referred in a sermon to Peter's poor treatment of his son, Aleksei 'broke off our correspondence; nor did I permit him to come to me, that I might not give room for suspicions'. Aleksei admitted that he ought to have written to Yavorskii, from abroad, as he had to the metropolitans of Rostov, Krutitsy, and Kiev, because the Austrians had bidden him to write to the 'chief of the clergy and laity'; 'yet I did not do it, for I knew him more particularly than the rest, and the suspicions would have been strong against him and me because of the sermon he had preached'.[1]

Aleksei's letters to the three metropolitans were treated as important evidence: in subsequent interrogations Peter's officials repeatedly examined the tsarevich concerning them; and the metropolitans of Rostov and Kiev, it will be seen, were arrested in consequence. In yet another confession, signed by Aleksei on 17 June, he declared that 'I constantly relied upon the people, and especially upon the Metropolitan of Ryazan', ever since his sermon, seeing thereby that he had an inclination for me, though I never talked of anything with him except what I have confessed before'.[2] Moreover, on 19 June Aleksei stated that another of his confessors had told him that God would forgive him for wishing his father's death, for 'we wish it too', and had permitted him to receive communion.[3] The confessor was unfrocked and interrogated. When confronted with Aleksei's testimony, he acknowledged the truth of it, claiming only that by the word 'we' he had not meant any particular group but rather 'the people, [who] when they drank [Aleksei's] health called him the Hope of the Russians'.[4]

Additional and more conclusive evidence of the clergy's participation in the Aleksei conspiracy was not included among the official documents of the trial, whose publication obviously was intended not only to justify Aleksei's condemnation but to discredit the opposition to Peter's regime and to serve as a warning to his enemies both at home and abroad. But the numerous letters and other relevant documents subsequently discovered in the archives and published by a historian[5] fully confirm the picture which emerges from the official documents, filling out as they do the background to the conspiracy and clarifying, in particular, the relations between the principal conspirators. And on the basis of all the evidence at the government's disposal Aleksei's confessor, Ignatiev, who had led the inner group of Aleksei's maternal and grandmaternal relations, former tutors, and courtiers, who for

[1] *Ibid.*, pp. 53–54. [2] *Ibid.*, pp. 75–76. [3] *Ibid.*, pp. 92–93.
[4] *Ibid.*, p. 93. [5] Pogodin, *op. cit.*

years had encouraged Aleksei's treasonous thoughts, who in turn had been encouraged by Peter's unhappy first wife, Evdokiya, Aleksei's mother, and who like so many of the clergy was opposed to Peter's ecclesiastical policies and way of life: Ignatiev was among those executed for their association with the condemned tsarevich. Similarly, Metropolitan Dositheus of Rostov was on Peter's orders broken on the wheel, beheaded, his body burned, and his head impaled and publicly exhibited; having been formally deposed by a group of clergy led by a reluctant Yavorskii, who murmured something about it being impossible without a patriarch, Dositheus confessed under torture to having had treasonous dealings with the tsarevich and his mother. Of the two other metropolitans who had received seditious letters from Aleksei, the aged (over 70) and partially paralysed Joseph Krokovskii of Kiev was arrested at Peter's command and brought under escort to St. Petersburg; but before he could reach the new capital to undergo an interrogation he collapsed and died in Tver. The metropolitan of Krutitsy emerged, for the time being, safely; he had taken part in the deposition of Dositheus in February and now, in late June, was among the episcopal participants in the grandiose funeral services held for Aleksei. And Yavorskii himself survived. It seems he had confined himself to expressing an 'inclination' for the tsarevich, and after the latter's flight abroad had had nothing to do with him. Yavorskii had not received a seditious letter from Aleksei. But the damage to his relations with the tsar caused by Aleksei's revelations, was done.

Yet it was Yavorskii who, to his credit, led the clergy in recommending mercy for the wretched tsarevich, which perhaps further displeased Peter. On 14 June, the day on which Aleksei was formally arraigned before a large assembly of notables, Peter asked the attending clergy for their written opinion, based on Scripture, as to 'what punishment my son's terrible crime, which resembles the sin of Absalom, has deserved'.[1] The opinion, signed by Yavorskii (first), Prokopovich (second), six other bishops, four archimandrites, and two priests, was duly submitted to the tsar on 18 June. The signatories stated that they had abstained entirely from judging Aleksei, 'for this matter manifestly lies under civil jurisdiction, and not ecclesiastical'; moreover, that 'in this matter our ecclesiastical judgment must be made according to the spirit, and not according to flesh and blood'. On the basis of these sentiments, and having adduced relevant extracts from Scripture, Yavorskii, Prokopo-

[1] *Trial*, pp. 67–68.

vich, Aleksei of Krutitsy, Theodosius Yanovskii, and the others submitted 'all this to the most high monarchical consideration, with all due obedience, that [the tsar] may do what is agreeable in his own eyes: if he punishes [Aleksei] in proportion to his guilt, he will have before him the examples set forth above from the Old Testament; if he is inclined to mercy, he has the example of Christ Himself. . .'.[1] The recommendation was phrased in the cautious, circumlocutory language characteristic of Yavorskii's utterances; but its message was unmistakable. It had no effect whatever on the outcome of the case. Within a week the tsarevich, who had been formally condemned by a grand assembly of 128 notables on 24 June, was dead.

III

THE FINAL PHASE (I), 1718–1721

The final phase of what has been called the politics of church reform under Peter may be said to have begun on 20 November 1718. For on that day an extraordinary interview took place in St. Petersburg between the tsar and Stefan Yavorskii, at the conclusion of which the former remarked, with reference to the filling of episcopal vacancies, that 'for the better management of such important matters in future, an Ecclesiastical College would seem appropriate'.[2]

Yavorskii had come to St. Petersburg from Moscow late in May 1718, in response to Peter's urgent summons, for the confrontation with Prokopovich and for Aleksei's trial. Now, in the interview, he complained of being detained in the new capital 'in a rented house, far from a church', in which it was impossible for him to live through the winter because of his illness: did the Great Sovereign intend that he should remain in St. Petersburg indefinitely? And what of the 'gracious promise', conveyed to him in Peter's own hand, that a house was to be prepared for him? If he were to move to St. Petersburg, how did the Great Sovereign intend that 'from such a distance' he should administer his own diocese, the patriarchal (Moscow) diocese, the Cathedral church, and ecclesiastical affairs? Who was to supervise the Moscow academy? To these questions Peter replied, somewhat testily, that Yavorskii had been told three years before 'about living here', but that

[1] Ustryalov, *op. cit.*, vi, pp. 518–523.

[2] The interview is recorded n a document dated 20 November 1718 and entitled 'Most High Resolutions to the submissions of Metropolitan Stefan of Ryazan" (*PSZ*, v, no. 3239 [pp. 594–595]).

he had delayed, gone off to the Ukraine (in the summer of 1716), and done nothing about moving; that a site had been prepared for him in St. Petersburg on which he was to build a house at his own expense, like any other bishop; that an auxiliary bishop was to be appointed to administer the Ryazan' diocese, while the affairs of the patriarchal domain were to be entrusted to the metropolitan of Krutitsy, as had formerly (i.e. before 1700) been the practice; that the academy had been provided for;[1] and, finally, that Yavorskii would be informed by letter of any matter that could not be decided in his absence. But Yavorskii persisted: were the bishops, then, to come to St. Petersburg (for the customary visit to the head of the church)? were they to come by turns? alone or by twos? how long were they to remain and where should they stay? He was told that the bishops were to come at regular intervals and that sites would be prepared where they were to build their houses; and that he should decide the rest. It was then that Peter declared, in response to still further questioning, that he was thinking of founding an Ecclesiastical College.

It had been a momentous occasion not only in Yavorskii's career, but in the history of the Russian church. For Peter had resolved that St. Petersburg was to become the ecclesiastical capital of Russia as well as the seat of the civil government. Moreover, his decision to create an Ecclesiastical College necessarily implied that he meant to abolish the patriarchate: thus, the whole of Part I of the *Ecclesiastical Regulation*, which was drafted in the latter part of 1718,[2] was devoted to an exposition of the reasons why administration by a college was to be preferred to the rule of a patriarch. But the task of composing the *Ecclesiastical Regulation*, as we know, was given to Feofan Prokopovich. Yavorskii had lost all influence. Shorn of the burden of his patriarchal

[1] By an edict of 15 March 1718 the Monastery Prikaz had been given control of the academy (*PSZ*, v, no. 3182 [p. 554]).

[2] Internal evidence indicates that Part I of the *Ecclesiastical Regulation*, if not the whole text, was written in the latter part of 1718 (see Verkhovskoi, ii, p. 28, n. 18). Verkhovskoi himself, however, urges that work on the *Regulation* was begun sometime during the month and ten days remaining in 1718 after Yavorskii's interview with Peter (20 November). His argument rests on the supposition that the idea of creating an Ecclesiastical College first occurred to Peter during the course of the interview, a supposition he bases on the hypothetical form of Peter's words – 'an Ecclesiastical College *would seem* appropriate': 'This form [of words]', Verkhovskoi writes, 'best shows the unexpectedness and novelty of the idea itself' (i, pp. 155–156). But Verkhovskoi attempts perhaps to date too precisely Peter's decisions to create an Ecclesiastical College and, consequently, to order that an *Ecclesiastical Regulation* should be drafted. It is perhaps enough to say that these decisions were taken sometime in the latter part of 1718 and were doubtless closely related in time.

responsibilities, and doubtless pleading ill health, he retired to Moscow, where except for occasional visits to St. Petersburg he remained until the day of his death, which occurred almost exactly four years later.

Impatience with Yavorskii's behaviour was only one factor which influenced Peter's decisions of late 1718. In an earlier chapter it was suggested that his discussions with churchmen like the Anglican Bishop Burnet or, more recently, the doctors of the Sorbonne had provided him not so much with specific models to imitate but with personal knowledge of alternatives to the system of church government that prevailed back in Russia. It was also suggested that over the years Peter had absorbed from various sources a conception of absolute monarchy that was more akin to contemporary western theories than it was to traditional Orthodox doctrine. In the *Military Statute* of 1716, we saw in an earlier chapter, it was explained that 'His Majesty is an autocratic monarch who need not account for his actions to anyone on earth, but as a Christian Sovereign has the power and authority to govern his realm and his territories according to his own will and at his own discretion'.[1] This theory was explicitly accepted by Yavorskii and the other representatives of the church when, in their opinion submitted to Peter in June 1718, they declared: 'The highest authority in the Tsardom is the Monarch, who cannot be liable to the judgment of his subjects, but does as he wills without any counsel from the lower ranks'; disclaiming any jurisdiction over the heir to the throne, the clergy had asked, rhetorically: 'who would make us judges over those that rule [*obladayut*] us?'[2] And with the creation of a standing army, necessitated by the long-drawn-out war with Sweden, the notion had arisen among Peter's entourage that the state was served by three distinct 'orders [*chiny*]' – military, civil, and ecclesiastical – over which the tsar, as an absolute 'Christian' monarch, had equal authority.[3] By 1718, in short, Peter was intellectually predisposed radically to transform the administration of the church (or of the state) when the opportunity, indeed the necessity of having to do so, seemed to present itself.

Moreover, not only Yavorskii and certain other bishops and priests,

[1] *PSZ*, v, no. 3006 (p. 325); also *ZAP*, no. 33 (pp. 48–51).

[2] Ustryalov, *op. cit.*, vi, pp. 519, 522.

[3] See the manifesto of 25 January 1721 announcing the establishment of the Ecclesiastical College, in Verkhovskoi, ii, p. 5. The theory of the three orders was also expounded by Prokopovich in his sermon of 6 April 1718 (discussed above, Chapter 1, esp. p. 59) and in his *Primer*, which was first published in 1720 (see below p. 284).

but the clergy as a whole had been discredited in Peter's eyes by the recent revelations of the Aleksei conspiracy, which had impressed on him the necessity of ensuring their future loyalty: many of the provisions of the *Ecclesiastical Regulation* attest to this fact. Peter doubtless perceived, too, that the provisional ecclesiastical government introduced in 1700–1701 could not endure forever; that prolonging the *mezhdupatriarshestvo* only begged the question; that in consequence of the numerous measures affecting ecclesiastical persons and property enacted since 1701, ecclesiastical and civil jurisdictions had become confused, to the detriment of good order and the state's best interests; and that the situation must at last be 'regulated' – if not by the election of a new patriarch, then by some other means. In 1717–1718 Peter had found it necessary to appeal to the patriarch of Constantinople for rulings (i) that his troops should be exempt from fasting in time of war and (ii) that Protestant converts to Orthodoxy need not undergo rebaptism.[1] The cost and inconvenience (if not the humiliation) attending this means of achieving politically desirable ends were doubtless not lost on Peter.[2]

Finally, it will have been noticed that in November 1718 Peter had not said, abstractly, that the administration of the church was to be altered, but rather, concretely, that an 'Ecclesiastical College' was to be created. Why a 'college'? The answer to this question suggests an additional element that influenced Peter late in 1718. For it is more than a coincidence that his decision to found an Ecclesiastical College occurred simultaneously with his introduction of the collegial principle into the civil government. In the mind of the legislator, the creation of an Ecclesiastical College must have seemed a logical extension to the 'ecclesiastical order' of the changes being wrought elsewhere. 'We should indeed be anxious', Peter proclaimed in January 1721, 'lest we appear ungrateful to the Most High if, having received such great assistance from Him in the reform of both the military and the civil orders, we should neglect the reform of the ecclesiastical; . . . and seeing no better means to this end than an administrative council, we

[1] *PSZ*, v, no. 3178 (pp. 550–552); no. 3225 (p. 586).

[2] Cf. Consett, who writes that among the reasons adduced in Part I of the *Ecclesiastical Regulation* for establishing the Ecclesiastical College 'probably one reason is conceal'd, which may [nevertheless] be apprehended: that he [Peter] designed to exempt himself and his country from a dependance on the Patriarch of Constantinople' (*op. cit.*, p. xvi). Also Weber (*op. cit.*, i, p. 238): 'Remittances of money made thither [to the patriarch of Constantinople] are now rigorously prohibited, the Czar being sensible of what prodigious sums his dominions were drained by the applications made to that See . . .'.

hereby establish an Ecclesiastical College'.[1] Similarly, in Part I of the *Ecclesiastical Regulation* it is pointed out that 'the Most Potent All-Russian Tsar... has established colleges, varying according to the business and needs of the state, for the good of the fatherland and of his dominions, in this year 1718'. 'And as a Christian Sovereign', the *Regulation* continues, 'having observed the needs of the ecclesiastical order and desiring that it should be better administered, he has also deigned to establish an Ecclesiastical College'.[2]

The institution of a regime of colleges was discussed by Peter with the Senate as early as 23 March 1715, as can be seen from a memorandum on the subject, in Peter's own hand, preserved in the Senate's archives.[3] And in an anonymous memoir submitted to Peter early in 1715 the institution of nine colleges was proposed, one of which was to be a 'College of Religion [*Kalegium Very*]'.[4] An ecclesiastical college is not referred to again in the documents until the record of Yavorskii's interview with Peter in November 1718. But meanwhile, in September 1715 Peter had ordered his general in Pomerania to obtain copies of Danish civil and military statutes and to find out about the colleges established there: 'how many [there were], the number of members in each, their functions and duties, salaries, ranks, and everything else, from the most important [detail] to the least...'.[5] By 1717 the institution of a regime of administrative colleges in Russia was considered a foregone conclusion. A report of General Bruce, promulgated by the Senate on 9 August of that year, announced that 'Whereas His Majesty the Tsar most graciously intends to establish state colleges in his Russian Realm, he has therefore been pleased to write to me [from Spa, where Peter had gone after his visit to Paris] in his own hand, ordering that suitable assessors [for the colleges] should be found'.[6] In December 1717 the presidents of the nine new colleges – including those of Foreign Affairs, Finance, Justice, War, Commerce, Mines and Manufactures – were named.[7] The presidents, it was also announced, were to form their

[1] Manifesto of 25 January, in Verkhovskoi, ii, p. 6.
[2] Verkhovskoi, ii, pp. 28–29.
[3] *ZAP*, no. 254 (p. 213). See Verkhovskoi, i, pp. 145–148, for a discussion of the few collegial 'projects' submitted to Peter before 1715. Verkhovskoi's subsequent discussion of the establishment of the civil colleges (pp. 148–150) is derived mostly from secondary sources; since he wrote, however, much more archival material has become available (published in *ZAP*) to provide a more accurate picture of the evolution of Peter's major reorganization of the central government in the years 1718–1722. The new material shows, *inter alia*, Peter's close personal participation in the whole process.
[4] *ZAP*, no. 330 (pp. 269–271).
[5] *ZAP*, no. 25 (pp. 44–45).
[6] *PSZ*, v, no. 3101 (pp. 506–507).
[7] *PSZ*, v, no. 3133 (pp. 527–528).

colleges 'in the new year [1718]', but were not to 'interfere with things' until 1719 (a date later deferred to 1720),[1] when 'they shall begin to govern'.[2]

Thus, by the end of 1717 provision for the establishment of a regime of colleges in Russia had been made. It remained to draw up their governing statutes. Heinrich Fick, one of the tsar's German advisers, was given overall charge of the task.[3] Peter's instructions were that 'all the Colleges are to be based on the Swedish Statute [*Ustav*]; but those points in the Swedish Regulation [*Reglament*] which are not suitable or are inapplicable to the situation [*situatsiya*] of this Realm, are in my judgment to be set aside'.[4] The lesson was not lost on Herr Fick. At the conclusion of a report submitted to Peter at this time Fick suggested, with reference to the drafting of the collegial statutes, that 'one could combine foreign models and regulations with local [ones]'.[5] Indeed, the resultant *Regulations*, promulgated over the next few years, can have had no exact equivalents in contemporary European legislation.

With regard to the institution of the collegial regime, therefore, it is perhaps safest to conclude that while the idea no doubt originated in Peter's acquaintance with foreign (especially Swedish) governmental practices, the actual implementation of the scheme in Russia contained only some distinctly foreign elements, most notably the new official jargon. At the same time, it must be stressed that the establishment of the colleges constituted a radical break with the traditional Muscovite system of government. But then that was the purpose of the whole operation. An official proclamation of December 1718 explained to the people that, 'wishing to neglect nothing that might promote just government', it was now the tsar's intention to endow civil affairs with the same 'good order' that had already transformed the military establishment, 'with fruits that are known to all'; that therefore 'colleges' had been created – 'Colleges, that is, bodies composed of many persons (in place of the *Prikazy*) in which the Presidents or Presiding-officers [*Prezidenty ili Predsedateli*] do not, like the old judges [*sud'i*: heads of *prikazy*] have the power to do as they please'. The further advantages of the collegial system would be apparent, the proclamation concluded, when their 'Regulations (or Statutes) are

[1] *PSZ*, v, no. 3255 (p. 601).

[2] *PSZ*, v, no. 3129 (p. 525).

[3] See LaVie's dispatch of 3 April 1718, in *SIRIO*, xxxix, p. 333; also, Fick's report to Peter promulgated on 11 June 1718 (*PSZ*, v, no. 3208 [pp. 573–575]).

[4] Decree of April 1718, in *PSZ*, v, no. 3197 (pp. 564–565); also *ZAP*, no. 51 (pp. 60–61): decree to the Senate to the same effect of 11 June 1718.

[5] *PSZ*, v, no. 3208 (p. 575).

published'.[1] And it was at this time (late 1718) that Peter divulged to Yavorskii his intention of founding an Ecclesiastical College.[2]

Allowing for the other factors that came into play, Peter's decision to found an Ecclesiastical College must have been influenced by his contemporaneous provisions for overhauling the civil administration. It was there that the specific idea of creating an 'Ecclesiastical College' must have originated. Yet neither the Ecclesiastical College that came to be, nor its governing statute, resembled their civil counterparts (or prototypes) in other than outward form. The Russian patriarchate, which the Ecclesiastical College was meant to replace, was not, for one thing, merely another governmental prikaz – a fact of which the first eleven members of the Ecclesiastical College were fully aware. In the following chapter it will be seen that their first order of business was to dispense with the name 'College' in favour of the more distinctive and dignified 'Most Holy All-Ruling Synod'.

Impatience with Yavorskii's conduct and intermittent opposition; a predisposition towards radical change; a belief that his power was absolute and that it extended equally to the 'ecclesiastical order'; a distrust of the clergy; an awareness of the need to resolve, after eighteen years, the question of the patriarchal succession; and a realization that the example of the civil colleges was relevant to the problem: all these factors certainly influenced Peter late in 1718, though the relative weight he gave to each is impossible to determine exactly. But having decided to found an Ecclesiastical College, Peter felt that his decision needed to be justified. And judging from the justification set forth in Part I of the *Ecclesiastical Regulation*, it was a distrust of the patriarchate as such, a belief in its potential for disrupting the tranquility of the state, that was the major factor which decided Peter to apply to the administration of the church the principle of collegial government.

By far the longest of the nine 'weighty reasons' adduced in Part I to prove that an Ecclesiastical College was the 'most perfect' form of government, 'better than one-man rule' and particularly suited to a 'Monarchical State, such as our Russia', is the one set forth under point 7. No single passage of the *Regulation* is more suggestive of the nature

[1] *PSZ*, v, no. 3261 (pp. 603–604); also *ZAP*, no. 60 (p. 66) – indicating that the passage defining the colleges was written by Peter himself.

[2] The second mention of an Ecclesiastical College in the legislative acts of Peter's reign occurs in his edict of 10 December (1718), whereby the Senate was informed that in future responsibility for ecclesiastical persons would devolve upon 'the Ecclesiastical College' (*ZAP*, no. 58 [pp. 64–65]).

and flavour of Peter's church reform, and it may therefore be quoted at length:

> The fatherland need not fear from an administrative council [the Ecclesiastical College] the sedition and disorders that proceed from the personal rule of a single church ruler. For the common folk do not perceive how different is the ecclesiastical power from that of the Autocrat, but dazzled by the great honour and glory of the Supreme Pastor [the patriarch], they think him a kind of second Sovereign, equal to or even greater than the Autocrat himself, and imagine that the ecclesiastical order is another and better State.

The author of the *Regulation* thus makes somewhat tendentious use of the traditional Byzantine-Muscovite theory of the parallel powers (tsar and patriarch), and perhaps alludes to the fact that during the middle years of the seventeenth century the patriarchs of Moscow did in fact assume the title 'Sovereign [*Gosudar'*]'. But the title had not been used by the patriarchs since 1667, when its last bearer, Patriarch Nikon, was deposed. The passage continues:

> Thus the people are accustomed to reason among themselves, a situation in which the tares of the seditious talk of ambitious clerics multiply and act as sparks which set dry twigs ablaze. Simple hearts are perverted by these ideas, so that in some matters they look not so much to their Autocrat as to the Supreme Pastor. And when they hear of a dispute between the two, they blindly and stupidly take sides with the ecclesiastical ruler, rather than with the secular ruler, and dare to conspire and rebel against the latter. The accursed ones deceive themselves into thinking that they are fighting for God Himself, that they do not defile but hallow their hands even when they resort to bloodshed. Criminal and dishonest persons are pleased to discover such ideas among the people: when they learn of a quarrel between their Sovereign and the Pastor, because of their animosity towards the former they seize on the chance to make good their malice, and under pretence of religious zeal do not hesitate to take up arms against the Lord's Anointed; and to this iniquity they incite the common folk as if to the work of God. And what if the Pastor himself, inflated by such lofty opinions of his office, will not keep quiet? It is difficult to relate how great are the calamities that thereby ensue.
>
> These are not our inventions: would to God that they were. But in fact this has more than once occurred in many states. Let us investigate the history of Constantinople since Justinian's time, and we shall discover much of this. Indeed the Pope by this very means achieved so great a pre-eminence, and not only completely disrupted the Roman Empire, while usurping a great part of it for himself, but more than once has profoundly shaken other states and almost completely destroyed them. Let us not recall similar threats which have occurred among us.

In an ecclesiastical administrative council there is no room for such mischief. For here the president himself enjoys neither the great glory which amazes the people, nor excessive lustre; there can be no lofty opinions of him; nor can flatterers exalt him with inordinate praises, because what is done well by such an administrative council cannot possibly be ascribed to the president alone. . . . Moreover, when the people see that this administrative council has been established by decree of the Monarch with the concurrence of the Senate, they will remain meek, and put away any hope of receiving aid in their rebellions from the ecclesiastical order.[1]

Behind the author's characteristic references to papal pretensions (quite irrelevant in a Russian context) plainly lay Peter's apprehension that a new patriarch should become a focus of opposition to his regime. In the light of the very recent revelations of the Aleksei conspiracy, the fear, and Prokopovich's evocation of the 'great calamities that [would] thereby ensue', seem partly justified. However, the accuracy of their prognostications is not in question, but rather the evidence the whole passage provides of the motives underlying Peter's reorganization of the administration of the church. And compared with this passage, the eight other 'weighty reasons' adduced in Part I of the *Ecclesiastical Regulation* appear more or less incidental, or merely rhetorical.

Thus: '1. In the first place, truth is more certainly discovered by a council than by a single person. . . . 2. And so far as there is more certain knowledge, there is greater power to act. For men are more inclined to accept and obey the decision of a council than the decree of a single person. The power of monarchs is autocratic, which God himself commands us to obey in good conscience: yet monarchs have their advisers, not only for the sake of better ascertaining the truth, but in order that disobedient subjects should not slander them by saying that they rule by force and caprice rather than by justice and truth. How much more so, then, should this be the case in church government, where the power is not monarchical and the ruler is forbidden to lord it over the clergy. . . .[2] 3. . . . it should be noted that a college is not some faction secretly joined to promote its own interest, but rather is composed of persons gathered together for the common good by order of the Autocrat after consultation with his advisers'.[3]

[1] For the whole passage, see Verkhovskoi, ii, pp. 31–32.

[2] Prokopovich alludes perhaps to I Peter 5:1–3: 'So I exhort the elders. . . . Tend the flock that is your charge, not by constraint but willingly, not for shameful gain but eagerly, not by domineering over those in your charge but by being examples to the flock'.

[3] Verkhovskoi, ii, pp. 29–30.

Points 4, 5, 6, and 8 refer in the same vein to the practical and moral improvements that were supposed to derive from collegial, as opposed to patriarchal, government. (Again, the accuracy or fairness of the implied criticisms of previous patriarchal administrations is not at issue here.) Thus: '4. . . . when one man rules, procrastinations and interruptions in business often occur because of the overwhelming demands made on the ruler or because of his sickness or infirmity; and when he dies business stops altogether. It is otherwise with an administrative council; if one member is absent . . . business continues its uninterrupted course. 5. . . . in a College there is no room for partiality, intrigue, or bribery: . . . should one member be prejudiced for or against a person on trial, the second, third, and so on will be free of any such prejudice. How could bribery prevail when matters are decided not arbitrarily but only after regular and serious consideration? For any individual member will be wary lest he be unable to show good cause for his opinion and so be suspected of having taken a bribe. This would be particularly true if the College were composed of persons who could not possibly conspire in secret, that is, of persons of different rank and station: bishops, archimandrites, igumens, and leading members of the secular clergy. . . . 6. Similarly, a College enjoys greater freedom of mind to administer justice, for unlike a single ruler it need not fear the wrath of the mighty: to put pressure on many persons . . . it is not so easy as on one man. . . . 8. Church and State will further profit from such an administrative council because not only each of its members, but the president himself, is liable to the judgment of his brothers, that is of the College itself, in case of notable transgression. This is not what happens when one Supreme Pastor rules, for he is unwilling to be tried by his subordinate bishops. . . . Hence it would be necessary to summon a general council to try him, which can only be managed at great trouble and expense for the entire country; and at the present time (when the Eastern patriarchs live under the Turkish yoke, and the Turks are more than ever wary of our State) it would seem impossible'.[1]

The last of the nine reasons set forth in Part I states that 'such an administrative council will become a kind of school of church government', from which 'the most suitable members will deservedly advance to the episcopal rank'. This 'reason' is clearly rather a declaration of policy, a policy which was in fact partially observed by Peter's government in subsequent years when filling episcopal vacancies. Reason 9,

[1] *Ibid.*, pp. 30–32.

and Part I as a whole, conclude with the sentence: 'Thus in Russia, with God's help, grossness will soon disappear from the ecclesiastical order, and the best results may be hoped for'.[1] We are reminded that a simple disinterested desire to reform the church cannot be discounted in any analysis of Peter's measures.

It will have been noticed that various passages of Part I of the *Ecclesiastical Regulation* gave further expression to the view that the sovereign's power is unique, absolute, and universally obligating. Yet it will also have been noticed that, ironically, this 'autocratic monarch who need not account for his actions to anyone on earth' found it necessary to provide his subjects with a lengthy justification of his decision to establish an Ecclesiastical College and to abolish the patriarchate. It was perhaps an indication of Peter's awareness of the magnitude of the changes he proposed to make.

The *Ecclesiastical Regulation* was completed and ready to be revised, ratified, and promulgated by the beginning of 1720. Attached to the final page of the *Regulation*'s rough draft is a piece of paper on which its author, Prokopovich, has written: 'All this herein set down the All-Russian Monarch Himself, His Most Sacred Majesty the Tsar, was pleased to have read in his own presence, and to consider and to amend, this 11th day of February 1720; and then, by decree of His Majesty, the Most Reverend Bishops and Archimandrites, conjointly with the All-Ruling Senators, also heard it and, upon due consideration, amended it this 23rd day of February, *in confirmation whereof they have ratified it with their own signatures, as follow*. And for the immutable execution thereof, after the signatures of *the aforementioned* Ecclesiastical and Senatorial personages present, His Majesty the Tsar Himself was pleased to sign it with his own hand'.[2]

The amendments in Peter's hand in the rough draft of the *Regulation*, and the asterisks placed by him at various points in the margins of the draft, as well as the numerous alterations in Prokopovich's own hand,[3] confirm that the tsar carefully went over the text with its author and that together they made their final revision on (according to Prokopovich) 11 February 1720.[4] But there is no evidence that the 'Ecclesiastical and Senatorial personages' referred to were expected to consider this

[1] *Ibid.*, p. 33.

[2] *Ibid.*, p. 76, no. 248. Except for the words in italics, these two sentences form the concluding paragraph of the final version of the *Ecclesiastical Regulation*.

[3] See the rough draft of the *Regulation* printed in Verkhovskoi, ii, pp. 27–105, *passim*.

[4] Cf. Verkhovskoi, i, p. 161.

momentous document so carefully. On receipt of Peter's decree of 23 February the first secretary of the Senate was thereby ordered to 'notify the most reverend bishops and the Senate that this project [*proekt*] of an Ecclesiastical College, here enclosed, is to be reviewed tomorrow'; the original decree, preserved in the Senate's archives, is minuted: 'Received this date [i.e. 23 February]'.[1] On 24 February, however, the Senate was sent another decree by Peter, commanding that 'whereas yesterday I heard from you that the project of an Ecclesiastical College was reviewed and everything favourably received by both you and the bishops, it is therefore appropriate that it be signed by you and the bishops and then confirmed by my signature'; this second decree was 'Received 25 February'.[2] In other words, it would appear that the senators and bishops who happened to be in St. Petersburg on 23 February were convened and heard the *Regulation* read to them, after which they amended and approved it, in the space of one, or at the most two days – even though the contents of the document were previously unknown to them and would have required, at a conservative estimate, some three hours merely to read aloud at a brisk, uninterrupted pace.[3] But of course the senators, not to mention 'the bishops', were not expected to have substantial objections to a 'project' that was communicated to them by the tsar himself. There is no doubt that at least Yavorskii, the first of the ecclesiastical persons to sign the *Regulation*, was opposed to the abolition of the patriarchate.

[1] *ZAP*, no. 83 (p. 81). See also *SIRIO*, xi, p. 400; and Runkevich, *op. cit.*, p. 120.

[2] *ZAP*, no. 84 (p. 81). Also *SIRIO*, xi, p. 400; and Runkevich, *op. cit.*, p. 121.

[3] Verkhovskii's printed edition of the *Regulation*, corresponding almost exactly in length to the manuscript version read by the senators and bishops, occupies seventy-five quarto pages. Prokopovich himself, in his letter to Markovich of 10 May 1720, claims that the draft of the *Regulation* 'was read [by the senators and bishops, or to them] twice in the course of two days', and that 'several new amendments' were then added (letter printed in Chistovich, *Feofan Prokopovich*, p. 47; also Verkhovskoi, i, p. 161). But these 'new amendments' were confined to a few supplementary notes to points 5, 6, 7, and 8 of the section concerning 'Lay Persons' (Runkevich, *op. cit.*, p. 21; cf. Verkhovskoi, ii, pp. 68–70), and did not in any way substantially alter the *Regulation*. Runkevich also suggests (*op. cit.*, p. 120, n. 4; p. 121, n. 5) that Peter's first order to the Senate, although dated 23 February, was in fact written on the night of 22 February; that the *Regulation* was then read in the Senate on the 23rd and again on the 24th (as Prokopovich, in the letter just referred to, implied); and that Peter's second order, dated 24 February, was actually written late that night, so that 'yesterday' referred to 'today [i.e. the 24th]'. The point of Runkevich's exercise, apparently, is to prolong the period of time that Peter might possibly have given the senators and bishops to read, review, and approve the draft *Regulation*. But there is no denying that Peter's order to sign it was received in the Senate on 25 February. Clearly, there had been little time (a maximum of two days) for those present seriously to consider its contents (cf. Verkhovskoi, i, pp. 161–162).

Nevertheless he was considered by Peter to have 'reviewed and favourably received' the document.

Apart from Yavorskii and Prokopovich himself, the first ecclesiastical signatories of the two final drafts of the *Regulation* included Theodosius Yanovskii, archimandrite of the Alexander-Nevskii monastery in St. Petersburg and an enthusiastic supporter of Peter's policies;[1] Bishop Pitirim of Nizhnii-Novgorod, the scourge of the schismatics and another of Peter's close clerical collaborators;[2] the aged bishops of Tver and Smolensk, who both died within little more than a year; Bishop Aaron of Karelia, Peter's appointee and *de facto* bishop of St. Petersburg; and Archimandrite Antonii of the Zlatoustovskii monastery, who in 1718 had been appointed by Peter to administer schismatic affairs.[3] The roll of the 'Ecclesiastical and Senatorial personages present' was completed with the signatures of seven (of a total of thirteen) senators, followed by that of Peter. The formality of signing the *Regulation* appears to have taken place in the Senate on 27 February.[4]

Peter's second order to the Senate, that of 24 February, had concluded: 'it would be best that two [copies of the *Regulation*] should be signed, one to remain here [in St. Petersburg] and the other to be sent for signing by the other bishops'. Accordingly, two copies of Prokopovich's rough draft were made and each was signed, as described above, by the senators and bishops and archimandrites who were present in St. Petersburg on 27 February; and by a further decree of the tsar, issued by the Senate on 9 March, Lt-Col. Davydov was commissioned to take the second copy to Moscow, where he was to collect the signatures of the local bishops. Simultaneously, decrees were sent by the Senate to those same bishops (of Krutitsy, Rostov, Suzdal', and Kolomna), requiring that they and the archimandrites and igumens of their dioceses should go to Moscow to sign the *Regulation* by 1 May, 'without fail'. Davydov was told by the Senate that on his arrival in

[1] For a résumé of Yanovskii's career, see below, pp. 166–169.

[2] For Pitirim, see below, p. 298.

[3] As mentioned above, p. 77. For Antonii, see also *Russkii biograficheskii slovar'*, ii, pp. 219–220. For the list of the original signatories of the *Regulation*, see Verkhovskoi, ii, p. 19. Runkevich also provides a list (*op. cit.*, p. 122), but includes in it the name of Archimandrite Ioan of the Transfiguration monastery in Kazan'. Ioan may have been there in the Senate on 23–24 February (as Prokopovich indicates in his letter of 10 March to Markovich, cited above, when he refers to *three* archimandrites being present); however, Ioan was not among the original signatories of the *Regulation*, but rather was the first of five senior clergy who apparently signed it soon after the eight original signatories had done so (see Verkhovskoi, ii, p. 19). Three of these five clerics (not including Ioan) were among the first eleven members of the Ecclesiastical College.

[4] Verkhovskoi, i, p. 164; Runkevich, *op. cit.*, p. 122.

Moscow he was to communicate his orders to Archimandrite Antonii of the Zlatoustovskii monastery, now head of the Prikaz of Ecclesiastical Affairs, and to Vice-Governor Voeikov, who were to cooperate with him in collecting the signatures. 'And when [a bishop or an archimandrite] has signed, having read the *Regulation* and the Tsar's decree, he is to return to his place'. If a bishop were ill and unable to travel to Moscow, Davydov was to go to him to obtain his signature and those of the heads of the local monasteries. Whoever refused to sign was to be reported to the Senate by name. It was indicated that Davydov was to treat the matter with urgency. The summonses to the bishops were sent in specially prepared packets labelled 'Edict to the Most Reverend ... concerning urgent state business'.[1]

Davydov arrived in Moscow on 4 April. On 6 April the metropolitan of Krutitsy and the archimandrites of the Moscow diocese signed the *Regulation* presented to them; and on 3 May the bishops of Rostov, Suzdal', Kolomna, and thirty-four archimandrites and igumens of their own and the Ryazan' dioceses signed. In June the Ukrainian bishops (of Chernigov and Pereyaslavl'; the see of Kiev was still vacant) and senior monastic clergy were ordered by the Senate, through Davydov, to report to Moscow for signing by 1 September; they did so on 6 October. Davydov then went south to collect the signatures of the bishops and archimandrites of Kazan', Astrakhan, and Vyatka at Kazan', where they had been told to assemble; and then, in November, north to collect those of the bishops and archimandrites of the Vologda, Kholmogory, and Ustyug dioceses at Vologda. He arrived back in St. Petersburg on 31 December and on 4 January submitted his copy of the *Regulation*, heavy with some eighty-seven signatures, to the Senate. Forty-eight archimandrites, fifteen igumens, five priests, and all nineteen incumbent bishops – with the exception of the metropolitan of Tobol'sk, who had been considered too far away to reach within the permitted time – had signed.[2]

Yet it would be unreasonable to deduce from this fact that the eighty-seven clerical signatories had approved of the *Ecclesiastical Regulation* presented to them by the tsar's representatives,[3] just as it

[1] The decree of 9 March is printed in *ZAP*, no. 87 (p. 83). For further details, see Runkevich, *op. cit.*, pp. 125–127.

[2] For details of the way in which the signatures were collected, drawn (apparently) from Davydov's reports to the Senate, see Runkevich, *op. cit.*, pp. 128–132.

[3] *Pace* Runkevich: 'The new form of central administration of the Russian church was thus accepted by the entire Russian church, in the person of its leaders, without a single objection ... an absolute majority ... unanimous ...' (*op. cit.*, p. 133).

would clearly be wrong to deduce from the appearance of Yavorskii's signature that he was in favour of it. It is by no means certain that the signatories had been given leisure to consider the document's contents: Davydov's successive reports simply state that the various clergy, 'having heard it, signed it'. Moreover, those among the signatories who may have opposed the abolition of the patriarchate no doubt swallowed their indignation after deciding, quite understandably, that in view of their experience of twenty-five years of Peter's rule gestures of defiance would be utterly futile. Memories of the Aleksei trial were fresh. As the *Ecclesiastical Regulation* itself confidently predicted, 'when the people see that this administrative council has been established by decree of the Monarch with the concurrence of the Senate, they will remain meek'.

For his part, Peter had obviously been concerned that the *Regulation* should appear to have the sanction of the church. However, he was not prepared to summon a council for that purpose, but rather had resorted to the methods described. And once the signatures had been collected, the project was to proceed swiftly. Among the papers of Peter's cabinet dating from late 1720 or early 1721 has been found a note which reads: 'About the Ecclesiastical College, here'.[1] According to a senatorial register of 'points' submitted for the tsar's resolution on 16 January 1721, the first concerned 'the signatures on the *Ecclesiastical Regulation* of the bishops and archimandrites'; Peter's reply was to order that a *zhalovan'e* – in this context a 'charter' or 'decree' – was to be prepared and submitted to him.[2] Accordingly, on 25 January a manifesto announcing the establishment of an Ecclesiastical College was promulgated, Prokopovich's rough draft of which had been corrected by Theodosius Yanovskii and in two places amended by Peter himself. In the margin opposite the words 'and seeing no better means to this end [i.e. the reform of the "ecclesiastical order"] . . . we hereby establish an Ecclesiastical College', Peter had written: 'because this is too great a burden for a single man whose power is not hereditary'. The amendment was duly incorporated into the final version of the document. And the last sentence of the final version of the manifesto also originated as an amendment by Peter to the draft: 'Upon taking office all members of this College must make an oath or promise on the Holy Gospels according to the form hereto affixed'.[3]

An oath was duly drawn up, based largely on the oath included in the *General Regulation* (*Generalnyi Reglament*), which by a decree of May 1719 was to be taken by all senators, members of colleges, and

[1] *ZAP*, no. 98 (p. 88). [2] *ZAP*, no. 100 (p. 89). [3] Verkhovskoi, ii, pp. 6–7.

provincial governors.[1] But there were appropriate differences between the two oaths. It was Prokopovich who introduced into the draft of the former a sentence which reads: 'I acknowledge on oath that the Supreme Judge [*Krainii Sud'ya*] of this Ecclesiastical College is the Monarch of All Russia himself, our Most Gracious Sovereign'.[2] The sentence was incorporated into the final draft of the oath, which was signed by Yavorskii, Prokopovich, Theodosius Yanovskii, and the eight other clerics who had been appointed members of the new College.[3] And their subscription to an oath which contained this sentence as well as a promise to 'defend unsparingly all the powers, rights, and prerogatives (or privileges) belonging to the High Autocracy of His Majesty' and to Peter's 'august and lawful successors', may be taken as marking the formal end of the independence of the Russian church and the beginning of its modern history. For Yavorskii, in particular, it marked the end of a road which had led from Kiev and the Jesuit colleges of Poland to his largely self-imposed isolation in his episcopal house in Moscow.

IV

STEFAN YAVORSKII: AN OBITUARY

Following Yavorskii's death late in the autumn of 1722, a contemporary panegyrist, Cyril Florinskii, prefect of the Moscow academy, acclaimed him as 'theologorum Phoenix, solidae eruditionis vertex'. 'In the Russian firmament', proclaimed his friend Archbishop Antonii of Chernigov in language typical of Yavorskii's own,

> he remains in the forefront, appearing as the morning star amidst the clouds. The Russian church was watered and irrigated by the abundant dew of his many labours and by his wise teaching; the ark of the Russian church, steered by Stefan's prudent administration, was not intimidated by a thousand Scyllae and Charybdes. Everyone in Russia, in their hearts and aloud, esteemed him as a virtuous, honourable, and worthy Guardian.

Yavorskii's contemporary biographer, in an appendix to the 1729 edition of *The Rock of the Faith*, called him a 'Pillar of the Eastern church, a true zealot . . . the model of a good pastor, a fine theologian'.[4]

[1] For the decree of May 1719, see *ZAP*, no. 72 (pp. 72–73). For the close correspondence between the oath of the Ecclesiastical College and that in the *General Regulation*, compare the text of the former, printed in Verkhovskoi, ii, pp. 10–11, with that of the latter, in *ZAP*, no. 400 (see pp. 483–484).

[2] Verkhovskoi, ii, p. 11, n. 23.

[3] *Ibid.*, p. 8.

[4] Quotations from Morev, *op. cit.*, pp. ii–iii.

But in view of the events of Yavorskii's career, a perhaps deliberate note of ambiguity is discernible in all these praises. For it is clear that by the time of his death Yavorskii, at least, regarded himself as a failure.

On 31 December 1720 (the day on which Davydov returned to St. Petersburg with the signed *Regulation*) Peter had ordered Yavorskii 'to proclaim the bishop of Pskov [Prokopovich], archbishop, and archimandrite Theodosius [Yanovskii], archbishop of Novgorod. Let it be done tomorrow.'[1] In January 1721 Yanovskii and Prokopovich were appointed by Peter, respectively, first and second vice-presidents of the new Ecclesiastical College. Yavorskii was named president, presumably to ensure an orderly transition from the old to the new regime. And he appears to have resisted his latest commission, as he had resisted his consecration as metropolitan of Ryazan' some twenty years before, and again to no avail. It has been suggested that for his part Yavorskii finally accepted the presidency in the hope that thereby he would be able to combat the 'protestant' influences emanating from his two vice-presidents.[2]

But having accepted the presidency, Yavorskii subsequently took little part in the Synod's proceedings. The Synod's journal for 1721 mentions him as present at meetings, which by statute were held three times a week, only twenty times in the whole of that year.[3] Indeed, in the late spring of 1721 Yavorskii proposed by letter to the Synod that contrary to its resolution of 21 May, made in his absence, the practice of commemorating the 'Eastern Patriarchs' in church services, which had been followed in Russia throughout the years of the *mezhdupatriarshestvo*, should be continued. In reply, the Synod on 12 June resolved to send to its president (who was back in Moscow) the tsar's decree forbidding him to 'communicate to anyone' his 'opinion' on the subject, his colleagues having rejected it as 'being neither weighty, nor forceful, nor beneficial, but rather most oppositional and disruptive of the peace of the church and harmful to the tranquility of the state'. The Synod somewhat justifiably objected to the fact that in February 1721 Yavorskii had formally acquiesced in the original resolution of the matter 'without indicating his contrary opinion' and then had waited until four months later to reveal it.[4]

In 1722 Yavorskii was alleged to have remarked to one Varlaam Levin, a monk from Penza who was tried by the Privy Chancellery

[1] *OAS*, i, appendix I, no. 15 (col. x).

[2] Korolev, *op. cit.*, p. 421.

[3] Runkevich, *op. cit.*, p. 167.

[4] *PSP*, i, no. 106 (pp. 143–147); no. 118 (pp. 165–166).

and executed that year for publicly calling Peter the Antichrist, that Peter was 'not the Antichrist, but an iconoclast'. 'Iconoclast', as we have seen, was a contemporary Russian euphemism for 'Protestant'. In July 1722 four members of the Synod visited Yavorskii in Moscow and informally tried him, by the side of his sickbed, for having made the remark. He denied the allegation.[1] And on 27 July he wrote a long apologetic letter to Peter which reads in part: 'I have waited not a little time to have an audience of Your Majesty. . . . and to lay my forlorn petition before your paternal mercy. For how many years have I worked for you and never transgressed your commands. . . . Now, as Your Majesty's face has been turned from me, I say in truth that I grow weak from grief and my illness worsens without surcease. Where are your former mercies, Lord! Why this change? . . . for my guilt, falling at Your Majesty's feet, I ask your merciful pardon'.[2] In August he composed a most pathetic poem of farewell to his books, three-quarters of which were in Latin.[3] Four months later he died.

Bookish, sickly, indecisive, a Latinizer, Yavorskii, perhaps without ever realizing it, was doomed to frustration from the outset of his long career as temporary head of the church. He had proved unsuited to the rigours of the politics of church reform under Peter. For all his compromises and intermittent acts of opposition, he had lived to witness both the abolition of the patriarchate and the triumph of 'protestantism' as personified by Feofan Prokopovich.

[1] See Runkevich, *op. cit.*, p. 169.

[2] Yavorskii's letter is printed in Chistovich, *Feofan Prokopovich*, pp. 108–111.

[3] Transliterated Slavonic and Latin versions of the poem are printed in Consett, *op. cit.*, pp. 447–451. On Yavorskii's library, see Lewitter, 'Peter the Great, Poland, and the Westernization of Russia', pp. 500–502.

CHAPTER FOUR

Politics and Administrative Reform, 1721–1725

In accordance with the tsar's manifesto of 25 January 1721 the Ecclesiastical College was ceremoniously opened, and then promptly renamed the Most Holy All-Ruling Synod, on 14 February; and its governing statute, the *Ecclesiastical Regulation*, was first printed the following September. The task of the present chapter is two-fold: to identify, in section I, the first members of the Holy Synod and to discuss their relations with Tsar Peter, and so to begin, as a link with the preceding chapter, an account of the politics of church reform during the last four years of Peter's reign; and secondly, to describe – in the next four sections – how the Synod coped with the numerous administrative problems with which it was faced but which were not anticipated in its governing statute. The Synod, it may be said, was commissioned by Peter both to reform and to administer the church; and it is the record of the Synod's attempt to discharge the latter commission, a task for which the *Ecclesiastical Regulation* provided it with little or no guidance, that is examined in these pages.

I

THE FINAL PHASE OF THE POLITICS OF CHURCH REFORM UNDER PETER (ii), 1721–1725

According to the *Ecclesiastical Regulation*, the members of the projected Ecclesiastical College were to be 'of various ranks: bishops, archimandrites, igumens, and archpriests – of whom three shall be bishops'.[1] In his manifesto of 25 January 1721 Peter announced that the College 'shall be composed of one president [*prezydent*], two vice-presidents [*vitse-prezydenty*], four councillors [*sovetniki*], and four assessors [*assessory*]': a total of eleven members, each of whom was to have one vote in deciding matters brought before the College.[2] In the latter part of January the first eleven members of the College were duly appointed – most of them directly by the tsar; a few on the recommendation of

[1] Verkhovskoi, ii, p. 72. [2] *Ibid.*, p. 7.

the College's president and vice-presidents – and their annual stipends specified;[1] and on 27 January the members took their oath of office.[2] They included the prescribed three bishops (Yavorskii of Ryazan', president; Yanovskii of Novgorod, first vice-president; Prokopovich of Pskov, second vice-president), four archimandrites, one archpriest, one priest who in due course became an archpriest, and two monks who were soon promoted to the rank of igumen.

The careers of Yavorskii and Prokopovich have been recounted in the preceding chapters. Theodosius Yanovskii should now be more fully identified. For his nomination to the see of Novgorod (then the richest and most prestigious in Russia) and his contemporaneous appointment as first vice-president of the Ecclesiastical College were the fruits of a long career of faithful service to the tsar; and together with Feofan Prokopovich, Yanovskii was to dominate the Synod during the first four years of its existence.

He was yet another son of the polonized lesser nobility of southwestern Russia and was born sometime in the 1650's.[3] From 1663 to 1673 he was a student at the Kiev academy. It is not known whether, like so many of his contemporaries, he went abroad to complete his education. In later life he seems to have enjoyed the reputation of a scholar, though he has left no literary evidence from which we may judge; and it is assumed by the authorities that intellectually he was not of a class with Yavorskii and Feofan Prokopovich.

While still a young man Yanovskii became a monk of the Moscow Simonov monastery, from which, in the wake of an altercation with his superiors, he was sent in irons to the Trinity-Sergiev monastery. There he attracted the favour of the archimandrite, Job; and when Job became metropolitan of Novgorod in 1697, he took Yanovskii with

[1] See Runkevich, *op. cit.*, pp. 134, 136–137. The president of the Ecclesiastical College was assigned an annual stipend of 3000R; the two vice-presidents, 2500R; the four councillors, 1000R; and the four assessors, 600R. The stipends were to be drawn from the revenues of the members' respective diocese, monastery, or church; but in January 1724 Peter conceded that state funds could be used to make up deficiencies from those sources, and that members' stipends need not include the fees they received for conducting services or the donations they received from their home institution (see *PSZ*, vi, no. 3712 [p. 312]; *PSP*, i, no. 225 [p. 279]; *PSZ*, vii, no. 4407 [pp. 198–199]; *PSP*, iv, no. 1158 [pp. 2–3]).

[2] As described above, pp. 161–162.

[3] For Yanovskii's biography, see the article with full bibliography by B. Titlinov in the *Russkii biograficheskii slovar'*, xxv (St. Petersburg, 1913), pp. 346–357; Chistovich, *Feofan Prokopovich*, pp. 74–87, 112–118, 159 ff.; Runkevich, *op. cit.*, pp. 177–206; and I. Ya. Moroshkin, 'Feodosii Yanovskii, arkhiepiskop novgorodskii', *Russkaya starina*, July 1887, pp. 1–34: October 1887, pp. 31–44: November 1887, pp. 273–296.

him. By 1704 the latter had become archimandrite of the Khutyn monastery and Job's principal assistant in the administration of the diocese. It was in Novgorod, moreover, that Yanovskii first became known to the tsar, who in the course of his military campaigns was often in the area. In Peter's campaign journal of 1704 it is recorded that 'on 7 May the Great Sovereign was pleased to go by boat with his suite, and with the metropolitan of Novgorod and other church dignitaries, from St. Petersburg to the new fortress on the island of Kotlin . . . [where] for three days there were festivities'.[1] No doubt Yanovskii was conspicuous among the clergy who attended the tsar on this occasion.

In the years that followed he came to play an increasingly important role in the ecclesiastical affairs of Russia. Both Metropolitan Job and the tsar appear to have credited him with exceptional administrative ability, a certain love of learning, and a willingness conscientiously to carry out orders. For his part, Yanovskii seems to have been energetic in fulfilling his duties, practical, well-versed in the important theological questions of the day, and ambitious. He was, evidently, a man who could sense which way the wind was blowing: who could move with the times. And Peter naturally made use of such men. In 1708 Yanovskii was sent to supervise the patriarchal press in Moscow, and soon thereafter was appointed 'ecclesiastical judge' in St. Petersburg with special responsibility for building churches and nominating clergy for the new capital and for the newly-conquered towns of the Baltic region. He had become, in effect, the head of a new diocese; and while in theory he remained subordinate to Metropolitan Job of Novgorod, in practice he was independent both of Job and of Stefan Yavorskii, the nominal head of the church.

In 1712 Yanovskii was named archimandrite of the Alexander-Nevskii monastery in St. Petersburg (founded 1710), which in 1715 was designated by Peter the training centre of the higher clergy of Russia.[2] In 1710, as we have seen, Yanovskii officiated at the wedding of Tsarevna Anna with her Lutheran duke. Moreover, he helped to compose the episcopal oath of 1716 and the manifesto of 25 January 1721. Indeed, after 1718 he exercised greater authority over the affairs of the church than did Yavorskii, whom he had openly opposed as early as 1712, when he participated in the Senate's condemnation of the metropolitan of Ryazan' for denouncing the activities of the fiscals. In 1714 Yanovskii had openly defended the heretic Tveritinov against Yavorskii's charges. Voicing the conservative reaction to Yanovskii's

[1] *PiB*, iii, pp. 614–615. [2] See above, p. 140.

rise to prominence, Tsarevich Aleksei was alleged to have said that 'because my father loves him, he imposes Lutheran ways on the people and decides everything'.[1]

On Yavorskii's death in November 1722 Yanovskii inherited his house in Moscow[2] but not his title of president of the Most Holy All-Ruling Synod. In matters of protocol, however, he now took precedence over all other bishops.[3] And although during the first four years of the Synod's existence he conceded the initiative in important business to Feofan Prokopovich, who was at least twenty years his junior and probably a much cleverer man, Yanovskii did play a consistently active role in Synodal affairs. Together he and Prokopovich formed a channel through which Peter frequently communicated his wishes to the Synod as a whole. In 1724 Yanovskii collaborated with Peter in drawing up the coronation rite for Empress Catherine,[4] a sign that he remained in high favour.

Yet it was during these years of his glory that the seeds of his fall were sown. The Synod's impatience with what it regarded as secular interference in its affairs or as affronts to its dignity – an impatience that was manifested (it will be seen) from the moment the Synod opened its doors – has been attributed largely to Yanovskii's influence.[5] In 1724 he was accused of misappropriating the large revenues of the Novgorod diocese. While Peter lived, nothing came of the accusation. But after the tsar's death in January 1725 the charge was revived. For in April 1725 Yanovskii publicly proclaimed that he was greater than Prince Menshikov and deserved equal access to the empress (Menshikov, Peter's life-long favourite, was the dominant figure at court during the reign of Peter's wife Catherine, 1725–1727); and Yanovskii's subsequent misfortunes were popularly ascribed to Menshikov's resentment of this 'insolence'.[6]

The immediate chain of events leading to Yanovskii's downfall began on 16 April 1725, when the Synod met to discuss arrangements for holding a requiem for the dead Tsar Peter. At the meeting Yanovskii angrily denounced the 'tyranny' whereby the secular authorities could order the Synod to say prayers. The other members did not share this interpretation of the government's request for a requiem, whereupon Yanovskii stated that he would cooperate in the matter only out

[1] Quoted in Chistovich, *Feofan Prokopovich*, p. 78.
[2] *SIRIO*, x, p. 509; also Runkevich, *op. cit.*, p. 177.
[3] Titlinov, 'Yanovskii', p. 352.
[4] *PSP*, iv, no. 1253 (pp. 107–109).
[5] Titlinov, 'Yanovskii', p. 353.
[6] See Consett, *op. cit.*, p. 115, note *a*.

of fear of being punished if he did not. But 'will God hear such prayers?' he challenged his colleagues, and on the day of the service refused to dine with the empress.[1] On 27 April he was arrested. Several days later the Prussian ambassador informed his king that 'the Archbishop of Novgorod, the first ecclesiastic of the realm, a conceited and very rich man, but foolish, is caught up in a very dangerous investigation; according to rumour, he has committed *crimes de haute trahison*'. The ambassador reported that it had been Yanovskii's intention 'to have himself made patriarch by unobtrusive means, to which end he proposed in the Synod . . . that the president [Yavorskii] was now dead, that the Emperor [Peter] had been a tyrant, that the Empress [Catherine I] could not preside over the church, and that, consequently, it was now for him to be president of the Synod; and he is said to have uttered many other seditious remarks'. But the Synod, the ambassador further reported, 'declared to him that they wished to hear nothing about his presidency, that what the Emperor had been [i.e. Supreme Judge of the Synod], the Empress now was, and that without her command they would do nothing. I am assured', the ambassador concluded, 'that he has been taken to the fortress and placed under guard for his madness, and that he now makes every conceivable gesture of submission in an effort to obtain his pardon, in which he is unlikely to succeed'.[2] He did not succeed. Yanovskii was publicly condemned on 12 May, having been denounced by Prokopovich and his colleagues in the Synod, the charges against him including treason and misappropriation of diocesan funds.[3] He was sentenced to life imprisonment in a monastery in Karelia, where less than a year later he died (5 February 1726).

As for the remaining eight members of the original Ecclesiastical College, Gabriel Buzhinskii, the first of the four councillors, was briefly identified in the previous chapter.[4] At the time of his appointment he was archimandrite of the Ipatskii monastery in Moscow. An outstanding preacher and skilled editor and translator, Buzhinskii was named 'protector' of the Moscow academy and press in 1721. On 20 March 1722 he was appointed by Peter 'to the place vacated by the present archimandrite of the Trinity monastery, who for many irregular actions has come under suspicion';[5] and in 1724 was proposed

[1] Titlinov, 'Yanovskii', p. 354.
[2] *SIRIO*, xv, pp. 284–285: Mardefeld to the king, 4 May 1725.
[3] For Yanovskii's trial, see esp. Chistovich, *Feofan Prokopovich*, pp. 157–184.
[4] Above, pp. 129 f.
[5] *PSP*, ii, no. 493 (p. 142).

by his Synodal colleagues for the vacant see of Kazan'. He continued to occupy the positions of Synodal councillor, protector of the Moscow academy and press, and archimandrite of the prestigious and wealthy Trinity-Sergiev monastery, until Peter's death, indicating that he remained in favour. It has been said, with good reason, that 'apologists of the old ways linked his name with those of Yanovskii and Prokopovich as the principal activists in the church reform of the time'.[1] In fact, during the first years of its existence the Synod was entirely dominated by these three Ukrainians of the Kiev academy, all staunch supporters of Peter's regime.

Comparatively little is known about the other three councillors.[2] Archimandrite Peter Smelich of the Moscow Simonov monastery, who was born in Serbia, seems to have acquired some education and to have enjoyed the favour of both Peter and Catherine. His enthusiasm for the regime is perhaps suggested by the fact that he signed the *Ecclesiastical Regulation* twice, once in St. Petersburg and again in Moscow.[3] He also seems to have enjoyed the reputation of an able bureaucrat, for in 1723 he was placed in charge of the Synod's Moscow office.[4] Perhaps for this reason Peter did not nominate him to a bishopric, although his name was put forward by the Synod in 1722.[5] The third of the original councillors, Archimandrite Leonid of the Petrovskii monastery in Rostov (nothing is known of his earlier life), was made archbishop of Krutitsy by Peter in March 1722,[6] while the last of the original councillors, Archimandrite Ierofei Prilutskii of the Donskoi monastery in Moscow, was appointed archimandrite of the important Novospasskii monastery in July 1721. In June 1724 Prilutskii was left in charge of the Synod's Moscow office, and later that year was recommended by the Synod for the vacant see of Suzdal'; he failed, however, to secure the tsar's approval of his nomination.[7]

The four assessors of the original Ecclesiastical College included Ioann Semenov, archpriest of the St. Petersburg Trinity cathedral, who began his career as a parish priest in Moscow. In March 1722 he was appointed archpriest of the Spasskii cathedral in Moscow, a post which

[1] Chistovich, *Feofan Prokopovich*, p. 90. In 1726 Buzhinskii was named bishop of Tver'; but before he was consecrated he was reappointed to the Ryazan' see, where in 1727 he took up his duties and in 1731, died.

[2] For details, see Chistovich, *Feofan Prokopovich*, pp. 89–97, and Runkevich, *op. cit.*, pp. 209–219.

[3] See Verkhovskoi, ii, pp. 19, 22.

[4] *PSP*, iii, no. 1041 (pp. 76–77).

[5] *PSP*, ii, no. 338 (pp.1–2).

[6] *PSP* ii, no. 338 (pp. 1–2).

[7] *PSP*, iv, no. 1314 (pp. 146–147); also Runkevich, *op. cit.*, p. 122.

had been vacant since 1718 when its last incumbent, Tsarevich Aleksei's former confessor, was executed.[1] But in 1723 Semenov appears to have somehow vexed the tsar, and was transferred to an administrative post in the Moscow diocese; he was not reinstated as an assessor of the Synod until after Peter's death.[2] Another of the original assessors, Peter Grigor'ev, was a priest of the Sampsonov church at the time of his appointment: sometime later in 1721 he was named archpriest of the Peter–Paul cathedral in St. Petersburg;[3] and he served in the Synod without distinction throughout the whole of the period under discussion.

The third of the assessors appointed early in 1721 was a Phanariot Greek named Anastasios Kontoeidēs. Kontoeidēs had taken refuge in Russia with his patron, Dimitrii Kantemir, hospodar of Moldavia (1710–1711), after the Turkish defeat of the Russian army at the battle on the Pruth (summer 1711). Prior to that time Kontoeidēs had served the Russian ambassador in Constantinople, Count Tolstoi, and by his own account had once been a preacher to the patriarch of Constantinople. After 1711, having come to Russia, he tutored Kantemir's children (including the celebrated poet, Antiokh), taught theology for a time at the Moscow academy, and worked at the Moscow press. In January 1721 he was appointed to the Ecclesiastical College, although, as he later admitted, 'I could speak only a little Russian'.[4] In November 1721 Peter decreed that for his 'loyalty and service in Constantinople' Kontoeidēs was to receive the annual stipend of a councillor (1000R instead of 600R).[5] But it was not enough. In February 1722 the Greek humbly petitioned the Synod to be given the monastic rank of igumen, since according to the *Ecclesiastical Regulation* (as we have seen) members were to be chosen from among the bishops, archimandrites, igumens, and archpriests, and he was at present the only member 'without a title'. The Synod promptly granted his request, ordering that he be made a monk, and then igumen, of the small Tolgskii monastery near Yaroslavl';[6] and thereafter Kontoeidēs was known by his Russian name 'Afanasii [Athanasius]'. By 1724 he had become archimandrite of the Spasskii monastery in Yaroslavl'.[7] Among the voluminous published documents covering the first four years of the Synod's existence, Kontoeidēs' name appears only twice: once, when in response to a

[1] *PSP*, ii, no. 469 (p. 121).
[2] Chistovich, *Feofan Prokopovich*, p. 97.
[3] *PSP*, i, no. 324 (p. 378).
[4] Quoted in Chistovich, *Feofan Prokopovich*, p. 95.
[5] *PSP*, i, no. 298 (p. 350).
[6] *PSP*, ii, no. 401 (p. 55).
[7] See *PSP*, iv, no. 1304 (p. 137).

report submitted by him in August 1721 the Synod took action against the few Franciscan friars serving the Catholic community in Russia, and a second time when in December 1725 he was named a Synodal councillor.[1]

The last of the Synod's original assessors was the priest-monk Varlaam Ovsyanikov, who in March 1721 was made igumen of the minor Ugreshskii monastery.[2] Ovysanikov was also appointed the first 'chief secretary [*obersekretar*]' of the Synod.[3] But in August 1721 the Synod resolved that Vice-President Yanovskii's personal secretary should become chief secretary;[4] while on 1 October the tsar himself, 'being present in the Synod', ordered that Timothy Palekhin, an official of the Chancellery for (army) Recruitment Affairs, should be named to the post.[5] Naturally Peter's will prevailed, and by a resolution of 1 January 1722 the Synod ratified Palekhin's appointment.[6] It was a defeat both for Yanovskii personally and for the principle of exclusive clerical rule; for although Palekhin was not made a member of the Synod itself, but only chief secretary, nonetheless a layman, one of the tsar's own *prikaznye lyudi*, had been placed in a key position within the Synodal administration. As for Ovsyanikov, sometime later in 1722 he was arrested; and in December 1723 Peter informed the Synod that an investigation had shown him to be guilty of 'considerable crimes, for which he must be tried. Therefore order him to be deprived of his priestly and monastic rank'.[7] In 1725 he was sentenced to life imprisonment in the Solovetskii monastery, where in 1732 he died.[8]

Thus during the first four years of the Synod's existence one of its original eleven members (Yavorskii) died, two others were sacked (the assessors Semenov, who was reinstated in 1725, and Ovsyanikov, whose fate was just described), and a fourth (the councillor Leonid) was promoted to the see of Krutitsy. During Peter's lifetime Yavorskii was not replaced as president of the Synod, indicating once again his deep distrust of all 'ambitious clerics'. Yet the *Ecclesiastical Regulation* stipulated that three of the Synod's members should be bishops; and in 1722–1723 a place in the Synod, and then a bishopric, were found for

[1] *PSP*, i, no. 176 (pp. 229–230); *Russkii biograficheskii slovar'*, ii, p. 371. He went on to become bishop of Vologda (October 1726) and then of Suzdal' (September 1735); he died in 1737.

[2] Chistovich, *Feofan Prokopovich*, p. 97.

[3] See *PSP*, i, no. 324 (p. 378).

[4] *PSP*, i, no. 190 (p. 245).

[5] *PSP*, ii, no. 337 (p. 1).

[6] *Ibid.*

[7] *PSP*, iii, no. 1150 (p. 231).

[8] Chistovich, *Feofan Prokopovich*, pp. 168–169, 179–180.

another of the tsar's long-standing ecclesiastical favourites, Theophylact Lopatinskii.[1]

On 21 February 1722 Peter abruptly ordered that Archimandrite Gennadii of the Chudov monastery in Moscow was to be sent to Archbishop Yanovskii of Novgorod and assigned by him to some other monastery.[2] Lopatinskii was given the Chudov monastery and appointed a councillor of the Synod. Then, in February 1723, Peter commanded the Synod to transfer Bishop Sylvester of Tver to the 'widowed' Ryazan' see (Yavorskii's old diocese), and 'to his place in Tver consecrate as bishop the Synodal councillor, Archimandrite Theophylact of the Chudov monastery, who is to remain in the Synod'.[3] It was a typical example of Peter's personal intervention in the matter of high ecclesiastical appointments, which had come to resemble a game of musical chairs. Lopatinskii's promotions could not have been sought by the Synod itself: his former opposition to Prokopovich was noted above;[4] and his name does not appear in a list of candidates for episcopal vacancies which the Synod submitted to the tsar in January 1722.[5] Moreover, after Peter's death, and in the wake of Yanovskii's fall (which Lopatinskii had helped to precipitate), it was Lopatinskii, and not Prokopovich, who became the dominant figure in the Synod until, with the accession of Empress Anna and her 'German' party, he in his turn fell, and went the way of all the 'ambitious clerics' of early eighteenth-century Russia. In 1735 he was sacked and arrested and in 1738 condemned and imprisoned. He was reprieved, after the accession of Elizabeth Petrovna and a reshuffle of influences at court, only a year before he died (1741). And with his death the last of the principal protagonists in the drama of Peter's church reform had passed from the scene.[6]

In sum, by June 1724, some six months before Peter's death, the Synod consisted of seven of its original eleven members plus four later appointments (i.e. Lopatinskii and three new assessors);[7] of five

[1] For Lopatinskii's earlier career, see above, p. 129. [2] *PSP*, ii, no. 421 (pp. 64–65).
[3] *PSP*, iii, no. 1011 (p. 45). [4] p. 134. [5] *PSP*, ii, no. 338 (pp. 1–2).
[6] See Titlinov, 'Lopatinskii', esp. pp. 459–464. For his rivalry with Prokopovich, see Chistovich's essay, *Feofan Prokopovich i Feofilakt Lopatinskii*.
[7] Two of the new assessors were appointed by the tsar in 1722. The first, the monk Feofil Krolik, who had done diplomatic service in Prague, was on his appointment to the Synod ordained successively deacon and priest and then, in 1723, was made archimandrite of the Chudov monastery in succession to Lopatinskii (*PSP*, ii, no. 403 [p. 56]; *PSP*, iv, no. 1304 [p. 137]). The second, Anastasius Mikhailov, was a Greek living in Moscow who signed himself without any ecclesiastical title whatever (he was, presumably, an ordinary

Ukrainians, three Great Russians, two Greeks, and one Serb; of ten monks (three were bishops and six were archimandrites) and a sole representative of the secular clergy (the Archpriest Peter).[1] As a group, therefore, they were hardly representative of the church they purported to rule. But this was, perhaps, inevitable. A truly representative body could not have been expected to carry out, much less to understand, the church reform that was called for in the *Ecclesiastical Regulation*. For the necessity of education, as we shall see in a following chapter, is the *Regulation*'s ruling idea; and 'learning [*uchenie*]' was one of the qualities that Peter required in potential members of his Synod. Among the clergy of contemporary Russia, however, 'learning' was the prerogative of monks, rather than secular priests; it was the prerogative of graduates of the Kiev academy, rather than those of the Moscow academy; it was the prerogative of immigrant Greeks and southern Slavs, rather than native Great Russians. In this sense it was inevitable that Peter should have entrusted the supreme administration of the reformed Russian church to a group of foreign monks.

But the dependence on foreigners (if not on monks) was meant to be temporary. When the educational reforms envisaged in the *Ecclesiastical Regulation* eventually took root, educated Great Russians would gradually replace the learned Ukrainians who had trained them. There is no indication, however, that the utter dependence of the members of the Synod on the tsar's good graces was intended to be anything other than a permanent feature of the new regime. Now, more than ever before in Russia, high ecclesiastical office and honours were in the gift of the tsar and his favourites, and a most dangerous precedent had been set. For under a less determined and reform-minded sovereign than Peter, ecclesiastical offices and honours, including membership of the Synod itself, were liable to become the object of intrigue and the reward of unscrupulous careerists.

It is not too much to say that Peter himself promoted to the Synod as enlightened a group of clerics as could be found in contemporary Russia. Prokopovich and Yavorskii, in particular, were churchmen of

refugee monk); he appears to have known no Russian and to have spent his time officially on leave (*PSP*, ii, no. 462 [p. 115]; *PSP*, iv, no. 1304 [p. 137]; see also Runkevich, *op. cit.*, p. 219). A third assessor appointed sometime before 1724 was Raphael Zuborovskii, another learned monk from Kiev, who by 1724 had also become archimandrite of the Kolyazin monastery (*PSP*, iv, no. 1304 [p. 137]; see also Smolitsch, *op. cit.*, pp. 415, 553, 570).

[1] *PSP*, iv, no. 1304 (p. 137).

European stature. Yet despite their learning and records of distinguished service – as teachers and preachers, as ecclesiastical administrators, or even as diplomats – the members of Peter's Synod did not enjoy his full confidence. Probably he doubted the depth of their loyalty to him and to his policies, and with some justification: Yavorskii's implacable, if discreet opposition was a known fact; the assessor Ovsyanikov was sacked and condemned for crimes against the state; and Yanovskii's true feelings were revealed very soon after Peter's death. It was for this reason, no doubt, that Peter declined to name a successor to Yavorskii as president of the Synod (Yanovskii was the obvious candidate); that he appointed a civil servant to be the Synod's chief secretary; and that, finally, he created the office of chief procurator of the Synod, entrusting it to one of his guards-officers. In view of the notoriety that this office later achieved, its origins should be carefully considered.

On 11 May 1722 Peter decreed that 'a good man, who shall be fearless and able to acquaint himself with the administration of Synodal affairs, is to be chosen from among the Officers and made Chief Procurator [*Ober-Prokuror*]'.[1] On 15 June the Senate informed the Synod that Colonel I. V. Boltin had been appointed to the post by the tsar, that an *Instruktsiya* had been drawn up for him in Peter's presence, and that the oath of office had been administered to him in the Senate.[2] On receipt of this information, the Synod requested the Senate to send it a copy of Boltin's instructions, so that it should know what duties he was to perform and be able to communicate this news to the subordinate departments of the ecclesiastical administration.[3]

According to Boltin's *Instruktsiya*, 'the Chief Procurator is obliged to sit in the Synod and strictly observe that the Synod fulfils its duties, and that all matters submitted for the Synod's consideration and resolution are dispatched truthfully, zealously, promptly, and in an orderly way....' The chief procurator was to keep a journal of the Synod's proceedings and was to see that the Synod's decisions were conscientiously carried out: 'he must determine who has received what [Synodal] decree, whether it was implemented within the prescribed time, and if it was not, he must discover the reason – an insurmountable obstacle, fear, or laziness – and promptly inform the Synod'. At the same time, the chief procurator was 'strictly to observe that the Synod conducts its business justly and impartially. And should he discover anything contrary to this [injunction], that very hour he must lay it

[1] *PSZ*, vi, no. 4001 (p. 676); *PSP*, ii, no. 609 (p. 266); *ZAP*, no. 136 (pp. 109–110).
[2] *PSP*, ii, no. 705 (p. 384). [3] *Ibid.*

openly before the Synod with a full explanation of how they, or certain among them, have not acted as they ought to have acted, in order that they might make amends. But should they not comply, that very hour he must protest, suspend business, and promptly report to Us [the tsar], if the matter is urgent; if it is not urgent, he will do as We command upon Our weekly or monthly visit to the Synod'. Yet regarding his duty promptly to inform the tsar of the Synod's misdemeanours, the chief procurator was enjoined to act 'discreetly and carefully, lest someone is wrongfully dishonoured'; and attached to the enjoinder is one of Peter's typical sanctions: 'should he submit an unjust report through fear, he will himself be punished according to the gravity of the matter'. 'Above all', stated Boltin's *Instruktsiya*, 'the Chief Procurator must observe that [the Synod] conducts its business truthfully and zealously. And should someone transgress in this, he is to be judged by the Synod; and all of the Procurator's reports are to be laid before the Synod in evidence, so that the trial may proceed accordingly'. The chief procurator was to be in charge of the Synod's chancellery. He was to be, concluded the tsar, 'Our eye and personal representative [*stryapchii*] for the affairs of the State'.[1]

It was suggested above that Peter created the office of chief procurator because he doubted the depth of the Synod's loyalty to him. Judging from Boltin's *Instruktsiya*, it is clear that Peter also distrusted the Synod's readiness to discharge its duties properly. But it should be pointed out that similar officials, under the overall supervision of a 'Procurator-General', had been attached to the civil colleges and even to the Senate, and that all these procurators were given instructions similar to Boltin's.[2] Indeed, in the closing years of his reign Peter

[1] *PSZ*, vi, no. 4036 (pp. 721–722); *PSP*, ii, no. 680 (pp. 356–358). Although in modern Russian the word *stryapchii* connotes an 'attorney' or 'advocate', in immediately pre-Petrine Russian it signified the holder of a lesser court rank who, according to Kotoshikhin, closely attended the tsar when he went to and from church, to the council chamber, when he dined or went hunting, when he went on campaign, etc.: in church the *stryapchii* might hold the tsar's cap and cloak, in the field, his breast plate, at other times, his sword etc. (see Kotoshikhin, *op. cit.*, p. 21). Thus in the above context Peter doubtless meant to indicate that the chief procurator was to be his personal representative in the Synod, as the old *stryapchii* was the tsar's personal attendant in the council chamber or in church; though the procurator did, to be sure, have the duty *inter alia* of an advocate – that is, of prosecuting erring members of the Synod.

[2] See the decree outlining the 'Duties of the Procurator-General' which was promulgated on 27 April 1722 (*PSZ*, vi, no. 3979 [pp. 662–664]). According to the Prussian ambassador, the regime of procurators was instituted by Peter primarily in an effort to expedite the transaction of business in the colleges, whose members, 'like lazy dogs who hunt badly, are much more eager to do nothing': in the Senate, the ambassador reported,

increasingly made use of officers and sometimes non-commissioned officers and even ordinary guardsmen in an attempt to enforce honest and efficient administration at every level of the government.[1] In this respect, therefore, the Synod had not been subjected by Peter to any special form of control.

Moreover, so far as the published record of its proceedings is any guide, during the first few years of the Synod's existence the interventions of its chief procurator were infrequent and largely perfunctory. In September 1722 Boltin reminded the Synod (his first recorded intervention) that according to the tsar's decree of February 1721 it was to meet every Monday, Wednesday, and Friday, and that on the other days of the week one of its councillors and two of its assessors were to meet to transact its business.[2] However, Boltin reported, while the Synod had duly met on the three appointed days, the prescribed meetings of three of its members had not taken place sufficiently often, 'whence proceed delays in the dispatch of business'; and Boltin respectfully suggested that in future the tsar's decree should be strictly observed. On 19 September, 'having heard' Boltin's report, the Synod resolved to mend its ways accordingly.[3] Thereafter the chief procurator's interventions were largely confined, as noted, to routine administrative matters.[4] And for his pains Boltin appears to have earned the Synod's gratitude: in January and again in September 1724 the Synod communicated to the Senate its 'opinion' that for his 'loyal service' Boltin should be given a bonus of 300R.[5] Not long after Peter's death Boltin retired. His successor, another guards-officer, served only for a brief period; and for the next eleven years (until 1740) the Synod managed to conduct its business without the help of a chief procurator.[6]

The Ecclesiastical College was formally opened on 14 February 1721. It is one of the few events not directly connected with either military

there were at the moment some 16,000 cases awaiting decision (Mardefeld's dispatch to the king of 20 March 1722, in *SIRIO*, xv, pp. 202–205).

[1] See M. Florinsky, *Russia: a History and an Interpretation* (New York, 1959–1961), i, p. 382.

[2] For the decree of February 1721, see *PSZ*, vi, no. 3742 (p. 358); and *PSP*, i, no. 6 (p. 35).

[3] For Boltin's report and the Synod's consequent resolution, see *PSP*, ii, no. 826 (pp. 518–519).

[4] See *PSP*, iii, no. 997 (pp. 30–31); no. 1070 (p. 106); also *PSP*, iv, no. 1282 (p. 122); no. 1299 (p. 133); no. 1372 (pp. 209–210); no. 1410 (p. 277); no. 1423 (p. 286).

[5] *PSP*, iv, no. 1160 (pp. 6–8); no. 1376 (pp. 221–222).

[6] See Smolitsch, *op. cit.*, p. 193. For the subsequent evolution of the office of chief procurator of the Synod into a virtual ministry of ecclesiastical affairs, see *ibid.*, pp. 194 ff.

or naval affairs that is described in the official history of Peter's reign: 'In the morning [of 14 February] His Majesty and the Ministers, as well as the bishops and other church dignitaries, attended the Liturgy in the Trinity cathedral [in St. Petersburg], at the conclusion of which a sermon was preached by the Archbishop of Pskov, Feofan Prokopovich, concerning the inauguration of the Ecclesiastical College. Thereafter everyone left the church and went to the Ecclesiastical College, where His Majesty ordained that this College was to be equal in dignity to the Senate and in church services was to be styled the Most Holy All-Ruling Synod'.[1] Similarly, the Synod's own journal opens with a brief account of how 'After services in the Trinity cathedral . . . His Most Illustrious Majesty the Tsar was pleased to attend in the Synod together with all the Ministers, at which time [seven] points were submitted to His Majesty by all the members of this Ecclesiastical Administration and to which His Majesty subscribed resolutions in His own hand'.[2] The first of the points submitted to Peter, as the official history indicates, concerned the correct formulation of the new body's title for use in church services, where it was to replace the traditional commemoration of the patriarch or – since the death of Patriarch Adrian in 1700 – of the 'Eastern Patriarchs': in response to the members' query, and having been assured that the title was 'not to be attributed to any one member in particular, but only to the body as a whole', Peter graciously conceded that the form 'the Most Holy Synod, or the Most Holy All-Ruling Synod', was henceforth to be used.[3]

His choice of words is highly significant. The term 'synod', widely used in both East and West to denote an assembly of clergy, was something of a neologism in Russian; perhaps it was first suggested to Peter by Feofan Prokopovich, who in Part 1 of the *Ecclesiastical Regulation* described the projected Ecclesiastical College as 'a permanent Synod or Sanhedrin [*Sinod ili Synedrion*]':[4] in any case, it served to distinguish the new body both from the new civil colleges and from church councils (*sobory*) of the traditional kind. The title 'Most Holy [*Svyateishii*]' had been formerly used only with reference to the patriarch, while 'All-Ruling [*Pravitel'stvuyushchii*]' was a distinction conferred by Peter on

[1] *Zhurnal*, ii, p. 151. The opening of the Synod is also described in the *St. Petersburg Gazette* of 15 February 1721 (see Pekarskii, *op. cit.*, ii. p. 536).

[2] *PSP*, i, no. 2 (p. 33).

[3] *PSP*, i, no. 3 (p. 33); also *PSZ*, vi, no. 3734 (p. 355).

[4] Verkhovskoi, ii, p. 29. Cf. also Prokopovich's letter to Markovich of 10 May 1720, in which he refers to the 'College or All-Ruling Synod provided for in the *Regulation*' (Chistovich, *Feofan Prokopovich*, pp. 46–50).

the Senate, alone among governmental institutions, to connote its all-embracing jurisdiction.[1] Thus Peter, by his resolution of the first of the points submitted to him on 14 February 1721, confirmed that the Synod was to succeed to the patriarchal dignity and was to be considered, as the official history puts it, 'equal in dignity to the Senate'. The degrading term 'Ecclesiastical College' was, accordingly, dropped from official usage.[2]

Peter's resolutions of the remaining six points submitted to him by the Synod on 14 February 1721 will be referred to in the following pages. But on 16 February, it should be noted, the Synod resolved to send copies of the resolutions to the Senate, the bishops, and to the archpriest of the Peter–Paul cathedral in St. Petersburg.[3] Indeed, Peter's resolutions of 14 February, together with the manifesto of 24 January 1721 and the *Ecclesiastical Regulation* itself, were to serve as the legal basis of the Synod's subsequent attempts to assert its jurisdiction over a wide range of matters. Thus the resolutions and the manifesto, as well as the Synod's oath of office, were included in all printed editions of the *Ecclesiastical Regulation*, the first of which was published at Peter's order on 16 September 1721.[4] And together these documents embodied the fundamental principles according to which the Russian church was to be governed for the next two centuries.

II

THE SYNOD TAKES OVER THE PATRIARCHAL DOMAIN

Late in February 1721 Metropolitan Ignatius of Krutitsy informed the Synod that on receiving his copy of the tsar's resolutions of 14 February he had ordered the Synod's name to be commemorated in church

[1] The title first appears in an edict of the Sovereign promulgated by the Senate on 10 January 1719 (*PSZ*, v, no. 3273 [p. 608]).

[2] Though in the first (September 1721) and all subsequent printed editions of the *Ecclesiastical Regulation* (the last of which was published in 1904) the term is retained, constituting a permanent reminder of the Synod's origins.

[3] *PSP*, ix, no. 3 (p. 34).

[4] *PSP*, i, no. 294 (p. 346); also T. A. Bykova and M. M. Gurevich, *Opisanie izdannii grazhdanskoi pechati (1708–1725)* (Moscow/Leningrad, 1955), no. 606 (pp. 335–338). See Verkhovskoi, i, pp. 206 ff. for the subsequent publishing history of the *Ecclesiastical Regulation*. It may be noted that a copy of the second edition of the *Regulation*, which was printed at Moscow on 14 June 1722 in the 'ecclesiastical type' (the first edition was printed at St. Petersburg in the new 'civil type'), is deposited in the Bodleian Library (Vet. H4e. 2.). It may also be noted that the only English translation of the *Regulation* and related documents, that by Thomas Consett, which was published in London in 1729, is based on the third Russian edition published at St. Petersburg on 18 January 1723.

services 'in the domain of the Most Holy Patriarch and in my own diocese'.[1] For the past two years, Ignatius reported, he had administered the ecclesiastical affairs of the patriarchate: was he to continue to do so?[2] In reply, the Synod ruled (8 March) that the patriarch's Ecclesiastical Prikaz was to be placed under the direction of a cleric appointed by the Synod, and that the Prikaz's staff and archives were to come under the Synod's own jurisdiction.[3] In March and April 1721 the Synod resolved that Ignatius was not to consecrate archimandrites and igumens for the monasteries of the 'former patriarchal domain', nor to transfer them from place to place, without the Synod's permission; that he was to continue to supervise the cathedral clergy of Moscow, but that none of these clerics could be deprived of his place or transferred to another without a Synodal order; and that candidates for ordination in the domain were to be 'sent to the bishops of other dioceses'.[4] And in the Synod's decree of 8 March Ignatius was told pointedly that 'in reports submitted to the All-Ruling Ecclesiastical Synod its title is to be set forth with no diminution, and it is to be obeyed absolutely in all things, in accordance with His Majesty's edict; for this Synod, since it is a Council [*Sobor*], possesses the patriarchal honour, power, and authority, neither more nor less'.[5]

As a matter of fact, Peter had never explicitly granted such 'honour, power, and authority' to the Synod, which in any case was not in the usual sense a *sobor*; and the sentence just quoted is an excellent illustration of the Synod's tendency to stretch the meaning of its founding statutes in an effort to assert its importance. Perhaps Ignatius saw through the pretence. In any case, early in June 1721 he was relieved of his duties and summoned to St. Petersburg by the Synod to face charges of, among other things, misappropriating a pair of 'grey German draught horses', which he was alleged to have given to 'the former Tsaritsa' in 1717 while he was bishop of Suzdal'. Ignatius claimed, in his defence, that he had only stabled the horses at the Pokrovskii convent in Suzdal', where the tsaritsa had lived since 1698, because his own stables had burned down; that the tsaritsa, it was true, had borrowed the horses

[1] *PSP*, i, no. 27 (p. 44).

[2] On 27 January 1719 the tsar had ordered him to assume control of the ecclesiastical affairs of the patriarchal domain, Ignatius stated in his report. Clearly, the order was a direct result of Peter's interview with Stefan Yavorskii on 20 November 1718 (described above, pp. 147–148); and Ignatius's report confirms that following the interview Yavorskii had been deprived of this responsibility.

[3] *PSP*, i, no. 27 (pp. 43–45).

[4] *PSP*, i, no. 37 (p. 50); no. 53 (pp. 77–78); no. 59 (pp. 84–85).

[5] *PSP*, i, no. 27 (p. 45).

to go to Moscow, but that now they were back in the episcopal stables in Suzdal'. The Synod, and behind it the tsar's Privy Chancellery, were not satisfied: the horses could not be found; and in any case the metropolitan appeared to have had extensive dealings with 'the former Tsaritsa'.[1] Indeed that, evidently, was the heart of the matter. Ignatius had been caught up in the ramifications of the Tsarevich Aleksei trial, which implies that at one time or another he had expressed opposition to Peter and to his policies and was now being punished. In June 1721 the Synod resolved that 'until the return to Moscow of the metropolitan of Krutitsy' the ecclesiastical affairs of the former patriarchal domain were to be administered by two itinerant Greek bishops assisted by two (Russian) archimandrites.[2] In January 1722 the see of Krutitsy was officially listed by the Synod as vacant.[3] In March, as mentioned above, one of the Synod's councillors, the Archimandrite Leonid, was named to the post; and in its preface to Leonid's *Instruksiya* the Synod referred to 'the late Ignatius, metropolitan of Krutitsy'. According to this document, Leonid was 'to govern this *Synodal domain* [italics mine] with respect to the ordination of clergy and the other matters subject to the jurisdiction of the Synodal Administration'.[4] In other words, the transition from 'patriarchal' to 'former patriarchal' to 'Synodal domain' had been completed and one more 'oppositionist' eliminated.

During the first four years of its existence the Synod made further provisions regarding the patriarchal – now Synodal – domain. In 1722 it established an 'Ecclesiastical Consistory [*Dukhovnaya Dikasteriya*, or, as it was first called, *Konsistoriya*]' which was given jurisdiction, under the Synod, over the clergy and ecclesiastical affairs of the domain.[5] The Synod also took steps to recover the so-called *stavropigial'nye* monasteries, 'since hitherto they were dependencies of the patriarch of

[1] *PSP*, i, no. 121 (pp. 169–171). 'The former Tsaritsa' refers no doubt to Peter's discarded first wife, Evdokiya, mother of the condemned Aleksei.

[2] *PSP*, i, no. 121 (p. 171). The order was confirmed in August: *PSP*, i, no. 181 (pp. 233–234).

[3] *PSP*, ii, no. 338 (pp. 1–2).

[4] *PSP*, ii, no. 508 (pp. 154–156); also *PSZ*, vi, no. 3954 (pp. 646–647).

[5] *PSP*, ii, no. 508 (pp. 154–156); *PSP*, iii, no. 1044 (pp. 78–83); *PSZ*, vii, no. 4190 (pp. 40–43). See also *PSP*, iii, no. 1054 (pp. 89–92); and *PSZ*, vii, no. 4249 (pp. 79–80). Some of the new Consistory's functions overlapped those of the Prikaz of Ecclesiastical Affairs, which previously had enjoyed exclusive jurisdiction over the clergy of the Moscow diocese. In December 1723 the Prikaz was subordinated to the Consistory, the first step in the former's liquidation.

Moscow'.[1] And having asserted its claim to the patriarchal succession, the Synod was obliged to dispose of the patriarchal household. In March 1721 the patriarchal choir was dispersed; some of the choristers were brought to St. Petersburg to sing in the Trinity cathedral; others, being 'educated', were put to work in the Synod as clerks.[2] In June the Synod resolved that for 'the better dispatch of business' the proceedings of the church council of 1667 and all subsequent 'articles and decrees' should be sent without delay from the 'former patriarchal household' in Moscow to the Synod in St. Petersburg, 'where they must always remain'.[3] The order was confirmed in September, except that now the Synod further resolved that 'all the effects of the former patriarchal household', and any 'ecclesiastical objects' which were at present in the 'custody' of Count Musin-Pushkin or of 'any other secular commander', should be handed over to the Synod.[4]

But the Synod was not to have its way so easily. Judging from the report of the Monastery Prikaz submitted to the Synod in August 1722, it seems that in 1707 a total of nearly 690 pounds of silver plate and gilded objects of all kinds had been collected from various episcopal and monastic households and deposited for safe-keeping in the patriarchal treasury, where they remained 'in chests, in the custody of the patriarchal treasurers', until the present time (1722).[5] It was over the disposition of this treasure that the Synod came into conflict with the secular authorities. In February 1722 Prince Menshikov informed the Senate that while by Peter's command the documents and records of the patriarchal household, together with all liturgical objects belonging to it, should be turned over to the Synod, as it had commanded, nevertheless any treasure not belonging to the patriarchal household should be disposed of by the Senate, whence 'ancient objects' would be consigned to the Synod and 'silver objects' to the government mint.[6] In August the Senate complained to the Synod that when attempting

[1] See *PSP*, i, no. 195 (p. 248); *PSP*, ii, no. 650 (p. 319), for examples.

[2] *PSP*, i, no. 30 (p. 47).

[3] *PSP*, i, no. 130 (pp. 181–182). See also *PSP*, i, no. 218 (p. 273): a Synodal order of 18 September requiring that the registers of decrees (*ukaznye knigy*) kept by the former patriarchal *prikazy*, which on Peter's orders had been deposited in 1719 in the Alexander-Nevskii monastery, should now be transferred to the Synod.

[4] *PSP*, i, no. 203 (pp. 253–255).

[5] *PSP*, ii, no. 793 (pp. 484–486).

[6] *PSZ*, vi, no. 3907 (p. 511); *PSP*, ii, no. 397 (p. 53); *PSP*, ii, no. 464 (p. 114). It may be noted that there was an acute shortage of specie at the time, as the Senate admitted in February 1723, when it announced that for an unspecified period of time all civil servants would be paid in kind – 'in Siberian [i.e. furs] and other treasury goods' (see *PSP*, iii, no. 1017 [pp. 46–47]).

to enforce the above order its agents had encountered resistance from the patriarchal officials, so that a supplementary order had had to be issued requiring the officials to comply under threat of immediate arrest. What, the Synod was now being asked from all sides, did it propose to do in the matter?[1] In reply, the Synod resolved that the Monastery Prikaz should send it the inventories of the disputed treasure, which it would then inspect; and 'if it [the treasure] must go to the Mint', the inventories would be sent to the Senate. But any 'curiosities' to be found among the treasure the Synod resolved to return to the custodians of the 'Synodal household'.[2] Obviously, the Synod was determined to gain undisputed possession of as much as possible of the church's treasure.

And in assuming control of the patriarchal household and domain the Synod became directly responsible for the lives and fortunes of some six thousand persons. It became the employer of the staffs of the three patriarchal *prikazy* (the 100 or so persons who worked in the Palace, Treasury, and Ecclesiastical Prikazy) and of the staff of the Moscow press (175 persons); it became the religious superior of the nearly 5000 monks and nuns living in monasteries and convents dependent on the patriarchate, of the 235 teachers and senior students of the Moscow academy, and of the 356 clerics and staff attached to churches and monasteries in and around Moscow.[3] In practice, the staffs of the *prikazy* and the press became, as we shall see, part of the one great bureaucracy of the state; while the clergy of Moscow and of the rest of the Synodal domain remained in the anomalous position of having no bishop until 1742, when the independent diocese of Moscow was finally reconstituted.[4] Similarly, the clergy and ecclesiastical affairs of the St. Petersburg region were managed by a special 'Ecclesiastical Administration' which was created by the Synod in 1721 and was directly subordinate to it.[5] It was only in 1742, again, that an independent diocese of St. Petersburg was created.[6]

[1] *PSP*, ii, no. 793 (pp. 484–486). [2] *Ibid.*

[3] Figures from a report sent by the Synod to the Senate on 12 November 1722 (*PSP*, ii, no. 901 [pp. 595–619]). These figures do not include the 74 persons employed by the newly formed chancelleries of schismatic affairs, ikon supervision, and inquisitorial affairs; nor do they include the staffs of the recently opened offices of ecclesiastical affairs in Moscow and St. Petersburg (about 60 persons), the 86 employees of the new St. Petersburg Press, or the 72 employees of the revived Monastery Prikaz: a total of some 292 bureaucrats, printers, painters, clerks, guards, and porters, who were also, by November 1722, directly dependent on the Synod.

[4] See Smolitsch, *op. cit.*, p. 360. [5] *PSP*, i, no. 60 (pp. 85–90).

[6] Smolitsch, *op. cit.*, pp. 359–360.

Late in 1721 the Synod ordered that the patriarchal palace in Moscow was to be cleaned and refurbished, the patriarchal Treasure House readied for members of the Synod's own staff, and the patriarchal horses and stables, 'which now belong to the Synod', maintained henceforth in good condition.[1] It seems that for some time the patriarchal stables had been used as an ammunition dump by the Munitions Chancellery; but now the ammunition was to be removed, since – as the Synod declared, once again stretching the meaning of the tsar's resolution – 'by His Majesty's edict of 14 February the former patriarchal household is to be subject to the Synod'.[2] In December 1721 Vice-President Yanovskii informed the Synod that by Peter's command the patriarchal wardrobe was to be distributed to needy churches or divided among the members of the Synod themselves, as they should decide.[3] In January 1722 the Synod resolved that 'in the Synodal palace in Moscow a throne is to be installed for His Imperial Majesty, and over it a *baldichino* of fine velvet with gold trimmings [is to be erected]; and for the Synod's sessions, a table with suitable decoration is to be designed and constructed'.[4] Nothing could have been more symbolic of the changes that had taken place in Russia. And in February 1722 arrangements were made for the manufacture of the Synod's official seal, which was to have both the Imperial arms and the Synod's full title imprinted on it.[5]

III

THE SYNOD AS THE SUPREME ADMINISTRATIVE AND JUDICIAL ORGAN OF THE CHURCH

The Synod was not content merely to take possession of the patriarchal household and to assert its jurisdiction over the ecclesiastical affairs of the patriarchal domain and the St. Petersburg region. For the fifth of the points submitted to Peter by the Synod on 14 February 1721 concerned the 'patriarchal, episcopal, and monastic estates, which for taxation and administrative purposes were subject to the Monastery Prikaz: are they to be subject to the [Synod] alone?' the tsar was asked. The Synod pointed out to Peter that the estates of the church had been 'brought to poverty and ruin by civil administrators'; that by its oath the Synod had 'sworn faithfully to serve His Majesty's interest no less

[1] *PSP*, i, no. 233 (pp. 284–5); no. 234 (p. 285).
[2] *PSP*, i, no. 234 (p. 285).
[3] *PSP*, i, no. 345 (p. 399).
[4] *PSP*, ii, no. 348 (p. 7).
[5] *PSP*, ii, no. 447 (pp. 91–92).

than the other Colleges'; and that 'in the *Ecclesiastical Regulation* it is laid down that such administrative powers belong to the Synod'. As a matter of fact, the *Regulation* contains no such explicit provision;[1] nevertheless Peter acceded to the Synod's request with a curt 'so be it'.[2] And armed with the tsar's resolution, the Synod promptly gave notice that it intended to exercise exclusive jurisdiction over all ecclesiastical persons and property in Russia.[3]

But it was not enough for the Synod merely to proclaim its intentions in this respect, and to demand, repeatedly, that the relevant organs of the secular government hand over to it their tax records and other documents relating to the estates of the church.[4] It was necessary for the Synod first to rescue the Monastery Prikaz from the oblivion to which it had been consigned by the tsar and then to transform it into a department of its own administration. As early as December 1718 Peter had indicated, in response to the Senate's inquiries regarding the integration of the various *prikazy* into the new collegial regime, that the Monastery Prikaz was to be liquidated: the bulk of its responsibilities were to devolve upon the new colleges of Justice, State Expenditure, and State Revenue, leaving the patriarchal Palace Prikaz in charge of the estates of the patriarchal domain and the projected Ecclesiastical College with judicial responsibility for all ecclesiastical persons.[5] By the summer of 1720 the administrative reorganization was completed, and in August of that year, some six months before the Synod had begun to function, the tsar decreed that the Monastery Prikaz had ceased to exist.[6] But on the basis of Peter's resolution of 14 February 1721, the Synod declared on 27 February that 'the Monastery Prikaz and the former patriarchal Palace and Treasury Prikazy, and the episcopal and monastic servitors of various ranks attached to them, as well as the clerks of the College of State Revenue who have lately been

[1] The *Regulation* provides only that the projected Ecclesiastical College was to keep 'records of the income and expenditure of all the most important monasteries in Russia' and that it was to be informed of any 'extraordinary expenditure' undertaken by them; that the College was to keep records of 'episcopal revenues'; and that it was to 'pay heed to who owns church lands and to how they are managed, and to what is done with the grain and money profits, if there are any' (see Verkhovskoi, ii, pp. 42, 73).

[2] *PSP*, i, no. 3 (p. 33); *PSZ*, vi, no. 3734 (p. 355).

[3] See esp. *PSP*, i, no. 64 (pp. 91–95); also *PSZ*, vi, no. 3749 (pp. 366–367); *PSP*, i, no. 25 (pp. 42–43); *PSZ*, vi, no. 3796 (p. 401); *PSP*, i, no. 127 (p. 179).

[4] *PSP*, i, no. 64 (pp. 91–93); no. 113 (pp. 159–160); no. 129 (pp. 180–181); no. 147 (pp. 198–200); no. 271 (pp. 326–327).

[5] *ZAP*, no. 58 (pp. 64–65).

[6] See Gorchakov, *O zemel'nykh vladeniyakh vserossiiskikh mitropolitov, patriarkhov i sv. sinoda*, pp. 448–449; also Milyukov, *op. cit.*, p. 453.

concerned with the affairs of these *prikazy*, are, for the sake of better management, to be brought under the control of the All-Ruling Ecclesiastical Synod'.[1] The Monastery Prikaz had been given a new lease of life. It was not, however, to enjoy the wide powers it had exercised during the twenty years of the *mezhdupatriarshestvo*.

In the spring of 1721 the Synod placed its own nominee, one Vasilii Ershov, a senior civil servant, at the head of the revived Monastery Prikaz.[2] In 1722 it took steps to separate the administration of the Synodal domain from that of the other estates of the church. In March of that year the former patriarchal Treasury Prikaz was removed from the control of the Monastery Prikaz and placed under the custodian of the former patriarchal sacristy, who was a cleric: the Synod explained that this was the traditional practice, and was now being revived, because the Treasury Prikaz (as we have seen)[3] derived its income from the taxes and tithes paid to the head of the church and because it dealt with other matters, such as the furnishing and consecrating of churches, 'which pertain only to the ecclesiastical order'. The Synod also provided that during its absence from Moscow (the Synod spent the whole of 1722 in Moscow) the Prikaz and sacristy were to be subject to the overall supervision of the Synodal councillor, Archbishop Leonid of Krutitsy.[4] Similarly, in July 1722 the Synod resolved that Leonid should supervise the former patriarchal Palace Prikaz: the senior official (*dvoretskii*) at the Prikaz, A. A. Vladykin, who had been appointed by the Senate in 1719,[5] was confirmed in his post with the modish title of 'Synodal Agent'; and the 'Synodal household and its villages, estates, and other properties', which 'formerly were maintained by the Most Holy Patriarchs', were to be administered henceforth only by this Prikaz. Only state taxes were, after collection by the Palace Prikaz, to be turned over to the Monastery Prikaz.[6]

Under the Synod, therefore, the Monastery Prikaz was to continue to function as the central government's agency for collecting taxes from the estates of the church. But it was also to retain some of its other powers. In September 1722, in a pronouncement designed to clarify

[1] *PSP*, i, no. 13 (p. 37).

[2] *PSP*, i, no. 88 (p. 114). The long-time head of the Monastery Prikaz, the powerful senator and privy councillor Count Musin-Pushkin, had retired sometime before 1720. In 1717, perhaps in recognition of his services at the Monastery Prikaz, he had been named president of the new College of State Expenditure (see *PSZ*, v, no. 3255 [p. 601]).

[3] Above, p. 107.

[4] *PSP*, ii, no. 472 (pp. 123–125).

[5] See Gorchakov, *O zemel'nykh vladeniyakh vserossiiskikh mitropolitov, patriarkhov i sv. sinoda*, p. 449 and appendix, p. 178.

[6] *PSP*, ii, no. 708 (p. 387); also *PSZ*, vi, no. 4045 (pp. 725–726).

the jurisdiction of the several departments of its administration, the Synod confirmed that the Monastery Prikaz had authority in no less than eight other, supposedly related, areas: (1) the administration of justice to ecclesiastical landlords and peasants (except those of the Synodal domain); (2) the adjudication of disputes between ecclesiastical landlords and their peasants; (3) the leasing of ecclesiastical lands (except those of the Synodal domain); (4) the distribution of retired and disabled soldiers among the monasteries; (5) the administration and financing of the almshouses; (6) the prosecution of anyone guilty of financial irregularities in the administration of ecclesiastical (but not Synodal) estates; (7) the apprehension and return of fugitive peasants found hiding on ecclesiastical estates; and (8) the apprehension of fugitive soldiers, recruits, and other 'suspicious persons' who had taken refuge on ecclesiastical estates.[1]

Yet the Monastery Prikaz lacked an adequate administrative apparatus for carrying out its various commissions – a situation conducive to that interference by the secular authorities which the Synod had expressly forbidden.[2] In February 1723, in an effort to repair the anomalies of its position, the Prikaz submitted a lengthy list of complaints and proposals to the Synod. It was pointed out, for one thing, that the Prikaz had not yet been designated a college, although it had the responsibilities of one, and was the 'most important administrative body under the Most Holy Synod'. The Prikaz complained, further, that while the civil colleges had adequate staffs, 'in many *gubernii* and provinces not one man has been sent from the Monastery Prikaz to collect taxes and to administer affairs; and there is no one to send'. The Prikaz proposed that forty tax-collectors (*sborshchiki*), each having 'no more than 5000 [peasant] households within his jurisdiction', and assisted by as many 'commissars', should, on the model of the College of State Revenue, be assigned to it, for without them 'it is impossible to collect taxes properly and to deal with other matters'. It was also suggested that the officials just mentioned should be assigned by provinces, rather than dioceses, for 'the College of State Revenue has apportioned taxes by *gubernii* and provinces, and collects them thus; therefore the Synodal command [*sic*] must find other ways of administering taxes, since a single diocese may cover many provinces and even *gubernii*'.[3] The Synod readily agreed to submit the Prikaz's proposals to the Senate. Indeed, as early as January 1722 it had ruled that 'reports

[1] *PSZ*, vi, no. 4081 (pp. 764–767); *PSP*, ii, no. 693 (pp. 366–372).

[2] See documents cited above, p. 185, n.3.

[3] *PSP*, iii, no. 1027 (pp. 57–63).

[*reporty*]' sent from the Monastery Prikaz to the Colleges of State Revenue or of State Expenditure, or indeed to any of the other colleges and chancelleries, should take the form of 'memoranda [*promemorii*]' rather than 'submissions [*donosheniya*]'. It was an important point of bureaucratic etiquette for, as the Synod had pointed out to all concerned, 'this Prikaz is subject to the Synod alone, and because of the importance of many of the matters it deals with, it is to be considered equal to a college'.[1]

In the latter part of 1723 a network of local tax-collectors, analogous to that of the College of State Revenue, was established under the Monastery Prikaz;[2] and in January 1724 Peter decreed that 'a college similar to the College of State Revenue' was to be established under the Synod.[3] The project of transforming the Monastery Prikaz into a college enjoyed the enthusiastic support of the Synod, over the Senate's objections, for the reason that if the Synod were to make good its claim to be 'equal in dignity to the Senate' it must, like the Senate, have colleges subordinate to it.[4] In 1724 the Synod was empowered by the tsar to notify the Senate and the 'entire ecclesiastical administration' that henceforth the head of the Monastery Prikaz was to be known as the 'president of the Revenue Office [*Kamer kontor*] of the Synodal Administration';[5] and on 14 January 1725, a fortnight before Peter's death, the Senate formally ratified the change.[6] In the politics of church reform under Peter the Synod could claim to have won a minor victory.

During the first four years of its existence the Synod also laid claim to extensive judicial authority. According to the *Ecclesiastical Regulation*, it was to have exclusive jurisdiction over disputes between bishops and was to act as a court of appeal for any cleric who should be 'notably wronged by his bishop'.[7] The *Regulation* also stipulated that bishops could not impose the sentence of anathema on a recalcitrant sinner without the prior consent of the Synod.[8] Moreover, while the bishops were authorized by the *Regulation* to impose the 'lesser punishment of exclusion or interdict [*otluchenie ili zapreshchenie*]', whereby 'a sinner is not publicly delivered up to anathema nor expelled from the flock of

[1] *PSP*, iii, no. 987 (pp. 19–20).
[2] See Milyukov, *op. cit.*, pp. 453–454, 464–466.
[3] *PSZ*, vii, no. 4567 (pp. 348–349).
[4] For the Synod's negotiations with the Senate concerning the project, see *PSP*, iv, no. 1374 (pp. 211–212); no. 1379 (pp. 225–226).
[5] *PSP*, iv, no. 1438 (pp. 299–300).
[6] *PSZ*, vii, no. 4632 (p. 401).
[7] Verkhovskoi, ii, p. 50.
[8] *Ibid.*, p. 45.

Christ, but is merely humbled by being excluded from participating with the faithful in common prayer and from entering God's churches, and for a period of time is forbidden to receive communion' – nevertheless an 'innocent man' so punished by his bishop was entitled to appeal to the Synod.[1] And the Synod was to have jurisdiction over 'anyone who should scorn, revile, or, what is worse, refuse to heed the teaching or preaching of the word of God without good cause . . . if the offence is great';[2] over 'doubtful' marriage cases referred to it by a bishop;[3] over cases of schism and heresy;[4] and over 'doubtful cases of conscience which might arise: for example, what is to be done when someone who has robbed a stranger wishes to make restitution but cannot do so, either through shame, or fear, or because the person from whom he stole has died; or what is to be done with a person who chanced to fall into bondage to a pagan, and to secure his freedom embraced their ungodly religion, and then returned to the Christian confession? These and other doubtful cases of conscience are to be brought to the [Synod].'[5] Or, as the *Regulation* itself concludes, 'To the jurisdiction of the [Synod] belong, briefly speaking, all those matters which formerly belonged to the jurisdiction of the patriarch.'[6]

Yet so far as the published record of its proceedings is any guide, the Synod did not, during the first four years of its existence, adjudicate any dispute between two bishops, decide more than a few 'doubtful cases of conscience', or hear any appeal from a cleric 'notably wronged by his bishop'. Nor did it concur in any sentence of anathema (the *Regulation* imposed such strict limitations on the exercise of this power by the bishops that they, no doubt, were loath ever to resort to it) or hear any appeal from an 'innocent man' wrongly excluded from church. No one was prosecuted before the Synod for having 'refused to heed the teaching or preaching of the word of God', unless it is thought that in trying cases of schism the Synod was fulfilling this particular provision of the *Ecclesiastical Regulation*. For during the years in question the Synod did try individual cases of schism as well as legislate new regulations, or confirm existing ones, governing the administration of 'schismatic affairs'.[7] And the Synod did hand down decisions in several 'doubtful' marriage cases.[8]

[1] Verkhovskoi, ii, pp. 47–48. [2] *Ibid.*, p. 67. [3] *Ibid.*, p. 71. [4] *Ibid.*, pp. 67–70. [5] *Ibid.*, p. 73. [6] *Ibid.*

[7] The Synod's administration of schismatic affairs will be examined in a later chapter.

[8] In this respect the Synod seems to have exercised its authority primarily to grant marital separations to influential persons. On 10 September 1722, for example, the Synod granted the wife of a certain nobleman a separation from her husband so that she might

It will be obvious that with regard to the exercise of its judicial authority the *Ecclesiastical Regulation* provided the Synod with little in the way of guidance. It explicitly defined only limited judicial powers for the Synod, some of which were, in the event, not exercised. Moreover, the meaning of the provision that the Synod should have jurisdiction over 'all those matters which formerly belonged to the jurisdiction of the patriarch' was, in the circumstances obtaining in 1721, by no means clear. Did the *Regulation* mean to imply that the traditional order of separate and exclusive ecclesiastical and secular jurisdictions should be restored, the legislation of the last twenty years notwithstanding? Or did the *Regulation* mean to confirm that the distinction drawn in 1700, and thereafter for the most part enforced, between the secular and ecclesiastical affairs of the church, should remain operative, and that the ecclesiastical courts should continue to have jurisdiction only over the latter? Nowhere in the *Regulation* is the judicial authority of the Synod and bishops in other than ecclesiastical matters referred to, except for the brief provision that 'if anyone steals church property, the [Synod] must prosecute him'.[1] Indeed, the *Regulation* specifically excluded from the Synod's jurisdiction cases in which 'a bishop or lesser servant of the church suffers an injury from some powerful lord'; in such cases the injured party was to seek redress 'not at the [Synod], but at the College of Justice, or at the Senate'.[2] In short, it was left to the Synod itself, on taking office, to attempt to define more precisely the actual scope of its judicial authority.

In one respect, at least, the task was not difficult. For no one seems to have doubted that the Synod should succeed to the jurisdiction over purely ecclesiastical matters which was formerly exercised by the patriarchs and, most recently, during the twenty-year *mezhdupatriarshestvo*, by the metropolitan of Ryazan'. Various provisions of the *Ecclesiastical Regulation* seemed to grant at least that much authority to the Synod. Moreover, according to the tsar's manifesto of 25 January 1721 the Synod was to 'administer all ecclesiastical affairs in the All-

enter a convent (*PSP*, ii, no. 512 [p. 160]; no. 801 [p. 497]). Similarly, in February 1722 the Synod granted Prince Aleksei Dolgorukov permission to send his wife to a convent (*PSP*, ii, no. 428 [pp. 70–71]; no. 522 [pp. 165–166]). But see also *PSP*, ii, no. 452 (pp. 97–99), for the Synod's decision in a complicated case of bigamy.

[1] Verkhovskoi, ii, p. 73.

[2] *Ibid.*, p. 74. This was something of an innovation. The *Ulozhenie* of 1649 had provided that in cases where a member of the service nobility caused injury to the patriarch or to a bishop, jurisdiction over the offender was to be shared by the tsar with the patriarch or bishop (*PRP*, vi, pp. 84–89; see also above, p. 101).

Russian Church'.[1] On this legal foundation the Synod promptly proceeded, as we have seen, to assert its jurisdiction over the ecclesiastical affairs of the patriarchal domain and over those of the St. Petersburg region. Yet it remained necessary to clarify what in fact constituted the 'ecclesiastical matters' over which the ecclesiastical courts, under the Synod, enjoyed jurisdiction, for which purpose the Synod submitted to the tsar, in April 1722, another list of 'points' for his resolution.

The Synod reminded Peter that 'the ecclesiastical matters which were subject to patriarchal jurisdiction, and then by His Imperial Majesty's edict to the Bishop [*sic*] of Ryazan', and which now, in accordance with the *Ecclesiastical Regulation*, are subject to the jurisdiction of the Synod, include: blasphemy, heresy, schism, magic [*volshebnye dela*], marriages of doubtful validity, and suits for divorce, which may be granted on the grounds of adultery, infidelity, or desertion by either party'. Peter confirmed that the ecclesiastical courts should have exclusive jurisdiction over all these matters with a characteristically curt 'so be it'. But he then ruled that sexual offences – rape, fornication, and incest – which hitherto had been subject to ecclesiastical jurisdiction only, should now be subject to the secular courts; equally, that cases of 'children begat in lechery' or of 'children born of parents united within the forbidden degrees of kinship', as well as cases of 'attempted marriage by children without their parents' consent', should now by adjudicated only by the secular courts. 'To the Synod' Peter assigned jurisdiction only over cases in which children or servants were forced to marry 'because of fear of their parents or of their master'. And Peter resolved that disputed wills were to be settled by a tribunal formed of members of the Synod and the College of Justice, whence persons found guilty of fraud – including, specifically, the parish priest who had registered the will – would be remanded to the civil courts for punishment.[2]

On this occasion the Synod also asked the tsar to indicate what sanctions were to be imposed for certain ecclesiastical offences. The *Ecclesiastical Regulation* specified (as the Synod pointed out to Peter) that anyone who 'openly blasphemes the name of God or Holy Scripture or the Church; or is a notorious sinner and is not ashamed of his deeds, but even boasts of them; or without good cause has not gone to confession or received Holy Communion for more than a year; or does anything in open contempt or mockery of God's law, and after

[1] Verkhovskoi, ii, p. 6.

[2] *PSZ*, vi, no. 3963 (pp. 650–652); also *PSP*, ii, no. 532 (pp. 173–177).

repeated admonitions remains contumacious and proud' – that such a person was liable to anathema.[1] But the *Regulation* did not consider that the imposition of anathema was in itself an adequate punishment for such offences, or that the matter ended there; for 'if the person excommunicated does not repent, and continues to scorn the church's anathema or to revile the bishop or another cleric, then the bishop shall submit a report of the matter to the [Synod] . . . [which] shall urgently request judgment from the appropriate secular authority or from His Majesty himself'.[2] So now, in April 1722, in response to the Synod's further 'points', Peter resolved (1) that persons guilty of blasphemy should be remanded to the secular courts, there to be sentenced according to law;[3] (2) that 'notorious sinners' should be tried by the Synod and the 'unsubmissive ones' handed over to the secular courts for punishment; (3) that non-confessors should be punished in accordance with existing regulations,[4] while persons who refused to receive communion should be tried by the Synod and punished by the secular authorities; and (4) that transgressors of the 'respect and obedience' due to the Synod, as well as those who 'arrogantly scorn ecclesiastical authority, giving great scandal to their lesser brethren', should be punished by the state. Peter also resolved that persons guilty of 'superstition' were to be punished by 'condemnation to the galleys for life together with slit nostrils'; that 'when someone, because of a sermon, becomes indignant with a priest – which sometimes happens when a person's conscience is pricked by a sermon – and then proceeds to take vengeance on the priest', the Synod was to prosecute 'such criminals according to the magnitude of the offence'; finally, that he, Peter, was to be informed by the Synod of any case in which 'an ecclesiastical person has been injured by a notable and powerful person' and has not received satisfaction in the secular courts.[5]

By the tsar's resolutions of April 1722, therefore, the traditional jurisdiction of the ecclesiastical courts was somewhat curtailed. Sexual offences, bastardy, disputed wills, and marriages without parental consent were no longer considered 'ecclesiastical matters' subject to adjudication by these courts. At the same time, the range of offences against religion for which the tsar's subjects were liable to punishment by the secular courts was broadened to include, not only blasphemy,

[1] Verkhovskoi, ii, p. 44. [2] *Ibid.*, p. 47.

[3] Peter no doubt referred to the relevant provisions of his father's *Ulozhenie*, for which see above, p. 76 and n.1. [4] For which see above, pp. 76–79.

[5] *PSZ*, vi, no. 3963 (pp. 650–652); *PSP*, ii, no. 532 (pp. 173–177).

schism, heresy, and non-confession, but also failure to receive communion and contempt of the Synod. Moreover, after April 1722 'notorious sinners' who remained 'unsubmissive', as well as persons guilty of 'superstition', were subject to some of the most cruel punishments that the state could impose. In sum, if Peter's concern that unfortunate children should be spared the harshness of ecclesiastical justice was once again demonstrated,[1] so also was his disposition to regard every form of religious non-conformity as a crime against the state.

While the Synod more or less successfully defined the scope of ecclesiastical jurisdiction, it was simultaneously obliged to find ways and means of enforcing respect for its own judicial authority within the church. This was done, most notably, by the institution of a regime of 'inquisitors' with quasi-judicial powers. The *Ecclesiastical Regulation* stipulated that 'for the more convenient dispatch of [certain] matters the bishops must direct that in every town inspectors [*zakashchiki*], or specially appointed supervisors [*blagochinye*], shall watch over [these] matters and report to them'.[2] But the business was not to be left to the bishops: on 1 March 1721 the Synod resolved that an 'archinquisitor [*protoinkvisitor*]' was to be attached to the Synod itself in St. Petersburg and another to the 'Ecclesiastical Administration' in Moscow, while lesser 'inquisitors' were to be appointed 'in all the dioceses of Great Russia';[3] and on 15 March the names of the two archinquisitors, both of them monks, were announced.[4]

According to the *Instruktsiya* given to the archinquisitor of Moscow late in 1721,[5] he and his subordinates were to convey the Synod's 'edicts and instructions' to every level of the ecclesiastical administration, 'in order that all should be informed of them and that no one, from the humblest official to the bishop himself, should presume to administer justice without [reference to the appropriate document]'. It is clear from the rest of the *Instruktsiya* that in judicial matters the archinquisitor and his subordinates were to act as prosecutors rather than judges. They were not to supplant the established courts; indeed, they were specifically forbidden to conduct judicial inquiries. On the

[1] Cf. above, pp. 95–96.

[2] Verkhovskoi, ii, pp. 40–41. It may be noted that opposite this sentence in the margin of Prokopovich's rough draft of the *Regulation* Tsar Peter placed five of his asterisks, indicating thereby that the proposal met with his warmest approval (see *ibid.*, p. 40, n. 90).

[3] *PSP*, i, no. 22 (pp. 41–42).

[4] *PSP*, i, no. 34 (p. 48). In April 1722 the post of archinquisitor of St. Petersburg was abolished by the Synod, leaving his colleague in Moscow as the 'sole archinquisitor for ecclesiastical affairs' (*PSP*, ii, no. 526 [pp. 168–169]).

[5] *PSZ*, vi, no. 3870 (pp. 467–476); *PSP*, i, no. 348 (pp. 401–408).

diocesan level, for example, the inquisitor was to attend judicial proceedings conducted by the bishop and to report their outcome directly to the Synod. In a word, the inquisitors were to act chiefly as the Synod's spies, and their wider responsibilities will be discussed presently.

By way of concluding our discussion of the Synod's judicial authority it may be mentioned, once again, that in September 1722 a lengthy document was issued explaining, 'for the information of all', what matters were subject to the jurisdiction of the various departments of the Synod's administration.[1] The document provides us with a convenient summary of the way in which ecclesiastical justice was administered, in theory at least, during the early years of the Synod's existence. The Synod had decided to issue the document because of the increasing number of petitions and suits relating to 'lesser matters' that were being brought to it, thus 'obstructing the dispatch of urgent matters which can be resolved only by the Synod'. For by decree of the tsar justice was to be sought from the Synod only 'in ultimate ecclesiastical matters, "ultimate" understood to mean matters above the jurisdiction of the other courts: that is, should someone who has submitted his case to a lower court, or to an episcopal court, not receive satisfaction . . . he is to petition and seek redress at the Synod, where ultimate justice [*krainaya uprava*] in such cases is to be secured'.[2] Accordingly, the Synod now insisted that anyone with a petition or suit concerning some matter subject to ecclesiastical jurisdiction (as defined by the *Ecclesiastical Regulation* and the tsar's resolutions of April 1722) was in the first instance to submit it to the ecclesiastical authorities of the town in or near which he lived. In cases concerning estate matters, ecclesiastical landlords or peasants were to submit their petitions to the provincial government authorities or, if these were far away, then to the nearest ecclesiastical authorities: if the decision of either of these courts was unsatisfactory, the petitioner was to appeal to his bishop; and if the bishop or his subordinates handed down an unjust decision, the petition was to be brought to the Synod. Finally, if someone were 'compelled' to bring an action against a member of the Synod or one of its officials, or against a bishop, he was to do so before the Synod.

[1] *PSZ*, vi, no. 4081 (pp. 764–767); *PSP*, ii, no. 693 (pp. 366–372); as cited above, p. 187.

[2] The Synod refers here to the manifesto of 25 January 1721, whereby the projected Ecclesiastical College was given jurisdiction over 'ultimate matters of ecclesiastical justice [*krainye dela dukhovnoi upravy*]' (see Verkhovskoi, ii, p. 6).

In other words, the Synod constituted itself the supreme ecclesiastical court of Russia, enjoying initial jurisdiction over 'ultimate' ecclesiastical matters and appellate jurisdiction over all others. But when defining the jurisdiction of the several departments subordinate to it, the Synod dealt with the whole range of their administrative responsibilities, as might be expected, given the confusion of administration and justice that was characteristic of contemporary Russian practice. Thus, by the terms of the document in question, the Synod confirmed that in addition to its other functions the Monastery Prikaz was to exercise, as noted above, certain judicial powers over the inhabitants of episcopal and monastic estates. Similarly, the Ecclesiastical Prikaz was to retain jurisdiction over important ecclesiastical cases as well as purely administrative responsibilities. The duties of the Treasury Prikaz, as its name implies, were primarily financial. But the Synod's Palace Prikaz was charged not only with administering the properties and other 'interests' of the Synodal household, and with collecting taxes from the Synodal domain, but also with administering justice to Synodal peasants. The Prikaz of Ecclesiastical Affairs (*Tserkovnykh del*) was concerned chiefly with disciplining the Moscow clergy and (since 1718) with administering schismatic affairs (both quasi-judicial functions), while the Prikaz of Inquisitorial Affairs directed the activities of the diocesan and local inquisitors. And over the activities of these six administrative-judicial *prikazy* the Synod claimed ultimate and – with regard to the secular government – exclusive jurisdiction.

It may seem from the preceding pages that by freely interpreting its founding statutes and the tsar's subsequent resolutions the Synod had largely succeeded in recreating that state within a state that Part I of the *Ecclesiastical Regulation* inveighed against; that under the Synod the administration of the Russian church had been restored to that independent position which Peter, and to some extent his predecessors, had laboured to suppress. But this was not, of course, the case. The Synod did not simply take up where Patriarch Adrian had left off, some twenty years previously. For by their oath of office the members of the Synod themselves had acknowledged the tsar as their 'Supreme Judge'; and the history of their relations with Peter reveals how completely they depended on his good graces. The Synod could do nothing without Peter's at least tacit consent; nor could it, by the same token, openly resist the tsar's interventions in its affairs.

Moreover, it should be noted that as an agency for collecting state taxes the Monastery Prikaz – 'the most important administrative body under the Synod' (so it described itself) – was subject to the Colleges of State Expenditure and of State Revenue,[1] and that after February 1723 this Prikaz, together with the other departments of the Synod's administration, was required to open its books to inspectors of the Office of State Control (*Revizion kontor*).[2] Indeed, the Synod itself was required to submit to the Senate annual accounts of the income and expenditure of its own household as well as of all the other ecclesiastical institutions of Russia.[3] It was in an effort to impose some order on ecclesiastical finances generally – for the purpose of determining 'how many poor people, orphans, monks, schools, and hospitals, as well as episcopal and monastic households, can be maintained' – that Peter consented in 1724 to the transformation of the old Monastery Prikaz into an enlarged, college-like institution.[4] Peter's long-standing policy of using 'surplus' ecclesiastical revenue for general social purposes, with its corollary of overall state control of ecclesiastical finances, was thus confirmed in the very last year of his reign. And neither the enlarged and renamed Monastery Prikaz, nor any other department of the 'Synodal command', was permitted to take part in the collection from ecclesiastical estates of 'taxes for the army'[5] – in the administration, that is, of the all-important 'soul tax', which in 1724 alone accounted for 54 percent of total state revenue, having replaced all other forms of direct taxation.[6]

During the first four years of its existence, therefore, the Synod succeeded in gaining only nominal control of the secular affairs of the church. In practice, it served merely as a convenient channel for conveying news of the government's numerous financial and tax regulations, troop levies, labour conscriptions, supply requisitions, etc. to the administrators of ecclesiastical estates.[7] Equally, the scope of its judicial authority was in practice greatly restricted by legislative action, by Peter's direct interventions, and by the continual interference of the secular authorities. Within the first few months of its existence, for example, the Synod had been granted exclusive jurisdiction over all

[1] See *PSP*, ii, no. 349 (pp. 7–8); *PSP*, iii, no. 1027 (p. 60); *PSP*, iv, no. 1313 (p. 145); no. 1327 (pp. 176–177).

[2] *PSZ*, vii, no. 4580 (p. 358); *PSP*, iii, no. 1007 (pp. 40–43).

[3] *PSZ*, vii, no. 4488 (pp. 274–275); *PSP*, iv, no. 1237 (pp. 97–99). See also *PSZ*, vii, no. 4567 (pp. 348–349).

[4] See *PSZ*, vii, no. 4567 (pp. 348–349); *PSP*, iv, no. 1374 (pp. 211–212).

[5] *PSZ*, vii, no. 4567 (p. 348); *PSP*, iv, no. 1235 (pp. 94–96).

[6] For the introduction of the soul tax, see above, p. 81.

[7] See *PSP*, i–iv, *passim*.

ecclesiastical persons in all but criminal cases (treason, robbery, and murder) and 'grave matters of state', a term that was defined by Peter to include anything that related to the country's trade or industry.[1] Similarly, as early as August 1721 the Synod had complained to the Senate that 'many' government officials were violating ecclesiastical jurisdiction, citing in support of its contention the case of the Archimandrite Andronika, a judge of the Novgorod diocese, who had been arrested and sent in irons to the Preobrazhenskii Prikaz (near Moscow) without reference to the Synod; 'and in other localities much harm is done to ecclesiastical persons, that is to the clergy and other dependants of the Synodal administration: priests, deacons, and lesser clerics are taken to the [secular] *prikazy* not only in grave matters of state, but also in civil actions, and are held under guard for a long time, causing them considerable harm and great exasperation'.[2] In November the Synod had taken the matter to the tsar, but without much success: Peter ruled, vaguely, that the Synod was to have jurisdiction over ecclesiastical persons in all but 'criminal matters [*kriminal'nye dela*]' and cases of 'evil-doing [*zlodeistvo*]', though for the unfrocking of clerics guilty of such offences 'the Synod is to be referred to'.[3]

And in the years that followed the range of offences for which clergy could be tried by the secular courts was broadened to include 'concealment of souls' from the census-takers[4] and the cutting down of trees in 'forbidden forests'.[5] At the same time, the secular authorities continued to interfere in the administration of justice to ecclesiastical persons: in January 1723 the Synod found it necessary to reiterate that 'persons of the ecclesiastical order accused of some crime are, except in grave state matters, to be tried by the ecclesiastical officials of the Synodal command, to whom the secular command is to communicate the details of the case. For by His Imperial Majesty's edict', the Synod insisted, 'ecclesiastical persons are not subject to the civil courts; nor may they be arrested and held anywhere until after their trial, when the ecclesiastical authorities may remand them to the civil authorities for interrogation'.[6] At one point, in a further attempt to secure its exclusive jurisdiction over the servants of the church, the Synod proposed to the

[1] *PSZ*, vi, no. 3761 (pp. 371–372); *PSP*, i, no. 64 (pp. 91–95); *PSP*, i, no. 76 (p. 105).
[2] *PSP*, i, no. 172 (pp. 221–222).
[3] *PSZ*, vi, no. 3854 (pp. 455–459); *PSP*, i, no. 312 (pp. 364–369).
[4] *PSZ*, vi, no. 3787 (pp. 391–394); *PSP*, i, no. 105 (pp. 138–143); *PSZ*, vi, no. 4113 (p. 784); *PSP*, ii, no. 865 (p. 560); *PSZ*, vii, no. 4519 (p. 293).
[5] *PSZ*, vii, no. 4176 (p. 27); *PSP*, iii, no. 1034 (pp. 67–68).
[6] *PSP*, iii, no. 996 (p. 30).

tsar that 'a College similar to the College of Justice should be created . . . [which] would be under the jurisdiction of the Synod'.[1] At first Peter seems to have favoured the proposal;[2] but nothing came of it. And the Synod was obliged to carry on that uneven struggle with the secular government for a recognition of its authority which is the subject of the next section of this chapter.

IV

THE SYNOD'S RELATIONS WITH THE GOVERNMENT

The *Ecclesiastial Regulation* did not provide the Synod with any grounds for claiming a special position in relation to the newly-reorganized central government. Indeed, with its reminder that 'this Administrative Council is established by decree of the Monarch with the concurrence of the Senate', and with its references to 'the other Colleges', the *Regulation* seemed to imply that the projected Ecclesiastical College was to be little more than the appropriate government bureau for administering ecclesiastical – as distinct from military or foreign – affairs. The implication was not lost on the members of the Ecclesiastical College: their first order of business on 14 February 1721, as we have seen, was to jettison the name 'Ecclesiastical College' and to assume with Peter's permission the more distinctive and dignified 'Most Holy All-Ruling Synod', a title which implied that in relation to the secular government the supreme administrative organ of the church was to occupy a position above the colleges and equal to the Senate. This position was explicitly confirmed by the second of Peter's resolutions to the points submitted to him on 14 February: the Synod's communications with the Senate, he ruled, were to be signed by all the members, while those with the colleges were to be signed only by secretaries, 'just as it is done in the Senate'.[3] The resolution was formally ratified by the Senate on 3 March.[4] But having thus acknowledged the Synod's equality, the Senate proved reluctant to behave accordingly.

On 3 May 1721 it was accused by the Synod of not having co-operated in securing administrative staff for the latter, whence 'from day to day business accumulates which it is impossible to dispatch'; the Senate was exhorted to attend to the business because by the tsar's

[1] *ZAP*, no. 161 (p. 122).
[2] See *PSZ*, vii, no. 4160 (p. 21); and *ZAP*, no. 164 (p. 125).
[3] *PSP*, i, no. 3 (p. 33); *PSZ*, vi, no. 3734 (p. 355).
[4] *PSZ*, vi, no. 3749 (pp. 366–367); *PSP*, i, no. 25 (pp. 42–43).

decree 'this All-Ruling Synod has the honour and power in the ecclesiastical government that the All-Ruling Senate enjoys in the secular'.[1] Obviously stung by the Synod's accusation, the Senate replied on 24 May that by Peter's command a secretariat had been formed for the Synod from the existing staffs of the Monastery and patriarchal *prikazy*, and that if the Synod were not satisfied with these arrangements it should have complained first to the Senate and not to the tsar (as the Synod apparently had done). For the Senate had acted in the matter 'as was thought fit, with vigilance for the improvement of the Sovereign's affairs and interests, and not contrary [to them]'. Moreover, the Synod was tartly reminded that by His Majesty's decree of 1711 the Senate enjoyed an overall authority in civil affairs which the Synod itself had acknowledged, and that 'in the times of the Most Holy Russian patriarchs' civil servants had been seconded to the ecclesiastical administration only by edict of the tsar's Razryadnyi Prikaz, 'though this Prikaz did not have the power and authority that the All-Ruling Senate now has'. And so the Senate belaboured the justification of its actions, concluding at last with the statement that civil servants could work in or under the Synod only with the Senate's permission, and that for certain offences Synodal officials could be tried by the Senate.[2]

The Synod promptly (31 May) retorted that it had exclusive jurisdiction over the ecclesiastical bureaucracy, and that 'by sending directives to Synodal servitors the All-Ruling Senate would trouble itself in vain'; furthermore, having signed the *Ecclesiastical Regulation*, the senators would know that the Synod was entitled to appeal directly to its 'Supreme Judge, His Majesty the Tsar'; etc.; etc. While conceding that in patriarchal times the tsar's Razryadnyi Prikaz had had a voice in the matter, the Synod reminded the Senate that 'this ecclesiastical administration founded by [Peter] is not like that of the patriarchs: it does not consist of only one person; nor does it govern in its own name, but rather by decrees of His Majesty, who as a Most Pious Monarch, and following the example of the ancient Christian Kings, has established Himself as Supreme Ruler and Judge of this Holy Synod'.[3] A few days later (5 June) the Synod rejected another of the Senate's communications, strenuously objecting to the fact that it took the form of a 'senatorial order [*senatskoe prikazanie*]', which suggested 'a diminution of the actual honour and equality with the Senate which was granted

[1] *PSP*, i, no. 82 (pp. 110–111).
[2] *PSP*, i, no. 112 (pp. 151–153).
[3] *PSP*, i, no. 112 (pp. 153–159).

to the Synod by His Majesty; for the All-Ruling Senate has communicated its order to the All-Ruling Synod as if to a subordinate, ignoring its equality and forgetting that it enjoys the patriarchal honour, power, and authority, and that orders were not sent by the secular government to the patriarchs'.[1]

The immediate outcome of the Synod's feud with the Senate was something of a victory for the Synod. After June 1721 it never again received 'orders' from the Senate; and when on 7 July the Synod forwarded to the Senate (admittedly for the second time) a request for twenty-eight additional staff for the Monastery Prikaz, the Senate fairly promptly (25 July) complied.[2] Furthermore, in September of that year Feofan Prokopovich informed the Synod that Peter had been pleased to order that 'if in future a communication should be sent from the Synod to the Senate, or vice-versa, which appears perplexing to either side', the matter was to be settled at a conference of two representatives from each body.[3] Peter personally confirmed the order in a letter to the Synod which he sent from Astrakhan in July 1722: 'if in future some matter arises which cannot be postponed, you will write to me about it, but only for our information; for you can decide the matter together with the Senate in anticipation of our approbation'.[4] It would seem that the Synod had in fact achieved a position of equality with the Senate, with the corollaries that for administrative purposes the Russian state was divided into ecclesiastical and secular spheres headed respectively by the Synod and the Senate, and that together these two bodies constituted, under the tsar, and particularly in his absence, the supreme governmental organ of the state. In the legislative documents of the last years of Peter's reign we often encounter the formula: 'The All-Ruling Senate and the Most Holy All-Ruling Synod, meeting jointly in the Senate, have resolved . . .'.[5] It was at joint conferences of the Synod and the Senate that the acts conferring the Imperial dignity on Peter were drawn up and then, on 22 October 1721, formally presented to him.[6]

But the Synod had won a battle, not the war. In order to make good

[1] *PSP*, i, no. 114 (pp. 160–161). [2] *PSP*, i, no. 171 (pp. 220–221).

[3] *PSP*, i, no. 207 (p. 257).

[4] *PSZ*, vi, no. 4051 (p. 737); *PSP*, ii, no. 716 (p. 403). See also *ZAP*, no. 139 (p. 111) for the original letter written and signed by Peter himself.

[5] The opening sentence of an important edict of May 1722 dealing with army recruitment (*PSZ*, vi, no. 3996 [p. 672]).

[6] *PSZ*, vi, no. 3840 (pp. 444–446); *PSP*, i, no. 278 (pp. 332–335).

its claim to equality with the Senate, as well as to discharge its duty of administering the church, the Synod felt obliged to reorganize and expand the ecclesiastical bureaucracy which it had inherited; and in the process of so doing it continually referred, by way of justifying its actions, to the example of the Senate and the civil bureaucracy.

The institution of a regime of ecclesiastical 'inquisitors' was mentioned above. In June 1721 the Synod rejected an attempt by the Senate to attach a 'fiscal' to the revived Monastery Prikaz, insisting that the latter was not a secular college, but a Synodal prikaz, and that the post in question properly belonged to one of its own inquisitors,[1] who were to be established in the ecclesiastical administration (as the Synod declared in July) on the 'model of the fiscals established in the secular government'.[2] According to the *Instruktsiya* given to the archinquisitor of Moscow, he and his subordinates were 'always to bear carefully in mind the [provisions of the] civil law regarding the duties and functions of the secular fiscals', which were, in brief, 'to make inquiries and to send reports and to make accusations in court' with the object of ensuring honest and efficient administration on all levels of the tsar's government; 'and while these [provisions] concern only the secular fiscals, nevertheless the ecclesiastical inquisitors are to act in accordance with the sense of them'. The Synod was careful, however, to stipulate that the inquisitors were not to send reports to the Senate, to the colleges or chancelleries, or to any lay person (except in certain financial matters) under pain of severe punishment: 'for this would be contrary to the respect [*respekt*] due the Most Holy All-Ruling Synod'. The inquisitors were to strive to promote 'the welfare of Holy Church, of the State, and of the people, for which they shall be rewarded by His Imperial Majesty's favour in proportion to the measure of their faithful service'.[3]

The Synod's first chief secretary, as we have seen, was the priest-monk Varlaam Ovsyanikov. As an assessor of the Synod Ovsyanikov received an annual stipend of 600R; but in December 1721 the Synod raised it to 1200R because that was the stipend of the Senate's chief secretary.[4] And in succeeding months and years this principle was widely applied by the Synod: its 'commissars', its *protokolist*, and its secretaries were all assigned annual stipends equivalent to those of their senatorial opposite numbers because – as the Synod never tired of

[1] *PSP*, i, no. 133 (pp. 184–186).
[2] *PSP*, i, no. 151 (pp. 206–207).
[3] *PSZ*, vi, no. 3870 (pp. 467–476); *PSP*, i, no. 348 (pp. 401–408).
[4] *PSP*, i, no. 325 (pp. 379–380).

pointing out – 'by the personal edict of His Imperial Majesty the Most Holy Synod is considered to have authority and power equal to that of the All-Ruling Senate'.[1] In the spring of 1722 the Senate announced that a councillor from each college, as well as a member of the Senate itself, were to open offices in Moscow;[2] the Synod was informed of the order and in due course it, too, established an office in Moscow under the direction of one of its councillors.[3] In 1724, having been informed by its chief procurator that 'in the secular command there has been established a special office for dealing with the reports of the fiscals', the Synod resolved that 'therefore such an office of inquisitorial affairs should be founded in the Synodal command'.[4]

Occasionally the Synod's efforts to achieve a kind of bureaucratic parity with the Senate reached absurd proportions. 'Having learned that for guard and investigative duties the Senate maintains a full company of dragoons, while the Synod has only forty-seven retired soldiers', the Synod decided in October 1722 to recruit an additional seventeen men from the retired soldiers regularly sent to it by the War College for distribution to the monasteries.[5] In October 1721 the Synod resolved to acquire 'three silver inkstands for the Synod's table of the kind they have in the Senate'.[6]

The measure of the Synod's initial success in reorganizing and expanding the ecclesiastical bureaucracy can be gauged from a report which it submitted to the Senate in November 1722.[7] The report indicates that in addition to the 310 persons employed in the administrative agencies subordinate to the Synod – the various *prikazy* and chancelleries of ecclesiastical affairs located for the most part in Moscow – there were no less than 222 persons attached directly to the Synod: a total which included, besides the members of the Synod themselves and their chief procurator (and his staff of six), the chief secretary and his staff of 97 secretaries, translators, 'chancellerists', and copyists; 6 archivists; 73 soldiers; 6 porters; etc. In its report the Synod requested that because of its expanding volume of business the number of staff employed in various grades of the ecclesiastical bureaucracy should be increased. At the same time it ordered that a *bol'shaya palata*, equal in

[1] *PSP*, i, no. 336 (pp. 384–385); *PSP*, ii, no. 798 (pp. 494–495); *PSP*, iv, no. 1163 (pp. 10–13).

[2] *PSZ*, vi, no. 3951 (pp. 644–645).

[3] *PSP*, iii, no. 1041 (pp. 76–77).

[4] *PSP*, iv, no. 1282 (p. 122).

[5] *PSP*, ii, no. 869 (p. 562).

[6] *PSP*, i, no. 280 (p. 336).

[7] *PSP*, ii, no. 901 (pp. 595–619).

size to the present Synodal house (*dom*), was to be built to contain its chancellery.[1]

But if by the end of 1722 the Synod had acquired an imposing bureaucratic machine which closely corresponded, in structure if not in size, to that of the secular government, it still was obliged to struggle to maintain the independence of this bureaucracy, to enforce compliance with its requests and orders, and to preserve the inviolability of ecclesiastical jurisdiction. From the first weeks of its existence the Synod had found cause to complain to the Senate of the disregard, opposition, and antagonism shown to it, or to its subordinates, by members of the secular government; and after 1722, as before, the Synod continued to receive reports of secular interference in, and contempt for, the ecclesiastical administration.[2] Indeed, at one point the Synod complained to the tsar himself of a general 'contempt for ecclesiastical authority' and, more ominously, of the 'increasing boldness of persons calling for the suppression of the ecclesiastical administration'. The Synod went on to complain that in 'Synodal affairs' its 'procedures and actions' were scorned by 'important and powerful persons', leading others, 'though unimportant and not powerful', to imitate them.[3]

It may be useful to quote one or two examples of the Synod's problems in this respect. In November 1722 the Prikaz of Ecclesiastical Affairs reported that during the previous summer the commanders of two Moscow regiments had ignored repeated orders to collect the statutory fines for non-confession from their soldiers. At first the commanders objected that to collect the fines would reduce the men to 'great poverty and misery'; then, when confronted by an under-secretary of the Prikaz and his aides, the commanders claimed to have received a special decree exempting soldiers from the fines. When the under-secretary and his men went to complain to the *ober-auditor* of the War College, the latter met them on the stairs and threatened to break their arms and legs if they attempted to 'take anything from me'. What, the Prikaz asked, did the Synod propose to do about the 'opposition of these regiments'? It was a most delicate problem. The Synod chose to abide by the letter of the law and on 5 December,

[1] *PSP*, ii, no. 807 (p. 500).

[2] See *PSP*, i, no. 12 (p. 37); no. 119 (pp. 167–168); no. 123 (pp. 171–175); no. 215 (pp. 269–270); no. 338 (p. 390); *PSP*, ii, no. 346 (pp. 5–6); no. 389 (pp. 45–48); no. 394 (pp. 51–52); no. 671 (p. 349); no. 751 (p. 443); no. 791 (p. 484); no. 921 (pp. 648–649); no. 946 (pp. 666–667); *PSP*, iii, no. 988 (pp. 20–21); etc.

[3] *PSZ*, vi, no. 3854 (pp. 455–459); *PSP*, i, no. 312 (pp. 364–369); no. 313 (pp. 369–370).

having noted that there was no evidence of a special decree exempting soldiers from the fines, it resolved to send the Prikaz's report of 'this audacity', together with a 'demand for satisfaction', to the Senate.[1] And on 17 December, having received further reports of similar 'obstructions', the Synod sent another, more general complaint to the Senate, 'with this declaration: that although by His Imperial Majesty's edicts ... the Synod is supreme in ecclesiastical affairs, and in particular is responsible for seeking out schismatics, and is deserving of equal respect with the Senate, nevertheless these edicts do not appear to be observed by the War College; for not only were the officers and soldiers requested by the Synod for seeking out schismatics not sent, and the necessary means for arresting these oppositionists not provided, but the decree [to this effect] which was repeatedly sent to the War College was not accepted, whereby both His Imperial Majesty's edicts and the Synodal administration have been rendered nugatory'.[2] On 9 January 1723 the Senate duly ordered that in future decrees from the Synod should be accepted by the War College and promptly carried out.[3]

The government's practice of using ecclesiastical buildings in Moscow for storing ammunition and for quartering troops was another matter that roused the Synod's ire. In November 1721 it ordered the War College to clear away the arms and munitions stored in the bishop of Rostov's house (*podvor'e*), and to return it to his use;[4] and in January 1722 it requested the Senate to direct that all the Moscow houses belonging to bishops or monasteries should cease being used to quarter troops.[5] On 3 February the Synod instructed the Monastery Prikaz to make an inventory of all these houses, with the aim of discovering what state they were in and how many remained in the hands of the secular authorities. On receipt of the Prikaz's report in April, the Synod immediately demanded that the Senate should issue an edict requiring that episcopal or monastic houses still in secular hands be promptly vacated and compensation paid to their rightful owners for restoration purposes.[6] It was no use. In October 1722 it was necessary to complain once again to the Senate that many ecclesiastical houses in Moscow had still not been cleared of their 'secular and military residents', and that even now some of the houses were being used without the Synod's consent to quarter troops.[7] The following month the Synod drew up a

[1] *PSP*, ii, no. 918 (pp. 644–645).
[2] *PSP*, ii, no. 939 (pp. 661–662).
[3] *PSZ*, vii, no. 4144 (pp. 9–10); *PSP*, iii, no. 983 (p. 18).
[4] *PSP*, i, no. 290 (pp. 343–344).
[5] *PSP*, ii, no. 356 (p. 13).
[6] *PSP*, ii, no. 603 (pp. 258–263).
[7] *PSP*, ii, no. 871 (p. 563).

'final protest' to be sent to the Senate, and threatened to send its soldiers to enforce the evacuation orders.[1] And in January 1723, in still a further attempt to clear the troops and stores from episcopal and monastic houses in Moscow, which 'despite the many demands of the Synod have not yet been vacated, causing destruction to these houses', the Synod directed that accounts of all damages be kept by their rightful owners and charged to the government. The same was to be done by the episcopal and monastic owners of occupied houses in the other towns.[2]

The matter is not referred to again in the printed legislation of Peter's reign, a fact which suggests either that the Synod gave up its attempt to recover the property in question or that the secular authorities eventually complied with its numerous requests, demands, and orders. But whatever the outcome, it is clear that Peter himself had not brought the weight of his authority to bear in the struggle; had he done so, the matter would have been settled, one way or the other, in the early months of 1721. Evidently Peter was prepared to hear the Synod's complaints, even to allow it to legislate; but so long as his army had need of the houses he was not prepared to enforce the evacuation orders. As in the matter of collecting fines from non-confessing soldiers, the Synod had (to repeat its taunt to the Senate) 'troubled itself in vain'. For nothing in the history of Peter's reign permits us to believe that, whatever the legal rights or wrongs of a case, he would have sided with the clergy and Synod against his soldiers.

In attempting to keep control of the ecclesiastical bureaucracy the Synod also encountered serious difficulties. In July 1721, as we have seen, it secured the transfer of twenty-eight civil servants to the Monastery Prikaz. But in granting the request, the Senate had somewhat ungraciously informed the Synod that should these civil servants, or any others who might later be transferred, report they had 'nothing to do', the Synod was to return them to the secular government.[3] In short, the Synod's staff requirements were rated low on the government's list of priorities, and civil servants assigned to the ecclesiastical administration were apt to be recalled at any moment. Already in August 1721 the Synod had to remind the College of State Revenue, which had just reclaimed several of its erstwhile under-secretaries from service in the diocese of Nizhnii-Novgorod, that only the Synod had

[1] *PSP*, ii, no. 903 (p. 620).
[2] *PSP*, iii, no. 971 (p. 6).
[3] *PSP*, ii, no. 171 (pp. 220–221).

jurisdiction over such persons.[1] Again, in March 1722 the Synod felt obliged to resist the Senate's attempt to transfer one of the secretaries concerned with the administration of schismatic affairs in Moscow to a department of the secular government.[2] In April, the Synod was informed by the bishop of Smolensk that the local governor had appropriated one of his secretaries without his permission.[3] And in May the Synod was merely notified by the Senate that Colonel Pleshcheev, who had been appointed to the 'investigation of schismatic and other affairs' in 1721, was now to become master herald (*Gerol'dmeister*).[4] At first the Synod opposed this transfer on the grounds that Pleshcheev was a Synodal official and could not be moved except at the express command of the tsar;[5] it then acquiesced in the matter (the necessary edict having been issued), at the same time lamely insisting that none of Pleshcheev's staff could be moved without its consent.[6] But less than a year later we find the Synod complaining to the Senate that Pleshcheev's staff had been summarily transferred;[7] and on 15 March 1723, tacitly admitting to complete defeat, the Synod requested the Senate to approve the nomination of a number of officials to replace Pleshcheev's staff at the Chancellery for the Investigation of Schismatic Affairs.[8]

Yet part of the Synod's problem in controlling the ecclesiastical bureaucracy was of its own making. In the summer of 1722 the College of State Expenditure announced that it had been commanded to obtain full particulars concerning the remuneration of all 'state ranks, whether high or low, employed in the Colleges and Chancelleries as well as in the *gubernii* and provinces'. The tsar, the College explained, wished to equalize the pay scales of all 'state ranks' and the Synod was asked to cooperate in the matter. The Synod promptly issued the necessary directives;[9] and in November it submitted a full report to the Senate coupled with a request for pay rises for nearly all ranks of the ecclesiastical bureaucracy, so that their stipends should be equal to those of the civil bureaucrats.[10] The Synod's ready compliance in this matter suggests that it, too, regarded the church's administrators as members

[1] *PSP*, i, no. 189 (pp. 243–245).
[2] *PSP*, ii, no. 465 (pp. 117–118).
[3] *PSP*, ii, no. 525 (pp. 167–168).
[4] *PSP*, ii, no. 679 (p. 356).
[5] *Ibid.*
[6] *PSP*, ii, no. 866 (pp. 560–561).
[7] *PSP*, iii, no. 1020 (p. 54).
[8] *PSP*, iii, no. 1031 (p. 65). At least three other contemporary instances of the Synod's apparently unsuccessful attempts to resist the transfer of ecclesiastical officials to the secular government may be found in the official documents: see *PSP*, ii, no. 746 (pp. 439–440); no. 854 (pp. 549–551); no. 927 (pp. 653–654).
[9] *PSP*, ii, no. 704 (pp. 383–384); no. 776 (pp. 465–466).
[10] *PSP*, ii, no. 901 (pp. 595–619).

of the one great bureaucracy. Indeed, in June 1722 the Synod complained to the Senate that its staff (*prikaznye sluzhiteli*) had not been included in a recently compiled 'table of ranks', even though it, the Synod, had previously asked that they be included on the grounds that 'Synodal *prikaznye sluzhiteli* are also engaged in His Imperial Majesty's affairs'.[1] The Synod of course welcomed the Senate's ruling (in October 1722) that the '*prikaznye lyudi* subordinate to the Synod and located in the dioceses, who are provided for by grants and maintained by state taxes', should, like the '*prikaznye lyudi* of the secular command', be exempt from the new soul tax.[2]

And as members of the one great bureaucracy the servants of the church shared not only the privileges, but also the liabilities, of civil servants, and were subject to the same regulations. When in February 1723 the Senate announced that 'because of the present shortage of specie' the tsar had commanded that 'all *prikaznye lyudi* and similar persons' would be paid in kind – in 'Siberian and other treasury goods [i.e. in furs, etc.]' – the order was sent to the Synod, which promptly took the necessary action with respect to its subordinates.[3] At this time, too, the Synod was informed that the new Office of State Control, which had been established by Peter 'for the sake of an orderly management of revenue and expenditure and for the inspection of all accounting matters', was to supervise ecclesiastical finances, including those of the Synod's own household; and according to its *Instruktsiya*, the Office of State Control was to regulate, in particular, the stipends of the ecclesiastical bureaucracy.[4] Even the stipends of the members of the Synod themselves were not secure. In January 1723 they received an edict from the tsar which read: 'it has been made known to us that the Monastery Prikaz, which is subject to the Synod, has not sent a large sum of money to the appropriate places, wherefore the poor soldiers of the field army have not been paid, some for nearly a year, others for more than a year.... For this reason, as long as the money is not forthcoming your stipends are not to be paid to you; nor are their stipends to be paid to your subordinates...'.[5] As might be expected, the Synod speedily responded to this particular gesture of Imperial capriciousness, pleading that the delay in question was the fault of the Senate and the College of State Revenue, who had not sent officers to

[1] *PSP*, ii, no. 681 (p. 358).
[2] *PSZ*, vi, no. 4104 (p. 781); *PSP*, ii, no. 849 (p. 546).
[3] *PSP*, iii, no. 1017 (pp. 46–47).
[4] *PSZ*, vi, no. 4127 (pp. 794–795); *PSP*, iii, no. 1007 (pp. 40–43).
[5] *PSZ*, vii, no. 4152 (p. 18); *PSP*, iii, no. 998 (p. 31).

collect the money; and Peter was respectfully reminded that those of the Synod's lay subordinates who had no other income than their stipends would be unable to survive without them.[1] In February Peter relented, but only with respect to the Synod's landless subordinates;[2] it was not until May 1724 that the members' own stipends were fully restored to them.[3]

The history of the Synod's relations with the secular government during the first four years of its existence suggests that in securing a position of equality with the Senate and of superiority to the colleges, the Synod had won but a formal victory. It is not merely that the Synod's judicial and administrative authority over the secular affairs of the church remained subject to regulation and control by various agencies of the secular government, leaving the Synod with exclusive jurisdiction over only a relatively narrow range of 'ecclesiastical matters'. Nor is it merely that the Synod was obliged to wage a constant struggle with the secular authorities to secure in practice a recognition of even that limited authority to which, in theory, it was entitled. Rather, on a more fundamental level, it is that both the statutory controls and the continual interference of the secular government were the inevitable concomitants of that reform of the church which had brought the Synod itself into being. Nothing could conceal the fact that the Synod was in reality a government bureau charged with administering the church in the name of the tsar. The Synod's grandiose titles, its status in the administrative hierarchy, its broad jurisdictional claims – all these were formalities, formalities which the secular authorities were not always disposed to observe.

Evidently the Synod was pleased to think that for administrative purposes the state was divided into ecclesiastical and secular spheres which were headed, respectively, by itself and by the Senate, each supreme in its own sphere and 'equal' to the other. It was a sort of modernized version of the traditional Byzantine theory of the parallel powers. But the conception, whether or not it is rightly ascribed to the Synod, was greatly at odds with reality. Time and again we encounter, in the Senate's communications with the Synod, the telling formulas: 'The Most Illustrious, Most Potent Peter the Great, Emperor and All-Russian Autocrat, being present this day in the Senate, has decreed: . . . and the Most Holy All-Ruling Synod is to do as His Imperial

[1] *PSP*, iii, no. 1004 (pp. 37–38). [2] *Ibid.*
[3] *PSP*, iv, no. 1267 (p. 115); no. 1280 (pp. 121–122).

Majesty has commanded'.[1] If the 'Supreme Judge' of the Synod chose to rule it through the Senate, the Synod, to be sure, could do nothing about it. Nor could it compel the tsar to honour his commitment to pay a 'weekly or monthly visit to the Synod',[2] and to rule it directly, and thus to confirm that equality with the Senate which the Synod so eagerly sought. To judge from the printed record of its proceedings, in the last four years of his reign Peter personally attended meetings of the Synod no more than half a dozen times. And so the Synod had no choice but to accept the government's directives concerning matters which nominally lay within its own jurisdiction and duly to forward them, under the seal of its formal approval, to the relevant departments of the ecclesiastical administration. The Synod could only insist that such directives should be communicated to it in the proper bureaucratic form: 'memoranda' from the Senate, 'submissions' from the colleges and other organs of the civil government.

For the Synod, it must be stressed, could not deny that it was 'established by decree of the Monarch with the concurrence of the Senate'. Nor could it, for this very reason, rightfully claim to be the successor of the patriarchs in any but the strictly temporal sense of the word. Indeed, it was the Synod itself that assured the tsar, on the day of its official opening, that it had 'sworn faithfully to serve His Majesty's interest no less than the other Colleges'; and it was the Synod who pointed out to the Senate, as we have also seen, that 'this ecclesiastical administration founded by [Peter] is not like that of the patriarchs . . . it does not govern in its own name, but rather by decrees of His Majesty, who . . . has established Himself as Supreme Ruler and Judge of this Holy Synod'. Everything, as the Synod well knew, depended on the will of the tsar, including the appointment and dismissal of the members of the Synod themselves.

Nothing illustrates more clearly its real position in relation to the secular government than the history of the Synod's unsuccessful attempt to gain exclusive control of its own bureaucracy. That the Synod should have reorganized the ecclesiastical administration on the model of the secular bureaucracy was not in itself a radical break with the past; the structure of the patriarchal administration of the seventeenth century, as we saw in an earlier chapter, was closely modelled on that of the tsar's government. Yet the patriarch himself, not unlike the tsar,

[1] *PSP*, i, no. 334 (p. 386); *PSP*, ii, no. 651 (pp. 319–320); etc.

[2] As expressed in his *Instruktsiya* to the chief procurator of the Synod in June 1722 (see above, p. 176).

had stood outside and above his administrative machine: he was, in the ecclesiastical sphere, the counterpart, indeed the 'equal', of the tsar in the secular; and this independent position of the patriarch, who could be removed from office (as the *Regulation* pointed out[1]) only at great trouble and expense, had been the ultimate guarantee of the independence of the church – of the autonomy, that is, of its adminstration. Peter changed all that. The creation of the Synod destroyed the independence of the ecclesiastical administration. And during the first four years of its existence the Synod itself more or less willingly cooperated in carrying out measures that completed the incorporation of the church within the framework of the newly absolute, secularized, bureaucratic state. By the time of Peter's death the ecclesiastical administration had become to all intents and purposes an integral part of the one, vast, centralized bureaucracy to which everyone, layman or cleric, was subject.

A rose by any other name is still a rose. The Synod's original name was more appropriate to its true nature: it remained, in reality, Peter's College of Ecclesiastical Affairs. And from this point of view the Synod's endeavour to assert a special position in relation to the secular government may be seen as an attempt to minimize, if not to conceal, the degradation which the church had suffered. For at least some of the individual members of the Synod – Yavorskii and Yanovskii, for instance – appear to have regretted the loss of the church's autonomy and to have striven, therefore, somehow to repair the damage.

V

OTHER ADMINISTRATIVE MATTERS

What uses were made, other than those already mentioned, of the reformed ecclesiastical administration? What other orders did it faithfully convey to the bishops, clergy, and people who still made up the long-suffering church? The Synod's administration of clerical, educational, and schismatic affairs during the first four years of its existence will be examined in the following chapters. We may conclude the present chapter with a brief discussion of the Synod's administration of certain other matters that fell within its purview. In this way, perhaps, the essentially bureaucratic nature of the Most Holy All-Ruling Synod will be seen more clearly and more light shed on the nature of Peter's church reform.

[1] See above, p. 156.

The Synod inherited from Yavorskii, and from the patriarchs before him, the office of chief priest of Russia – though not, of course, in the liturgical or sacramental sense: the Synod as such could not officiate at services. But 'by edict of His Majesty the tsar and by command of the Synod' it was ordered, in May 1721, that 'throughout the Russian state the Tsar's coronation day, as well as His birthday and nameday, are to be commemorated with public prayers: in execution whereof the Synod has sent decrees to all the bishops'.[1] Similarly, in January 1722 the Synod issued decrees regulating the form of the prayers for the health of the tsar and his family that were to be used in 'all church services throughout the Russian state': the titles 'Emperor' and 'Empress' were to replace 'Tsar' and 'Tsaritsa'; and Peter's name was always to be followed by the epithet 'the Great'.[2] In December 1722 Peter ordered the Synod to compose new prayers 'to the holy Orthodox Prince Alexander Nevskii' which were to be printed and distributed to all the churches in Russia for use 'in all services'.[3] It was the Synod that took charge of arrangements for bringing Nevskii's remains to St. Petersburg for internment in the monastery newly dedicated to his memory.[4] The ceremony took place on 30 August 1724 in the presence of the tsar, who on that occasion decreed once again that special prayers and hymns to Nevskii should be composed for printing and distribution throughout Russia. Peter also commanded that in future the saint's feastday should be observed on 30 August instead of 23 November, 'as was hitherto the custom'.[5] The thirteenth-century soldier-hero of old Rus' had become, with the Synod's dutiful cooperation, the patron saint of the St. Petersburg empire. Thus in June 1724 the Synod resolved that in painting ikons of Alexander Nevskii 'no one on any account is to portray this saint as a monk . . . but rather in the garments of a Great Prince'.[6] It was symbolic, indeed, of the saint's new status and of the baroque religiosity of Peter's new state.

During the early years of its existence the Synod issued decrees concerning the painting and veneration of ikons generally. On this subject the *Ecclesiastical Regulation* stipulated only that the Synod was 'to observe what is written in the consecration oath of the bishops',[7]

[1] *PSZ*, vi, no. 3783 (p. 390); *PSP*, i, no. 85 (p. 113).

[2] *PSZ*, vi, no. 3882 (pp. 481–483); *PSP*, ii, no. 361 (pp. 15–17).

[3] *PSP*, ii, no. 936 (p. 660).

[4] *PSZ*, vii, no. 4241 (pp. 74–75); *PSP*, iii, no. 1065) (pp. 101–103). The Synod also designed, and paid for, the magnificent silver reliquary which was constructed to contain the saint's remains.

[5] *PSP*, iv, no. 1347 (p. 188). [6] *PSP*, iv, no. 1318 (p. 148). [7] Verkhovskoi, ii, p. 35.

according to which the latter undertook to make annual visitations of their dioceses to ensure, among other things, 'that holy ikons are not idolatrized and false miracles attributed to them, which gives cause for slander by the enemies of Orthodoxy'.[1] On this somewhat slender legal foundation the Synod proceeded to rule (in February 1722) that 'miracle-working ikons found in private houses are to be investigated by the ecclesiastical authorities': those previously certified as 'genuine' were to be seized and taken to the nearest large church or monastery and their certificates of authenticity sent to the Synod for inspection; and 'on no account' were such ikons to remain in private houses.[2] The following year the Synod ordered that the 'great number of little domestic ikons' to be found in the churches of Russia should be removed by their owners, and the custom of taking them there discontinued, because this was done 'not for the sake of beautifying the churches, but only to preserve [the ikons]; however it is most unfitting that churches should be treated as repositories of domestic ikons'.[3] Moreover, at a joint meeting of the Synod and the Senate in August 1722 Peter himself commanded that 'ikons are to be painted in accordance with ecclesiastical customs and the Acts of the Council [of 1667]', and that to ensure that this was done a 'superintendent [*sic*]' of ikon painters, responsible to the Synod, was to be appointed.[4] One Ivan Zarudnev was named to the post;[5] and within weeks of his appointment the Synod informed the Senate that Zarudnev had no less than thirty-six painters working under him.[6] However, in addition to painting ikons according to a closely regulated pattern, Zarudnev's artists were given another task. In January 1723 the Synod was informed by the Senate that the tsar was displeased with all the 'pictures of His Imperial Majesty and the Empress which out of ignorance have been unskilfully painted'; Zarudnev was to collect up all such pictures and bring them to the Synod, while his artists were to paint portraits of the emperor and his consort 'by studying the work of the [western European]

[1] *PSZ*, v, no. 2985 (p. 194).
[2] *PSP*, ii, no. 423 (p. 65).

[3] *PSZ*, vii, no. 4154 (p. 19); *PSP*, iii, no. 999 (pp. 31–32). The Synod had already ruled that 'no images of any kind are to be taken for any reason from the monasteries and parish churches ... to private houses' (*PSZ*, vi, no. 3910 [p. 512]; *PSP*, ii, no. 419 [p. 64]).

[4] *PSZ*, vi, no. 4079 (pp. 762–763); *PSP*, ii, no. 534 (pp. 177–180); no. 777 (pp. 466–468).

[5] See his *Instruktsiya*, dated 31 October 1722, in *PSP*, ii, no. 885 (pp. 575–576). The council of 1667, as the Synod noted, had commanded that 'over the ikon painters there is to be appointed a skilled artist and good man from the ecclesiastical order, who shall be their elder [*starosta*], that is their *nachal'nik* and *dozorshchik*'. But until Zarudnev's appointment, apparently, the council's decision had not been acted on.

[6] *PSP*, ii, no. 901 (p. 614).

masters, and with attention and assiduous care'. In future only such 'official' portraits were to be sold and displayed.[1]

The painting and veneration of ikons were not the only old customs to be regulated by the Synod. The Synod's war on what it considered superstitious practices will be discussed in a later chapter. But it may be noted here that in October 1723 the Synod took action to implement the tsar's decree that 'no little houses [*budki*] for the reading of the psalter are to stand over the graves in parish churchyards; rather, such prayers are to be said inside the churches'.[2] At the same time, the Synod forwarded to the bishops the tsar's command that only 'important persons' should be buried in urban churchyards; everyone else was to be buried 'outside the towns . . . because of the harmful vapours which emanate from bodies which are sometimes infected'.[3] On Pete 's orders the Synod also issued detailed regulations governing the manufacture and sale of candles for use in the churches.[4] And in these numerous prohibitions and regulations the Synod or Peter frequently invoked rational or practical or aesthetic criteria to justify their actions. Indeed such justifications, or 'explanations' as they were called by the lawmakers, were a conspicuous feature of the legislation of the latter years of Peter's reign generally, and were part of that 'ubiquitous tutelage' of the people undertaken by his government in a 'conscious effort to lead [them] towards prosperity and well-being'.[5]

Under the Synod, too, an attempt was made to enforce more attentive participation in church services. 'On consideration of the idle conversation of people in church during the time of services, and mindful of His Imperial Majesty's edict forbidding it in the churches of St. Petersburg', the Synod resolved in January 1723 that henceforth during services the people were not to converse, nor to pray aloud, nor to kiss the ikons, but rather were to 'confine themselves to reading and singing the services, and [were] otherwise to maintain silence'.[6] The Synod also instructed the bishops and other local ecclesiastical authorities not to accept petitions nor to conduct any business – 'except the most urgent affairs of state' – during the time of services, since it was up to them to set a good example.[7] Nor did the Synod neglect to

[1] *PSZ*, vii, no. 4148 (pp. 16–17); *PSP*, iii, no. 986 (p. 19).

[2] *PSZ*, vii, no. 4339 (p. 143); *PSP*, iii, no. 1133 (p. 216).

[3] *PSP*, iii, no. 1123 (p. 208); no. 1130 (p. 215).

[4] *PSZ*, vi, no. 3746 (p. 362); *PSP*, i, no. 17 (p. 39); no. 18 (p. 40); *PSP*, iii, no. 931 (p. 655); *PSZ*, xl, appendix, no. 4490a (p. 1); *PSP*, iv, no. 1251 (p. 107); no. 1256 (p. 110).

[5] As Bogoslovskii (*Oblastnaya reforma*, esp. pp. 1–13) shows.

[6] *PSZ*, vii, no. 4140 (p. 6); *PSP*, iii, no. 974 (pp. 11–12).

[7] *PSZ*, vii, no. 4169 (p. 25); *PSP*, iii, no. 1010 (p. 44).

regulate the collection of offerings during church services, which was to be done (according to a decree of July 1723) by clerics and trusted lay elders: two bags were to be used, one to receive offerings 'for the needs of the church', the other 'for the hospital fund'. Accounts were to be kept of every collection, and an annual report of the proceeds was to be sent to the bishop and thence to the Synod.[1]

The *Ecclesiastical Regulation* explicitly forbade the practice of maintaining priests and private churches (or chaplains and chapels, in the western sense) by lay persons 'except the family of His Majesty the Tsar'; for 'this is unnecessary, and is done only for ostentation, and is a reproach to the ecclesiastical order. Let the lords go to the parish church, and not scorn their brethren in the Christian community, though they be their peasants'.[2] While the Synod allowed certain exceptions to this rule,[3] it also took steps to enforce it, and in April 1722 issued a decree prohibiting private chapels: 'the lords can go to the parish church, as is specified in the *Ecclesiastical Regulation*'.[4] In time the ruling was modified to permit 'important persons' to keep the necessary liturgical objects for administering the sacraments in their houses, for the benefit of invalids unable to get to church; 'but on no account will special clergy be maintained in these houses . . . services will be conducted by the parish priest'.[5]

The prohibition of private chapels linked on to a policy which had been pursued by Peter's government for more than twenty years: the prohibition of 'superfluous' ecclesiastical buildings.[6] In April 1722 the Synod required that all the parishes of Moscow should draw up inventories of all their buildings and submit them to the Synod, which would

[1] *PSZ*, vii, no. 4277 (pp. 96–97); *PSP*, iii, no. 1084 (pp. 124–125).

[2] Verkhovskoi, ii, p. 70.

[3] In April 1721 it granted the petition of Count P. M. Apraksin, who had asked for permission to keep his chapel and priest because of his age and infirmities (*PSP*, i, no. 75 [pp. 103–104]). In his petition Apraksin took the trouble to point out that his sister, 'the Tsaritsa Martha Matveevna of happy memory', had lived in his house; that he had served the tsar in many senior capacities for many years; and that as recently as 6 April (his petition was submitted on 14 April) Archbishop Theodosius Yanovskii had celebrated the Liturgy in his chapel and had told him that in order to keep it he must petition the Synod. No doubt these facts influenced the Synod's favourable response. For other exceptions to the prohibition of private chapels, see *PSP*, no. 959 (pp. 681–682); no. 961 (p. 684).

[4] *PSZ*, vi, no. 3964 (pp. 652–653); *PSP*, ii, no. 533 (p. 177). See also *PSZ*, vii, no. 4187 (p. 33); and *PSP*, ii, no. 607 (pp. 264–266): decrees of 1722–1723 confirming the prohibition.

[5] *PSZ*, vii, no. 4320 (p. 130); *PSP*, iii, no. 1120 (p. 203); no. 1132 (p. 216); *PSP*, iv, no. 1295 (pp. 130–131).

[6] For the earlier legislation to this effect, see above, p. 85.

decide which were 'superfluous'.[1] In June the Synod was made responsible for deciding all petitions concerning the building or rebuilding or repairing of churches in stone, which hitherto had been entirely prohibited.[2] In October the Synod ruled, once more on Peter's orders, that no new ecclesiastical construction be undertaken without its permission, 'since any reasonable man knows how contrary to the glory of God is the maintenance of superfluous churches and a multitude of priests'.[3] The Synod, or rather Peter, was evidently attempting to stabilize the number of churches in Russia; and judging from available statistics, the attempt succeeded.[4]

In assuming control of the Monastery Prikaz the Synod assumed overall responsibility for the rudimentary social services that the Prikaz administered. During the first four years of its existence the Synod was therefore obliged to deal with numerous reports relating to the administration and financing of the Moscow surgical hospital and school, and to the special military hospitals (*lazarety*).[5] Similarly, the Synod was required to devote a portion of its time to the problems of the almshouses.[6] With regard to these institutions, the Synod did not introduce any notable changes of policy: Bidlo's hospital and school were rebuilt after a disastrous fire and maintained at their former capacities; and the number of almshouses (93) and of their inmates (4411), as well as the total of the inmates' annual grants (13,000R), remained remarkably constant in the years 1721 to 1725, according to the reports regularly submitted to the Synod by the Monastery Prikaz.[7]

[1] *PSZ*, vi, no. 3964 (pp. 652–753); *PSP*, ii, no. 533 (p. 177); no. 607 (pp. 264–266).

[2] *PSP*, ii, no. 662 (p. 334).

[3] *PSZ*, vi, no. 4122 (pp. 791–792); *PSP*, ii, no. 868 (pp. 561–562); *ZAP*, no. 138 (p. 111).

[4] In 1722 there were some 15,761 churches in Russia, serving a population of about 14 millions, or approximately one church for every 903 inhabitants. In 1738 there were an estimated 16,901 churches, and a population of nearly 16 millions, or approximately one church for every 980 inhabitants. In other words, between 1722 and 1738 the total number of churches remained relatively constant; that is, the increase in the number of churches was proportionate to the increase in population. (Statistics on number of churches from Smolitsch, *op. cit.*, p. 709; population estimates from Blum, *op. cit.*, p. 278.)

[5] *PSP*, i, no. 61 (p. 90); no. 95 (p. 123); no. 237 (pp. 288–290); *PSZ*, vi, no. 3962 (pp. 649–650); *PSP*, ii, no. 531 (pp. 172–173); no. 539 (pp. 184–188); no. 551 (pp. 196–197); no. 652 (p. 320); no. 670 (pp. 346–347); no. 795 (pp. 487–488); *PSP*, iii, no. 1070 (p. 106); no. 1112 (pp. 150–152); no. 1118 (pp. 200–202).

[6] *PSP*, i, no. 309 (pp. 361–363); *PSP*, ii, no. 789 (p. 483); no. 901 (pp. 616–619); no. 932 (p. 656); *PSP*, iii, no. 1093 (pp. 135–139); *PSP*, iv, no. 1235 (pp. 90–97).

[7] See the documents just cited, nn. 5, 6. For the Monastery Prikaz's administration of the hospitals and almshouses in the years prior to 1721, see above, pp. 90–92.

Nor did the Synod, during the first four years of its existence, introduce any significant innovations in the other areas of social welfare covered by existing legislation.[1] Decrees were issued providing for the care of illegitimate children[2] and for the maintenance of the wives and widows of soldiers who had been recruited from ecclesiastical estates.[3] Regarding the practice of public begging, the *Ecclesiastical Regulation* ordained that the Synod was 'earnestly to consider the best means of extirpating this evil' – which the *Regulation* condemned at great length – and to 'establish sound rules for alms-giving; for in this we err greatly'.[4] While the Synod never got down to composing such rules, it did take steps to enforce the existing anti-begging laws, and thus to fulfil the *Regulation*'s provision.[5]

Yet there was one area in the field of social legislation in which the Synod, under Tsar Peter, did introduce significant innovations. In 1721 it ruled, in response to a petition from the College of Mines, that 'Swedish prisoners in Siberia, who are skilled in mining matters and have sworn faithfully to serve His Majesty, as well as those who should henceforth enter His service, are hereby permitted to marry Russian women without changing their [Lutheran] faith; provided that before the wedding they undertake in writing to do nothing whatever to induce their Russian wives to accept their faith, and also promise, in writing, that any children born of the marriage will be baptized and brought up in the Orthodox faith'.[6] And in 1724 the Synod promulgated the tsar's decree requiring that before the marriage of their children or servants the respective parents or guardians or masters must swear an oath that they consented to the marriage, that the persons about to marry 'ardently' wished to do so, and that no form of pressure had been brought to bear on them. 3600 copies of this remarkable document were printed at the Synod's order for distribution to the various branches of the secular government and to the bishops.[7] In

[1] For which, see also above, pp. 92 ff.

[2] *PSP*, ii, no. 838 (p. 532); also *ZAP*, no. 121 (p. 100).

[3] *PSP*, i, no. 243 (pp. 292–293); *PSP*, ii, no. 355 (pp. 12–13); *PSP*, iv, no. 1235 (p. 96). See also *PSP*, ii, no. 901 (p. 616).

[4] Verkhovskoi, ii, pp. 74–75.

[5] *PSP*, ii, no. 518 (p. 164); no. 932 (p. 656).

[6] *PSZ*, vi, no. 3778 (pp. 383–387); no. 3798 (pp. 401–402); no. 3814 (pp. 413–419); *PSP*, i, no. 131 (pp. 182–183); no. 154 (p. 208); no. 173 (pp. 222–227); no. 183 (pp. 236–240); no. 333 (p. 386). However the Synod forbade marriages between the tsar's Orthodox and Lutheran (Baltic) subjects according to the Lutheran rite (*PSP*, ii, no. 848 [pp. 542–546]).

[7] *PSP*, iv, no. 1157 (pp. 1–2); no. 1172 (pp. 22–23). See also *ZAP*, no. 128 (p. 103), which indicates that the essence of this law was first drafted under Peter's personal supervision in April 1722.

enacting both of these reforms of the marriage laws, however, the Synod was responding to pressure from the government, and did not itself initiate the changes. Rather, the Synod provided a theoretical (canonical and scriptural) justification for the reforms and the appropriate means for carrying them out.

Lastly, by way of concluding this discussion of the Synod's administration of various matters that came within its purview, it may be noted that in May 1721 Peter ordered the Synod to assume 'specific responsibility' from the College of Foreign Affairs for all churches of the 'Roman, Lutheran, and Calvinist confessions' located within the boundaries of the Russian state. The Synod was to keep detailed records concerning these churches: when they were built, where they were located, what clergy were attached to them, who was permitted to worship in them. In particular, all clergy of these confessions who were living in St. Petersburg had to register 'without delay' at the Synod; it was implied that henceforth only registered clerics would be considered as 'authorized' to perform their various religious duties.[1] The Synod had become, in short, the executor of Peter's long-standing policy of limited toleration for foreign non-Orthodox Christians living in Russia.[2] In 1724 it ratified the appointments of seven French Franciscans who were to serve the Roman Catholic communities of St. Petersburg, Kronshtadt, Riga, and Revel, having first stipulated that the Franciscans were not to proselytize among the native populations and that no other Catholic priests were to be allowed in these areas.[3] Similarly, during the years 1721–1724 the Synod formally approved the appointment of pastors for the Lutheran churches of the newly-conquered Baltic provinces, on condition that before taking office the pastors should 'swear an oath of loyalty to the Emperor according to [their] faith'.[4] Indeed, the Synod found itself in the somewhat anomalous position of having to give its consent, for reasons of state, to the building of new Lutheran churches in the Baltic region as well as additional schools 'for teaching young people the precepts of Evangelism'.[5] It would seem

[1] *PSZ*, vi, no. 3790 (pp. 395–396); *PSP*, i, no. 107 (pp. 147–148).

[2] See above, esp. pp. 72–73.

[3] *PSP*, iv, no. 1207 (pp. 65–68). See also *PSP*, i, no. 176 (pp. 229–230) *PSZ*, vii, no. 4376 (p. 176); *PSP*, iii, no. 1148 (p. 230); *PSP*, iv, no. 1291 (pp. 128–129).

[4] *PSP*, i, no. 149 (pp. 203–205); no. 167 (pp. 217–218); *PSP*, ii, no. 572 (pp. 218–220); *PSP*, iv, no. 1184 (p. 40); no. 1226 (pp. 82–83); no. 1302 (p. 136); no. 1320 (p. 149); no. 1330 (p. 179).

[5] *PSP*, iii, no. 1060 (pp. 98–99); no. 1142 (pp. 223–224).

that, among foreign Christians living in Russia, only the Armenian merchants of Moscow were to be denied freedom of worship 'lest', as the Synod declared, when justifying its order to close down their church, 'they convert Russian folk from Christian piety to their sophistical faith and cause temptation or humiliation to the Holy Church'.[1] The Synod's action in the case of the Armenian merchants reveals once again the political basis of Peter's policy of religious toleration: the Armenians, unlike the Roman Catholics, had no foreign Power to protect them; nor did they, like the Lutherans of the Baltic provinces, have any treaties with the tsar to protect their rights.[2]

In view of the evidence cited above, it is possible to regard the Synod not only as the embryonic ministry of social welfare, but also as the embryonic ministry of religion of the new, secular state. An Orthodox patriarch at the head of the Russian church could not have been expected to direct the affairs of other Christian confessions. But a government bureau, such as the Synod clearly was, could assume such a task, if that were the will of the tsar. The transformation of the supreme administration of the Russian church into an agency of the tsar's government was the single most important result of Peter's church reform, and this fundamental fact must not be lost sight of in our detailed discussions of the Synod's activities.

[1] *PSP*, iii, no. 1045 (pp. 83–84); no. 1144 (pp. 224–225).

[2] It must be noted that while the Synod was closing the Armenian church in Moscow, the tsar was offering refuge from the Turks to Patriarch Isaiah and his Armenian flock 'in Our newly-acquired Persian provinces lying along the Caspian Sea', where they might 'abide in tranquility and practise their Christian religion according to their own rite without hindrance' (*PSZ*, vii, no. 4357 [p. 157]). Thus, politically desirable Armenian settlers were guaranteed the religious freedom denied their co-religionists living in Moscow.

CHAPTER FIVE

Reform and the Clergy, 1721–1725

Peter's pre-1721 legislation affecting the clergy was discussed in a previous chapter.[1] There, it was shown how from the earliest years of his reign Peter took resolute action to suppress their traditional economic and judicial privileges. It was shown that beginning with measures designed to clear the streets of Moscow of unattached, impoverished, or fraudulent clerics Peter's government had proceeded to impose unprecedented restrictions on the monastic clergy; that in an effort to maximize the number of potential recruits for the army his government had decreed new regulations covering the selection and ordination of priests and deacons; and that in the years after 1716 it had manifested an increasing propensity to regard the secular clergy as its agents, enlisting their services in the campaign to impose uniform religious discipline on all subjects and in the official effort to 'root out criminals, bandits, fugitive soldiers, and similar persons'. In 1721, however, Peter introduced another and potentially more radical policy: that of 'reforming' the approximately 86,300 monastic and secular clerics who constituted what was known to contemporary Russian officialdom as the 'ecclesiastical order [*dukhovnyi chin*]'. This new policy was announced in the manifesto of 25 January 1721, which proclaimed that the all-seeing eye of the tsar had perceived 'many irregularities and great deficiencies in the affairs of the ecclesiastical order'; that 'having assumed the responsibility of reforming the ecclesiastical order, and seeing no better means to this end', he had established an 'ecclesiastical administrative council'.[2] On 14 February 1721 Peter agreed that this 'council' should henceforth be called the Most Holy All-Ruling Synod.

The present chapter is an attempt to describe how the church reform of Peter the Great affected the clergy of Russia. Thus, in the following pages the provisions of the *Ecclesiastical Regulation* relating to the clergy are examined in the context of the legislation enacted or merely implemented by the Synod between the time of its official opening in

[1] Chapter 2, esp. pp. 76–79, 82–83, 97ff. [2] Verkhovskoi, ii, p. 6.

February 1721 and that of Peter's death in January 1725. The chapter is divided into three sections which deal, respectively, with the bishops, with the secular clergy, and with the monasteries.

I

REFORM AND THE BISHOPS; THE QUESTION OF THE SYNOD'S CANONICAL VALIDITY

Prior to 1721, it will be remembered, Peter introduced a number of measures which directly concerned the twenty or so bishops of the Russian church.[1] The various charters granting individual members of the hierarchy extensive judicial and financial privileges in their respective domains were abrogated. At the same time, the bishops were subjected to numerous special taxes, forbidden to construct superfluous buildings, and required to submit annual accounts of their income and expenditure to the tsar's government. Moreover, during the middle years of Peter's reign various members of the hierarchy were obliged to hand over their entire revenue to the Monastery Prikaz or to the

[1] During the period of Peter's reign there were some twenty-six dioceses under the jurisdiction of the Moscow or 'All-Russian' patriarchate. This number includes the four Ukrainian sees (Kiev, Chernigov, Pereyaslavl', and Mogilev: the latter, founded in 1632, was in Polish territory, but was under the jurisdiction of the metropolitan of Kiev); the see of Irkutsk (founded 1707); and the short-lived see of Karelia (1714–1721). This total does not however include the very short-lived metropolitanate of Azov (1700–1701) or the diocese of Tambov, which between 1701 and 1722 was administered by the metropolitan of Ryazan' and in 1723 was joined to the Synodal domain (the Moscow diocese). For the see of Tambov's fortunes, see *PSP*, iii, no. 1015 (p. 46); for a handy list of all the dioceses of the Russian church, with their founding dates, etc., see Smolitsch, *op. cit.*, pp. 705–709.

Under Peter, therefore, three new sees were established, reflecting the contemporaneous expansion of the state: Irkutsk in the east, Azov in the south, and Karelia in the west; but only one of these sees, Irkutsk, survived Peter's death. It should also be noted that owing to the often prolonged vacancies which Peter left in the Russian hierarchy, the actual number of bishops at any one point in his reign was something less than the total number of sees. Thus in 1720 only nineteen bishops, a number which included all the incumbent bishops with the sole exception of the metropolitan of Tobol'sk, signed the *Ecclesiastical Regulation* (see above, p. 160).

In January 1725 the Synod itself drew up a classified list of the sees of Great Russia (see *PSP*, iv, no. 1448 [pp. 308–309]). The first class of sees so listed, those in which there were 'more or less 1000 churches, but more than 500', included: Novgorod, Rostov, Krutitsy, Ryazan', Belgorod, and Vologda. The dioceses of the second class, which contained 'between 200 and 500 churches', included: Kazan', Nizhnii-Novgorod, Suzdal', Tver, Kolomna, Kholmogory, and Voronezh. The third class of dioceses – those with less than 200 churches – included: Astrakhan, Tobol'sk, Pskov, Smolensk, Vyatka, and Ustyug. This list of sees, totalling nineteen, did not include those of Moscow, Azov, Tambov, Irkutsk, Karelia, or the four Ukrainian dioceses.

provincial governments, whence fixed stipends were paid to them for the upkeep of their households. In the autumn of 1715 two decrees appeared which clearly were designed to ensure that only monks who were known to the tsar should become bishops. And the government's legislation making ecclesiastical persons liable to the civil courts for an increasing number of offences, as well as its measures designed to regulate the careers of the secular clergy and to make them its agents, imposed, in effect, new limitations on the bishops' traditional authority over their subjects.[1]

The origins of many of these measures, particularly of those relating to episcopal finances, were linked, it was suggested above, to the exigencies of Peter's war effort. Others, such as the abrogation of episcopal charters and the curtailing of the jurisdiction of the episcopal courts, can be viewed as the outgrowth of tendencies originating in the reigns of Peter's predecessors. Yet one of Peter's pre-1721 measures, the introduction of the episcopal oath of 1716, was entirely unprecedented, and was unconnected with his war effort. The oath, which embodied the essentials of much of Peter's pre-1721 legislation affecting the church, was in effect an oath of loyalty to the tsar and to his policies, and may well have been seen by the bishops for what it was: a portent of Peter's resolve eventually to reform the church in a way that would further restrict episcopal authority.[2]

For the 'duties of bishops' are the subject of a lengthy passage of the *Ecclesiastical Regulation* of 1721.[3] Under this heading, the *Regulation*'s author, the newly-consecrated Bishop Feofan Prokopovich of Pskov, adduced some seventeen points which he considered worthy of his colleagues' attention. The first of these points no doubt reassured the more conservative members of the hierarchy: 'Every bishop is to have by him the [canons of the] ecumenical and local councils and is to know thoroughly what is prescribed in them for his own order as well as for all of the lower clergy'. It was only when he came to the last of these points that a conservative bishop might have experienced the pangs of doubt: 'Let every member of the hierarchy, whatever his rank, whether he is simply a bishop, or an archbishop, or a metropolitan, know that he is subject to the [Synod] as the supreme authority; that he is to obey its decrees, submit to its judgment, and be content with its decisions'.

[1] For Peter's pre-1721 legislation affecting the bishops, see above, pp. 80–83, 84–86, 87–88, 98–99, 100 ff., 140–141.

[2] For the episcopal oath of 1716, see above, pp. 141–142.

[3] See Verkhovskoi, ii, pp. 39–51, for all subsequent quotations from, or references to, the *Ecclesiastical Regulation*'s provisions regarding the duties of bishops.

A conservative bishop might well have worried whether this provision did not conflict with the earlier injunction to observe the conciliar canons. Indeed, he might well have doubted whether Peter's whole scheme of reform, based as it was on an arbitrary and radical reorganization of the supreme administration of the church, was, canonically speaking, valid. On this point the pragmatic and overtly political justification of the reform set forth in Part I of the *Ecclesiastical Regulation* would not have allayed his fears.[1]

The question of the canonical validity of Peter's church reform could not be ignored by his chief clerical collaborators. Thus the Synod was wont to insist, as we saw in the preceding chapter, that it had succeeded to the 'patriarchal honour, power, and authority, neither more nor less'. And in May 1721 it issued a lengthy justification of the first of the tsar's resolutions of 14 February, whereby he had commanded that the Synod be commemorated in all church services in place of the 'patriarch or patriarchs'.[2] This remarkable document was written the year before by Feofan Prokopovich, as he informed his friend Markovich in a letter dated 10 May 1720: 'I am now writing a treatise in which I explain how and when the patriarchate was established in the church and how, in the course of 400 years, the church was governed without patriarchs, and how some churches still to this day are not subject to a patriarch. This work I conceived as a defence of the [Synod] which is to be established, so that it should not appear to be something new and unusual, as will inevitably be contended by ignorant people of ill will'.[3]

Accordingly, Prokopovich's 'treatise' is based, not on an appeal to canon law, but on an appeal to reason, which was intended to prove, by means of a tendentious reading of ecclesiastical history and an arbitrary definition of liturgical commemorations, that the four Eastern patriarchs should not be 'publicly, particularly, and perpetually' commemorated in Russian churches, as 'some people have argued', because (1) this was not the practice 'among the Greeks themselves' ('What greater proof do we need than this? We cast an eye to the Greeks, and by the Greeks we are taught'); (2) this had not been the practice in Russia during the time of the Russian patriarchs; and (3) this was not compatible with the independent status of the Russian church, since a 'public, particular, and perpetual commemoration shows the

[1] Part I of the *Regulation* was discussed at length above (pp. 153 ff.).

[2] *PSP*, i, no. 106 (pp. 143–147); *OAS*, i, appendix, no. 24 (cols. CCXXXV–CCXLIV).

[3] Letter quoted in Chistovich, *Feofan Prokopovich*, p. 48.

subordination of the commemorator to the authority commemorated'. Yet Prokopovich could not conceal the fact that the creation of a collegiate body of clergy to rule an autocephalous church was without precedent in the long history of Orthodox Christendom; that, in other words, the example of Greek or previous Russian practices was wholly irrelevant to the situation in which the Russian church now found itself. Nor could Prokopovich's impressive rhetoric conceal the fact that the most telling of his arguments was simply one from authority – from, in this case, the authority of the tsar: it was the 'supreme judgment of our Monarch himself' that the practice of commemorating the Eastern patriarchs, which had been followed in Russia throughout the twenty-year *mezhdupatriarshestvo*, should be discontinued and the name of the Synod commemorated instead. Faced with an argument of such force and simplicity, the bishops, clergy, and people of Russia would have had no choice but to swallow any misgivings that they might still have entertained. It was shown in an earlier chapter how when one member of the hierarchy, Metropolitan Stefan of Ryazan', the president of the Synod himself, took exception to the terms of this document (which had been issued in his absence), he was promptly rebuked by his colleagues for being 'most oppositional and disruptive of the peace of the church and . . . the tranquility of the state', and was forbidden by order of the tsar to 'communicate to anyone . . . his contrary opinion.'[1]

And it was in an effort to vest the Synod with some sort of canonical validity that Peter himself appealed to the Orthodox patriarchs of the East for their formal recognition of the new administrative head of the Russian church.[2] The patriarchs' reply, dated 23 September 1723, was received by the College of Foreign Affairs in December and thereafter conveyed to the Synod. It consisted of two nearly identical letters, one from Patriarch Jeremiah of Constantinople, written on behalf of himself and the patriarchs of Jerusalem and Alexandria, and the other from Patriarch Athanasius of Antioch. Both letters 'confirmed, ratified, and declared' that the Synod established by Peter, 'is, and shall be called, our holy brother in Christ'; and the patriarchs enjoined all Orthodox clergy and people to submit to the Synod 'as to the four Apostolic thrones'.[3] In July 1724 the Synod, 'having inspected the letters from Tsargrad [Constantinople]', resolved to send copies of them

[1] See above, p. 163.

[2] Peter's *gramota* to the patriarchs of 30 September 1721 is printed in Verkhovskoi, i, pp. 678–679.

[3] See *PSZ*, vii, no. 4310 (pp. 101–103); *PSP*, iii, no. 1115 (pp. 160–162).

to the Senate and the secular government; and one week later similar copies were sent by the Synod to all the bishops, with orders that they be read 'in all monastic, cathedral, and parish churches before the congregation'.[1]

We can only surmise the patriarchs' reasons for thus legitimizing Peter's church reform. For one thing, in Peter's letter to the patriarchs the role played by the Russian clergy as a whole in the creation of the Synod was somewhat exaggerated; and it was an essential part of the Eastern Orthodox tradition that one autocephalous church did not interfere with the affairs of another. Moreover, in his letter Peter had assured the patriarchs that he had instructed the Synod to rule the Russian church 'in accordance with the unalterable dogmas of the faith of the Holy Orthodox Catholic Greek Church', and that he had ordered the Synod to correspond with the patriarchs and to seek their 'advice' in 'all ecclesiastical matters'. From the patriarchs' point of view there were also the obvious political considerations: the tsar of Russia was the sole independent ruler in the Orthodox world, the traditional dispenser of alms and, more recently, the protector of Orthodox interests in the Holy Land: his requests could not be refused easily. And the true nature of Peter's church reform – the transformation of the supreme administration of the Russian church into an agency of the tsar's will and the consequent bureaucratization of the church – was not perhaps as plain to contemporaries as it is to us. But more important than any of these considerations, it must be noted that on 28 September 1723 Patriarch Jeremiah sent a second letter to Russia, this time directly to the Synod, enclosing an exposition of the Orthodox faith which had been ratified earlier that month at a council meeting in Constantinople and signed by Jeremiah himself, the patriarchs of Jerusalem and Antioch, and eight other Greek prelates.[2] The exposition was prefaced by still another letter from the patriarchs, in which they 'advised' the Synod that

> as you have received from the beginning and until now have preserved and professed with your whole heart and soul the dogmas of the Orthodox faith maintained by our Eastern Holy Christian Church, so henceforth remain steadfast and unshakeable in these same holy dogmas, ordinances, commandments, and royal statutes of the church which you administer, lest in some form you should accept other proposals and explanations than the said

[1] *PSP*, iv, no. 1331 (p. 179); no. 1337 (p. 182).

[2] *PSP*, iii, no. 1115 (pp. 162–163). The exposition of the faith, in eighteen articles and three questions and answers, is printed in the original Greek and in Russian translation in *ibid.*, pp. 165–194.

exposition of the Divine Dogmas of the holy and Orthodox faith, which [dogmas] were scrupulously examined and defined in ancient times by the holy ecumenical councils and by the divinely-inspired holy fathers and given to our holy Catholic Church. . . . to them it is not permitted to add or to subtract anything.[1]

The enclosed exposition of the faith was the most recent authoritative statement of Orthodox doctrine then in existence;[2] and by sending it to the Synod at this time, in the immediate wake of their letters of recognition, the patriarchs of the East had discharged their duty of ensuring that the doctrinal bond of the Orthodox communion should be preserved.

And yet, it may be doubted whether the late Patriarch Dositheus of Jerusalem, on whose Confession the patriarchs' exposition of the faith was based, and whose relations with Peter were discussed above,[3] would have granted such prompt and unqualified recognition to the Synod. Indeed, for the next two centuries the canonical validity of Peter's church reform remained, unofficially, an open and vexed question, to be revived and passionately debated and finally decided, in the negative, at the church council of 1917–1918, the first church council to be held in Russia since Peter's time.[4]

Among the remaining points of the *Ecclesiastical Regulation* which dealt

[1] *Ibid.*, pp. 164–165.

[2] The exposition had been drawn up, as the patriarchs informed the Synod, in reply to certain 'proposals and questions of persons in Great Britain' which had been forwarded to Constantinople by the Synod; and the patriarchs instructed the Synod that 'should you have the intention of writing to [these persons], then without fail write precisely thus; that the teaching of our Eastern Church is exactly that revealed and set forth in . . . our exposition of the Orthodox faith; according to it and no other is union possible' (see *ibid.*, p. 165). The 'persons in Great Britain' referred to were a group of Anglican Non-jurors who had been in correspondence with the patriarchs since 1716, in the hope of establishing communion between themselves and the Orthodox church. The correspondence was maintained – after 1721 via the Synod in Russia – until 1725: see G. Williams (ed.), *The Orthodox Church of the East in the Eighteenth Century, being the Correspondence between the Eastern Patriarchs and the Nonjuring Bishops* (London, 1868). The exposition itself was based on the Confession of Patriarch Dositheus of Jerusalem, which had been ratified in 1672 by the council of Jerusalem (also known as the council of Bethlehem); and the Confession has recently been judged 'a document of primary importance in the history of modern Orthodox theology' (Ware, *op. cit.*, p. 108; Ware also lists the Confession and the patriarchs' exposition of the faith among the thirteen 'chief Orthodox doctrinal statements since 787' [p. 211]).

[3] pp. 124–126.

[4] See A. Wuyts, S.J., 'Le Patriarcat russe au concile de Moscou de 1917–1918', *Orientalia Christiana Analecta*, cxxix (Rome, 1941), which is based on the published minutes of the council. See also J. S. Curtiss, *Church and State in Russia, 1900–1917* (New York, 1940).

with the duties of bishops, some simply confirmed the relevant provisions of canon law or of Tsar Peter's earlier legislation. Bishops were to 'know the degrees of lineal and collateral kinship, and who may or may not enter into wedlock according to the commandments of God (in Chapter 18 of the Book of Leviticus) and of the Church (in the patristic and imperial [Byzantine] canons)'; and in order that a bishop should be able to discharge this and other of his duties, 'the requisite canons are to be read to him at table, although sometimes this may be dispensed with, as on great feastdays or in the presence of distinguished visitors or for some other good reason'. Similarly, 'there are canons forbidding bishops to linger for long away from their dioceses': thus, if a bishop were detained by 'some essential need, such as service in the capital or some other valid cause', he was to appoint a 'prudent and honourable archimandrite or igumen' to administer the affairs of his diocese. The *Regulation* also confirmed that a bishop was to observe 'that which at his consecration he promised on oath to observe, that is, to see that monks do not wander about aimlessly, that superfluous churches, lacking congregations, are not built, that false and invented miracles are not attributed to holy ikons, etc.'[1] And the *Regulation* provided, as we have seen, that the Synod was to keep 'books containing [the accounts of] episcopal revenues'.

However, during the first four years of its existence the Synod was unable to gain effective control of the economic life of the church, as we saw in the preceding chapter; and it may be noted here that twice during these years, in 1721 and again in 1724, the Synod was unable to provide the Senate with any data concerning episcopal finances in particular.[2] It was left to the Monastery Prikaz, which was subordinate to the secular government as much as to the Synod, to collect state taxes (except the new soul tax) from episcopal landlords and to pay the bishops their annual stipends.[3] The principle of at least indirect control

[1] The *Regulation* refers to, indeed quotes, the episcopal oath of 1716 (for which see above, pp. 141–142).

[2] See *PSZ*, vii, no. 4488 (pp. 274–275); *PSP*, iv, no. 1237 (pp. 97–99); and *PSZ*, vii, no. 4567 (pp. 348–349).

[3] In November 1722 the Monastery Prikaz reported that it was paying some sixteen bishops a total of 25,810R in annual stipends (*PSP*, ii, no. 901 [p. 616]). The Synod itself, however, appears to have exercised some discretion over the exact amount of the stipends to be paid to individual bishops: see *PSP*, i, no. 199 (pp. 25–252); *PSP*, ii, no. 659 (pp. 332–333); *PSP*, iii, no. 1047 (p. 86); no. 1063 (pp. 99–100). These government stipends formed only a part of the total annual income (from rents, feudal dues, church fees, etc.) of the bishops in question, and seem to have been directed to the poorer ones.

of episcopal finances by organs of the tsar's government, a principle which had been implemented as early as 1696, remained in force.

The *Ecclesiastical Regulation* also prescribed new rules for the bishops to follow. For instance, if a bishop were unwilling to report to the Synod that he was incapacitated by reason of old age or illness, his diocesan officials were to send the report, whereupon the Synod would decide 'whether to send an *administrator* [*sic*] to the diocese or to consecrate a new bishop'.[1] As a measure 'most conducive to the reform of the church', the *Regulation* provided for the institution of a system of schools 'for the sons of the clergy or others destined for the priesthood' which were to be maintained by the bishops.[2] 'And in order that the bishops should not begin to complain that it would be a burden for them to support' these schools, the *Regulation* stipulated that they were not to 'maintain superfluous servants, nor to build unnecessarily (except profitable buildings, like mills, etc.), nor to augment their priestly vestments or personal wardrobes beyond what is appropriate to their dignity'. The *Regulation*'s provision regarding the establishment of a regime of ecclesiastical 'fiscals' was mentioned above.[3] But because the proposed officials could not be trusted to 'ensure that priests and monks and others . . . keep the laws relating to them',[4] the *Regulation* further ordained that 'every year, or once in two years, the bishop should go round and visit his diocese'. The 'great example of the Apostle Paul' in this respect was cited; and a detailed list of regulations governing the conduct of an episcopal visitation was then adumbrated. The regulations were in essence an amplification of the provisions of the episcopal oath of 1716 and require no further comment here.

In the passage of the *Ecclesiastical Regulation* concerning their duties the bishops were also treated to Feofan Prokopovich's views on the nature of episcopal authority:

> Every bishop should be aware of the measure of his dignity and should not think too highly of it. For the work is indeed great; but in Scripture no high honour is ascribed to this dignity: thus the Apostle, demolishing the Corinthians' inflated opinion of their pastors, states that pastoral work owes the whole of its success and its fruits to God himself working in the hearts of men ('I planted, Apollos watered, but God gave the growth'); that for this growth

[1] Opposite this sentence in the margin of Prokopovich's rough draft of the *Regulation* Peter himself placed three asterisks, indicating thereby that the provision met with his particular approval (see Verkhovskoi, ii, p. 40, n. 89).

[2] This provision will be discussed in the following chapter.

[3] See p. 193.

[4] 'for these fiscals, out of friendship for their benefactor, or for a bribe, conceal much . . .'.

> no man is to be commended ('so neither he who plants nor he who waters is anything, but only God who gives the growth').[1] In the same place, pastors are called merely the stewards of God and stewards of his mysteries,[2] which they will be if they faithfully abide in that work. Indeed pastoral work is external only – preaching, exhorting, reproving, in season and out of season, and administering the sacraments; but the internal work of turning hearts to repentance and to a renewed life belongs to God alone, by his grace invisibly working through the teaching and sacramental ministry of the pastors as through an instrument. . . . God commands that good presbyters be considered worthy of double honour, especially those who labour in teaching and preaching (1 Timothy 5).[3] Yet such honour is to be moderate, and not excessive and considered equal to the Tsar's. Pastors must not seek it or extort it from their subordinates, but be content with the honour which is freely given.

Most of Prokopovich's fellow bishops would not perhaps have quarrelled with this definition of episcopal authority, though they might well have found it inadequate, especially when compared with the relevant passage of the Confession of Patriarch Dositheus: 'The dignity of the bishop is so necessary in the Church that without him neither the Church nor the name Christian could exist or be spoken of at all. . . . He is a living image of God on earth . . . and a fountain of all the sacraments of the Catholic Church, through which we obtain salvation'.[4] Prokopovich neglected to point out in the *Ecclesiastical Regulation* that the Orthodox church was a hierarchical church, and that an essential element in its structure was the 'Apostolic succession' of its bishops. Indeed, the passage just quoted may be taken as an example of that element of selective omission in Prokopovich's theology which encouraged his enemies to charge him with 'protestantism'.

But the author of the *Ecclesiastical Regulation* was chiefly concerned 'to restrain', as he put it, 'the excessive glorification of bishops', especially when this 'glorification' seemed to rival the honour that was rightfully rendered to the tsar alone. And so it was proposed that bishops, 'so long as they are in good health, should not be supported by the elbows when walking', as was the custom,[5] and that 'their subordinates should not prostrate themselves before them, thus willingly and shamelessly flattening themselves on the ground, and with guile, so as

[1] Prokopovich quotes 1 Corinthians 3:6–7.

[2] Cf. 1 Corinthians 4:1.

[3] Cf. 1 Timothy 5:17.

[4] Quoted in Ware, *op. cit.*, pp. 252–253.

[5] Consett notes that in his observation the custom was no longer followed (*op. cit.*, p. 42); this was, perhaps, a direct result of the *Regulation*'s injunction.

to obtain a rank they do not deserve and to conceal their animosity and villainy'.[1] Moreover, 'it follows from this that a bishop should not be high-handed and precipitous, but forbearing and judicious in the exercise of his power to bind, that is to excommunicate and to anathematize'. Prokopovich then outlined the complicated procedure that was to be followed by the bishops before imposing the penalty of anathema on a recalcitrant sinner, a penalty which could not in any case be imposed without the written consent of the Synod.

The *Ecclesiastical Regulation* also provided, as we saw in the previous chapter, that disputes between bishops should be settled by the Synod and that any cleric could appeal to the Synod if 'notably wronged' by his bishop, although a severe punishment was promised to anyone 'who should dare falsely to accuse his pastor'. The bishops were further required to submit any 'difficult or perplexing case' to the Synod and to send to it bi-annual reports of the 'state and conduct of their dioceses, even if all should be well'. And should a bishop report that all was well and it then transpired that 'some superstition or manifest impiety' had occurred in his diocese, he would be summoned to stand trial before the Synod for his negligence.

On 8 November 1721 the Synod resolved that copies of the newly-printed *Ecclesiastical Regulation* should be sent to all the bishops, so that each would 'know how to conduct himself and what he must guard himself against'. At the same time, the Synod sent copies of the *Regulation* to the archinquisitors, so that they should know 'what the duties of bishops and others consist of, what they are to inspect, and what transgressions they are to look for'.[2] Indeed, according to the *Instruktsiya* given to the archinquisitor of Moscow at this time, he and his subordinates – the 'provincial inquisitors' assigned to every diocese – were to ensure that the 'holy canons, the *Ecclesiastical Regulation*, His Majesty's decrees, and the Synod's decisions' were observed by the bishops and that the Synod's 'honour, power, and authority' were respected by them.[3] The institution of the regime of inquisitors provided the Synod with a means of maintaining a constant surveillance

[1] 'And the pastor who receives such marks of esteem and feeds on such homage', Prokopovich adds, 'imagines that his whole task is to be led about like an untrained horse, and of his true work is ignorant'. However this sentence has been crossed out in the rough draft and does not appear in the other manuscript and subsequent printed editions of the *Ecclesiastical Regulation* (see Verkhovskoi, ii, p. 43 and n. 114).

[2] *PSP*, i, no. 294 (p. 346).

[3] *PSZ*, vi, no. 3870 (pp. 467–476); *PSP*, i, no. 348 (pp. 401–408).

over the administration of ecclesiastical affairs and of supervising, in particular, the activities of the bishops.[1]

For the Synod desired, quite naturally, that the bishops should acknowledge its supreme authority, which was not only like that of a patriarch but was an emanation of the power of the tsar himself. Thus in March 1721, as we have seen, Metropolitan Ignatius of Krutitsy was told pointedly that the Synod was to be obeyed 'absolutely in all things, in accordance with His Majesty's edict; for this Synod . . . possesses the patriarchal power, honour, and authority'.[2] In November 1721 Metropolitan Sylvester of Tver was required to 'answer the Synod, in terms of the strictest truth, as to why he disregarded a decree sent to him by the most Holy All-Ruling Synod . . . and as to why he conducts himself as if he were not subordinate, but equal to the Synod': Sylvester had apparently ignored a recent decree concerning the maintenance of military hospitals in his diocese, and had sent his communications to the Synod in the form of 'memoranda [*vedeniya*]' rather than 'submissions [*donosheniya*]'.[3] In short, the Synod had assumed an unrestricted right to dictate to the bishops which they, in turn, were in no position to challenge. Especially after the recognition granted to the Synod in 1723 by the Eastern patriarchs, which dealt the last (if unintentional) blow to the traditional order of church government in Russia, the Russian bishops had no one to whom they could appeal. Patriarchs and church councils, hitherto the embodiments of supreme ecclesiastical authority, were things of the past. It is not surprising, therefore, that apart from the two cases just mentioned the printed record of the Synod's proceedings for the years 1721–1725 contains no other reference to a case of episcopal insubordination.

On the contrary, during these years the bishops dutifully submitted to the Synod a host of reports concerning a wide range of matters which were coupled with requests for the Synod's instructions.[4] In most cases the Synod's response was simply to enjoin observance of the relevant provisions of the civil or ecclesiastical law. In some cases, however, its considered judgment was required. In the case of a licentious priest of the Smolensk diocese, for instance, the Synod ruled that pending further investigation by the colonel of the local garrison and by the Smolensk episcopal prikaz (which had referred the case to the Synod), the priest could celebrate matins and vespers but not the liturgy.[5] In January 1722 the bishop of Suzdal' submitted a list of some

[1] For the inquisitors, cf. above, pp. 193–194, 201.
[2] See above, p. 180.
[3] *PSP*, i, no. 302 (pp. 354–357).
[4] *PSP*, i–iv, *passim*.
[5] *PSP*, i, no. 292 (p. 345).

twenty 'doubtful' cases for the Synod's resolution: what was to be done with the daughter of a certain *pomeshchik* who had been molested by him and then incarcerated in a convent? what was to be done with the unmarried daughters of two prominent persons who were being held in a local convent for killing their children at birth? how was the law prohibiting the bringing of ikons from church to private houses to be applied in certain cases? etc.[1] The Synod granted to one bishop additional funds for his school, to another an increased annual stipend, to a third permission to rebuild two of his churches.[2] It advised the bishops as to how to deal with schismatics, heretics, and other non-conformists.[3] It delimited episcopal jurisdiction,[4] forbade any bishop to leave his diocese without its permission,[5] provided for the burial of deceased bishops and for the temporary administration of their dioceses.[6] In all these ways the bishops acknowledged their subordination to the Synod while the Synod, in turn, exercised its right to rule them.

Perhaps the Synod's most effective means of controlling the bishops was its power, under the tsar, over episcopal appointments. This matter is not referred to in the *Ecclesiastical Regulation*, except for the statement that the Synod was to be 'a kind of school of church government' from which the 'most suitable members will deservedly advance to the episcopal rank'.[7] Thus, the fourth of the points submitted to Peter by the Synod on 14 February 1721 concerned the exact procedure to be followed in filling episcopal vacancies: 'is the [Synod] to choose a bishop, and upon reporting [its choice] to His Most Sacred Majesty the Tsar, to consecrate him and dispatch him to his diocese?' In reply, Peter resolved that the Synod was to 'choose two persons, and him whom we designate, consecrate and dispatch'.[8] Yet in the following years neither the *Regulation*'s provision nor the tsar's resolution of 14 February was strictly adhered to by Peter. Between 1721 and 1725 only two members of the Synod were promoted to episcopal rank.[9] As for the ruling that

[1] *PSP*, ii, no. 476 (pp. 127–130).

[2] *PSP*, i, no. 21 (pp. 40–41); *PSP*, ii, no. 659 (pp. 332–333); *PSP*, iii, no. 1134 (pp. 216–217).

[3] See below, pp. 298–300.

[4] *PSZ*, vi, no. 4081 (pp. 764–767); *PSP*, ii, no. 693 (pp. 366–372).

[5] *PSP*, ii, no. 559 (pp. 208).

[6] *PSP*, i, no. 101 (pp. 133–136); *PSP*, iv, no. 1238 (pp. 99–100); no. 1243 (pp. 103–104); no. 1269 (p. 116).

[7] Verkhovskoi, ii, p. 33.

[8] *PSZ*, vi, no. 3734 (pp. 355–356); *PSP*, i, no. 3 (pp. 33–34).

[9] Archimandrite Leonid, to the see of Krutitsy, in 1722, and Theophylact Lopatinskii, to the see of Tver, in 1723 (see above, pp. 170, 173).

the tsar would nominate one of two candidates presented to him by the Synod to fill a given episcopal vacancy, we have only to consider the case of Archbishop Antonii of Chernigov, whose future was summarily decided by Peter on the very day – 14 February 1721 – that he issued the said ruling: to the question of whether Antonii, who had fallen under a cloud for 'protecting seditious agitators', was to be allowed to return to his diocese, Peter replied that he was to be disciplined by the Synod and then transferred to the see of Tobol'sk to replace the aged incumbent.[1] The Synod duly ratified Antonii's new appointment.[2]

Similarly, of the twelve candidates submitted to the tsar by the Synod in January 1722 to fill six episcopal vacancies,[3] only four were nominated by Peter and consequently consecrated.[4] Peter had decided, for political reasons, to leave one of the sees (Irkutsk) vacant;[5] and to the sixth vacancy, in the Smolensk diocese, he appointed, 'with the blessing of the Most Holy All-Ruling Synod', a newly-arrived Greek bishop.[6] In February 1723 Peter commanded the Synod to transfer Bishop Sylvester of Tver to the 'widowed' see of Ryazan' and to appoint to Sylvester's place in Tver Archimandrite Lopatinskii.[7] Ironically enough, in August 1721 the Synod had rebuked the bishop of Suzdal' for applying for a transfer to a more comfortable see ('lest I, living in great need, should die an untimely death from grief') on the grounds that episcopal transfers were uncanonical.[8]

In other words, after 1721, as before,[9] Peter continued to intervene directly in the matter of episcopal appointments. And if prior to 1721 this direct intervention was contrary to tradition, after 1721 it was contrary to his own laws. But what was more important for the fate of the church was the fact that with the creation of the Synod and the promulgation of the resolution of 14 February 1721 the tsar's absolute control of episcopal appointments was firmly established in law. After 14 February 1721 no bishop could be consecrated without the prior and explicit approval of the tsar; and after that date no one could hope to become a bishop without having first attracted the tsar's attention or that of his agents or favourites. Indeed, the Synod's control under the

[1] *PSZ*, vi, no. 3734 (pp. 355–356); *PSP*, i, no. 3 (pp. 33–34).
[2] *PSP*, ii, no. 388 (p. 43). [3] *PSP*, ii, no. 338 (pp. 1–2).
[4] See *PSP*, ii, no. 508 (pp. 154–155); no. 650 (p. 319); no. 659 (pp. 332–333); no. 671 (p. 347).
[5] See above, p. 67. [6] *PSP*, ii, no. 460 (pp. 110–114). [7] See above, p. 173.
[8] *PSP*, i, no. 168 (pp. 218–219). Episcopal transfers 'from a smaller see to a greater' were uncanonical (Pavlov, *op. cit.*, p. 344).
[9] See above, pp. 123–124, 134 ff., 138 ff.

tsar of episcopal appointments tended to reduce the bishops to the status of Synodal deputies in much the same way that the provincial governors had been reduced by Peter's administrative reforms of 1718–1722 to the status of deputies of the central government.

II

REFORM AND THE SECULAR CLERGY; THE CURIOUS HISTORY OF THE SUPPLEMENT TO THE *Ecclesiastical Regulation*

The so-called 'Supplement [*Pribavlenie*]' to the *Ecclesiastical Regulation*, which contains nearly a hundred injunctions relating to the secular and monastic clergy, has a curious history. We know that it was written by the author of the *Regulation*, Feofan Prokopovich; that originally it was intended by him to form an integral part of the *Regulation* proper; and that it was completed by him in the early part of 1720. Our most conclusive evidence in this respect is Prokopovich's letter to his friend Markovich of 10 May 1720, in which he relates that he has finished writing a '*Regulation* for the Ecclesiastical College or Consistory which consists of the following eight parts: . . . (5) regulations for priests, deacons, and others; (6) regulations for monks; . . .'.[1] But these two parts were not included in Prokopovich's rough draft of the *Regulation*, although a fragment of his manuscript entitled 'On the priests, deacons, and other clergy' survives[2] to prove, in conjunction with his letter to Markovich, that the missing parts had been written by him by the early part of 1720. And for some reason – perhaps for lack of time – these two parts were not, like the rest of the *Regulation*, amended by the tsar and Prokopovich on 11 February 1720, reviewed by the bishops and senators on 23–24 February, signed by Peter and the others on 27 February, and ratified by the rest of the higher clergy in the following months of that year.[3]

The oversight, if such it was, was corrected by the Synod very soon after it took office. The earliest of four surviving manuscript versions of what came to be known as the Supplement to the *Regulation* is signed by the original members of the Synod and counter-signed by 'the Assessor and Chief Secretary, the Priest-Monk Varlaam Ovsyanikov';[4] since Ovsyanikov was made an igumen in March 1721,[5] his

[1] Prokopovich's letter is printed in full in Chistovich, *Feofan Prokopovich*, pp. 46–50; and this portion of the letter is quoted in the original Latin in Verhovskoi, i, p. 161.

[2] The fragment is printed in Verkhovskoi, ii, pp. 81–82.

[3] As described above, pp. 157 ff.

[4] For the four MSS., see Verkhovskoi, ii, pp. 77–81.

[5] As noted above, p. 172.

signature here as 'the Priest-Monk' indicates that this version of the Supplement was thus ratified by the Synod within the first month of its existence. A slightly modified copy of this version (the second of the surviving manuscripts just referred to) was sent to the printers and published as the Supplement to the first edition of the *Ecclesiastical Regulation*, which appeared in St. Petersburg in September 1721 and was sent to the bishops the following November.

But this, alas, was not the end of the matter, for on 19 November 1721 we discover the Synod ordering that a 'printed copy of the *Ecclesiastical Regulation*, except for the Supplement composed in the Synod, is to be sent to the Senate'.[1] Moreover, one of our authorities had access to two copies of the first edition of the *Regulation*: in one he found the Supplement, in the other he did not – a fact which prompted him to conclude that the *Regulation* was first published complete with the Supplement but was then, 'in view of a protest from Peter', issued without the Supplement.[2] In other words, sometime in the autumn of 1721 the publication of the *Regulation* was interrupted for as long as it took to remove the Supplement; and sometime during the winter of 1721–1722 a new manuscript copy of the excised Supplement (the third of the surviving manuscripts referred to above) was made and submitted to Peter, presumably at his command, for his inspection.[3]

This third manuscript version of the Supplement contains no less than twenty-one individual notes and subscripts in Peter's own hand, some of which were incorporated more or less verbatim into the final version of the Supplement (the fourth of the surviving manuscripts) which was sent back to the printers.[4] Moreover, this same third copy was further amended by Peter and by Prokopovich, perhaps with the participation of the whole Synod, in the spring of 1722: among the papers of his cabinet has been found an edict written by Peter which contains additional amendments that the Synod was instructed to include in the Supplement: the edict is dated 19 March 1722;[5] and the penultimate paragraph of the final version of the Supplement states that 'this Supplement to the *Ecclesiastical Regulation* His Imperial Majesty himself was pleased to have read in his own august presence and to amend in his own hand; and having approved of all that is written herein, he commanded it to be printed and published in the last days of April and the first days of May of this year 1722'.[6] However, in its

[1] *PSP*, i, no. 314 (p. 370).
[2] Verkhovskoi, ii, pp. 206–207.
[3] *Ibid.*, pp. 198–199.
[4] *Ibid.*, pp. 79–80; and pp. 83–105 *passim*.
[5] *ZAP*, no. 121 (p. 100).
[6] Verkhovskoi, ii, p. 105.

final form the Supplement contains a reference to a Synodal act of 17 May, a fact which indicates that Peter, who left St. Petersburg early in May to begin his Persian campaign, had entrusted Prokopovich and the Synod with the responsibility of drafting the final version for the printers. According to a resolution dated simply 'May 1722', the Synod, 'having considered this Supplement to the *Ecclesiastical Regulation* which was composed in the Synod in accordance with His Imperial Majesty's decree . . .; and having notified His Imperial Majesty of this Supplement; and having received his Majesty's personal considerations and amendments and his permission to print it, hereby resolves to print it in the same way and in the same quantity that the *Ecclesiastical Regulation* was printed, and to distribute them to all the dioceses'.[1] Thus the final version of the Supplement was printed at the Moscow press on 14 June 1722 and bound with the second edition of the *Regulation*, which had been printed, but not published, in February.[2] A third edition of the *Regulation*, complete with the Supplement, was published in Moscow in January 1723;[3] except for the introduction of Peter's Imperial title it was identical with the second edition and served as the basis of all subsequent (1738, 1749, etc.) editions.

Our account of the history of the Supplement to the *Ecclesiastical Regulation* reveals, once again, Peter's close personal participation in the drafting of the major ecclesiastical legislation of his reign. Moreover, the final version of the Supplement differs considerably from the version that was published in the autumn of 1721; indeed, it will be seen shortly that some of the Supplement's most radical and eventually notorious provisions affecting the clergy were added to it, under Peter's supervision, in the spring of 1722. Now it has been speculated that the original Supplement was excised from the *Regulation* because, although Peter 'no doubt' was familiar with its contents, he objected to the fact that it had been published without his 'formal approval'.[4] In view of the nature and extent of the amendments introduced under Peter's supervision, however, it is clear that he was deeply interested in the substance of the document. The history of the Supplement to the *Ecclesiastical Regulation*, it must be emphasized, confirms the suggestion put forward at various points in the preceding pages, namely, that Peter himself played the decisive role in the church reform that we associate with his name.

* * *

[1] *PSP*, ii, no. 596 (pp. 240–255); no. 597 (p. 255).

[2] Verkhovskoi, i, p. 208; ii, pp. 80–81.

[3] *Ibid.*, i, p. 208.

[4] *Ibid.*, pp. 202–204.

The final version of the Supplement contains some thirty 'regulations [*pravila*]' which were intended to provide for a 'reform [*ispravlenie*]' of the secular clergy.[1] A preface to these regulations states that if the clergy would but follow the injunctions of St. Paul, 'the Church would not need further regulations and statutes'. But

> since in the course of time the clergy became corrupt, the holy fathers, in the various councils, issued many regulations [*pravila*: canons] for their reform, in accordance with the needs of the times. And since all these statutes are included in the books of the councils, they need not be set forth here. Yet since special infirmities are visible in the clergy of our Russian church, it is fitting that in addition to the above [canons] special remedies should be devised, after the example of the ancient fathers, so that the bishops should know what they must watch over with regard to their clergy, the clergy the straight path of their vocation, and the Most Holy Synod be better able to discharge its great responsibility of supervising the ecclesiastical order.

Thus, in the spirit of reformation movements everywhere, the author of the Supplement claims scriptural and patristic sanction for the ensuing regulations governing the activities of the secular clergy; and the clergy were assured that the prescribed 'remedies' were designed to help them remain true to their vocation. Yet formulas such as these had introduced some of the most radical and unprecedented provisions of Peter's ecclesiastical legislation. Contemporary Russian churchmen might well have been wary of what now was to come.

The first six regulations dealt with the necessary qualifications for ordination. To prevent unqualified persons from entering the priesthood 'for no other reason than to have greater freedom and a better living', no one was to be ordained who had not been educated in one of the projected episcopal schools; and until such schools were established, candidates for ordination were to learn by heart certain 'little books on Christian faith and law and the duties of each order'.[2] Equally, before ordination a candidate for the secular priesthood was to secure a testimonial from his future parishioners certifying that they knew him to be a 'good man; more precisely, that he is not a drunkard, that he is a good administrator, that he is neither a slanderer nor a

[1] See Verkhovskoi, ii, 83–93, for all subsequent citations from the Supplement regarding the secular clergy. Verkhovskoi's critical edition of the Supplement is based on the MS. amended by Peter, which Verkhovskoi then collated with the other MSS. mentioned above. The differences between the various versions he has indicated in his notes.

[2] Provision for the composition of these 'little books' and for the institution of a system of episcopal schools is made in Part II of the *Regulation* proper, and will be discussed in the following chapter.

quarrelsome or violent person nor an adulterer, and that he has not been convicted of a criminal offence'. Also, before his ordination the stipend or property that the priest would receive was to be agreed in writing between him and his parishioners. The candidate was to be examined by a 'discerning person' – designated, presumably, by the bishop – as to whether he was a 'hypocrite and feigns humility . . . and relates his own dreams and visions or those of others; for from such a person what can be expected but the spreading of old wives' tales and pernicious tares in place of sound doctrine'. And after his ordination the new parish priest was to remain for a while at the bishop's house for instruction in the ecclesiastical offices, during which time he was to make his own copy of these regulations and of certain passages of the *Ecclesiastical Regulation* proper so that in future he could not 'excuse himself' by reason of ignorance of his own or his parishioners' duties. On leaving the bishop's house the new priest was to declare in writing that he would abide by these regulations, his copy of which he would be obliged to show to the bishop when the latter visited his parish. Finally, at the time of his ordination the candidate was 'publicly to curse by name all schismatic groups, and swear an oath that he will not conceal by his silence any secret schismatics he may discover in his parish through their absence from holy communion or through other signs, but will report them in writing to his bishop'.[1]

This last regulation is one of five in the Supplement which deal specifically with the duties of parish priests in regard to non-conformists. When a priest went to hear the confession of a sick person and to give him communion, he was to hear the confession in private but was to administer communion in the presence of the people of the house and of his own attendants: 'this is because some impious priests . . . only pretend to give communion to a sick person in private, so as to conceal thereby a schismatic'. For such 'godlessness', a priest was to be unfrocked and remanded to the secular courts for corporal punishment, and the schismatic whom he had thus concealed was to forfeit his property to the crown. Moreover, whoever reported such 'evil-doers' was to be rewarded with 'a half or a third of the forfeited property'. Priests who accepted bribes from non-conformists to register their infants as legally baptized would be 'similarly dealt with'. And 'as the pastor of those

[1] By a decree of the tsar in February 1722 these regulations laying down the conditions for ordination were sent by the Synod to all the bishops (see *PSZ*, vi, no. 3911 [pp. 512–513]; *PSP*, ii, no. 439 [pp. 86–87]). Presumably the decree was issued to ensure that the regulations should be implemented before the Supplement itself became available.

entrusted to his care, a priest must ensure that schismatic monks and teachers, those sycophantic hypocrites,[1] do not enter the house of one of his parishioners; and should he discover such persons, he is to apprehend them and send them to the bishop's house, under pain of such penalty as the bishop may determine'. But this last provision was amended by Peter himself to read: 'under pain of unfrocking and civil punishment'.[2]

Similarly, to the first of these regulations – that requiring that at his ordination a candidate was to swear an oath that he would denounce any schismatics he found in his parish – Tsar Peter himself added a line which in a slightly modified form was incorporated in the final version of the Supplement. Peter's amendment reads: 'Besides the above-mentioned oath, [the candidate] must take an oath of loyalty to the Sovereign, and must report any opposition as well as those things he is commanded by these regulations to report, even though someone relates them in confession, yet neither repents nor abandons his intention: this matter is clearly explained below under point 11'.[3] Indeed point 11 of the final version of the Supplement, which was drafted in response to another of Peter's marginal notes,[4] consists of the following passage, which in view of its radical nature and subsequent notoriety should be quoted in full:

> If during confession someone discloses to the priest an unfulfilled but still intended criminal act, especially [one] of treason or rebellion against the Sovereign or the State, or an evil design against the honour or health of the Sovereign and the family of His Majesty; and disclosing such an evil intention shows that he does not repent of it but indeed justifies his intention and does not forsake it, and confesses it not as a sin but rather to be confirmed in his intention by the assent or the silence of his confessor, which [fact] may be discovered in this way: if the confessor orders him in the name of God to wholly desist from his evil intention and he is silent and apparently dubious, or justifying himself appears unchanged in this respect, the confessor must not only not give him absolution and remission of his openly confessed sins (for it is not a true confession if someone does not repent of all of his sins), but must promptly report him at the prescribed places pursuant to the personal decree of His Imperial Majesty promulgated on 28 April of the present year 1722 ... in virtue of which, for words reflecting on the high honour of His Imperial Majesty and prejudicial to the State, such villains are

[1] Such terms of abuse, as will be seen in the following chapter, were typical of the Synod's utterances concerning schismatic teachers.

[2] See Verkhovskoi, ii, p. 91, n. 43.

[3] For Peter's amendment, see *ibid.*, p. 84, n. 9.

[4] *Ibid.*, p. 85, n. 22.

commanded to be apprehended with all dispatch and brought to the designated places.[1]

Therefore should someone reveal in confession an evil intention of which he does not repent, the confessor must, pursuant to this decree of His Imperial Majesty, immediately report him. However in this report he is not to disclose the grave matter revealed in this confession, because by the said decree it is commanded that such villains who will have been shown to have uttered evil [i.e. treasonous] words are to be interrogated only in the Privy Chancellery and in the Preobrazhenskii Prikaz; rather, in his report the confessor is secretly to relate that such and such a person (having revealed his name and rank) harbours an evil design against the Sovereign . . . a design of which he does not repent and from which great harm would ensue, and that for this reason he must be apprehended forthwith and placed under arrest.

And since by the said decree it is commanded that informers or accusers are to be placed under honourable arrest and then [released] on bail or, if no bail is forthcoming, may be sent under escort to the said Privy Chancellery or to the Preobrazhenskii Prikaz—the confessor, having made his report and given surety for himself, is, on receiving his instructions, to proceed without delay to the designated place and there, where such crimes are investigated, to declare everything he has heard about this evil intention explicitly, without hesitation, and concealing nothing.

And having thus obliged the clergy to violate the secrecy of confession and to appear in court as witnesses against their spiritual children, Peter's clerical collaborators proceeded to justify this extraordinary injunction, maintaining that

By his declaration the confessor does not dislcose the confession he has heard nor violate the canons,[2] but rather fulfils our Lord's teaching, expressed thus: If your brother sins against you, go and tell him his fault, between you and him alone; if he listens to you, you have gained your brother, etc.; if he still does not listen, tell it to the church.[3] And from this it may be deduced that if the Lord commands that such a sin of brother against brother, even one such offence, or one similar to it, of which the sinner does not repent but perseveres in not listening, is to be told to the church, how much more then is it a duty to report and declare a criminal intent against the Sovereign or against the body of the church and the evil consequences thereof.

[1] For the decree of 28 April 1722, whose contents are summarized here, see *PSZ*, vi, no. 3984 (p. 666). The 'designated places' were the tsar's Privy Chancellery and the Preobrazhenskii Prikaz, which had, as the decree states, exclusive jurisdiction over cases of treason.

[2] According to the canon law then supposedly in force in Russia, priests were absolutely forbidden to divulge anything heard in confession, even to another priest (Pavlov, *op. cit.*, pp. 245–246).

[3] Cf. Matthew 18:15–17.

Moreover, every priest should remember that in the certificate of ordination given to him by the bishop who ordained him he is admonished by the latter, in accordance with the ancient tradition of the fathers, to bind the consciences of those who have confessed to him and to remit sins prudently, according to the canons, etc., 'and by our episcopal blessing and command to bring to us the gravest and most difficult cases to judge'.

And if it is ordained from olden times that these gravest and most difficult cases, which are already confessed with repentance to the priest, should be brought to the bishop, how much more then must an unrepented and criminal intent against the Sovereign or the State be reported.

And by such a report the confession is not violated, since the revealing of an intended crime which the person confessing does not wish to forsake nor impute to himself as a sin is neither a confession nor part of a confession, but a cunning contrivance conducive to the seduction of his conscience, the total ruin of such villains, and the perdition of the confessor who conceals their criminal intention.

This has already been demonstrated in actual cases not only in previous years, but also in the present year: whereof a special announcement of the Most Holy Synod to the confessors and priests has been printed, of which all are commanded to have a copy and in which what every confessor must do concerning the necessary deposition in such cases is precisely explained and sufficiently ratified.

Thus, with perverse logic, it was argued that black was white, that something a priest had heard in confession had not been heard in a 'true confession', that the uttering, in confession, of what could be construed as a treasonous remark, was 'neither a confession nor part of a confession'. The political motives underlying the drafting and issuing of this injunction are obvious. And in its 'special announcement' of 17 May 1722, which contained the whole of the passage quoted above, the Synod, inspired by Peter, recounted the 'actual cases' which, they said, demonstrated that certain confessions were in reality 'a cunning contrivance . . .':

There was a typical case of such artful cunning in recent years, when the criminal Talitskii intimated to his priest in confession his most wicked intention, *namely: to write a letter by means of which he wished everywhere to incite sedition, insisting that it was right* and not to be forsaken; and the priest, although this [intention] disgusted him, nevertheless gave him communion, and did not report it to the appropriate authorities. . . . *and this criminal proceeded to carry out his intention. And should he not have been caught in the act, what blood and disasters would have issued therefrom; and to what wickedness the sacrament of penance had been put by Talitskii and his confessor.*

> Then again, most wicked of all and completely unprecedented, in 1718 it was revealed that another confessor not only did not report what had been told to him, but even forgave the person for it, and conspired with him in an evil plot, namely: the son of His Imperial Majesty, the Tsarevich Aleksei, revealed in his testimony that during confession he had told his confessor that he wished his Father were dead; and this confessor forgave him in the name of God and said that he, too, wished He were dead, which this former confessor himself admitted under interrogation . . .; and for this evil deed he [the confessor] was put to a well-deserved death.

The trial and execution of 'Grishka' Talitskii, whose crime it was to distribute leaflets in which the imminent end of the world was predicted, Moscow called Babylon, Peter himself denounced as Antichrist, and the people forbidden to serve the tsar or to pay his taxes, took place, as we have seen, in 1700–1701.[1] The memory of Talitskii's crime had remained fresh in Peter's mind for more than twenty years: the words in italics in the passage just quoted were inserted into the draft of the Synod's announcement by the tsar himself. The trial of the unfortunate Aleksei, together with its wider ramifications, including the execution of his confessor, was also discussed above.[2] Yet the Synod, in this announcement of 17 May 1722, recounted yet another relevant case of 'evil-doing' which, it was said, 'has caused great scandal not only to the Orthodox but has been viewed with horror by all the foreigners, as an instance of the depravity of our church'.[3] Thus,

> On 19 March of the present year 1722 a certain evil-doer, on arrival at the town of Penza, publicly uttered many evil things against the most high honour of His Most Illustrious Imperial Majesty, and most pernicious words against the State, about which an investigation is now under way in the Privy Chancellery. But from this investigation it has already appeared that this evil-doer had intimated these evil words to his priest in confession, who did not in any way forbid them but indeed assented to some of them, as now this unfrocked priest has himself confessed under interrogation.[4]

The 'evil-doer' in question was, as we know, a monk from Penza named Varlaam Levin, who was tried and executed in 1722 for publicly calling Peter the Antichrist. Indeed, the investigation of Levin's case also resulted, not only in the arrest and unfrocking of his confessor, but

[1] See above, p. 130. [2] pp. 143 ff.

[3] Thomas Consett, the Anglican chaplain in St. Petersburg, was one such foreigner (see Consett, *op. cit.*, p. 140).

[4] For the 'Announcement of the Most Holy All-Ruling All-Russian Synod to the entire ecclesiastical order of the Russian State' of 17 May 1722, see *PSZ*, vi, no. 4012 (pp. 685–689); also *PSP*, ii, no. 557 (pp. 203–206), which indicates Peter's amendments to the text.

in the informal trial by the Synod of the ailing Metropolitan Stefan Yavorskii, who was alleged to have remarked to Levin that Peter was not the Antichrist, but an 'iconoclast'.[1] Clearly, it was Peter's increasing preoccupation, amounting to an obsession, with the problem of opposition to his regime that had led the Synod to introduce the extraordinary injunction requiring priests to violate the secrecy of confession; that had resulted, moreover, in the death of Tsarevich Aleksei and others; that had resulted, indeed, in Peter's decision to reform the church and was now undermining the good and positive elements of that reform.[2]

On Peter's orders the Synod's announcement of 17 May was separately printed and published 'so that it should not be delayed in printing with the other [regulations of the Supplement]'; it was to be distributed to all the clergy 'as soon as possible, in order that they should be promptly informed of it and know how to conduct themselves in such matters and not excuse themselves by ignorance'; and to the announcement was appended the oath which 'every priest must have a copy of and commit to memory'.[3] The priests were to regard the oath and the announcement as matters of the 'utmost importance'. Indeed, according to the announcement itself, 'should any priest in possession of this document not act in conformity with it, he will be treated as a criminal, deprived of his rank and property, and condemned by a civil court, after severe corporal punishment, to the galleys; and should the case be an important one, he will be executed'. Such a priest was to be considered 'as an oppositionist, as a conspirator in the wickedness, indeed as a protector of the enemies of the State'. On the other hand, 'those confessors who report unrepented evil intentions . . . will be deservedly rewarded for their loyalty by His Imperial Majesty's favour'. The oath that the priests were to memorize corresponded closely to the Synodal oath of office, which in turn was modelled on the oath of office taken by the civil servants of the state.[4] But by their oath the priests also pledged themselves to discharge their duties in accord-

[1] See above, pp. 163 f.

[2] The full significance of popular (including clerical) opposition in the history of Peter's church reform has yet to be demonstrated. The matter is touched on here and elsewhere in this book and more systematically explored by O. F. Kozlov, 'Reforma tserkvi Petra I i otkliki na nee v russkom obshchestve v pervoi polovine XVIII v.', *Vestnik Moskovskogo universiteta*, no. 5 (1968), pp. 86–92.

[3] *PSZ*, vi, no. 4012 (p. 685); *PSP*, ii, no. 557 (p. 203). See also Bykova and Gurevich, *Opisanie izdanii napechatannykh kirillitsei, 1689–1725*, no. 164 (pp. 241–242).

[4] See above, pp. 161–162

ance with the terms of their ordination certificates, of the *Ecclesiastical Regulation*, and, in particular, of the attached announcement concerning confession, which they were to observe 'without any addition of falsehood and without employing any cunning artifices, fearing deprivation of honour and life and mindful always of the incorruptible judgment of God'. The priests swore further 'never to have dealings with schismatics from the church nor to make use of anything that has to do with them.[1] Rather, all schismatic sects . . . I curse and disown, and not only all such pernicious sects, but all who tolerate them; and with my whole strength I will seek out and denounce the schismatics in my parish . . . and report them in writing to my bishop and to the appropriate authorities, fearing grave punishment for not fulfilling this my duty'.

Lastly, the Synod's announcement of 17 May 1722 contained what came to be point 12 of the final version of the Supplement to the *Ecclesiastical Regulation*. This point ordained that

> Priests must report not only an intended evil which will be carried out, but also a public scandal which has already occurred: if anyone anywhere should invent or fabricate in any way a false miracle, and then spread rumour of it, which by simple and ignorant folk is accepted as true; and should the inventor then reveal his invention in confession but show no repentance thereof nor promise to make public disclosure of it (lest the ignorant accept this fraud as true): then this falsehood, being taken by the ignorant for the truth, would be added to the number of genuine miracles and in time be confirmed in the mind and memory of everyone. Therefore the confessor must report this to the appropriate authorities without the slightest delay, so that such a fraud should be cut short and the people, deceived by this fraud, should not err in ignorance and accept falsehood as the truth.

It was pointed out that the perpetration of such falsehoods not only violated the second Commandment ('Thou shalt not take the name of the Lord thy God in vain'), but led 'foreigners to rebuke piety', a remark which betrays once again the sensitivity to western opinion of Peter and his chief clerical collaborator. And so in addition to the part they were to play in stamping out opposition to the regime, confessors were also required to participate in the Synod's campaign to eradicate superstition.

The Supplement contains five more regulations governing the administration of the sacrament of penance. Confessors were instructed to consult their bishop about any sin they found 'difficult . . . to decide

[1] This referred to ikons, liturgical objects, etc. that may have been venerated or used by schismatics.

how grievous it is, and what correction and penance it deserves'. They were forbidden to become 'overweening and rude' to a penitent in confession or to 'demand something in return for absolution or for waiving the penance'. A priest was never to reveal in a quarrel the sins of a person who had confessed to him, and was to 'guard in every way against quarrelling with his spiritual children, lest by emitting a reproach against them a bystander should think he knows what he says from confession'. And in response to yet another of the tsar's marginal notes,[1] the author of the Supplement quoted at length from the works of various of the church fathers in an attempt to show that the 'canons relating to penances are not unalterable, but are left to the judgment of the confessor, who must consider what kind of a person the penitent is, whether he truly repents, and what kind of penance he is able to bear – lest a severe penance, instead of acting as a cure, should become for him the poison of despair'. Peter had noted that 'many priests stand on the service book like blind men and anathematize and appeal to what is written, and thus for twenty or more years do not give communion to a penitent even though he desires it; moreover at the very hour of his death they do not do it, as I myself have seen happen, saying that without penance it is impossible; but he cannot do a penance because he is sick, and death does not wait'. Hence it was now prescribed that the penance of a temporary deprivation of communion could not be imposed by a confessor without the permission of his bishop. The Supplement somewhat ruefully observed that, in any case, 'at the present time, not only does [such a penance] no longer strike fear in many persons, but the lazy welcome it, secret schismatics very much desire it, and hypocritical sinners, in confession, deliberately seek it'.

The Supplement includes twelve other regulations concerning the duties, discipline, and conditions of service of the secular clergy.

> Especially must priests know how to intimidate with [threats of] Divine retribution anyone who in confession appears cold, without feeling, and argumentative; how to raise up someone stooped in despair and to fortify his trust in the grace and mercy of God; how to instruct a sinner to break his habits; how to visit and comfort the sick; how to strengthen the dying; and how especially to fortify those condemned to death and to assure them of Divine mercy: truly these are the most important duties of priests.

Yet because it was 'not to be expected' that the poorly-educated clergy of Russia could perform these duties properly, the author of the

[1] See Verkhovskoi, ii, p. 85, n. 22.

Supplement proposed that the 'services for the above-mentioned occasions should be written down; and having been learned by the priest, he could then recite them from memory or read them aloud from little books to the sick, the dying, the condemned, etc.' Happily for the 'sick, the dying, the condemned, etc.', the Synod, during the first four years of its existence, never got down to composing such little books of prescribed prayers for any and all occasions; and it must be assumed that in their poorly-educated way the ordinary parish clergy continued to comfort, as best they could, their unfortunate brethren.

Priests, deacons, and the lesser clergy were forbidden under pain of severe punishment to hold services 'at places reputed to be miracle-working but not certified as such by a council'. Moreover, priests were not to bargain with their parishioners over baptisms, weddings, and funerals, but were to be content with what was given them. Nor was a parish priest to allow another priest to celebrate the liturgy in his church unless the latter could produce a certificate from his bishop attesting that he was validly ordained and had been given leave to travel; it was Peter who added here that the priest 'must also, so far as possible, strictly forbid talking during services and the liturgy, and on leaving the church must openly rebuke an offender, however high his rank'.[1] A priest was not to employ more than one of his sons as a cantor or sexton in his church, and then only with the consent of his parishioners and the express permission of his bishop: other sons were to be 'given to another church or to another honest occupation'. Priests were not to attach themselves of their own accord to army regiments as chaplains;[2] nor were they to go to private houses to sing vespers or matins, for 'the priest is the leader and celebrant of public worship in the church of God, and especially of the unbloody sacrifice and of the other sacraments, which cannot be administered without a priest. What reason is there to invite a priest to a private house for services which can be done without him? And why so great a distinction between the powerful and wealthy person and the poor brethren, to whose houses the priests never go for services? In truth this is to provoke, rather than supplicate God'.[3]

[1] *Ibid.*, p. 90, n. 41. See above, p. 213, for a brief discussion of the Synod's efforts to enforce the tsar's injunction.

[2] One of the Synod's first actions on taking office was to assume direct control of the appointment and discipline of army and navy chaplains: see *PSZ*, vi, no. 3759 (pp. 370–371); *PSP*, i, no. 35 (pp. 48–50); no. 166 (p. 217); *PSP*, ii, no. 369 (p. 23); no. 381 (pp. 33–36); no. 519 (p. 164); no. 630 (pp. 299–303); *PSP*, iv, no. 1334 (pp. 180–181).

[3] This regulation obviously linked on to the provision of the *Ecclesiastical Regulation* and

Still another of the Supplement's regulations was concerned with clerical decorum. The bishops and other authorities were to see that 'priests and deacons are not disorderly and that lesser clerics are not noisy and drunk in the streets or, what is worse, rowdy in church'. The clergy were not to chant simultaneously several different prayers or to behave boorishly at table or to 'regale themselves when visiting'. They were not – 'an intolerable disgrace' – to engage in the national pastime of fisticuffs.[1] And bishops were to ensure that their clergy maintained a proper appearance: 'more precisely, that their outer garments, though poor, should be clean; and one should not be black and another coloured. And they should not walk about bareheaded nor lie down in the streets to sleep nor drink in the taverns nor boast of their capacity for drink when visiting'.

The Supplement also provided that every parish priest was to keep a detailed register of the births, baptisms, marriages, and deaths of all his parishioners. Every four months the number of births and deaths was to be sent to the bishop, who was to forward this information to the Synod. However in November 1723 and again in February 1724 the Synod was obliged to issue further, more particular instructions concerning the keeping of parish records, since 'none of these registers have been received by the Synod'.[2] The Synod was perhaps unrealistic, if not contradictory, in supposing that the mass of boorish, quarrelsome, and poorly-educated priests portrayed in the Supplement would be capable of compiling such data.

The remaining regulations of the Supplement concerning the secular clergy were connected with a long-standing policy of Peter's government: the elimination of 'superfluous' clergy.[3] It was noted in the Supplement that canon 6 of the Council of Chalcedon 'forbids the ordination of priests and deacons who are not attached to churches, and does not permit those who are nevertheless ordained to perform any of the offices of priest or deacon'. While it was true that in Russia unattached clergy were not ordained, 'nevertheless many are ordained

the Synod's subsequent legislation prohibiting the maintenance of priests and chapels in private houses (discussed above, p. 214).

[1] *ne khrabrstvuyut v boyakh kulachnykh.* Consett describes this activity as 'a play in winter, where the vulgar people push at the breasts of each other with their fists . . . an annual diversion of the populace at which sometimes the greatest men in the country are present as spectators' (*op. cit.*, p. 157).

[2] *PSP*, iii, no. 1143 (p. 224); *PSP*, iv, no. 1218 (pp. 78–79, 332); also *PSZ*, vii, no. 4480 (pp. 266–267).

[3] For Peter's earlier efforts in this field, see above, pp. 97 ff.

above the requirements of a particular church; and many, having abandoned the church to which they were appointed, wander from place to place, which is an irregularity comparable to [the ordination of unattached clergy]'. On this pretext it was ruled that lay persons were not to harbour unattached priests and that bishops were not to ordain more clergy than was strictly necessary. Moreover, the bishops were to 'apprehend and punish those [clerics] who have abandoned their churches. And should they not wish to return to their churches and to discharge their duties in a regular and orderly way . . . then they are to be deprived of the priesthood'. And in the years that followed the Synod introduced further measures designed to enforce the regulations against vagrant or fraudulent clerics adumbrated in the Supplement.[1]

But this was not the end of the matter. In the margin of his copy of the Supplement Tsar Peter had noted: 'The number of priests, deacons, and other clergy assigned to each church must be specified exactly, since many are fleeing from service or taxes and are accepted into the clergy'.[2] The tsar's note, somewhat amended, was duly added to the final version of the Supplement: 'Superfluous clergy are not to be ordained for any reason; since many who are ordained and accepted into the clergy are fleeing from [state] service, the number [of clergy] is to be promptly specified by decree'. And the Supplement further provided that 'whereas it is the intention of His Imperial Majesty to apportion a sufficient number of parishioners to every church, and to specify that every parishioner must annually give to the clergy enough to provide them with an adequate living, the Most Holy All-Ruling Synod must therefore take counsel, pursuant to His Imperial Majesty's decree, with the secular authorities, and must execute this said intention. And when this has been done, priests will not seek the least bit more for their offices than the fixed remunerations, unless out of the goodness of his heart someone should want to give more'.

[1] See *PSP*, ii, no. 766 (pp. 455–456); no. 947 (pp. 667–669); also *PSZ*, vi, no. 4136 (pp. 814–815). Related measures include the Synod's decision of June 1721 to cooperate with the police in controlling the comings and goings of clerics in St. Petersburg (*PSP*, i, no. 16 [p. 163]); and the decision, made at the suggestion of Chief Procurator Boltin, to forbid the clergy of St. Petersburg to attend public assemblies at the palaces of the tsar 'and other important persons' (*PSP*, iv, no. 1423 [p. 286]). Moreover, in January 1723 the Synod introduced new and strict regulations governing the movements of 'priests and monks who come from Greece to beg alms and go about in the guise of holy men'; such 'suspicious wanderers' were to be detained at the borders and interrogated according to a prescribed questionnaire, after which only those with the necessary documents from their religious superiors would be allowed to proceed to their destinations in Russia (*PSP*, iii, no. 980 [pp. 15–16]; no. 1001 [pp. 34–35]; *PSZ*, vii, no. 4149 [p. 17]).

[2] See Verkhovskoi, ii, p. 91, n. 54.

The Synod very promptly took steps to execute 'this said intention' of the tsar. Well before the finished Supplement was printed (June 1722) the Synod resolved (18 April) that on consideration of the 'increase in the number of parish clergy, and [of the fact] that since the death of the last Russian patriarch [in 1700] many persons have been and are being ordained . . . not for the sake of ecclesiastical service, but to avoid state service' – that detailed reports of the number of clergy and the parishes to which they were assigned should be compiled in the Synodal domain and in all the dioceses and sent to the Synod. The reports were also to indicate where there were 'empty' churches, or churches 'without services'. And the Synod's resolution forbade any increase in the number of churches or clergy without the express permission of the Synod.[1]

Furthermore, in August of that year, in response to a 'memorandum' from the Senate, the Synod established the exact number of clergy that were to be attached to the cathedrals and parish churches of Moscow and the other towns; any clergy in excess of the fixed numbers were to be considered as 'superfluous' and were to find 'vacant places' in churches with less than their quota of clergy.[2] In March of the following year (1723), however, the Senate decreed, at the Synod's request, that clergy who thus found themselves 'superfluous' and could not immediately find new places were not to be unfrocked and turned out of their parishes, though their sons and grandsons were still to pay the

[1] *PSP*, ii, no. 548 (pp. 194–195). In a memorandum to the Synod in Peter's own hand, dating from the spring of 1722, this entry appears: 'Daily services in churches where there are people, and from time to time in the others; and according to this the number of priests' (memorandum printed in *ZAP*, no. 186 [pp. 137–138]). The memorandum also includes the following entries: 'Priests and deacons for divine services . . . and lesser clergy – apportion by the number of parishioners, so that there won't be any superfluous [clergy]'; 'Concerning the stipends of parish priests'. There are half a dozen other entries, relating mostly to the monasteries, which will be discussed presently. The existence of the memorandum confirms once again that Peter himself closely supervised the drafting of the reforms embodied in the Supplement and related legislation.

[2] *PSZ*, vi, no. 4072 (pp. 756–757); *PSP*, ii, no. 745 (pp. 438–439). According to this decree, episcopal churches (*sobory*) were to be staffed by one archpriest, two sacristans (*klyuchari*), five priests, one archdeacon, four deacons, two cantors, and two sextons, while the episcopal households were to comprise forty-one lesser clerics, choristers, clerks, and other officials. In the other main churches (*sobory*) there were to be one archpriest, two priests, two deacons, two psalmists (or cantors), and two sextons. In the large parish churches, serving from 200 to 300 households, there were to be two or three priests and no more than two cantors and sextons; in the smaller parish churches, serving 100 to 150 households, there were to be one priest, one cantor, and one sexton. Thus, parishes were to consist of at least 100 households – or perhaps 500 to 1000 parishioners – and each parish priest was to have no more than one cantor and one sexton under him.

soul tax.[1] Indeed, the soul tax proved to be the government's chief means of controlling the number of clergy. For it was on the basis of the census taken as a preliminary to imposing the soul tax that the Synod, acting in concert with the Senate, fixed the number of clergy and the size of their parishès; and thereafter only 'actually serving clergy' and their sons were exempt from the soul tax: the sons and other male relations of 'superfluous' clergy were to be enrolled to pay the tax as townsmen or as peasants of the local landlord, unless they chose to enter the civil or ecclesiastical bureaucracy or to become domestic servants, in which case they, too, would be exempt from the tax.[2] These stern regulations were confirmed by Peter's government in 1723 and again in 1724, when the soul tax was first collected.[3] It is worth noting, as a further instance of the application of these regulations, that in January 1725 the Senate ruled that priests and deacons attached to the chapels (*chasovni*) found in hamlets belonging to newly-settled landowners in the Azov province were not to be considered as 'actually serving clergy', and that they and their sons were to pay the soul tax.[4] There was to be no escape from the government's drive to fix absolutely the number of clergy in Russia.

In sum, the principal objectives of Peter's reform of the secular clergy, as it was embodied in the Supplement and related legislation, were these: to eliminate 'superfluous' clergy; to fix the number of 'actually serving' clergy; to ensure that the 'ecclesiastical order' should no longer serve as a haven for fugitives from state service; and to provide for the apprehension and punishment of vagrant or fraudulent clerics. At the same time, the reform legislation enacted in the years 1721 to 1725 manifests, once again, the propensity of Peter's government to make the clergy its agents in various, usually invidious ways. They were forced to cooperate in the campaign to suppress superstition and religious dissent; they were obliged to supply the government with the vital statistics of their parishioners (of, in fact, the Russian population); they were required, not only to take an oath of loyalty to the tsar and to his policies, but to administer in their churches the oath of loyalty

[1] *PSZ*, vii, no. 4186 (pp. 32–33).

[2] *PSP*, ii, no. 513 (pp. 160–162); *PSZ*, vi, no. 4035 (p. 720); *PSP*, ii, no. 674 (pp. 350–351); no. 745 (pp. 434–437).

[3] *PSP*, iii, no. 1029 (pp. 64–65); no. 1121 (pp. 203–208); *PSZ*, vii, no. 4515 (pp. 289–291).

[4] *PSZ*, vii, no. 4627 (pp. 398–399).

required of all classes 'except the peasants';[1] they were required, after 1721 as before, to read to their congregations on Sundays and feastdays the government's decrees on a wide range of political and economic matters;[2] and, most significantly, they were required, in their capacity as confessors, to cooperate in suppressing opposition to the regime. This is not to deny, however, that the legislation under question also included an element of reform in the more purely beneficent or moral sense, in the sense of a disinterested attempt to eliminate petty corruption and clerical abuses and to improve the standards of clerical behaviour. The key to this aspect of the reform was thought by Peter's government to lie in improved clerical education, and the attempt to implement this policy will be discussed in the following chapter. But the clergy were also enjoined to dress properly, to behave in public with dignity, to refrain from bargaining with their parishioners over the performance of religious rites, to impose penances prudently, to comfort sinners, the sick, the dying, and the condemned, and to desist from catering to the rich and powerful at the expense of their poorer parishioners. Regulations designed to prevent morally unfit persons from entering the priesthood were introduced. Yet somehow, in the mass of legislation subsequently enacted or implemented by the Synod, in the press of the politics of church reform under Peter, this moral aspect of clerical reform that was embodied in the Supplement appears to have been largely neglected. During the remaining years of Peter's reign no serious effort to enforce a moral reform of the clergy, apart from improving their education, appears to have been made. It was perhaps beyond the power of Peter's government, or of any government anywhere at any time, to impose such a reform, to do anything more than publish the numerous admonitions, exhortations, injunctions, and regulations contained in the Supplement. But whatever the reason, it must be recorded that a general reform of the clergy in the moral sense remained very much a secondary objective of Peter's government.

It is not within the scope of this book to attempt to assess the effects of Peter's effort to reform the secular clergy. Intensive research in, among other things, the record of the Synod's proceedings in the years after 1725 would doubtless throw light on this problem. Yet it may be provisionally observed that elements of Peter's reform – the clergy's exemption from the soul tax and their duty to act in various

[1] See *PSP*, ii, no. 466 (p. 118); no. 471 (pp. 122–123); no. 677 (p. 354).

[2] See *PSP*, ii, no. 339 (pp. 2–3); no. 749 (pp. 441–442); no. 756 (pp. 447–448); no. 794 (pp. 486–487); no. 846 (pp. 541–542); etc.

ways as government agents – undoubtedly worked to identify them with the increasingly oppressive state and thus to divide them from the people they served. If in general Peter's legislation powerfully reinforced the division of Russian society into government and landlords on the one side, and everybody else on the other, there can be no doubt to which side of the yawning social gap the ordinary parish clergy – the representatives of the church in the daily lives of the people – were being drawn.

On a more concrete level, there is evidence that at least in the short term a major aspect of Peter's church reform – his attempt to stabilize the number of secular clergy – failed miserably. If between 1722 and 1738 the number of churches in Russia remained relatively constant,[1] during the same period the number of secular clergy more than doubled,[2] an increase that was proportionately far in excess of the concurrent increase in the general population. Perhaps there were far fewer 'superfluous' parish clergy than Peter and his collaborators supposed. Or perhaps by exempting *all* sons of 'actually serving' clergy from the soul tax, Peter's government had unwittingly ensured that places in the church would always be found for them. For the bureaucracy could not be indefinitely expanded to accommodate them; and their alternative was to be reduced to the status of tax-paying townsmen or peasants. In this situation, the sons of the clergy, like their fathers, were unlikely to surrender voluntarily their inherited and relatively privileged position in society.

III

REFORM AND THE MONASTERIES

The basic objectives of Peter's reform of the monastic clergy were similar to those of his reform of the secular clergy. With the promulgation of the Supplement to the *Ecclesiastical Regulation* (June 1722) and of subsequent, related measures, a renewed effort was made both to reform the monasteries in the moral sense and to put them to various social uses. At the same time, an attempt was made not merely to stabilize the number of monastic clergy, but drastically to reduce it. The attempt appears to have succeeded. Between 1724 and 1738 the total number

[1] See above, p. 215 and n. 4.

[2] From a total of 61,111 priests, deacons, and cantors in 1722 to a total of 124,923 in 1738 (see Smolitsch, *op. cit.*, p. 710).

of monks, nuns, and novices in Russia was nearly halved,[1] a fact which contrasts sharply with the result of Peter's concurrent attempt to control the number of secular clergy. But then monks and nuns did not breed sons and daughters for whom places in the church would have to be found. And short of a wholesale dissolution of the monasteries and convents (which Peter seems never to have contemplated), their number of inmates could be greatly reduced by the simple device of restricting the entrance of new-comers. This, in essence, was Peter's policy.

The final version of the Supplement comprises some sixty-two regulations designed to 'reform' the monastic order, 'which in olden times was a mirror and model of repentance and reform for all Christians, but which at the present time is corrupted by many disorders'.[2] The very first of these regulations states that 'no one under thirty years of age is to become a monk'. Equally, the last of the regulations stipulates that a woman could not become a nun 'until she is sixty, or at least fifty, years of age'. Army deserters were not of course to be accepted into the monasteries; but properly discharged soldiers could enter only after a three-year period of probation. Peasants could not be accepted unless they had leave of their masters and (virtually an impossible condition) knew how to read and write. A married man could not be accepted except by leave of his bishop and of the Synod. A son could not 'abandon' his parents to enter a monastery without their consent; nor could parents compel their son to enter a monastery against his will. Debtors and fugitives from justice were not to be accepted; and 'so that this should not occur, no one is to be accepted . . . who has come from another diocese and is not known by honourable persons'. Civil servants and ecclesiastical bureaucrats could not become monks without the written permission of their superiors. Benefactors of monasteries could not themselves become monks ('an idle and mischievous custom') unless they, too, first underwent a three-year period of probation and then were personally approved by the local bishop. (Nor could monasteries accept presents from such benefactors until they had completed the prescribed period of probation.) It was specified that the convents were also to observe these regulations. In short, only single men (or women) of at least thirty (or fifty) years of age and who were able to read and write could enter a

[1] From a total of 25,207 in 1724 to a total of 14,282 in 1738 (see Smolitsch, *op. cit.*, p. 713).

[2] See Verkhovskoi, ii, pp. 94–105.

monastery (or convent), provided that they could also prove that they were neither deserters, criminals, debtors, nor interested benefactors and had the permission of their families, superiors, or masters to do so.[1]

No doubt these regulations, when put into practice, would have sharply curtailed the number of novices accepted by the monasteries and convents, and so in the course of time would have contributed to that drastic reduction in the monastic population which was mentioned above. But Peter's government also took steps to stabilize the present number of monastic clergy. By a decree of May 1722 the Synod confirmed the long-standing rule that monks and nuns were not to travel from monastery to monastery or from convent to convent 'without a decree'; nor were monastic superiors, under pain of severe penalties, to accept any 'new-comers' for an unspecified period of time. Also, by the same decree, all monasteries and convents were to provide the Synod with detailed lists of their inmates: their names, dates and places of birth, social class, dates of profession, their function in the community, and any handicraft they might know, 'so that the Most Holy Synod can see the number of inmates in any monastery as in a looking-glass'.[2] The order to submit the detailed lists was repeated in an edict of the tsar communicated to the Synod in January 1723, with the additional stipulation that monthly reports of any deaths in the monasteries and convents were also to be sent to the Synod.[3] Moreover, the Supplement itself prescribed that 'for the sake of better devotion' monasteries and convents with fewer than thirty inmates were to be amalgamated with a nearby community, and that the churches of these monasteries and convents were to be converted to ordinary parish churches. Accordingly, at the suggestion of Vice-President Yanovskii the Synod in July 1722 ordered that a survey be taken of the underpopulated monasteries of the Novgorod diocese with a view to

[1] But what, Archbishop Varlaam of Kiev asked the Synod in May 1722, was to be done with well-educated Ukrainians from Polish territory or from the Kiev academy who wished to become monks but were under thirty and unable to support themselves during the prescribed period of probation? The Synod replied that the provisions of the Supplement were to be observed 'unalterably', and that any exception to these rules could be made only by decree of the Synod after careful consideration of the case (*PSP*, ii, no. 671 [pp. 348–349]). Had such regulations been rigidly applied in their youth, a sizable proportion of the Synod itself (including, most notably, Feofan Prokopovich) might never have achieved their present eminence.

[2] *PSP*, ii, no. 626 (pp. 295–296). The Supplement itself (promulgated June 1722) provided that the superior of every monastery was to keep such a record (*zapisnaya kniga*) of his monks.

[3] *PSZ*, vii, no. 4151 (p. 18); *PSP*, iii, no. 997 (pp. 30–31).

enforcing their amalgamation with the 'important monasteries of this diocese'.[1] In the following months and years the Synod initiated similar action with regard to the under-populated monasteries of the other dioceses.[2] And the last of the Supplement's regulations concerning the monasteries simply stated that 'no new monasteries or convents are to be built without the knowledge of the Most Holy All-Ruling Synod'.

The Supplement also includes some nineteen provisions regarding the internal discipline of the monasteries. Monks were to confess and to receive communion at least four times a year. They were never to be idle, but were to practise 'an art such as carpentry or ikon-painting and [an amendment by Peter][3] other things that are not contrary to the monastic life; and nuns are to knit and to sew, to weave lace, etc.'[4] The monasteries were to retain a strictly limited number of servants, some of whom should be assigned to the care of the sick. Monks were not to receive guests without the permission of their superior. Nor were they to visit the houses of laymen or convents or other monasteries, or even to go to town, except with their superior's written permission, which was to be granted no more than four times a year. And if a monk had to travel to another diocese or to St. Petersburg, he was to obtain a pass not only from his superior, but from his bishop as well, without which he was liable to immediate arrest by the ecclesiastical or civil authorities. Monks were forbidden to sell the monastery's produce, 'for this is a most shameful and dishonourable practice'. They were to eat not in their individual cells but in the common refectory, and all were to have equal portions of food, drink, and clothing; for 'monks must live a life in common, according to the canons of the holy fathers'. Women were not to be allowed into the cells of the monks or even of the superior, lest this give rise to 'reproach and censure by

[1] *PSP*, ii, no. 702 (pp. 381–382).

[2] *PSP*, ii, no. 883 (pp. 573–574); *PSP*, iii, no. 1091 (pp. 133–135); *PSZ*, vii, no. 4456 (p. 249); *PSP*, iv, no. 1371 (pp. 208–209).

[3] See Verkhovskoi, ii, p. 97, n. 90.

[4] The Synod took prompt action to implement Peter's amendment concerning the nuns. In August 1722 it ordered that some forty-four expert seamstresses from the village of Pokrovskoe, who had been brought to St. Petersburg to work in the spinning mill, should now be distributed among the convents of Moscow and the other towns, where they would train the nuns (*PSP*, ii, no. 747 [p. 440]). The Monastery Prikaz was to pay for 'materials and instruments' for the nuns (*PSP*, ii, no. 825 [p. 518]). It may also be noted that in his handwritten memorandum to the Synod of early 1722 (referred to above, p. 248, n. 1), Peter had commanded: 'About the nuns: instead of field-work, spinning; and it should begin this winter'.

foreigners or by our own people'. In every monastery some of the monks should learn 'not only to read the Scriptures but to understand them'; and these monks were to be ordained priests and promoted to positions of authority. No monk was to do any writing whatever in his cell without the express permission of his superior. Nor was he to receive any letters, nor even to keep ink and paper in his cell, without permission, under pain of corporal punishment, 'since nothing so ruins monastic tranquility as vain and useless writing'.

This last regulation, which had originally been enacted by Peter's government as early as 1701,[1] was confirmed in yet stricter terms by the tsar's edict of 19 January 1723, which was ratified and signed by the Synod.[2] The inclusion of this regulation in the Supplement, which was not in its original version,[3] as well as the promulgation of the confirmatory edict, were further expressions of Peter's current obsession with the problem of internal security. In April 1722 the Synod, 'having observed that among the cases brought before us many monks have had the audacity to utter treason against the person of His Imperial Majesty, and that when questioned about this in the Synod not only deny that their words carried such a grave meaning but admit that they are unaware of the force of such words and of the decrees of His Imperial Majesty describing in detail the import of such words' – having observed this, the Synod resolved to send printed copies of the relevant decrees to all the monasteries, in order that the monks should 'know the gravity of words and deeds against His Imperial Majesty, and knowing this would not dare to use such words or to excuse themselves by ignorance. ... and in order to refresh the memory, these decrees are to be read out each month in every monastery in the hearing of all the monks'.[4]

But it must not be forgotten that despite his obsession with the problem of opposition to his regime Peter was personally committed to the attempt to reform the monasteries, to the effort to restore them to their pristine purity that was embodied in some of the Supplement's provisions. In January 1724, just a year before he died, he sent to the Synod a lengthy treatise on the origins and duties of the monastic life. To the treatise was appended a further list of regulations which were written with Prokopovich's help and were designed to guide 'those who in conscience wish to lead the monastic life' as well as to provide that 'there should be (as is the ancient custom) monks worthy for the

[1] See above, p. 99. [2] *PSZ*, vii, no. 4146 (p. 16); *PSP*, iii, no. 984 (pp. 18–19).
[3] See Verkhovskoi, ii, p. 99, n. 106.
[4] *PSZ*, vi, no. 3971 (pp. 657–658); *PSP*, ii, no. 547 (p. 193).

episcopal order'.[1] But like his attempt to reform the secular clergy, it was perhaps beyond Peter's power to enforce a thorough-going reform of the monasteries. His treatise of January 1724 remains a testimonial of his hopes and aims in this respect: a primary document in the brief history of Peter's vigorous but abortive attempt to revive and reform Russian monasticism.

In addition to the above-mentioned regulations of the Supplement, nuns in particular were to observe seven special injunctions. They were 'never' to leave their convents, 'not to go to monasteries or to parish churches or even to join in a religious procession'. Every convent was to be 'permanently enclosed' and was not to be entered by anyone except on certain occasions, such as the celebration of the liturgy in the convent church, when lay people could be admitted by a carefully circumscribed route but had to be kept well apart from the nuns; 'and to avoid suspicion [this was Peter's amendment],[2] no one, whether layman or cleric, is ever to be allowed to go to the cells of the nuns'. It was specified that not even members of the Imperial family could receive nuns in their houses. And in the latter part of 1722 and again in 1723 these stringest regulations were confirmed by special decrees of the Synod.[3]

Of course exceptions had to be made. In December 1722 the Synod permitted Helen Naryshkina (a relation of the tsar) and 'other such nuns from distinguished families' to keep their servants and to receive 'notable persons of the male sex' and other visitors and relations.[4] In 1723 Bishop Pitirim of Nizhnii-Novgorod pointed out to the Synod that the absolute prohibition against nuns going abroad imposed intolerable hardship on convents which had no estates or industries and hence had to purchase their food and other necessities in the outside world. The Synod therefore allowed that depending on the size of the convent two or more nuns 'of honest and blameless lives' could leave the convent 'at suitable times, between the offices', to obtain the convent's necessities; but no other nuns, it was reiterated, could go abroad for any reason; and those who had been chosen as emissaries to the outside world were to be 'zealously watched by their superior,

[1] *PSZ*, vii, no. 4450 (pp. 226–230); *PSP*, iv, no. 1197 (pp. 56–60). The original draft of the treatise, in Peter's own hand, survives: see *ZAP*, no. 191 (pp. 141–142), also Verkhovskoi, ii, pp. 128–151. See also Chistovich, *Feofan Prokopovich*, pp. 139–140.

[2] Verkhovskoi, ii, p. 100, n. 109.

[3] *PSZ*, vi, no. 4112 (p. 784); *PSP*, ii, no. 855 (p. 551); *PSP*, iii, no. 981 (p. 16).

[4] *PSP*, ii, no. 954 (pp. 673–678).

their confessor, and the [local] inquisitor, lest under the guise of necessity some suspicious activity should take place'.[1] In July 1724 – another exception to the rules – the Synod ordered, in response to repeated petitions from the Admiralty College, that nuns were to be regularly sent by the local convents to 'supervise the linen and the female workers' in the naval hospitals of the St. Petersburg region.[2]

Several of the Supplement's provisions concerned the superiors themselves of the monasteries. Indeed, it was on them that the success of the projected reform of the monastic clergy largely depended. Thus it was provided that monastic superiors should be men 'of good morals, experienced in the ascetic life, well-versed in Scripture and in the laws of monasticism', and that they were to be 'concerned with the salvation of the souls of the brethren, and not with building stone walls or accumulating riches'. It was also provided that on taking office monastic superiors were to swear an oath. The regulation concerning the oath was first promulgated by the Synod in February 1722; and the oath was first administered by the Synod to a newly-elected archimandrite in April.[3] The oath closely corresponded to the Synod's oath of office, except that in addition to swearing loyalty to the tsar the new archimandrite or igumen undertook to observe the provisions of the *Ecclesiastical Regulation* and its Supplement and any decisions handed down by the Synod.

The Supplement clearly implied that in conformity with tradition the monks of a given monastery were to elect their own superior. In an earlier chapter, however, it was seen that the headship of a leading monastery was always to be found for a member of the Synod. Indeed, in the first years of its existence the Synod, acting on the tsar's direct orders or on its own initiative, not only appointed, but also sacked, the heads of several important monasteries.[4] It was not long before the Synod declared, in June 1723, that 'on consideration of the archimandrites installed in all the monasteries since the death of Patriarch Adrian [in 1700], henceforth archimandrites and igumens are not to be promoted to the places of deceased archimandrites and igumens without the Most Holy Synod's permission, which is to be sought by sending the usual written submission'.[5] The order was repeated in April

1 *PSP*, iii, no. 1079 (pp. 119–120).
2 *PSP*, iv, no. 1329 (p. 178).
3 *PSZ*, vi, no. 3912 (p. 513); *PSP*, ii, no. 426 (pp. 68–69).
4 *PSP*, i, no. 296 (pp. 347–349); *PSP*, ii, no. 493 (p. 142); no. 580 (p. 225); *PSP*, iv, no. 1263 (pp. 113–114).
5 *PSP*, iii, no. 1061 (p. 99).

1724.[1] The Synod's control of the appointment of monastic superiors, and the policy of imposing on the monasteries politically reliable outsiders or court favourites, had been firmly established.

Lastly, the Supplement provided that monasteries with more than enough income to supply their own needs were to devote their surplus to the building of hospitals for sick and aged persons, who were to be looked after 'for the glory of God and in accordance with the methods laid down in the Naval Statute'. Almost the whole of this provision was added to the Supplement in response to Peter's hand-written order to the Synod of 19 March 1722.[2] But in his order Peter also stated that in these comparatively wealthy monasteries 'there should not be more than, say, two-thirds monks, and a half would be sufficient, since the fewer the monks and the more skilled they are, the better; they can maintain more pilgrims and sick people in the hospitals'. According to Peter, the number of inmates in a given monastic hospital was to be determined by the monastery's income, of which half should go to the monks and the rest considered as surplus to be used to maintain the hospital. 'It is fitting', said Peter in his order, 'that the brethren should serve the sick and keep the hospitals clean and orderly'. In a note dating from a month or so after he issued the order, he put the matter even more baldly: 'Of monks there are to remain however many are necessary to serve the sick; the others are to feed themselves by working in the monasteries' fields like ordinary working people [*delovye lyudi*]'.[3] In the last months of his life Peter followed up this revolutionary impulse with various measures intended to provide for the establishment not only of hospitals but of special schools and orphanages in the monasteries and convents; and, typically, he entrusted one of his guards-officers, Captain Bashakov, with the execution of these plans.[4] But there is no evidence that the project ever got beyond the preliminary stage of surveying the revenues of various monasteries: it appears to have died with Peter.

Yet another of the great tsar's schemes for using the monasteries was carried well beyond the planning stage. As early as 1719, as we have

[1] *PSP*, iv, no. 1239 (p. 100).

[2] *ZAP*, no. 121 (p. 100). Unaware of the written order's existence, Verkhovskoi surmised that the provision was included in response to an oral instruction from Peter (ii, pp. 79–80).

[3] *ZAP*, no. 152 (p. 118).

[4] *PSZ*, vii, no. 4426 (p. 207); no. 4516 (p. 291); *ZAP*, no. 199 (pp. 146–147); *PSP*, iv, no. 1279 (p. 121); no. 1284 (p. 124); no. 1309 (pp. 142–143); no. 1379 (p. 226). Captain Bashakov later retired, briefly, to a comfortable berth as chief procurator of the Synod.

seen, Peter inaugurated the policy of billeting retired soldiers in the monasteries.[1] The philosophy underlying this policy is perhaps nowhere better expressed than in a letter written by Menshikov, Peter's favourite, back in September 1706, where he proposed to the tsar that monks should be placed on stipends equivalent to those of ordinary garrison soldiers. 'In truth', wrote Menshikov,

> it is right, for as compared to soldiers monks are always superfluous. The former have wives and children, they serve and work, they have no peace. But monks, what more do they need than bread and water? They themselves have laid this down, so that they might follow the holy fathers, who despised money. Thus they ought to live by [this precept].[2]

And so, in the spring of 1722, Peter, with whose own views on monasticism we are familiar, confirmed in a written instruction to the Synod that 'in addition to the poor and to foundlings, retired soldiers are to be put in the monasteries'.[3] He even seems to have conceded that in order to maintain aged and disabled veterans the monasteries should retain, as a matter of right, all the revenues from their estates.[4] The Synod, however, was bent on frustrating the scheme, or at least on mitigating the hardship it supposedly imposed on the monasteries.

In April 1721, assuming jurisdiction in the matter, the Synod ordered that henceforth monasteries were not to accept retired soldiers sent to them by the government without an edict from the Synod.[5] The order was confirmed in April and again in May.[6] However in March of the following year the Senate ruled that 'officers and other ranks who are certified by the War College as no longer fit for service because of age or infirmity, and have no means of subsistence and wish therefore to enter a monastery either as monks or as residents, are to be remanded to the Synod'.[7] At first the Synod complied with the Senate's ruling, ordering the Monastery Prikaz to distribute these retired soldiers among the monasteries and to ensure that they were properly cared for.[8] But then in August and again in September 1722 the Synod complained to the Senate of the great financial burden incurred by many monasteries in fulfilling this duty. The Synod further complained that of the

[1] See above, p. 92.

[2] Ustryalov, *op. cit.*, iv, II, p. 434: Menshikov to the tasr, 26 September 1706.

[3] *ZAP*, no. 186 (pp. 137–138).

[4] See *PSZ*, vi, no. 3962 (pp. 649–650); *PSP*, ii, no. 531 (pp. 172–173).

[5] *PSP*, i, no. 81 (pp. 109–110).

[6] *PSP*, i, no. 70 (p. 97); no. 100 (p. 133).

[7] *PSP*, ii, no. 513 (p. 162). Confirmed by Senate decree of 31 July 1722 (*PSZ*, vi, no. 4066 [p 754]).

[8] *PSP*, ii, no. 536 (p. 180); no. 595 (p. 240); no. 738 (p. 428).

'great number' of retired soldiers sent to it for distribution among the monasteries, many did not qualify for retirement to a monastery under the terms of the Senate's ruling; that in 'but a brief period' it had been sent 373 men 'who could be dispatched to monasteries only with difficulty, since the monasteries are maintained by fixed grants according to the number of monks'.[1] As a matter of fact, if a report submitted to the Synod at this time by the Monastery Prikaz may be accepted as accurate, only eighty-one monasteries, or perhaps 10 percent of the total, continued to receive fixed grants.[2] The rest were, in accordance with Peter's edict of 1720, fully in control of their estates and revenues.[3]

Still, in September 1722 the Synod took the matter to the tsar: 'Since it has now been determined that the monasteries should maintain hospitals for the care and support of disabled dragoons and soldiers . . . the Synod therefore prays that monastic estates with all their revenues be returned to the monasteries, since without them it would be impossible to found and maintain the hospitals'. Peter, as noted above, granted this request, or rather confirmed once again that the monasteries were to retain immediate control of their properties and income. At the same time, however, he ruled that ordinary soldiers lodged in the monasteries were to receive the same portion of money and food as the monks; that junior officers were to receive a portion and a half; and that senior officers were to receive stipends commensurate with their former pay. The monasteries were also to provide housing for married soldiers who should need it; and soldiers who could do so were to help to run the monasteries. And should a monastery claim to have no money to divert to these purposes, it was to send some of its monks away to other monasteries and to fill their places with retired soldiers.[4] Thereafter, in 1723 and again in 1724, the Synod was content to confirm these regulations, choosing to think that they had been enacted 'by agreement of the Synod with the Senate'.[5] But the Synod had

[1] *PSP*, ii, no. 759 (pp. 449–550); no. 836 (p. 531).

[2] *PSP*, ii, no. 901 (pp. 616–619). The Prikaz reported that 52 monasteries of the Synodal domain, with a total of 1940 monks, received annual grants averaging 413R per monastery, and that an additional 29 monasteries in the other dioceses received average annual grants of 223R. Cf. the estimate noted above (p. 87, n. 1), that by 1710 approximately 2500 monks in some 80 monasteries, or perhaps 10 percent of the total number of monasteries, were supported by fixed stipends paid to them by the Monastery Prikaz out of monastic revenues.

[3] *PSZ*, vi, no. 3659 (p. 248); discussed above, p. 87.

[4] *PSZ*, vi, no. 4107 (p. 782).

[5] *PSP*, iii, no. 1026 (p. 57); *PSP*, iv, no. 1224 (p. 81); no. 1233 (pp. 88–89).

asserted its authority, its right to a say in the matter, and had confirmed the monasteries in possession of their estates and revenues, only to acquiesce in carrying out Peter's policy of using the monasteries as permanent rest homes for the veterans of the Swedish war.

CHAPTER SIX

Reform and Education, 1721–1725

I
CLERICAL EDUCATION

Education, it was thought by Peter and his principal collaborators, was the key to their church reform in its wider, beneficent, and moral sense. 'This is most conducive to the reform of the church', the *Ecclesiastical Regulation* states forthrightly: 'that every bishop should have in or near his house a school for the sons of the clergy or others destined for the priesthood'. The students were to be fed and taught free of charge and their books supplied by the bishop; equally, 'for the teacher or teachers themselves the bishop shall provide food and a stipend of money from the episcopal treasury'. 'Obtuse' students, or those who proved 'sharp-witted but perverse, obstinate, and incurably lazy', were, after an appropriate period of probation, to be expelled from the episcopal schools, 'having been deprived of all hope of ordination'. For 'only pupils educated in the episcopal schools (as soon as, with God's help, there are enough of them) are to become priests or, should some of them choose the monastic order, then archimandrites or igumens, unless there should appear some grave impediment to them'. Moreover, 'if a bishop ordains a person who is not from one of these schools, or makes a monk of him, having passed over an educated man without good cause', he was liable to punishment by the Synod. And in the margin opposite these lines in the rough draft of the *Ecclesiastical Regulation* Peter himself placed no less than five of his asterisks, indicating thereby that these provisions met with his enthusiastic approval.[1]

Indeed, fully a fifth of the text of the *Ecclesiastical Regulation* is devoted to a prolonged passage concerning 'the schools, and in them the teachers and students, as well as church preachers'.[2] The passage

[1] See Verkhovskoi, ii, pp. 41–42 and nn. 94, 95, 99.

[2] See *ibid.*, pp. 51–65, for all subsequent quotations from or references to this passage.

opens with a brief and striking statement of what may be regarded as the official rationale of Peter's church reform:

> It is known to the whole world how inadequate and feeble was the Russian army when it lacked proper instruction, and how immeasurably its strength was increased and beyond all hope became great and awesome when our Most Potent Monarch, His Majesty Tsar Peter the First, trained it with appropriate regulations.[1] The same may be said of architecture, medicine, government, and all other things. And especially may it be said of the administration of the church. When the light of learning is lacking, it is impossible that the church should be well run, that it should not be disorderly and subject to numerous ridiculous superstitions, as well as dissensions and the most absurd heresies.

But having shown that 'learning [*uchenie*]' was essential to the well-being of the church, the author of the *Regulation* felt obliged to defend himself against both the prejudices of the Old Muscovite enemies of learning and the sophistries of the Latinizers, those votaries of the dominant scholasticism of the Kiev and Moscow academies.[2] Thus, with regard to the former, 'many say, but wrongly, that learning is responsible for heresy. For besides the ancient heretics, possessed not by learning but by arrogant stupidity . . . have not our Russian schismatics become so madly possessed because of their rudeness and ignorance?' Moreover,

> Although learned men have created heresies, such as Arius, Nestorius, and others, yet their heresy was born not of learning but of a poor comprehension of Scripture, and grew and was strengthened by malice and pride, which prevented them from altering their wrong opinions even on perceiving the truth, and in opposition to their consciences. And though by their learning they were able to compose sophistries, that is cunning and subtle arguments, nevertheless he that attributes this evil simply to learning would have to say that when a physician administers poison to someone the science of medicine is at fault; that when a trained soldier with skill and strength commits an act of violence, military science is at fault. . . . And if learning were harmful to church or state, then the best Christian persons would not have engaged in it and would have forbidden it to others; but we see that all our ancient teachers studied not only Scripture, but also secular philosophy. . . .

[1] The author of the *Ecclesiastical Regulation* refers no doubt to the *Military Statute* of 1716 – the first of the great reform laws enacted under Peter (see *PSZ*, v, no. 3006 [pp. 203–453]) – and earlier, related measures.

[2] The 'learned Greeks' who were prominent in Moscow during the previous half-century had all but disappeared in the revolution to 'Latin learning' inaugurated about 1700 (cf. above, p. 93).

For learning that is good and well-grounded is beneficial both to the fatherland and to the church as the root and seed and foundation.

On the other hand, with reference to the Latinizers, who obviously did value learning, Prokopovich pointed out that 'there is a kind of learning which is unworthy of the name but is still considered true learning by otherwise intelligent people'. Thus

Many people often ask, in what school[1] was such and such a person; and on hearing that he was in rhetoric, philosophy, or theology, for that reason alone consider him a superior person, wherein they are often mistaken. For from good teachers not everyone emerges well taught, either because of the obtuseness of his mind or his indolence, or more especially because the teacher is but little or less than little versed in his subject.

The author of the *Regulation* alludes to the 'many schools'[2] in which 'rhetoric and philosophy and the other disciplines exist in name but not in fact', and concludes:

Men who have tasted such so to speak shadowy and chimerical learning are, of uneducated persons, the most stupid. For though living in darkness they imagine themselves fully educated, and supposing they have nothing more to learn they neither wish nor even think to read books and to study further. But an educated man, despite his regular education, is never satisfied with what he has learned and will never desist from studying, though he live for as long as Methuselah. . . .

Not only are these ill-grounded sophists not beneficial to society, the fatherland, and the church, but they are extremely harmful. They humble themselves excessively before the authorities. . . . They are prone to rebellion. . . . When they theologize, it is impossible for them not to fall into heresy; by their ignorance they would soon betray themselves. And they are never willing to change their expressed opinions, lest they show themselves not to know everything. But among the wise this adage has been affirmed: it is the property of a wise man to change his opinions.

In so many words did Prokopovich dismiss and condemn his own enemies and those of Peter and his policies. And having provided the rationale for a reform of clerical education, and having anticipated the objections both of those who were opposed to learning as the root of heresy and of those who erroneously assumed that they possessed it, the former professor and rector of the Kiev academy outlined some twenty-two regulations concerning the institution and running of an

[1] Prokopovich here uses the word 'school [*shkola*]' in the sense of an academic faculty or branch of study. [2] *Uchilishcha*, or 'schools' in the sense of institutions of learning.

academy (*akademiya*) and a further twenty-six regulations relating to the establishment of a 'seminary [*seminarium*] for the instruction and education of boys, such as those that have been established in foreign countries'. The details of these numerous regulations need not detain us. Suffice it to say, with regard to the projected academy, that some of the regulations covered the examination, appointment, and duties of the teachers; that others contained advice on methods of instruction which their author had found 'very successful'; that still others concerned the duties of the rector and prefects and the internal discipline of the academy, which was to be under the overall supervision of the Synod; and that one of the regulations – the only one to have merited the mark of Peter's explicit approval – provided that 'fiscals may be appointed who would observe whether everything in the academy proceeds in an orderly way'.[1] The regulations concerning the academy also included a proposed course of study:

> 1. Grammar, together with geography and history; 2. Arithmetic and geometry; 3. Logic or dialectics, which is the same discipline under two names; 4. Rhetoric and poetics; 5. Physics, supplemented by a brief course in metaphysics; 6. The short Politics of Pufendorf,[2] if it be judged necessary: and it may be added to dialectics; 7. Theology.

A year was to be devoted to each subject, and two to theology. Latin was to be the principal language of instruction, but Greek and Hebrew were also to be taught 'if teachers can be found'. Regarding the theology course in particular, Prokopovich took care to provide that

> the principal dogmas of our faith be taught, and God's law [*zakon Bozhii*]. He who would teach theology must be learned in holy Scripture and able to expound correctly its true essence and to corroborate all the dogmas with scriptural evidence. And for help in this matter he should diligently study the writings of the holy fathers, especially of those of the fathers who studiously wrote on dogma out of a need to combat the heresies that had arisen in the church.... Similarly, the acts and deliberations of the ecumenical and local councils are most useful.... And while a teacher of theology may seek assistance from modern authors of other faiths, he must not imitate them and give credence to their expositions, but only accept their guidance in the arguments they employ from Scripture and the ancient teachers, particularly

[1] Opposite this provision in the rough draft of the *Regulation* Peter placed three of his asterisks (see Verkhovskoi, ii, p. 57, n. 172).

[2] No doubt the *Politia brevis* of Samuel Pufendorf, which is a condensed version of his magisterial two-volume work *De officio hominis et civis secundum legem naturalem* (Lund, 1673). Prokopovich's large library contained three copies of the latter as well as other of Pufendorf's works (see Verkhovskoi, i, p. 124; also ii, v, pp. 23, 27, 28, 31, 39, 40, 42, 43).

as regards those dogmas wherein other faiths agree with us. However their arguments are not to be credited lightly, but rather examined to see whether such and such a quotation is to be found in Scripture or in the writings of the fathers, and whether it has there the sense in which they use it. . . . Thus a teacher of theology must not teach according to foreign expositions, but according to his own understanding.

In other words, with the exception of maths and physics and the optional course in Pufendorf's *Politia brevis*, the curriculum to be followed in the projected academy was more or less that which had been used in the Kiev and Moscow academies for many years. The author of the *Ecclesiastical Regulation* seems to have been concerned less with introducing a radically new course of study than with ensuring that the works of 'modern foreign authors' should be used critically and that both the traditional and the newer disciplines be properly taught by qualified teachers to diligent students. Moreover, the latter were to include, not only the sons of the clergy, but also the sons of the 'better civil servants', if that were the tsar's will.[1] And on completion of the course the students 'will be presented to His Majesty the Tsar and by His Majesty's decree appointed to various duties'. Thus while the projected ecclesiastical academy was intended primarily to train the higher clergy of Russia, it would also help to educate the tsar's administrators. A graduate of the academy was to 'receive preferment for either ecclesiastical or civil promotions above an uneducated man; and a great penalty will be incurred by those authorities who do otherwise'.

Similarly, the twenty-six regulations concerning the projected seminary covered questions of organization and internal discipline. A house was to be built 'on the model of a monastery'; it was to be large enough to accommodate fifty or sixty boys and the necessary staff and was to be under the direction of a rector, who would be responsible to the Synod. It was stipulated that the 'regulations pertaining to the teachers, students, and course of study described above with respect to the academy are to be observed here'. Indeed, the author of the *Ecclesiastical Regulation* believed the institution of a seminary to be more urgent – more 'necessary and beneficial' – than the founding of an academy: he explicitly stated that if the seminary could find the

[1] This was not really a new idea. In 1701 Peter had ordered the metropolitan of Kiev to admit 'sons of Russian people of all ranks and from all parts of the country' to the Kiev academy (*PSZ*, iv, no. 1871 [pp. 173–174]). And the student bodies of both the Kiev and Moscow academies had for some years included a small proportion of laymen, sons of the nobility or of ecclesiastical or civil bureaucrats in training, inevitably, for government service.

qualified teachers and undertook to teach the curriculum outlined above, 'then the seminary and the academy will be together'. In other words, Prokopovich was apparently proposing the creation of an institution of learning similar to those that already existed in Moscow and Kiev.

But the new seminary, or academy, or academy-cum-seminary, which was to be located, presumably, in the new capital, was to be different in certain significant respects from these older institutions. Not only were maths and physics and an optional course in Pufendorf's *Politia brevis* provided, as we have seen, but 'either military or ecclesiastical history' was recommended for reading aloud in the seminary's refectory. Moreover, 'on the first two or three days of every month the lives of celebrated men of learning – the great teachers of the church as well as the ancient and modern philosophers, astronomers, rhetoricans, historians, etc. – will be read aloud'. The recreation of the 'seminarists [*seminaristy*] – thus the students of this house are to be called' – was to include 'diversions which combine pleasure with some useful instruction: for example, navigation in regulation boats, geometrical exercises, construction of regulation forts, etc.'. Frequent 'theatricals, disputations, comedies, and rhetorical exercises' were to be organized for the purpose of 'inculcating that discipline and resolution, that is that honourable boldness, which is essential for preaching the word of God and for diplomatic affairs'. A military metaphor was used to describe the seminary's daily routine: 'like soldiers at the beat of a drum, the seminarists will, at the sound of a bell, proceed to the performance of whatever is appointed for that hour'. This description of the projected seminary clearly reveals the author's own taste for 'secular learning' and, equally, his sensitivity to the political realities of Petrine Russia – to, above all, the prejudices and preoccupations of the tsar himself, the creator of a modern Russian army and the conqueror of the Swedes.

Graduates of the new seminary who appeared 'most suitable for ecclesiastical affairs' were to be preferred by their bishops for all positions of authority in the church, 'unless some notable vice should appear in a seminarist which is not the invention of slanderers'. But on leaving the seminary every seminarist was to 'take an oath in the seminary chapel in the presence of his brother students, to the effect that he desires to be faithful to His Majesty the Tsar and to His successors and is prepared to serve in any appropriate capacity to which he is summoned by decree of the Sovereign'. The discussion of the projected seminary concludes with an expression of hope that 'from such education and instruction great benefit will accrue to the fatherland'. It is not too much to say that the needs of the state, rather than those of the church, were uppermost in the mind of Prokopovich the educationalist.

The last ten regulations of the passage of the *Ecclesiastical Regulation* under discussion concern 'preachers of the word of God'. Except for the provision that no one was to presume to preach who had not been trained in the projected academy and certified by the Synod, these 'regulations' clearly were designed as general guides for the practising preacher. They embody the advice of an opponent of the florid, baroque style of preaching; of an authority skilled in rhetoric and the arts of oratory: advice which was based, no doubt, on Prokopovich's own observations of contemporary Russian practices.[1] Thus, 'it is most unbecoming of preachers, especially when young, to speak of the sins of the authorities, or to accuse the congregation to its face, as for example: "you have not the fear of God"; "in you there is no love of neighbour"; "you are not merciful"; "you cheat one another". Rather should they speak thus, in the first person plural: "we have not the fear of God"; . . .' And 'preachers act foolishly who raise their eyebrows and arrogantly shrug their shoulders while saying nothing in their sermon from which one could gather what it is they are wondering at. The prudent preacher strives so far as possible to show by his speech and his every gesture that he thinks little of his own wit or eloquence; and therefore it is appropriate to mix in brief expressions of humble self-disparagement, such as: "I pray you not to consider who speaks"; "what testimony of myself can I give you other than that I am a sinner"; "trust in the word of God, for what I strive to propound is from holy Scripture and not of my own invention"; and similar expressions'. Or: 'It is most unbecoming for a preacher to rock back and forth, to wave his arms about, to lean from side to side, to jump up and down, to chortle; equally, it is unbecoming to weep and wail; rather, however agitated in spirit, it is becoming so far as possible to restrain the tears. For all such [practices] are superfluous and not in good taste and disturb the congregation'. Preachers were prudently advised to study the sermons of St. John Chrysostom and to preach of 'repentance, amendment of life, and submission to the authorities, especially to the supreme authority of the Tsar'.

In the last years of Peter's reign various measures were taken to imple-

[1] Cf. Chistovich, *Feofan Prokopovich*, p. 604.

ment the provisions of the *Ecclesiastical Regulation* regarding clerical education. A month after its official opening the Synod submitted to the tsar a memorandum drawn up by Vice-President Prokopovich concerning the projected seminary. With respect to the 'location of this house', Prokopovich reported that after a diligent search he had found eight possible sites in and around St. Petersburg of which the most suitable was, in his opinion, the house at present occupied by the tsar's collection of curiosities: his *Kunstkamera*. Prokopovich proposed that a large stone house be built on this site, and outlined a plan for it. He also urged that any foreign teachers who might be appointed should be confined to teaching secular subjects – languages, philosophy, history, etc. – 'and not dogmatic theology', lest they 'teach something contrary to our faith'. Prokopovich requested the tsar's permission to call the seminary 'Peter's Garden [*Sad Petrov*] or, according to foreign usage, Peter-garten', in order to 'honour its great founder' and to celebrate 'his great devotion to the common good'. He also advised that the 'great and liberal academy' projected in the *Regulation* should not be built yet; 'when God blesses the seminary, then from among those educated in it will come teachers able to teach and to run the great academy'.[1]

The brief covering letter submitted to the tsar by the Synod with Prokopovich's memorandum indicates that Peter had already approved the project, and that he intended to assign to it the very site which Prokopovich had selected; and in its letter the Synod now petitioned that the site and money for building the seminary be made available 'this year'.[2] But while Peter's *Kunstkamera* was duly transferred to its permanent quarters on the Vasil'evskii Island, to become Russia's first public library and museum, plans for building the seminary were somehow shelved. In June 1721 the Synod assured the Admiralty College that by the tsar's decree and in accordance with the *Ecclesiastical Regulation* 'a seminary is to be founded in St. Petersburg wherein, among other subjects, arithmetic and geometry will be taught'.[3] A note to the Synod in Peter's own hand, which dates from the spring of 1722 and includes the entries: 'one monastery should be for the seminary'; 'money for the seminary and the academy, etc.', suggests that Peter continued to be interested in the project.[4] Yet as late as

[1] Prokopovich's memorandum is printed in Pekarskii, *op. cit.*, i, pp. 561–564.

[2] The letter, dated 15 March 1721, was found among the papers of Peter's cabinet attached to the memorandum (see *ibid.*, p. 561).

[3] *PSP*, i, no. 120 (pp. 168–169).

[4] *ZAP*, no. 186 (pp. 137–183).

August 1724 the Synod resolved to submit to the tsar another detailed report concerning the 'establishment of a seminary in St. Petersburg as provided in the *Ecclesiastical Regulation*'. The Synod's resolution indicates that still another building had been designated by Peter for the seminary, but that at present part of the building was filled with artillery stores.[1] Finally, near the end of 1725, a month or two before Peter died, the upper classes of the grammar school founded in the Alexander-Nevskii monastery in 1721 by Theodosius Yanovskii were reconstituted the 'Slavonic–Greek–Latin seminary' of St. Petersburg.[2]

The compromise regarding the projected seminary, as well as the decision to abandon (as Prokopovich himself had advised) the plan to found an ecclesiastical academy, no doubt represented inevitable adjustments of the *Regulation*'s somewhat grandiose schemes to contemporary Russian realities. No doubt, too, the project of an ecclesiastical academy was sacrificed to Peter's ambition to found a wholly secular academy of sciences on the French and Prussian models, a project to which he had turned with renewed enthusiasm in the last years of his reign.[3]

During the first four years of its existence the Synod also took steps to implement the *Regulation*'s provisions concerning the institution (or revival) of a system of episcopal schools for the training of clergy. In June 1721 it informed the Admiralty College that sons of the clergy were no longer to be enrolled in the College's 'cipher schools', since in accordance with the *Regulation*'s provisions they were now to attend the episcopal schools.[4] In November 1721 the Synod secured Peter's explicit consent to this ruling, which in effect abrogated his earlier order requiring the sons of the clergy to attend the cipher schools and hence deprived the latter of a principal source of their students.[5] In January 1722 the Synod confirmed that 'uneducated' priests were not to be appointed to the churches of Moscow.[6] And in May it issued a lengthy

[1] *PSP*, iv, no. 1339 (pp. 182–183).

[2] See Chistovich, *Istoriya S. Petersburgskoi dukhovnoi akademii*, p. 12.

[3] For Peter's academy of sciences, which is not to be confused with Prokopovich's 'great academy', see A. I. Andreev, 'Osnovanie akademii nauk v Peterburge', in Andreev (ed.), *Petr Velikii: Sbornik statei*, pp. 284–333.

[4] *PSP*, i, no. 120 (pp. 168–169). The institution of the cipher schools was mentioned above (p. 94).

[5] *PSZ*, vi, no. 3854 (pp. 455–459); *PSP*, i, no. 312 (pp. 364–369). It has been estimated that sons of the clergy accounted for 45 percent of the total enrolment of the cipher schools during the first ten years of their existence (1715–1725): see Florinsky, *op. cit.*, i, p. 407.

[6] *PSP*, ii, no. 370 (p. 24).

declaration which was intended to clarify, once and for all, the educational obligations of the clergy.

Citing the relevant provisions of the *Ecclesiastical Regulation* and various of the tsar's decrees, the Synod declared (in May 1722) that sons of the clergy who were exempt from the soul tax were to attend the episcopal schools and only then (the bishops were reminded) were they to be ordained to vacancies in the church; that, accordingly, they were to be freed of the obligation to study 'secular sciences' – arithmetic and geometry – in the cipher schools; but that, 'since for training in grammar the teaching of arithmetic is indispensable, teachers appointed to the episcopal schools are to give instruction in both arithmetic and the most necessary parts of geometry, in order that both of these disciplines, needed by both church and state, should be learned'; and finally, that 'because of the lack of adqquate teachers for the most important subjects, that is theology and philosophy, as well as for the most necessary languages, some of the clergy enrolled in the episcopal schools were to study only mathematics, grammar, and the contents of a new religious primer. In sum, the Synod declared that

> having established the episcopal schools in accordance with the *Ecclesiastical Regulation*, the bishops are to inform the clergy of their diocese that their sons are freed from the cipher schools . . . and that they shall be taught in the episcopal schools, whence a better and reformed clergy is to be hoped for. . . .
>
> And should any son of a cleric who has been exempted from the soul tax and is being trained for the priesthood in one of these schools prove to be lazy and negligent, for that very reason he is to be deprived of all hope of ordination and ecclesiastical service, and for his sloth joined to those sons of the clergy who, as superfluous and redundant . . . are obliged to pay the soul tax. This they are to be clearly shown, so that knowing it they should not become lazy but zealously apply themselves to their studies.[1]

The Synod's declaration represented yet another attempt to adjust the *Regulation*'s proposals to contemporary Russian realities: for lack of adequate teachers, theology, philosophy, and languages were to be dropped from the curriculum of the episcopal schools; for the sake of the needs of 'both church and state', arithmetic and geometry were to be added to it. Still, all sons of the clergy were to possess at least an elementary education as a condition for ordination, a step that was itself a brave departure from previous practices.

* * *

[1] *PSZ*, vi, no. 4021 (pp. 697–699); *PSP*, ii, no. 648 (pp. 314–318); also *PSP*, ii, no. 624 (pp. 290–293).

But it was one thing for the Synod to issue such a declaration, and another to see that it was carried out. The reluctance of the secular authorities to release the sons of clergy from the cipher schools was one of the problems that soon arose. In the latter part of 1722 and again in 1723 the Synod brought the matter to the Senate, and a number of decrees were promulgated confirming, for the benefit of all concerned, the provisions of the *Regulation* and those of the Synod's subsequent declaration.[1] There was also the problem of forcing the bishops to comply: in November 1722 the Synod ordered that a census of the sons of the clergy was to be taken in the Synodal domain and in all the dioceses; and having taken the census, the bishops were promptly to enrol them in the episcopal schools.[2] The textbooks prescribed for use in the schools had to be printed and distributed.[3] And teachers had to be found: in October 1723 the Synod resolved that in dioceses lacking qualified teachers three persons from among the sons of the clergy or local civil servants were to be chosen by examination and sent to the episcopal school in Novgorod for training in the 'art of teaching grammar'; practising teachers in the other dioceses were also to be sent to Novgorod as 'observers'; during their stay in Novgorod the trainees and observers were to be maintained at the expense of their bishops; and on completion of the course they were to return to their dioceses and instruct the sons of the local clergy.[4] And although the bishops were to maintain the schools out of diocesan revenues, in November 1724 the Synod found it necessary to confer with the Senate about ways and means of providing supplementary funds.[5] Labouring under the heavy burden of taxes and controls imposed on them by the government, the bishops themselves were, evidently, unable to find the wherewithal to implement this vital aspect of Peter's church reform.

In 1723 Archbishop Yanovskii of Novgorod raised yet another problem for the Synod to consider. Of the 500 persons receiving tuition in his diocese, Yanovskii reported, only the 'smallest fraction' – some thirty students – were not sons of the clergy. He urged the Synod to consider the educational needs of the gentry, the merchants, and the civil servants; and the Synod resolved to communicate his report to the Senate.[6] The Senate responded by proposing that since the tsar had

[1] *PSZ*, vi, no. 4105 (p. 781); *PSP*, ii, no. 850 (p. 546); *PSZ*, vi, no. 4126 (pp. 792–794); *PSP*, ii, no. 900 (pp. 594–595); *PSZ*, vii, no. 4291 (pp. 105–106); *PSP*, iii, no. 1098 (p. 142); no. 1108 (pp. 148–149).

[2] *PSP*, ii, no. 896 (p. 585).

[3] For the Synod's efforts to deal with this problem, see below, pp. 276 ff.

[4] *PSP*, iii, no. 1131 (pp. 215–216).

[5] *PSP*, iv, no. 1434 (pp. 294–295).

[6] *PSP*, iii, no. 1097 (pp. 141–142).

recently decreed that arithmetic and geometry could be taught either in the cipher schools or in the new episcopal schools, the former should be joined to the latter. This dramatic proposal was accepted by the Synod as workable in Novgorod but not elsewhere, since 'in the other dioceses episcopal schools have not yet been founded'. And so to ensure that 'instruction should be under a single direction' and that 'reading and writing should be learned together with the science of ciphers', the Synod and the Senate agreed to implement the proposal in Novgorod, provided that the mathematics teachers continued to be paid by the Admiralty College and that the sons of all classes were eligible for enrolment.[1] It was, from the Synod's point of view, an admirable solution: the church's virtual monopoly of elementary education had been assured, and the beginning of the end of Peter's experiment in compulsory secular education – the cipher schools – was at hand.

Equally, by the end of Peter's reign the church's preponderant position in the restricted world of Russian higher education was also secure. Apart from the Naval Academy (whose enrolment declined from a peak of 394 students in 1724 to 180 in April 1725)[2] and a few highly specialized schools with a small number of students, the ecclesiastical academies of Moscow and Kiev remained the only institutions of higher learning in Russia. The latter, which in 1727 had a total enrolment of 654 students,[3] was under the jurisdiction of the metropolitan of Kiev, who in turn was, like any other bishop, subject to the Synod. The Moscow academy, which in 1727 had a total of 505 students,[4] had been placed under the jurisdiction of the Monastery Prikaz in 1718;[5] in February 1721, however, it came under the direct authority of the Synod.[6] The Synod had decided that the Moscow academy was to train the sons of the Moscow clergy 'without exception' and that only graduates of the academy were to be ordained for service in the Moscow region.[7] In 1723 Peter commanded that all literate monks between the ages of twenty and thirty in all the monasteries of Russia were to come to Moscow to study for a time at the academy.[8] It would seem that the government had decided that the

[1] *PSP*, iv, no. 1262 (pp. 112–113).

[2] See Florinsky, *op. cit.*, p. 405. Cf. above, p. 94, n. 2 for the origin of the Naval Academy.

[3] Pekarskii, *op. cit.*, i, p. 109.

[4] *Ibid.*, pp. 110–111.

[5] *PSZ*, v, no. 3182 (p. 584).

[6] *PSZ*, vi, no. 3741 (p. 358); *PSP*, i, no. 5 (p. 35). See also *PSP*, i, no. 8 (pp. 109–110); no. 137 (pp. 188–189); and *PSZ*, vi, no. 3802 (pp. 405–406).

[7] *PSP*, i, no. 109 (pp. 149–150); no. 139 (pp. 190–192); no. 192 (p. 246).

[8] *PSP*, iii, no. 1099 (p. 142); no. 1137 (pp. 217–218).

Moscow academy was to educate the higher clergy of the entire church, a decision which was, perhaps, a consequence of the shelving of plans for building a new ecclesiastical academy or a seminary in St. Petersburg.

Yet it should be noted that despite this re-emphasis on its important role the Moscow academy had fallen, as a result of Peter's policies and of his neglect, into a state of physical and psychological depression. In May 1721 its rector, Theophylact Lopatinskii, reported that since by the tsar's decree the monastery which supported the academy had been deprived of all its properties and subjected to heavy taxes, the 'students and staff are exhausted, and we have nothing'; the new stone building, which had been ordered in 1718, was only begun in 1721 and remained as yet unfinished.[1] Furthermore, in January 1722 the academy's prefect reported that whereas in previous years they had received a generous supply of firewood from the patriarchal Palace Prikaz, the supply had in recent years been reduced by two-thirds; that while last year the supply had been restored to half the original allotment, the promised firewood still (in January) had not materialized; 'and because of the cold the students are unable to sit out the hours appointed for instruction in the unheated buildings'.[2] The Synod resolved, in conference with the Senate, that the costs of finishing the stone building, of supplying the firewood, and of paying regular stipends to the students and teachers were to be borne by the Monastery Prikaz: by, in effect, the government.[3] And because it supplied the academy with its means of subsistence, the government felt free to make use of its students – or so it would seem: several of the academy's reports to the Synod in the early 1720's indicate that a high proportion of its graduates, whether by choice or under compulsion, went into state service.[4] The prefect of the academy also had cause to complain to the Synod that many of his students had simply 'fled' or been reclaimed by their former masters before completing their studies.[5] It was no doubt for all of these reasons that the Kiev academy, on which the Moscow academy depended for its teachers, was reluctant to send its graduates there, and had to be ordered to do so by an express command of the Synod.[6]

As for the situation with regard to the other schools of the church, the picture was not so black as the Synod suggested in 1723, when in response to the Senate's proposal for merging the episcopal and cipher

[1] *PSP*, i, no. 139 (pp. 190–192). [2] *PSP*, ii, no. 367 (pp. 21–22).

[3] *PSP*, i, no. 139 (p. 192); *PSP*, ii, no. 367 (p. 22); *PSP*, iv, no. 1232 (p. 88).

[4] *PSP*, ii, no. 451 (pp. 96–97); *PSP*, iv, no. 1164 (p. 13). See also Pekarskii, *op. cit.*, i, pp. 108–109. [5] *PSP*, i, no. 305 (pp. 358–359).

[6] *PSP*, iv, no. 1169 (pp. 19–21).

schools it had replied that, except in Novgorod, 'episcopal schools have not yet been founded'. In February 1724, for example, Bishop Pitirim of Nizhnii-Novgorod reported that since 1722 some 132 sons of the clergy in his diocese had completed the course of primary instruction prescribed in the *Ecclesiastical Regulation*, and that another 295 persons were at present enrolled in his school. In reply to Pitirim's report, the Synod resolved to send him a formal letter of praise 'in recognition of the good administration of his office, since by his report it is evident that in the school attached to his episcopal house a great number of sons of the clergy have been or are being educated'.[1] And elsewhere, too, the situation was full of promise. In July 1727 the government required the Synod to furnish it with information regarding the 'episcopal schools maintained in accordance with the *Ecclesiastical Regulation*', an order which the Synod duly forwarded to the bishops.[2] Fortunately, their more or less informative replies have survived to provide us with some statistical evidence of the spread of education among the clergy in the 1720's.[3]

To be sure, the bishops of Krutitsy, Voronezh, Pereyaslavl', and Astrakhan reported that they did not as yet have any schools in their dioceses because, quite simply, they could not afford them. The schools which had been started in two dioceses – in 1723 in Suzdal'; in 1725 in Ustyug – had been closed a few years later owing to the loss of their teachers, the death of the bishop (of Ustyug), or the shortage of grain (in Suzdal'). Moreover, apart from the academies of Kiev and Moscow only the episcopal school of Belgorod and the school of the Alexander-Nevskii monastery in St. Petersburg provided anything more than the most elementary course of study. The schools in the other dioceses provided instruction only in Slavonic grammar and in religion, although the episcopal school of Nizhnii-Novgorod gave a course in Greek and a cleric in Kolomna taught Latin grammar. Many of the bishops' reports indicated that a high proportion of their students never completed even the elementary course and became clergy: of fifty-two students who entered the Kazan' episcopal school in 1723, only thirteen became clerics (only two of them priests), while fourteen had simply 'fled'; similarly, of the forty-five students enrolled in the episcopal school of Vologda in 1724, no less than twenty-seven were for some reason subsequently enrolled to pay the soul tax, with the loss of clerical status that that implied. After the local cipher school was

[1] *PSP*, iv, no. 1238 (pp. 83–84). [2] *PSP*, vi, no. 2004 (pp. 61–62).

[3] The bishops' reports are printed in Pekarskii, *op. cit.*, i, pp. 109–121.

merged with the episcopal school of Ryazan' (founded in 1724), fifty-nine of its original ninety-six students 'left voluntarily'.

Still, when all is said and done the bishops' reports do indicate that in 1727–1728 a total of some 3100 students, the great majority of them sons of the clergy, were enrolled in the episcopal schools of Russia and were thus receiving at least a rudimentary education. Even the distant diocese of Tobol'sk in Siberia could boast of an episcopal school with fifty-seven students and two teachers (though one of the latter, a foreigner who wrote in Latin letters, complained that his students were 'extremely obtuse'). Indeed it was a hopeful beginning. Despite all the difficulties, despite even the fact that Latin scholasticism remained entrenched in the academies, only the most reactionary critics of Peter's reform could have regarded this beginning as an unwelcome development. And within ten years, it may be noted, the number of students in the episcopal schools had increased to 5000 and seventeen seminaries, with a total enrolment of 2589 students, had been founded.[1]

II

POPULAR EDUCATION; THE *Primer* OF FEOFAN PROKOPOVICH

Mention was made in the preceding section of a certain religious primer that was supposed to be used in the episcopal schools. According to the *Ecclesiastical Regulation*, the students were if possible to 'learn by heart' the primer and one other book, 'when such books shall have been printed'.[2] The books themselves are discussed in an earlier passage of the *Regulation*, where the author posed for himself the question 'whether there is in our country sufficient instruction for a Christian reform'.[3] By way of answering his question, Prokopovich argued that

> because few know how to read books, and of the literate few can gather from Scripture all that is necessary for salvation, the people require the guidance of the best educated men; and therefore the pastoral order was instituted by God to teach from holy Scripture the flock committed to its care.
>
> But since in proportion to the great number of people in the Russian church there are few priests who could preach from memory the dogmas and laws of holy Scripture, it is absolutely essential to have some short little books,

[1] See Florinsky, *op. cit.*, p. 406, n. 4; and Smolitsch, *op. cit.*, p. 711. For the history of two of the early seminaries, see Chistovich, *Istoriya S. Peterburgskoi dukhovnoi akademii*, esp. pp. 12–74, and S. K. Smirnov, *Istoriya Troitskoi lavrskoi seminarii* (Moscow, 1867), pp. 5 ff.

[2] Verkhovskoi, ii, p. 41.

[3] *Ibid.*, pp. 36–39.

> clear and intelligible to the ordinary man, which would include everything necessary for popular instruction, and that selections from these books should be read to the people in church on Sundays and feastdays.

The first of the proposed little books would treat of the 'most important dogmas of our faith as well as the commandments of God comprised in the Decalogue'. A second would deal with the 'duties pertaining to each order'. A third was to consist of a 'collection of plain-speaking sermons by various of the holy teachers on the most important dogmas, and particularly on sin and virtue and on the duties pertaining to each order'. The first two books were to be based on 'arguments drawn from holy Scripture itself, brief and comprehensible to everyone', while the third was to confirm what was expounded in the first two, 'in order that no one should think that we have invented this teaching, having put aside the teaching of the holy fathers'.

The last words just quoted, which were crossed out in the rough draft of the *Regulation* and hence do not appear in its subsequent editions,[1] reveal their author's concern that his innovations should seem to have the sanction of traditional authority. For Prokopovich was well aware of the fact that, as he put it, 'there exists a fair number of such books'; and among the catechisms and 'sermons on morality of certain great and holy teachers' he explicitly mentions the *Homologia* or *Orthodox Confession*, a catechism which is usually ascribed to the mid-seventeenth-century metropolitan of Kiev, Peter Mogila. However, Prokopovich points out, these works 'are written in Greek and are intelligible only in that language; their Slavonic translations have become obscure and are understood with difficulty even by an educated man, while for an ordinary ignorant person they are completely incomprehensible'. Furthermore, they 'contain many sublime theological mysteries and refer to many things ... which no ignorant person would know how to employ to his own benefit'. The *Orthodox Confession*, in particular, 'is long, and cannot readily be memorized by ordinary people; moreover it is not written in the vernacular and therefore is not very comprehensible to them'. It was in any case 'impossible to have these books in all the village churches, while in the towns only the rich churches can afford them'. Thus the author of the *Regulation* explains the necessity of composing the three little books referred to above, books which were to be studied by candidates for the priesthood and regularly read to the people in church so that they

[1] See *ibid.*, p. 38, n. 80.

should 'hear everything necessary for their instruction' and should know, more precisely, 'God's commandments to shun evil and to do good'. And if 'anyone should still persist in depravity, he would have no justification in the sight of God, and the blame would not rest on the pastoral order, which will have done its duty to promote his salvation'.

Prokopovich's criticism regarding the *Orthodox Confession* is echoed by a contemporary English visitor, the Reverend Consett, who remarked that while the *Confession* was an 'excellent summary of the Christian religion, abating some points wherein we Protestants think it our duty to differ from them', it 'could only effect and reach the learned of the country'; the 'simple and ignorant folk were in no respect better for it because it remained for some time only in MS. and came into very few hands, and is wrote in a sublime stile in the Slavonian tongue'; and this, Consett felt, was a major reason why 'not only the vulgar have very little knowledge of the doctrines of the Christian religion, but even many of their priests'.[1] It would seem that Consett agreed with Prokopovich's assessment of the sorry state of catechetical instruction in Russia and would have concluded with him that something new was needed. Yet it should be noted that the *Orthodox Confession* which they both criticised on practical grounds had been, since its first appearance in 1640, repeatedly approved by the authorities of the Greek and Russian churches, and has been ranked by later students among the chief Orthodox doctrinal statements of all time.[2] It should also be noted that both abridged and complete editions of the *Confession* had been published in Russia, in a Slavonic purged of Polish

[1] Consett, *op. cit.*, pp. xii–xiii.

[2] E. J. Kimmel (ed.), *Monumenta fidei Ecclesiae Orientalis* (Jena, 1850), i, pp. L–LXXV; Macaire (Metropolitan Makarii), *Théologie dogmatique orthodoxe*, trans. anon. (Paris, 1859), i, pp. 78–79. See also the article on catechisms by B. Gruzdev in *Pravoslavnaya bososlovskaya entsiklopediya*, ix (St. Petersburg, 1908), pp. 207–210; the introduction to A. Malvy and M. Viller (eds.), 'La Confession Orthodoxe de Pierre Moghila: texte latin inédit', *Orientalia Christiana*, x (Rome, 1927); M. Jugie, 'Moghila, Pierre', in *Dictionnaire de théologie catholique*, x (Paris, 1928), cols. 2063–2081; and Ware, *op. cit.*, p. 211. The *Confession* was written, originally in Latin, under the direction of Metropolitan Peter Mogila and approved by a council meeting in Kiev in 1640; after careful revision, a Greek translation of the *Confession* was approved by the council of Jassy in 1642. Abridged editions of the *Confession* were printed in Polish and in Slavonic at the Kiev Monastery of the Caves in 1645 (see Pekarskii, *op. cit.*, ii, pp. 342–343). A complete edition first appeared in Amsterdam, in Greek, in 1662; this edition included a commendatory preface by Patriarch Nectarius of Jerusalem and was subsequently approved by the council of Jerusalem of 1672. In the course of the next ten years the *Confession* was republished in Holland, and in 1691 was once again approved by a council of the Orthodox church, this time meeting in Constantinople. The Greek text was published together with the Latin at Leipzig in 1695, and by itself in Moldavia in 1699.

and Rutherian elements, since 1649.[1] Indeed, in July 1696 that generally conservative, suspicious old Muscovite Patriarch Adrian had personally sent a copy of the newly-printed Moscow edition of Mogila's *Confession* to Tsar Peter.[2]

To be sure, the complete version of the *Confession* is 'long', as Prokopovich contended: it contains, in the form of questions and answers, a detailed exposition of the Nicene Creed and commentaries on the Lord's Prayer, the Beatitudes, and the Ten Commandments; it includes learned disquisitions on the attributes of God, on Providence, predestination and free will, on the orders of angels and the degrees of perfection in heaven; on the seven sacraments, the spiritual and corporal works of mercy, the various virtues and vices, and the different kinds of sin. And so on. But in 1718–1720, when Prokopovich was writing the *Ecclesiastical Regulation*, the *Confession of* Peter Mogila was, as noted above, one of the two or three most authoritative expositions of the Orthodox faith then in existence. It was available, and had been widely used, in Russia.[3] It could have been newly abridged, its language updated and simplified, and then printed and distributed exactly as Prokopovich proposed to do with his own little books. Further investigation of the history of these little books will suggest that the author of the *Ecclesiastical Regulation* had other, unstated reasons for wishing to discard the *Orthodox Confession* of Peter Mogila.

Only one of the little books described in the *Regulation* was actually written and published during Peter's reign. It was an elementary catechism composed by Prokopovich himself with a view to fulfilling, presumably, the *Regulation*'s provision for a little book that would treat of the 'most important dogmas of our faith as well as the command-

[1] An abridged Slavonic version of the *Confession* was published in Moscow in 1649, and the complete version in 1696: this edition included a preface by Patriarch Adrian of Moscow authorizing its use in 'all Orthodox Great, Little, and White Russia' (see Gruzdev, *op. cit.*, p. 210; see also the edition complete with Adrian's preface which was printed at Moscow in 1709, a copy of which is deposited in the British Museum [3505. df. 25]). Complete Slavonic editions were printed at Kiev in 1712 and frequently thereafter (Gruzdev, *op. cit.*, p. 210; also Pekarskii, *op. cit.*, p. 275). An abridged version of the 1712 Kiev edition was published in Chernigov in 1715 (*ibid.*, p. 156).

[2] *PiB*, i, no. 103 (pp. 80–82, 586–587). In the memoir of an episcopal official of Kholmogory it is noted that in October 1692 five *inozemtsy* were received into the church by the enlightened Archbishop Athanasius (Peter's friend) after an interrogation 'according to the catechism of Peter Mogila' (see Golubtsov, *op. cit.*, p. 249).

[3] Cf. Lewitter, 'Poland, Ukraine, and Russia in the Seventeenth Century', p. 419.

ments of God comprised in the decalogue'.[1] Thus in his letter to his friend Markovich of 10 May 1720, in which he recounted the various literary projects he had recently completed, Prokopovich mentions, in addition to the *Regulation* itself, a 'brief exposition of the Ten Commandments, with an explanation of the Nicene Creed and of the Lord's Prayer. This little book will be published as a primer for the instruction of youth [*dlya pervogo uchenii otrokom*].'[2] Indeed, as early as 1 March 1720 a *Primer for the Instruction of Youth, with Letters and Syllables, as well as a Brief Explanation of the Ten Commandments, the Lord's Prayer, the Creed, and the Nine Beatitudes* was printed at the Alexander-Nevskii monastery in St. Petersburg, the first book ever to be printed at the monastery's new press.[3] And although the *Primer* does not bear the name of its author, there can be no doubt that it was written by Feofan Prokopovich.[4]

The fourteen-page 'Preface' to the *Primer*,[5] which is addressed to

[1] Verkhovskoi notes (i, pp. 395–396) that the place of the third little book described in the *Regulation* was taken by a collection that was published by the Synod in 1780 under the title (I translate the Russian) *Brief Lessons from Various of the Holy Fathers and Teachers.* Similarly, an *Instruction on the Particular Duties of Every Christian*, which appeared in 1787, was acknowledged by the Synod as the second of the little books described in the *Regulation.* But since, as Verkhovskoi points out, these two books were never widely used, their publication did not really fulfil the *Regulation*'s provisions.

[2] Letter printed in Chistovich, *Feofan Prokopovich*, pp. 46–50.

[3] See Bykova and Gurevich, *Opisanie izdanii napechatannykh kirillitsei*, no. 133 (p. 121); also Pekarskii, *op. cit.*, ii, p. 479. In Russian the *Primer* is entitled: *Pervoe uchenie otrokom. V nemzhe bukvy i slogi. Tazhe: Kratkoe tolkovanie zakonnago desyatosloviya, Molitvy Gospodni, Simvola very, i devyati blazhenstv.*

[4] The authorities mentioned in the previous note attribute the work to Prokopovich; and apart from Prokopovich's own reference to just such a work in his letter to Markovich cited above, there are at least two other contemporary references to the *Primer* which ascribe it to him. In a note to the third of his satires, the poet Antiokh Kantemir gives a brief account of his friend Prokopovich's life, and lists among the latter's published works a *Primer for the Instruction of Youth* (*Pervoe uchenie otrokom*), which Kantemir describes as a 'catechism of the Orthodox faith' (see A. Kantemir, *Satiry i drugiya stikhotvorcheskiya sochineniya . . . s istoricheskimi primechaniyami* [St. Petersburg, 1762], p. 39; or F. Ya. Priima and Z. I. Gershkovich [eds.], *Antiokh Kantemir; Sobranie stikhotvorenii* [Leningrad, 1956], p. 100). Equally, in 1736 another of Prokopovich's friends, the historian and civil servant Tatishchev, recommended the 'little book written by the Most Reverend Feofan Prokopovich, entitled *Pervoe uchenie otrokom . . .*' (see N. F. Demidova [ed.], 'Instruktsiya V. N. Tatishcheva o poryadke prepodavaniya v shkolakh pri Ural'skikh kazennykh zavodakh', in *Istoricheskii arkhiv*, v [1950], p. 170).

[5] I am grateful to the Librarian of the Lenin Library in Moscow for supplying me, through the kind agency of Mr. J. S. G. Simmons, with a microfilm of the twelfth impression of the *Pervoe uchenie otrokom . . .*, which was printed at the Alexander-Nevskii monastery press in November 1724; and hereafter I quote from this copy of Prokopovich's *Primer.* An outline of the contents of the *Primer*, based on a copy of the ninth impression (printed August 1723) which is in the library of the Academy of Sciences of

'pious parents, teachers, guardians, masters, and all others who exercise paternal authority over children', contains a concise statement of the basic philosophy of Peter's church reform in its specifically moral sense:

> The whole moral life of man depends, pious Christians, on the education received in adolescence: as the boy is, so the man shall be. If sound schooling and the fear of God (which is the beginning of wisdom) are inculcated in youth, it may be hoped that in maturity a person will be good; equally, if in youth he is defiant and unrestrained, there can be little hope that he will lead another and better life; for such rarely happens.
>
> And we have seen this to be true not only with regard to individual persons, but with regard to whole nations. Where a people abide in goodness, there, it is to be noted, the children receive good instruction; and where there is much quarrelling, animosity, duplicity, thievery, violence, and other forms of immorality, it cannot be doubted that there the children do not receive good instruction. Childhood is as it were the root whence both good and evil grow throughout the whole of life. The reason for which is this: because of the sin of our first parents, we are inclined from birth to evil. . . . Thus what good can be expected where there is no good instruction for children?

On the basis of these sentiments, Prokopovich proceeded to describe

how such education is lacking in Russia. There are many conscientious and

the USSR, may be found in Bykova and Gurevich, *Opisanie izdanii napechatannykh kirillitsei*, pp. 259–260.

It may be noted that the *Primer*, less its literal and syllabic exercises and the commentary on the Beatitudes, was translated into German soon after it first appeared (see Pekarskii, *op. cit.*, ii, p. 550, who gives the German title but not the date or place of publication). On the basis of this German edition the work was translated into English by J. T. Philipps and published in London in 1723 and again in 1725 under the title *The Russian Catechism* (copies of both editions are deposited in the British Museum [1018. h. 17; 1018. f. 26]). But apart from the archaic quality of his English, Philipps's translation is, when compared to the Russian original, very often inaccurate or misleading; and this fact, coupled with his garbled version of the *Primer*'s history and his obviously tendentious purpose in translating it (see pp. i–ii and 102–106 of the 1723 edition), seriously undermine its usefulness as a primary historical source.

But Philipps's translation has been used, uncritically, by a recent student of Peter's church reform: see G. Bissonette, 'Peter the Great and the Church as an Educational Institution', in J. S. Curtiss (ed.), *Essays in Russian and Soviet History in Honor of G. T. Robinson* (Leiden, 1963), pp. 3–19; Bissonette's article is a condensed version of chap. v of his unpublished Ph.D. thesis, 'Pufendorf and the Church Reforms of Peter the Great' (Columbia, 1961): coincidentally, perhaps, the passages from the Philipps's translation that Bissonette quotes (article, pp. 14–15; thesis, ff. 279–280) correspond exactly to those quoted in C. Tondini's polemical study *The Popes of Rome and the Popes of the Oriental Church* (London, 1871), pp. 84–86. And among the principal authorities on the reign of Peter or on his church reform, only Verkhovskoi makes more than passing reference to the *Primer* of Feofan Prokopovich. But Verkhovskoi's discussion (i, pp. 391–393) is brief and somewhat perfunctory; and his quotations from the 'Preface', his only quotations from the *Primer*, are taken from a secondary source (*viz.* Pekarskii, *op. cit.*, i, pp. 178–179).

> apparently good people among us who, not knowing the power and law of God, do not know many of their sins, and remain without fear. They know, for example, the commandment: 'Honour thy father and thy mother'; but how many know the force of this commandment, who is to be understood by the name of father, and what is commanded by the verb 'honour' . . . ? And the same may be said concerning the other commandments.
>
> How can such people educate children? And what of the many others who remain in such darkness and ignorance that they have not heard of the law of God, and place all piety in external rites and physical exercises, never thinking that the foundation of true piety lies in believing in God the Saviour and in observing his law in fear and charity. . . .

Moreover, it was a 'false opinion' to hold that the education of youth consists only in teaching them to read and write, which some people regard as the highest wisdom; for they might not understand what they read, or take the trouble to understand it, or use it for their own improvement. Indeed, some such poorly-educated persons invented 'evil doctrines, and create schism among the people: who could count the number of wicked little books produced by their pens!' And so,

> Since many among us who exercise paternal authority themselves know little of the law of God, there has arisen a need for a little book explaining the ten commandments given by God. For although a few such books already exist in Russia, they are written in the high Slavonic dialect and not in the vernacular;[1] and our youth have not been instructed by these books, wherefore until now they have been deprived of the education appropriate to them.

Thus, finally,

> Having perceived such a need in his people, and having been grieved at heart by the impiety of his subjects, the All-Russian Monarch . . . began diligently to consider how to establish in Russia an efficacious and indispensable rule for the education of youth. And God inspired him with this most wise counsel: to order that a little book clearly explaining the law of God, the creed, the Lord's Prayer, and the nine beatitudes should be written and printed together with a primer, so that in learning their letters the children may learn not psalms and prayers but these explanations; and having been thus instructed in religion and the law of God, they could read with profit the psalms and prayers. And in accordance with His Majesty's command this little book has been written and printed.

In addition to the section of literal and syllabic exercises, the *Primer*

[1] For details of the various Slavonic primers containing moral and religious instruction that were published in Russia prior to 1720, see Bykova and Gurevich, *Opisanie izdanii napechatannykh kirillitsei*, nos. 2, 5, 15, 34, 63, 107; Pekarskii, *op. cit.*, i, pp. 173–178; and B. Unbegaun, 'Russian Grammars before Lomonosov', *Oxford Slavonic Papers*, viii (1958).

contains, as promised in the 'Preface', a lengthy exposition of the Ten Commandments in the form of questions and answers, a phrase by phrase devotional commentary on the Lord's Prayer, a brief 'explanation' of each article of the Nicene Creed, and an essay on the Beatitudes. The last is a pious and unremarkable exhortation to lead a Christian life of humility, submissiveness, justice, and purity; it was highly commended by Peter himself in a letter to the Synod in July 1722[1] and was subsequently published as a separate little book to aid the faithful in their devotions and so to promote religious reform.[2] The brief 'explanations' of the articles of the Nicene Creed seem, so far as they go, not incompatible with traditional Orthodox teaching as embodied, say, in the *Confession* of Peter Mogila, although in the political-ideological conflicts of the years after Tsar Peter's death (which lie outside the purview of the present study) Prokopovich's enemies were to charge that they contained 'foreign' or 'heretical' or 'Protestant' elements.[3] As for the commentary on the Lord's Prayer, the following passage is illustrative:

> Give us this day our daily bread. Give us, merciful Father, all that is necessary to support our life: wholesome air, an abundance of the fruits of the earth, and thy blessing on our labours. Bless the government. Grant health and long life to our Most Blessed Sovereign Peter the Great, Emperor and All-Russian Autocrat, and to all his court and army. Grant that the chief lords [*bolyare*] may be utterly loyal. Preserve all the higher and lower officials in love and harmony....

And this tendency to subordinate piety to the interests of the state

[1] *ZAP*, no. 138 (pp. 110–111); Pekarskii, *op. cit.*, ii, p. 552.

[2] See Pekarskii, *op. cit.*, pp. 550–553; and *PSP*, iv, no. 1162 (pp. 9–10).

[3] It may be noted that a critique of certain 'loca obscura' in the *Primer* was written soon after it was published, and before Peter's death, by Prince Dimitrii Kantemir, the former hospodar of Moldavia who had fled to Russia in 1711 and had later served the tsar as soldier, diplomat, and senator. Prokopovich took the trouble to reply to the critique in a lengthy letter addressed to Kantemir's clerical protégé, Anastasios Kontoeidēs, who was one of the first members of the Synod (as noted above, pp. 171–172). Apart from the question of the Orthodoxy of Prokopovich's doctrine of original sin, the critique was largely concerned with pedagogical questions. It did not induce Prokopovich to alter the *Primer* in any way; nor did it affect the *Primer*'s subsequent success. Kantemir died in August 1723; and his polemic with Prokopovich remains a footnote to the history of Peter's church reform. The critique, and Prokopovich's rejoinder, are printed in Chistovich, *Feofan Prokopovich*, pp. 50–57; for an analysis of the polemic, see D. E. Izvekov, 'Odin iz maloizvestnykh literaturnykh protivnikov Feofana Prokopovicha', in V. Kashpirev (ed.), *Pamyatniki novoi Russkoi istorii*, i (St. Petersburg, 1871), pp. 1–35, and, more recently, P. P. Panaitescu, *Dimitrie Cantemir, viata şi opera* (Bucharest, 1958), pp. 202–208.

is even more clearly evident in the detailed, practical, and highly didactic exposition of the Ten Commandments – the so-called 'law of God [*zakon Bozhii*]' – which forms the longest and most remarkable section of the *Primer*. For example:

> Question: Are soldiers and judges to be considered transgressors of the commandment 'Thou shalt not kill' when they put a man to death?
> Answer: No; for judges only execute the power entrusted to them by God. Nor do soldiers transgress this commandment when they slay the enemy; for they are only doing their duty when, in defence of their country and in obedience to their Sovereign, they kill the enemy. It is the duty of kings to see that war is undertaken for just and substantial causes.

Or again:

> Question: What is ordained by God in the fifth commandment ['Honour thy father and thy mother']?
> Answer: To honour all those who are as fathers and mothers to us. But it is not only parents who are referred to here, but others who exercise paternal authority over us.
> Question: Who are such persons?
> Answer: The first order of such persons are the supreme authorities instituted by God to rule the people, of whom the highest authority is the Tsar. It is the duty of kings to protect their subjects and to seek what is best for them, whether in religious matters or in the things of this world; and therefore they must watch over all the ecclesiastical, military, and civil authorities subject to them and conscientiously see that they discharge their respective duties. This is, under God, the highest paternal dignity; and subjects, like good sons, must honour the Tsar.

The second order of persons enjoying paternal authority, the *Primer* explained, are the 'supreme rulers of the people who are subordinate to the Tsar, namely: the ecclesiastical pastors, the senators, the judges, and all other civil and military authorities'. The ecclesiastical authorities were to 'guide the people along the path to salvation; the civil, to dispense justice; the military, to teach sound military doctrine, to lead skilfully, and to incite valiant deeds'. The remaining orders of persons vested with paternal authority included parents – 'though first in the natural order, the first two orders [mentioned above] have responsibility for the common good, and therefore greater dignity' – other relations, teachers, lords, and masters, to all of whom children or students or servants or the people generally owed love, honour, obedience, and loyal service. And the *Primer* provided certain maxims to guide the faithful in the performance of these duties. 'Aged persons enjoy paternal authority, though civil authority takes precedence over age; for a young king is a father to his aged subjects'. Or:

> Question: What is to be done when one paternal authority commands one thing, and another forbids it?
> Answer: When neither of them has authority over the other, you must look not to the persons who command, but to what is commanded. For instance: if your master commands you to do something with regard to the service you owe him, and your father forbids it, obey your master and not your father. But if one authority is superior to the other, obey the superior: thus if your master or father commands you to do something that is forbidden by the civil authorities, obey neither your father nor your master. And if the civil authorities order you to do anything that the Tsar forbids, obey the Tsar.

Thus in the *Primer* of Feofan Prokopovich, which was intended to educate children in the 'will of God' and to promote a 'Christian reform', the idea of an absolute state is merged with the more traditional doctrine of paternal authority which Prokopovich had first publicly expounded in his sermon of Palm Sunday 1718.[1] In the *Primer*, a hierarchy of power is erected which culminates, 'under God', in the tsar, to whom the ecclesiastical, civil, and military authorities of the state were subject and to whom all the lesser 'orders of paternal authority', and their subjects, owed ultimate obedience. To be sure, the *Primer* also attempted to enlighten the people and to improve their religious and moral standards: superstition, defined as the attributing of a 'power to do good or evil to persons or things which in truth have no such power', and rebaptism (which was practised by some schismatics), were explicitly condemned. So, too, were bribery, simony, the promotion of unqualified persons to positions of authority ('as a result of which the people suffer'), dishonest business practices, all forms of slandering and backbiting, and the rendering of 'true worship', instead of appropriate forms of 'respect', to ikons. Overly scrupulous Orthodox Russians were assured that it was permissible to have sexual relations with their wives. But it is difficult to avoid the conclusion that the chief pedagogical purpose of the *Primer* was to instil a respect for all forms of authority, especially that of the tsar (or state). The things of God, the people were being taught by Prokopovich, were the things of Caesar, and vice-versa: the two could not be distinguished.

And in this respect the *Primer* stands in marked contrast to the

[1] See above, p. 58.

Confession of Peter Mogila. In his commentary on the Lord's Prayer, for example, Mogila confines himself to a prayer for spiritual and physical foods, with no mention of the government. Furthermore, in his explanation of the commandment to honour father and mother, Mogila *first* discusses the duties of children towards their parents, which 'even natural reason would teach us', and then shows that the words father and mother embrace all those 'from whom we receive any benefit, as our spiritual fathers, our teachers, masters, relations, kings and officials, and the like'. Not only is the order of Mogila's hierarchy noteworthy, but equally his final exhortation: 'we must be careful that nothing be done contrary to the glory of God or his most holy commandments, always remembering that we must obey God rather than our parents, as Christ says (Matthew 10:37): "He that loveth father and mother more than me is not worthy of me". And the same is to be understood of all our superiors'.[1] It is no wonder that Prokopovich wished to discard the *Orthodox Confession* of Peter Mogila: its doctrine that the things of God sometimes take precedence over the obedience owed to 'all our superiors' was obviously incompatible with the doctrine of the absolute state.

Prokopovich's *Primer*, it was noted above, was first printed in March 1720. It was reprinted in May 1721. It was reprinted again in June 1722. Indeed, in the space of four years it was printed and reprinted a total of no less than twelve times at the Alexander-Nevskii monastery in St. Petersburg, once in Moscow, and once in Chernigov.[2] The number of copies printed each time (the *tirazh*, in Russian) was 'large';[3] and already by the end of Peter's reign there were perhaps 16,000 copies in circulation.[4] Obviously the demand for the *Primer* was great, and not surpris-

[1] I quote from J. J. Overbeck's *The Orthodox Confession . . . of Peter Mogila* (London, 1898), which is a modernized version of the eighteenth-century English translation by P. Lodvill.

[2] See Bykova and Gurevich, *Opisanie izdanii napechatannykh kirillitsei*, nos. 133, 136, 172, 189, 190, 190a, 193, 208, 209, 210, 211; and Pekarskii, *op. cit.*, ii, pp. 479, 514, 548–550, 595, 617, 694.

[3] Bykova and Gurevich, *Opisanie izdanii napechatannykh kirillitsei*, pp. 260–261.

[4] We know that 2000 copies of the *Primer* were printed in January 1722 (third impression): see *PSP*, iv, no. 1162 (pp. 9–10); but as Pekarskii notes (*op. cit.*, ii, p. 550), normally the maximum *tirazh* printed at the Alexander-Nevskii monastery press was 1200, and multiplying this number by the number of printings, we get the approximate total of 16,000 copies. For the history of the *Primer*, see also N. A. Konstantinov, 'Nachal'noe obrazovanie v Rossii pervoi poloviny XVIII veka', in Konstantinov and Struminskii (eds.), *Ocherki po istorii nachal'nogo obrazovaniya v Rossii* (Moscow, 1953), pp. 44–46. The *Primer*, Professor Konstantinov points out, was repeatedly reprinted without alteration

ingly. In 1722 the Synod ordered that in accordance with the relevant provisions of the *Ecclesiastical Regulation* copies of the *Primer* were to be sent to all the dioceses, where they were to be used in all the episcopal schools and studied – indeed 'memorized' – by all the clergy, so that the 'benefit to be derived from introducing this instruction should not be delayed' and so that the clergy should 'not only know [the fundamentals of] the faith and the law of God, but be able to answer questions concerning them'.[1] Moreover, in February 1723 the Synod resolved that passages from the *Primer* were to be read in all the churches of Russia during the Great Lent, in order that 'parishioners preparing for confession and communion may, on hearing the commandments of God and their explanations, examine their consciences, and be better disposed to a true repentance'.[2] It was not of course to be expected that the great mass of ordinary Russians could make use of the *Primer* to inform themselves or to instruct their children; that would have been to presume a degree of popular literacy that was achieved in Russia only in our own century. And so it was prudently provided by the Synod that the people should hear the official explanation of 'God's law', with its insistence on the duty of submission to the tsar and his officers, regularly read to them in their parish churches.

There is additional evidence that from the early years of his reign Peter was personally concerned with improving the moral and religious education of his subjects, and that in later years a number of books, besides the *Primer*, were planned for this purpose. The record of Peter's interview with the dying Patriarch Adrian in October 1700 indicates that he was apprehensive lest foreigners taken into Russian homes as tutors should, as he put it, 'teach their heresies to the little children along with their lessons in the liberal arts, which does harm to our children and to our holy church'.[3] In a letter of 1714 to Metropolitan Stefan Yavorskii concerning the latter's work *The Rock of the Faith*, Peter suggested that to the book 'should be added . . . moral instruction for the simple folk concerning holy ikons, so that they should know what is against the teaching of the church'.[4] An anonymous memorandum submitted to Peter in 1715 proposed that special schools should be

throughout the eighteenth and first quarter of the nineteenth centuries, a fact which moves him to observe that 'unquestionably we must consider Prokopovich's book to be of extraordinary importance in the history of Russian pedagogy'.

[1] *PSP*, ii, no. 579 (pp. 223–224); no. 648 (pp. 314–318); no. 913 (pp. 636–637).

[2] *PSZ*, vii, no. 4172 (p. 26); *PSP*, iii, no. 1012 (p. 45).

[3] *ZAP*, no. 4 (pp. 33–34).

[4] See above, pp. 130–131.

founded in which the pupils would be taught about the 'creator and His creatures; and in order that this should be taught sufficiently, religious instruction is needed . . .'.[1] An entry in one of Peter's notebooks dating from 1718–1719 indicates that he was thinking about the composition of 'some sort of little rule' that could be read to the peasants in church 'for their instruction'.[2] Indeed, the surviving manuscript of a little catechism by Feofan Prokopovich includes a preface, dated February 1717, in which he explains that 'wishing to serve his Majesty the Tsar and the needs of the people' he had composed 'this little book of Christian instruction'; but that since it exceeded the tsar's request for 'brief and simple instruction, suitable for the education of youth', he was going to write another which 'will be a third or a fourth the size of this one'.[3] By the spring of 1720, as we have seen, Prokopovich had written his *Primer*, which was promptly printed and distributed for use in the episcopal schools.

Yet it was not enough. Plans were laid, at Peter's urging, for a new Slavonic translation of the Bible.[4] In a note to the Synod in 1722 Peter ordered that a manual of religious instruction be compiled for the use of confessors, so that the sacrament of penance (always of concern to the tsar) should be properly administered.[5] Early in 1723 the Synod was instructed by Peter to arrange for the collection, translation, and printing, 'for the sake of learning and guidance', of Roman Catholic, Lutheran, and Calvinist catechisms.[6] In September 1723 the Synod was informed that a copy of the 'long Protestant catechism' had been obtained from the authorities in Riga and was now to be translated into Slavonic.[7] These foreign catechisms were no doubt

[1] *ZAP*, no. 330 (pp. 269–271).

[2] *ZAP*, no. 62 (p. 67).

[3] The preface is printed in full in Verkhovskoi, i, pp. 389–390.

[4] *PSZ*, v, no. 3365 (p. 697); *PSP*, iii, no. 969 (p. 4); no. 982 (pp. 16–18); *PSP*, iv, no. 1199 (p. 61); no. 1305 (p. 141); no. 1348 (pp. 188–189); no. 1365 (p. 206); no. 1388 (pp. 247–248). The only complete Bible available in Russia at the time was first printed in 1581 at the Ostrog academy (in White Russia) and then in 1663 in Moscow. It was based on the Latin Vulgate and contained many errors as well as, by now, archaic Slavonic words. Under Peter a Slavonic edition of the New Testament only, based on the current Dutch Bible, was printed at the Alexander-Nevskii monastery press. It was not until 1751 that the new Slavonic edition of the complete Bible that Peter had ordered was printed. (See I. Chistovich, *Istoriya perevoda Biblii na russkii yazyk* [St. Petersburg, 1875], pp. 15 ff.)

[5] *ZAP*, no. 186 (p. 138); Verkhovskoi, i, p. 390.

[6] *PSZ*, vii, no. 4143 (p. 9); *PSP*, iii, no. 976 (p. 15); no. 1023 (pp. 51–52); *ZAP*, no. 160 (p. 122).

[7] *PSP*, iii, no. 1106 (p. 148); *ZAP*, no. 171 (p. 127). The 'long Protestant catechism' referred to was, presumably, *Der Grosse Katechismus* or *Catechismus Maior* of Martin Luther, which was first published in 1529: for both the Latin and German texts of this work, see J. T. Müller, *Die Symbolischen Bücher der Evangelisch-Lutherischen Kirche* (Güter-

intended by Peter to serve as models for an exposition of the Orthodox faith which should finally displace (as Prokopovich's little *Primer* of 1720 did not) the *Confession* of Peter Mogila. Peter referred to this project, among other things, in a letter of 19 April 1724, which was conveyed to the Synod by Prokopovich together with an order that it should be acted on without delay:

> Most Holy Synod! I have for a long time urged in conversation, and now in writing, that brief precepts be composed for the people (since we have very few educated preachers), as well as a book in which it would be explained what is the unalterable law of God [*zakon Bozhii*], what are the counsels and traditions of the fathers, what things are essential and what is done only as a matter of ritual, and what is unalterable and what has been changed according to time and place; so that everyone should know each thing's relative importance.

Peter went on to describe more fully the two projects which, by his own account, he had long had in mind:

> Concerning the first [the precepts], it seems to Me that they should be simply written, so that the simple peasant and his wife could understand them; but for the townsfolk they could be more elegantly phrased, for the pleasure of the listeners, as seems appropriate to you. And in these precepts the straight path of salvation would be explained, and in particular [the virtues of] Faith, Hope, and Charity (for about the first and the last they know very little, and that incorrectly; while of the middle one they have never heard); for they put all their hope in church singing, fasts, and prostrations, and other such things—and also in building churches, in candles and incense. They consider that the suffering of Christ was due only to a single original sin; but salvation is obtained by one's own efforts.
>
> Concerning the second, the book that is to be composed, it seems to me that it might be best to begin with a catechism, and to add to this successively the other things that are to be found in the church, with simple explanations; and also to add when and by whom and for what reason these things were brought into the church.

Peter's letter[1] provides another illustration of his basic religious outlook in the last years of his life and, in particular, of his attitude towards the

sloh, 1907), pp. 373–512. Luther also wrote a shorter version of his catechism (see *ibid.*, pp. 347–371), which perhaps inspired (as Verkhovskoi speculates, i, pp. 388–389) Prokopovich's own efforts in this field.

[1] *PSZ*, vii, no. 4493 (p. 278); *PSP*, iv, no. 1246 (pp. 104–105). See *ZAP*, no. 195 (pp. 143–144) for the original of the letter in Peter's own hand; also *ZAP*, no. 196 (p. 144) for Prokopovich's covering letter to the Synod. Peter's letter is also printed in Verkhovskoi, i, pp. 390–391.

religion of his subjects.[1] The letter also substantiates our claim that Peter was personally interested in the moral aspect of his church reform. But neither of the projects mentioned in the letter, nor those that we mentioned above, ever came to fruition. And for the next hundred years Prokopovich's little *Primer* remained the basic textbook of religious and moral instruction in Russia.

III

SUPERSTITION AND RELIGIOUS DISSENT; CENSORSHIP

The campaign to eradicate superstition and religious dissent was another aspect of Peter's church reform which may be studied in the context of his government's effort to educate the people in, as the phrase went, the 'straight path of salvation'.

Under the terms of the episcopal oath of 1716 the bishops were obliged to make regular visitations of their diocese in order to ensure, among other things, that 'superstition' was not practised.[2] The *Ecclesiastical Regulation* confirmed that a bishop was to 'observe that which at his consecration he promised on oath to observe, that is . . . that false and invented miracles are not attributed to holy ikons, that a close watch be kept for *klikushi*, etc.'[3] The *Regulation* also provided

[1] Cf. the discussion above, pp. 25–28.

[2] *PSZ*, v, no. 2985 (pp. 193–194).

[3] Verkhovskoi, ii, p. 40. Consett (*op. cit.*, p. 38 and note) translates the term *klikushi* into 'squawkers', whom he describes, perhaps from personal observation, as 'persons that feign themselves bewitch'd, screeming and shricking with the utmost distraction to move the compassion of spectators to give them money'. But *klikushi* were moved by other motives as well. In the tsar's edict of 7 May 1715, which provided for the apprehension, arrest, and interrogation of *klikushi* 'wherever they appear', a typical case, perhaps, is recounted: on a certain day in November 1714, in the Cathedral of St. Isaac in St. Petersburg, during the time of the liturgy, the wife of a certain carpenter, Barbara Loginova, 'shrieked [*krichala*] as though demented; and when questioned she said she was not demented but shrieked as though mad only because nearly a year ago now she was with her husband Elisei and brother-in-law Stafei Luk'yanovich as guests of Michael Makoveev, who is also a carpenter; and in the house of this Michael the carpenter Grigorii came to blows with her brother-in-law, the said Stafei Luk'yanovich, and beat her Stafei both in the house and out in the road; and she carried him off, and went home. And thereafter this Barbara began to meditate on how to take vengeance on this carpenter Grigorii for beating her brother-in-law; and she resolved to shriek as though mad and to denounce this Grigorii for despoiling her, and in this way to ruin him. And after the above-mentioned brawl she began from that week to shriek two or three times weekly, and as though demented she shrieked that this Grigorii had violated her; and on the above-mentioned day, being in the church of St. Isaac the Dalmatian during the time of a service, she similarly began to shriek. . . . But no one has despoiled this Barbara, and she has shrieked fraudulently, and in this lies her guilt' (*PSZ*, v, no. 2906 [pp. 156–157]). For a brief historical

that the ecclesiastical fiscals were to 'watch over all this and report to the bishop if such things have appeared anywhere',[1] a provision which was confirmed in the *Instruktsiya* given to the archinquisitor in 1721.[2] Furthermore, according to the *Regulation* the Synod itself was to investigate whether 'everything is done correctly and in accordance with Christian law'; it was to investigate, in particular, 'those fictions which lead a man to wicked practices or deeds and set before him models dangerous to salvation'. A few examples of such 'fictions' were cited; 'and how far these and similar tales lead men from the path of salvation, anyone with but a little knowledge of Orthodox doctrine and a good conscience will acknowledge, not without a sigh'. The *Regulation* went on to condemn various inappropriate, doubtful, harmful, wicked, shameful, or ungodly customs and practices: to condemn, 'in a word, everything that can be described as superstitious, that is, anything which is superfluous and unnecessary for salvation, which is devised by hypocrites merely out of self-interest, and which, captivating simple folk, and like snowdrifts impeding progress along the straight path to truth, is [now] to be investigated'.[3] We have just seen that superstition, defined as the attributing of a 'power to do good or evil to persons or things which in truth have no such power', was also condemned in the *Primer* first published in 1720 and thereafter widely used by teachers and preachers.

During the first few years of its existence the Synod itself tried a number of individual cases of alleged superstition. In September 1721 it heard the case of a certain minor cleric of the Novgorod diocese who had lit the candles and sprinkled holy water and burned incense before the ikons in his church in the 'dark of the night' and then, the next day, had claimed that all this was the work of the ikons and had spread word of it throughout the town 'as if it were something miraculous, never seen nor heard of', thus 'enticing light-minded and imprudent people' to believe it: citing Scripture, the *Ecclesiastical Regulation*, and the relevant passages of the *Primer* and the episcopal oath, the Synod resolved to remand the cleric to the College of Justice for 'civil punishment' on condition that this punishment be administered before the church in Novgorod where he had committed his crime and that he should then be publicly executed; and in December the College of

account and scientific analysis of the phenomenon of *klikushestvo*, see *Nauka i religiya*, 3 (1968), pp. 46–49.

[1] Verkhovskoi, ii, pp. 40–41.

[2] *PSZ*, vi, no. 3870 (pp. 467–476); *PSP*, i, no. 348 (pp. 401–408).

[3] Verkhovskoi, ii, pp. 34–36.

Justice ruled that death was to be by fire.[1] In May 1722 the Synod resolved that a certain monk was to be unfrocked, tortured, and condemned to the galleys for life for having spread tales (according to the deposition of the Prikaz of Inquisitorial Affairs) of his visions of St. Zacharius.[2] A peasant woman of the Smolensk diocese who claimed to have had visions of Christ and his angels was ordered by the Synod to be flogged and returned to her master: the woman's confessor had attested that she was not a schismatic but a regular communicant of his church; and so, 'because of her simplicity', the Synod took no further action, except to require her to promise that if in future she had visions she would tell no one.[3] By an oral decree of the tsar, which was conveyed to the Synod for execution by its two vice-presidents, a certain 'silver chest with an engraved image of Christopher the Martyr' was to be taken from the house of a secretary of the Monastery Prikaz and remade into an 'appropriate church vessel'; and the 'pieces of ivory contained in it under the guise of relics' were to be deposited in the Synod's 'Cabinet of curiosities [*Kunsht-kamor*]'. The Synod further resolved that a notice was to be composed 'with this declaration: that these and similar superstitions, which were practised before there were ecclesiastical inquisitors, and which were brought to Russia by Greeks, are now being eradicated by the Synod with great care'.[4]

The severity of the sentences imposed by the Synod on persons accused of superstition (the secretary of the Monastery Prikaz excepted) indicates the seriousness, if not the fanatical intolerance, with which it regarded the matter. In April 1722 the Synod requested the tsar to lay down a general rule as to what should be done when 'someone for his own interest, or for the sake of vain-glory, orders a priest deceitfully and slyly to publicize some miracle by means of *klikushi*, or in some other way creates superstition': Peter resolved that henceforth the punishment for superstition was to be 'condemnation to the galleys for life together with slit nostrils'.[5] Yet the Synod also attempted to *educate* the people out of their old ways, and thus to eradicate superstition at its source. In April 1721, for instance, it issued a notice declaring that 'in the Russian realm, in both the towns and villages, there is a certain disorderly custom which proceeds from ignorance', namely:

> whoever misses matins during Easter Week is, by way of a penalty, dunked in the river or in a pond; and though the simple folk do this as a form of

[1] *PSP*, i, no. 250 (pp. 301–307).
[2] *PSP*, ii, no. 612 (pp. 272–273).
[3] *PSP*, ii, no. 906 (pp. 662–623).
[4] *ZAP*, no. 158 (p. 121).
[5] *PSZ*, vi, no. 3963 (pp. 650–652); *PSP*, ii, no. 532 (pp. 173–177).

entertainment, this idle pastime is nonetheless not only injurious to health, but contemptuous of human life. For by being unsuspectingly dunked in deep water, people sometimes flounder or drown; and by a sudden drenching with water sleepy and befuddled persons lose their wits. And this is done as though in remembrance of disgusting idols, among which was the idol Kupalo, to whom on a certain day the people offered a sacrificial victim who had been bathed by them, as described at length in the Kievan chronicle. But since in those [medieval] times the Russian people had still but imperfectly received the holy Orthodox faith, which had not been firmly implanted in them, and which now by the mercy of God shines forth in holiness, they could not forsake this ignorant custom. Therefore this impious and injurious custom must be eradicated....

Parish priests were commanded to exhort their flocks to desist from this custom, so that 'henceforth it should cease to exist in the Russian realm'.[1]

Similarly, and in a more serious matter, the Synod at Peter's behest issued an 'admonition' to the people which begins:

It has been made known to the Most Holy All-Ruling Synod that there are many people to be found who from ignorance or stupidity, or from their own extreme wickedness, voluntarily wish themselves evil, as their own worst enemies, and vainly deprive themselves of health and life. Seduced by the single word suffering [*stradanie*], they delight in miserable torment and death, never considering that heedless and unlawful suffering of itself can gain them no martyr's crown but only augment the punishment, spiritual and physical, temporal and eternal.

The Synod, pained by the spectacle of those who 'proceed by vain and pernicious acts to their own destruction', and 'striving to protect the sheep of Christ's flock', judged it 'prudent to pronounce on this subject by means of this admonition, so that everyone should know that not any suffering, but only that which proceeds lawfully, that is, from the ground of familiar truth, of the eternally valid dogmas, and of God's unalterable law, is beneficial and pleasing to God . . .'. The admonition was promptly printed and ordered to be read every month in the churches, the market places, and wherever else 'many people gather', in order that 'this admonition, composed for the general welfare, should be known to all, and that no one should excuse himself by reason of ignorance'. The basic motive for issuing the admonition is perhaps revealed in a reference, which occurs about halfway through the text, to persons who uttered 'disdainful, abusive, and slanderous' remarks against the tsar, 'our Orthodox Monarch', and who 'for such godless

[1] *PSZ*, vi, no. 3771 (p. 377); *PSP*, i, no. 58 (p. 84).

audacity suffer till the blood comes and are not ashamed, imagining that their suffering is honourable and glorious'.[1]

Other admonitions were directed by the Synod to religious dissenters. Indeed, in the minds of Peter and his chief clerical collaborators, treason, opposition, and religious dissent, and ignorance and superstition, were closely related phenomena which could be eradicated not only by violent means, but also by moral suasion. This attitude is clearly reflected in the admonition promulgated by the Synod in January 1722:

> We have lately discussed the instruction and correction of the numerous ignorant persons, and how they might be converted to true piety and the straight path to salvation, having been led from superstition, that is from that which is not in accordance with the word of God but rather with light-minded and foolish old wives' tales. . . .
>
> There are two kinds of such persons: those whose hearts are malicious and melancholic, who without hesitation give instruction as though it were sound and truly based on the word of God. . . . And those who are in opposition not from evil intent but because of prejudice, for which reason the most enlightened teaching, if contrary to their opinions, is not accepted. . . .
>
> Therefore the Most Holy Synod, taking pity on these ignorant ones for having lost the way and perished in such great numbers [having perished, that is, largely as a result of official persecution], and desiring that such ignorance should be extirpated from the hearts of sons of the Russian church, exhorts all sincere lovers of Orthodoxy, and in the name of God enjoins them, to include among their daily prayers devout entreaties to the all-merciful God, that these hard hearts may be softened and transformed by the Holy Spirit into a willing ear, an enlightened mind, and a benevolent receptacle of sound doctrine. . . .
>
> And the Most Holy Synod prays for all who sincerely desire the truth, and is assiduously deliberating as to how permanent is the soul-destroying injury to the ignorant man of today who, lacking proper instruction, has wilfully, but unwittingly, chosen his opinions; for to judge the truth for oneself is the seed of all heresies and leads to eternal damnation, as is known to all from past events. . . .

There follows, in a few scornful sentences, the familiar, indeed the official version of the origin of the great church schism of the 1660's, which is attributed to the stubborn ignorance and blindness of those who would not accept the revised service books of the official church

[1] *PSZ*, vi, no. 4053 (pp. 742–746); *PSP*, ii, no. 588 (pp. 232–235). The admonition was written by Feofan Prokopovich.

but rather persisted in using the old, corrupted texts and in practising their religion in accordance with them. And there then follows a remarkable passage, which was inserted by Peter himself, concerning the unfortunate 'Grishka' Talitskii, who had clearly become in Peter's mind the prototype of all who opposed and reviled him, and called him Antichrist:[1]

> In 1701 the criminal Talitskii, in an attempt to incite sedition, wrote with great wickedness and rebellious cunning a scornful and false letter concerning the coming of the Antichrist. His teaching was followed by a certain Ivan Savin, who, amazingly, suffered great torments rather than accept spiritual instruction, and for his misdeed was condemned to death, which this Savin received with joy. But at the time of execution, by fire, Talitskii could not bear it, and having confessed his fault was taken away; and seeing this, Savin asked the guards why he had been taken away, from whom he discovered that Talitskii had confessed. Then he asked that he too might be taken away, and that he might see Talitskii; and when this was granted, he asked him why he had confessed. Then Talitskii told him in great detail that everything he had taught him was false. Oh, into what distress this Savin fell! And with what tears he ranted and raved at Talitskii for bringing him to such a misfortune, for he had gladly suffered for what he believed to be true. (Whence it is easy to see how such foolish and unthinking people, out of ill-grounded zeal, hold to their own opinions, oppose the truth, succumb to falsehood, and blindly condemn themselves to physical and spiritual misfortune.)

'Contemplating such destructiveness', the Synod proposed, as the 'most suitable means of curing the injury', that anyone who found a perplexing matter in any of the published books, or in any of the books that might in future be published, should come to the Synod and 'make known his doubt without suspicion or fear'. In the Synod, the 'doubt will be explained by means of holy Scripture; and the doubter is to be satisfied with this resolution of his doubt'. And this 'admonition from the Most Holy All-Ruling Synod to the entire Russian Orthodox Church' was to be printed in Moscow and distributed to all the dioceses without delay.[2]

Only a short time later, in the spring of 1722, the Synod, 'having deliberated on the growth of schism in the Great Russian realm and on

[1] The Talitskii case was referred to above, pp. 130, 240–241.

[2] See *PSP*, i, no. 349 (pp. 408–410) for the original *proekt* of the admonition drafted sometime in December 1721, with Peter's insertion written in the margin. For the final version, see *PSZ*, vi, no. 3891 (pp. 493–495); *PSP*, ii, no. 377 (p. 28); no. 385 (pp. 40–42). For information regarding the printing of the admonition, see Bykova and Gurevich, *Opisanie izdanii napechatannykh kirillitsei*, no. 147 (pp. 228–229); no. 156 (p. 237).

the maintenance, in secret, in private houses, of schismatic false teachers', issued what was in effect a challenge to these teachers to come forward and debate their differences. The Synod, it was announced,

> has no intention of detaining or of affronting [these teachers]. It earnestly desires freely to discuss their opposition with them. And that they might appear at the Synod for this discussion without any fear or apprehension whatever, the Most Holy All-Ruling Synod has judged it wise to proclaim this publicly with printed notices, so that these schismatic teachers should openly show themselves and observing only the rules of courtesy, and refraining from boorish behaviour, give free voice to their opinions.
>
> And should they, in discussion, acknowledge a troubled conscience, and desire to return to the Holy Church, not under constraint but from the promptings of their own conscience; and should they desire to unite themselves with the Most Holy Synod and the entire Church, they will be fervently received on their renunciation of their former opposition. And those who prove disinclined to such a conversion, and desirous of maintaining their former opinions, will be given unrestricted freedom. . . .

The remaining sentences of this extraordinary announcement indicated, however, that unconvinced schismatic teachers would be 'free' merely to return to their homes or to their wanderings and to submit once more to the penal regulations governing religious non-conformity. Indeed, after specifying the time limits within which they were to come forward to discuss their 'opposition', the Synod roundly declared that thereafter schismatic teachers were liable to arrest and execution by the civil authorities. For 'so long as they were, and are, only tolerated, so long is it unknown whether their consciences are confused and unable to distinguish falsehood from truth, or whether, aware of their falsehood and wickedness, they have become teachers among the simple folk for the sake of vain honour and a good feeding'.[1] The Synod, it is clear, could conceive of no other reason for schism, or heresy, or 'opposition' – for religious non-conformity – than black ignorance, which could be dispelled only by the 'light of learning';[2] otherwise, refusal to convert to the official church was the result of wickedness, avarice, or vanity, which must be severely punished. Thus, with a sort of deadly consistency, the Synod with one hand

[1] *PSP*, ii, no. 380 (pp. 32–33); *PSZ*, vi, no. 3925 (pp. 518–520); *PSP*, ii, no. 450 (pp. 94–96). The announcement was, as usual, to be read in all the churches on Sundays and feastdays.

[2] Cf. the passages of the *Ecclesiastical Regulation* quoted above (pp. 263–264): 'When the light of learning is lacking, it is impossible that the church . . . should not be subject to numerous ridiculous superstitions, as well as dissensions and the most absurd heresies . . .'.

invited religious dissenters freely to discuss their doubts while with the other it threatened to cut off the heads of those who, after discussion, remained unconvinced of the error of their ways.

There is no evidence that in response to the Synod's appeals the dissenters or their teachers came flocking to Moscow or St. Petersburg to discuss their doubts and differences with the exalted representatives of the official church. The teachers, in particular, were obdurate. In January 1725 the Synod issued a 'pastoral admonition to Orthodox Christians against false teachers and propagators of schism and superstition' which opens with a reference to the invitation to the schismatic teachers of 1722 and with a complaint that, since then, 'not one of them has appeared before the Synod'.[1] At their trials and public punishments for 'contempt of God's church', these same teachers, these 'iniquitous defenders of the old faith', had fervently accepted death rather than hear the Synod's 'justifications and proofs, which are based on holy Scripture'. What was their reason for choosing not to hear, for not appearing before the Synod? 'If', as Peter himself wrote – 'If they have true justification for [their beliefs], why don't they appear, when there is no need for any fear? There are two reasons for it: so as not to forsake their false opinions; so as not to be deprived of the filthy profit they gain from simple folk'. And so the teachers were utterly condemned by Peter's government for being 'conscienceless, godless, unwilling to perceive the light'; and all Orthodox Christians were warned not only to guard themselves against these 'dogs, villains, sycophants, and teachers of evil', but to denounce them to the Synod for trial 'in accordance with the Sovereign's justice'. Eight thousand copies of this admonition were to be printed for distribution to the ecclesiastical and secular bureaucracies and to all the parish churches, where it was to be read (the Synod commanded) on Sundays and feastdays.[2]

And in this latest admonition, the Synod professed to be greatly concerned with the violent extremes to which the 'superstition' of the schismatics led them, some of whom, 'having forgotten the fear of God, and scorning His law and the natural and civil law, set themselves on fire; and simple folk are led to self-immolation, and the people of God are innocently delivered up to a terrible death, temporal and

[1] *PSZ*, vii, no. 4635 (pp. 404–406). See *PSP*, iv, no. 1436 (pp. 296–298) for the draft of the admonition, dated 14 December 1724, which was written by Theophylact Lopatinskii and amended by Peter.

[2] For the printing of the admonition, see Bykova and Gurevich, *Opisanie izdanii napechatannykh kirillitsei*, nos. 212–213 (pp. 272–273).

eternal, as' – Peter added – 'has recently happened in Siberia and along the Dvina'.[1] But to us there perhaps seems, in the end, little to choose between the desperate fanaticism of the oppressed and the calculated fanaticism of the oppressor: between the excessive enthusiasm of the élite proponents of a reformed or enlightened religion, emboldened by the tsar's support, and the mistaken enthusiasm of the numerous adherents of the old ways.[2]

The Synod's endeavour to educate religious dissenters was not confined to issuing general admonitions and invitations to debate. If the schismatics would not come to the Synod, the Synod would go to the schismatics: it would send representatives, in effect missionaries, to convert them to the true religion. Such missionaries had been active in the diocese of Nizhnii-Novgorod, where there was an especially heavy concentration of schismatics,[3] for several years. In 1719 Archimandrite Pitirim, who had helped to draft the new anti-schismatic legislation of 1718,[4] became bishop there; and under his direction a school of missionaries was formed whose distinctive feature was that they were all, like Pitirim himself, former schismatics who had converted to Orthodoxy in their maturity. In 1721 the Synod requested Pitirim to send one of his chief assistants for schismatic affairs, the monk Filaret, to St. Petersburg, where he would have the special duty of arguing with 'schismatic oppositionists of the Holy Church', who 'have increased among the All-Russian people'.[5] At the same time, the Synod

[1] Four cases of self-immolation by fire which occurred in 1722–1724 are cited in the admonition: in two cases the number of dead was apparently unknown; in the third, 25 men and women died; in the fourth, 145 men, women, and children were burned to death in a hermitage near Tobol'sk.

[2] The utter irreconcilability of the two sides may be seen by comparing the so-called 'Pomorian Replies', a defence of the old rites and service books which was written in 1723 by teachers of the well-organized and industrious Vyg community (Olonets region, near the White Sea coast) of priestless Old Believers, with the refutation of the 'Replies' written by Theophylact Lopatinskii, on behalf of the Synod, at about the same time: see A. Sinaiskii, *Otnoshenie russkoi tserkovnoi vlasti k raskolu staroobryadstva v pervye gody sinodal'nago upravleniya (1721–1725)* (St. Petersburg, 1895), pp. 68–158. See also V. I. Malyshev (ed.), 'The *Confession* of Ivan Filippov, 1744', *Oxford Slavonic Papers*, xi (1964), pp. 17–27; J. Sullivan and C. L. Drage, 'Poems in an unpublished Manuscript of the *Vinograd rossiiskii*', *Oxford Slavonic Papers*, New Series, i (1968), pp. 27–48; and S. A. Zenkovsky 'The Ideological World of the Denisov Brothers', *Harvard Slavic Studies*, iii (1957), pp. 49–66 for studies of the remarkable Vyg community and its leaders about this time.

[3] In 1718 it was officially estimated that in 'all the most important towns' of the diocese there was a total of more than 200,000 schismatics (see P. S. Smirnov, *Spory i razdeleniya v. russkom raskole v pervoi chetverti XVIII veka* [St. Petersburg, 1909], p. 31).

[4] See above, pp. 76–77.

[5] *PSP*, i, no. 152 (pp. 207–208).

sent several priests to Nizhnii-Novgorod to be trained by Pitirim as missionaries to the schismatic communities in other parts of Russia. The local Orthodox clergy, whose task it was to convert the dissenters of their own parishes, were not, it was thought, sufficiently educated.[1]

But the missionaries sent by the Synod to work among the schismatic communities of the Starodubskii district (in the Ukraine), at Petrozavodsk (Olonets region), and elsewhere were few and not greatly successful.[2] It has been estimated that in the early years of the eighteenth century as many as 20 percent of the tsar's Russian subjects were schismatics;[3] and between 1718, when the official lists of non-confessors and schismatics were first compiled,[4] and 1725, the number had, if anything, increased.[5] And so simultaneously with its endeavour to educate the schismatics the Synod launched an intensified effort to enforce the existing regulations governing the registration and taxation of dissenters and non-conformists, regulations which were introduced by Peter's government, as we have seen, in 1716.[6] Immediately on taking office in February 1721 the Synod took steps to establish its overall responsibility for the administration of schismatic affairs.[7] It also promptly took action to secure its control of the fines collected from religious dissidents for not performing their 'Christian duties' to

[1] For Pitirim and his school of missionaries, see Sinaiskii, *op. cit.*, pp. 26–27, 49–65. It may be noted that for his 'zeal in seeking out schismatics and in admonishing and converting them to the Holy Church' Pitirim was promoted by Peter to the rank of archbishop in 1724 (*PSP*, iv, no. 1287 [pp. 125–126]).

[2] Sinaiskii, *op. cit.*, pp. 28–48, 65–68.

[3] See M. Cherniavsky, 'The Old Believers and the New Religion', *Slavic Review*, xxv (March 1966), p. 4. In addition to a highly interesting account of the life and ideology of the Old Believers (schismatics) based partly on manuscript sources, Cherniavsky's article provides many bibliographical references concerning the history of the schism. Cherniavsky does not, however, refer to the important works by Sinaiskii and Smirnov, cited above; and his account of government policy towards the schismatics, perhaps the single most important factor which determined the course of their history, is thin.

[4] See above, pp. 76–77.

[5] See Sinaiskii, *op. cit.*, pp. x, 302. It will be remembered from our discussion above that the Synod itself several times referred to such an increase: for instance, in its invitation to the schismatic teachers of 1722 the Synod had expressed concern about the 'growth of schism in the Great Russian realm' (quoted above, p. 295); or again, in 1721 the Synod informed the tsar that 'according to reports from Moscow, the number of schismatics has significantly increased, while in some parishes there is no one to be found except schismatics' (see *PSZ*, vi, no. 3854 [pp. 455–459]; *PSP*, i, no. 512 [pp. 364–369]).

[6] See above, pp. 76 ff.

[7] *PSZ*, vi, no. 3734 (pp. 335–356); *PSP*, i, no. 3 (pp. 33–34); no. 4 (p. 34); no. 103 (p. 138); *OAS*, i, appendix, no. 11 (col. CXIV); *PSZ*, vi, no. 3854 (pp. 455–459); *PSP*, i, no. 312 (pp. 364–369).

confess and receive communion at least once a year.[1] Moreover, in addition to missionaries the Synod dispatched regular army officers to the major dioceses to seek out schismatics 'with the utmost zeal'; from those who refused to convert to the official church, the officers were instructed to exact the prescribed fines.[2] The Synod also redefined, for the guidance of the secular and ecclesiastical officials concerned, the regulations imposing on schismatics severe penalties for failing to register with the authorities, important civil disabilities (they were banned from holding office and from appearing in court as witnesses against a member of the official church), double taxes, special fines, and other restrictions.[3] In short, during the first four years of its existence the Synod made a determined effort to contain, if not to exterminate, religious dissension in Russia by every means short of the large-scale physical persecution which Tsar Peter had long ago forsaken.[4]

But by rejecting the policies either of physical persecution or of complete toleration, and by employing instead the methods just described, Peter's government only ensured that the schismatics would survive as a distinct group in Russian society. For goaded by official oppression and by the logic of their own beliefs, and abetted by the reluctance of the secular authorities to enforce the regulations,[5] the dissenters stubbornly refused to convert: they went into hiding, became occasional conformists, fled to the borderlands or even abroad, or, in

[1] *PSP*, i, no. 15 (pp. 38–39); *PSZ*, vi, no. 3785 (pp. 390–391); *PSP*, i, no. 103 (p. 138); *PSP*, iv, no. 1223 (p. 81); *PSZ*, vii, no. 4526 (p. 300); *PSP*, iv, no. 1278 (p. 121); no. 1281 (p. 122).

[2] *PSP*, i, no. 89 (pp. 115–118); no. 92 (p. 121); no. 128 (pp. 179–181); no. 202 (p. 253); *PSP*, ii, no. 394 (pp. 51–52); *PSP*, iii, no. 972 (pp. 6–11); no. 1036 (pp. 69–73); *PSP*, iv, no. 1288 (pp. 126–127). Occasionally the Synod had to restrain the predatory zeal of its officers, who were liable ruthlessly to abuse peasants suspected of being schismatics or arbitrarily to confiscate or despoil their property (see *PSP*, i, no. 269 [p. 325], for instance).

[3] See esp. *PSP*, i, no. 52 (pp. 66–77); no. 148 (pp. 200–203); *PSZ*, vi, no. 4009 (pp. 671–681); no. 4052 (pp. 737–742); *PSP*, ii, no. 721 (pp. 407–411).

[4] For further discussion of the Synod's administration of schismatic affairs in the years 1721–1725, see Sinaiskii, *op. cit.*, pp. 178–301.

[5] The Synod frequently found cause to complain to the tsar, the Senate, or the War College of the refusal of the civil or military authorities to cooperate in enforcing the anti-schismatic legislation: see *PSP*, i, no. 202 (p. 253); *PSP*, ii, no. 394 (pp. 51–52); no. 425 (pp. 66–68); no. 918 (pp. 644–645); no. 939 (pp. 661–662); *PSP*, iii, no. 983 (p. 18); *PSZ*, vii, no. 4144 (pp. 9–10); *PSP*, iv, no. 1386 (pp. 237–246). The extent of the Synod's problem in this respect is indicated by the fact that in 1724 an ikon portraying Archpriest Avvakum, the early leader of the schismatics, was found hanging in the Chancellery for the Investigation of Schismatic Affairs itself. The Synod ordered the ikon to be publicly burned and a purge of the chancellery undertaken (*PSP*, iv, no. 1398 [pp. 257–258]).

relatively small numbers, registered to pay the double tax. They were persuaded of the error and wickedness of their ways neither by reason nor by force. And the more extreme among them persisted in their utter abhorrence and condemnation of Peter and all his works, and confidently predicted the imminent end of this world.[1]

Another of the Synod's functions, one which was closely related to its educational responsibilities and to its efforts to suppress religious dissent, was its power of censorship. In October 1720 the Senate decreed that because of the appearance in recent years of books containing certain irregularities – 'prayerbooks have been clandestinely printed in Chernigov for some schismatics; in a theology book printed in 1710 there appears much Lutheran opposition [*protivnost'*]' – that because of these 'irregularities', the monastery presses of Kiev and Chernigov were to print only 'church books' which had previously been published (and therefore approved by the central ecclesiastical authorities).

> And prior to printing [the Senate continued], these old church books are to be corrected in accordance with the church books used in Great Russia, and made to agree with them perfectly, so that all differences and local idioms should be eliminated.
>
> And no other books, whether old or new publications, are to be printed in these monasteries without prior notification to the Ecclesiastical College and without its permission, in order that books adverse to the Eastern church and not in Great Russian print should not appear.[2]

The Senate's decree was confirmed by the Synod within a week of its taking office: the Moscow (former patriarchal) press and the new Alexander-Nevskii monastery press, the Kiev and Chernigov presses, 'and the other presses of the All-Russian realm', were, by the tsar's decree, to be subject to its authority, 'whence permission is to be requested for the printing of books; and without this permission no book is to be printed'.[3] And in fact a sentence of the *Ecclesiastical Regulation* provided that 'should someone write a theological treatise on some subject, he is not to publish it, but first to present it to the [Synod]; and the [Synod] must consider whether there is anything in the treatise contrary to Orthodox doctrine'.[4]

[1] See esp. Smirnov, *Spory i razdeleniya v russkom raskole v pervoi chetverti XVIII veka*, pp. 145 ff. for the anti-Petrine and apocalyptic effusions of the extreme schismatic sects.

[2] *PSZ*, vi, no. 3653 (pp. 244–245).

[3] *PSZ*, vi, no. 3741 (p. 358); *PSP*, i, no. 5 (p. 35); no. 9 (p. 36).

[4] Verkhovskoi, ii, p. 73.

The Synod took its power of censorship seriously. In July 1721 it set up a special office under the direction of one of its members 'for a better supervision of the presses'.[1] The following month it confirmed once again the Senate's decree of October 1720 and also provided that two copies of all books printed at the presses should be sent 'for inspection and consideration' to its special office, where one copy was to be permanently deposited. Nor could second impressions of any book be issued without the Synod's permission. And 'now, everywhere, the title-page is to printed thus: by the most gracious permission of the Great Sovereign Tsar and Great Prince Peter the First, All-Russian Emperor, and with the consent of the Most Holy All-Ruling Synod, this book [title] is printed in the town of [name] at the [name] monastery. . .'.[2]

Censorship in the service of an official ideology, one of the more characteristic features of the modern absolute state, was thus firmly established in Russia in the closing years of Peter's reign. And Peter's action in conferring this power on the Synod reminds us, once again, of what was at once the fundamental fact and the single most important result of his church reform: the transformation of the supreme administration of the Russian Orthodox church into an impersonal department of the Imperial government.

[1] *PSP*, no. 153 (p. 208).

[2] *PSP*, i, no. 197 (pp. 248–249).

Epilogue

Peter the Great, All-Russian Emperor and Father of the Fatherland (so he was officially styled after October 1721), died slowly and most painfully, his body gradually poisoned by the urine it could not dispose of, a condition diagnosed by the doctors as strangury but greatly complicated by its victim's chronic venereal disease.[1] During his last days Peter's sickbed was surrounded, at his request, by the remaining members of his family, by his intimates and closest collaborators, and by his guards-officers, who perhaps alone among all his subjects felt for him, their chief, the first soldier of the realm, 'unendliche Liebe und Respect'.[2] His final agony Peter endured in an atmosphere heavy with the grief and terror of his entourage (the succession had not been settled), with the plottings of the magnates, and with the prayers of the priests, an atmosphere punctuated by the proclamation of increasingly generous decrees of clemency for those who had run afoul of the tsar's police. When death finally came on the night of 28–29 January 1725 'it was so quiet and peaceful in this great city', the Prussian ambassador reported from St. Petersburg, that 'all evening it was impossible to find a single person in the streets'.[3] The ambassador went on to describe the almost palpable gloom that had descended on the court and the capital. It was one of those rare times in modern history when for a few hours, if not days, the affairs of a great state were in suspense. The heart of the beast was dead.

Soon the question of Peter's interment arose, and Prokopovich, aware no doubt of the symbolism involved, of the fact that Peter was at once the last Muscovite tsar and the first Russian emperor, was among those who insisted that the dead man be buried in the church of the Peter-Paul fortress in St. Petersburg, and not with his predecessors in Moscow. Feofan Prokopovich: of all the clerics whom Peter had favoured and promoted and with whom he had worked Prokopovich

[1] For a very detailed account of Peter's death see the dispatches of the French ambassador, Campredon, in *SIRIO*, lii, especially pp. 427 ff.

[2] 'Undying love and respect': the phrase occurs in Ambassador Mardefeld's dispatch to the Prussian king of 31 January 1725(see *SIRIO*, xv, p. 252).

[3] *Ibid.*, p. 255.

had proved the most assiduous in seeking his 'interest', the most loyal to his person and policies, the most articulate in his defence, the most adroit in explaining and justifying his actions. Prokopovich may not have perceived 'the mystical reality of the Church'.[1] But he was the most intelligent and literate churchman of the Petrine era. It was fitting that he should have preached the sermon at the great tsar's funeral, which took place on 8 March.

Even then, even after nearly six weeks of mourning, it is said that it took Prokopovich an hour to get through his sermon, his eulogy, his monody (it is only three printed pages, or about a thousand words, in length), so often was he interrupted by his own expressions of grief and by the lamentations of his distinguished audience, which began after he had hardly uttered his first words:

> What is this? To what pass have we come, oh Russians? What do we see? What are we doing? We are burying Peter the Great! . . .

It is a simple measure of Peter's stature in life that among his survivors his death should have caused such a stoppage of the mind.

And it was in his funeral oration of 8 March 1725[2] that Prokopovich, turning to the representatives of the clergy, exhorted them to behold in the dead emperor their David and their Constantine. 'The Synodal administration is his work', he reminded them; 'his written and oral instructions', he suggested, were the proof of 'his solicitude'.

> Oh how this heart did groan at the ignorance of the path of salvation. How great was his zeal against superstition, hypocrisy, and schism. . . . And how great in him was the desire to promote improvement among the clergy, true religion among the people, and the most appropriate reform in everything!

Of course we may interpret these words of Prokopovich in a number of ways: as representing their author's sincere conviction; as representing objective reality or, as it now was, historical truth; or as a propaganda blast in the political and ideological conflicts of post-Petrine Russia. Or we may take them simply with a grain of salt, admitting, that is, that Prokopovich's rhetoric did not wholly obscure the truth about the religious cares and convictions and policies of that figure and creature of power whom he so adulated. And we may note that when explaining his comparison of Peter with David and Constantine Prokopovich mentioned first Peter's creation of the Synod. It was not,

[1] G. Florovskii, *Puti russkogo bogosloviya* (Paris, 1937), p. 92.
[2] Printed in Eremin, *op. cit.*, pp. 126–129.

perhaps, accidental. As was suggested frequently in the preceding pages, this was the essence of the church reform of Peter the Great.

In the preceding pages it was pointed out that Peter, tsar of Moscow and All Russia by birth, was by upbringing a soldier and artisan who early in life acquired a lasting taste for foreign ways and a disposition to radical reform. In maturity he was also impatient and lacking in self-control. To his practical, utilitarian cast of mind was joined a grossness of character that could turn him, all too often, into a brutal and cruel tyrant. Yet he was untiring and selfless in the pursuit of what he considered the good of the state. And he ruled, as it happened, at a time of profound cultural crisis and of dire military threats from abroad. Thus it was that the successful prosecution of the Swedish war became the dominant concern of his foreign policy, while reform in the face of any and all opposition – reform of styles of dress and of the alphabet, of the calendar and of architecture, of traditional commercial and industrial policies, of the tax law, above all of the army and, finally, of the state apparatus – came to dominate his domestic programmes. These are some of the aspects of Peter's character and some of the facts of his reign which help, it was suggested, to make his church reform intelligible.

For during the first twenty or so years of the reign Peter's ecclesiastical policies, though frequently innovative, were nonetheless conceived and implemented far more in response to his need for money and manpower than from any disinterested desire to reform the church. In 1718, however, Peter's hardheaded and reformist attitudes were joined by the abstract wit and disposition to radical change of Feofan Prokopovich, and together they turned to the pressing question of the patriarchal succession. It seems inevitable that their solution should have been revolutionary, political in inspiration and outlook, contrary to Muscovite traditions, and therefore opposed by the many people who saw in it, rightly, yet another sign of the collapse of their old way of life. Throughout the decisive years of Peter's church reform, from 1718 to Peter's death in 1725, it was Prokopovich who gave concrete expression to the impulsive dictates of the tsar, who then imposed their schemes on church and society. It would be difficult to exaggerate the influence of Feofan Prokopovich. As the chief ideologist of the Petrine system, as the original propagator of the myth of Peter the Great, as the era's foremost champion of secular learning, above all as the author, in the literal sense of the word, of Peter's church reform, he perhaps is after Peter himself the most important figure of early modern Russian history.

For of all the achievements of Peter's reign his church reform constituted the most decisive break with the past. The abolition of the patriarchate, an institution of great prestige and economic, social, and political importance – an institution that potentially was, therefore, a focus of opposition to the ever more exigent, impersonal, secularized, absolute state – destroyed the age-old autonomy of the Russian church and left the emperor with no possible rival for his subjects' loyalty. It left them with no independent court of appeal, no alternative source of justice, no hope of escape from the tsar's power. The simultaneous creation of the Holy Synod, a governing committee of the tsar's appointees, provided the means whereby the administrative apparatus of the church was incorporated in, indeed swallowed up by, the much larger bureaucracy of the state, a virtual absorption of the church by the state which for all intents and purposes was completed by the time of Peter's death. And because his church reform was in this essential sense so integrally a part of his contemporaneous reform of the central governmental machine, in order to undo the former it would have been necessary to undo the latter, and to displace the class which exploited and supported it, a revolution which it would have been far beyond the capacities of Peter's disjointed, bewildered, benighted opposition to mount.

But while carrying out the bureaucratization of the Russian church the Synod introduced other reforms, also in the name of the tsar. And if the Synod's reforms under Peter tended to turn the monasteries into veterans' hospitals, bishops into provincial deputies for ecclesiastical affairs, and the secular clergy into a force of policemen, government spies, registrars of vital statistics, and teachers of a stern morality of submission to authority, there were, on the other hand, its more or less successful attempts to spread education among clergy and people, to dispel superstition, to eliminate the grosser clerical abuses, to divert some ecclesiastical funds into social welfare projects, to halt the building of excess churches, and to prohibit the acceptance of insincere candidates for the priestly or monastic life. The Synod's persecution of religious non-conformity, perhaps the least admirable of its activities under Peter, is understandable only within the context of a time when the doctrine that a state should have only one form of Christianity practised within its borders could justify official intolerance and hypocrisy on, to our way of thinking, an absurd and distressing scale.

Apart from the vital role it played in the creation of a modern state and in the consequent secularization of society, it may be noted again, with regard to the long-term consequences of Peter's church reform, that the *Ecclesiastical Regulation* and related documents embodied the fundamental principles according to which the Russian church was governed until 1918. While Peter's efforts to reduce the number of monks and nuns appear to have been successful, his policies helped (no doubt unintentionally) to swell the ranks of the secular clergy with the sons of priests and deacons unwilling to forsake their relatively privileged position in society. They also worked (again, no doubt, unintentionally) to divide the secular clergy from the people they served, the mass of impoverished, taxpaying peasants. Peter's policies affecting the economic life of the church, though they fell short of outright confiscation of church lands, may still be seen as having set the stage for the large-scale secularization of ecclesiastical wealth which took place about forty years after his death. Indeed there is after all the incalculable effect on Peter's successors of his personal example in dealing with ecclesiastical and religious matters. But only further research in the Synod's records and other primary sources for the years after 1725 will provide the necessary basis for a discussion of the wider and deeper effects of the church reform of Peter the Great. That is the subject of another book.

Bibliography

The list which follows includes all the books, articles, unpublished papers or theses, and original sources quoted or referred to in the foregoing pages. It also includes a few other works which were not directly quoted or referred to but which were consulted and found useful in preparing this book. Sources or works which were examined but found to contain nothing of value or relevance here, are not listed. Nor are those which were cited on the authority of others, in which cases acknowledgment was made in a footnote.

A word on the historical literature devoted to Peter's reign and especially to his church reform (full titles and other details will be found in section II-B of this bibliography). On the church reform, as noted in my preface, Verkhovskoi's rare and most valuable volumes, replete with bibliographical information and with the texts of expertly edited original documents, remain, after more than half a century, the principal work and a monument, moreover, to pre-Revolutionary Russian historical scholarship. Verkhovskoi's two volumes constitute the indispensable starting point for students of Peter's church reform and indeed one of the few indispensable works on any aspect of the reign. Among the other, only more or less scholarly and often polemical pre-Revolutionary works specifically concerned with Peter's church reform, Runkevich's must be singled out: written from the standpoint of a conscientious Synodal *chinovnik* whose interpretations frequently do not stand the test of historical objectivity, his monograph is nonetheless rich in factual material drawn from sources (e.g. the archives of the Alexander-Nevskii monastery) which may now be lost. Given the importance of his subject in the history of the reform, Chistovich's old but magisterial study of the life and times of Feofan Prokopovich should be mentioned here. Post-Revolutionary Russian historians have produced nothing of value on the church reform of Peter the Great: the author of the relevant ten-page essay in the standard, 800-page *Ocherki istorii SSSR: Rossiya v pervoi chetverti XVIII v; Preobrazovaniya Petra I* does not even refer to (was unaware of?) Verkhovskoi's volumes. And the section on Peter in the first volume of Kartashev's history of the Russian church is somewhat polemical in tone and based only on secondary sources. But Soviet scholars have produced work of high scholarly standard and great interest on other aspects of Peter's reign. In addition to the growing monographic literature (on Peter's economic policies, political ideology, use of the police, etc.) and to the excellent collections of primary sources (including, notably, succeeding volumes of Peter's letters and papers, the earliest of which were published under the old regime, and the first of several projected volumes of legislative documents), there are on the reign as a whole new and copiously annotated editions of the relevant volumes of Solov'ev and Klyuchevskii, the *Ocherki* just mentioned, and several chapters of the third volume of the new *Istoriya SSSR* published by the Institute of History of the Academy of Sciences. Among pre-Revolutionary works devoted to the Petrine era mention must also be made of the still authoritative monographs of Milyukov and Bogoslovskii (on fiscal and monetary policy and on the second reform of the provincial administration, respectively), the voluminous eighteenth- and nineteenth-century works of Golikov and Ustryalov, which contain much primary material not elsewhere available, and the five posthumously published volumes of Bogoslovskii's *Petr I: materialy dlya biografii.*

Outside Russia the history of Peter's reign and church reform have aroused most serious interest among German scholars. The second volume of Stählin's *Geschichte Russlands* contains what B. H. Sumner considered 'an excellent account of Peter's life and reign', while Professor Wittram's two-volume study of *Peter I, Czar und Kaiser* is, as I suggested earlier, the most recent, comprehensive, and authoritative study of the subject in any language. Apart from valuable articles on aspects of the career of Feofan Prokopovich, Stupperich has contributed a short monograph on Peter's ecclesiastical policies which despite the limited use of original sources presents some fruitful ideas. And Smolitsch's massive study of the Russian church during its 'Synodal period (1721–1917)', the first of a projected two volumes on the subject, includes a sound first chapter on the Petrine reform. Voltaire's two-volume history of Peter's reign remains the most positive and stimulating study of a serious nature in French, though Milioukov's lengthy analysis of the reforms in the first volume of the collaborative *Histoire de Russie* is perhaps the most useful. More recently, Miss Simone Blanc has published several intricately worked articles on Petrine subjects in various of the French learned journals, including one devoted to the Russian church 'at the dawn of the Enlightenment'. In English, apart from Sumner's shrewd little book, we have, for a detailed and comprehensive study of Peter's life and reign, only the two volumes of Schuyler's very old-fashioned work. The 125 or so pages which Florinsky devotes to Peter in his celebrated history of Russia are of considerable interest; but their usefulness is undermined not only by Florinsky's quite deliberate decision to exclude any discussion of his sources, but also by his curiously hypercritical attitude towards (among others) Tsar Peter. There is nothing in English on Peter's church reform as a whole, and almost nothing of value on any aspect of it.

Two useful translations of the *Ecclesiastical Regulation* (they cannot of course be substituted for Verkhovskoi's critical edition of the original text) are: that into (now archaic) English by Thomas Consett, of the January 1723 edition, with commentary and notes which themselves constitute a primary source of some importance; and that into French by Tondini, who based his work on the

1861 Synodal edition of the *Ecclesiastical Regulation* compared with the text printed in the *PSZ* (1830) and with a Latin translation (which Tondini also published) printed at St. Petersburg in 1785. (For a note on the earliest French translation of the *Ecclesiastical Regulation*, see section 1 below.)

I. MANUSCRIPT SOURCES

British Museum: Additional MSS. 33573 (letters of Thomas Hale to his brother Bernard).

——: Additional MSS. 31128, 37355; and Stowe MSS. 223 (dispatches of Ambassador Charles Whitworth, many of which are not printed in the *SIRIO*).

French Foreign Ministry Archives, Paris: 'Correspondance politique: Russie', vols. 2, 8, 9, 10, 12 (dispatches of H. LaVie and M. Campredon, many of which are not printed in the *SIRIO*, and other important documents).

——: 'Mémoires et documents: Russie', vol. 3, doc. 14 (anon. memoir 'Sur la négotiation entamée lors du voyage du Czar Pierre I à Paris pour la réunion de l'Église Greque à l'Église Cat.e Romaine').

Bodleian Library, Oxford: Bodl. MSS. Add. D. 23, ff. 10, 12 (letters of Bishop Burnet to Dr. Fall).

A note on the earliest French translation of the *Ecclesiastical Regulation*. My search of major Paris archives uncovered two translations, one in the National Archives (Série K, carton 1352, dossier 72), the other in the Foreign Ministry Archives ('Mémoires et documents: Fonds divers [Russie]', vol. 1, no. 5). They are entitled, respectively, 'Ordonnance du Czar pour son clergé' and 'Ordonnance de Pierre Premier pour la réformation de son Clergé'. The two texts are virtually the same; despite minor variations in spelling and the slightly different titles, they are quite clearly the work of a single translator. Yet each is written in a different hand. On the face of it, therefore, one must be a copy of the other; and there is enough circumstantial evidence to suggest that most probably the NA translation is a copy of that in the FMA, moreover that the latter was done in St. Petersburg within a year or two of the publication of the first editions of the *Ecclesiastical Regulation* and probably at the instance of Campredon, the French ambassador, who would have sent it back to Paris in the regular diplomatic bag. If this much is true, then most probably the NA copy was made in Paris soon thereafter (i.e. in the early 1720's) for circulation among the priests and ladies of the court and their friends – among those personages about the place, that is, who might have been interested in it but who would not in the normal course of things have had access to government papers. The NA manuscript – a carefully bound folio of a hundred or so pages written in a neat, flowing hand – certainly looks like a copy; and it is to be found in a carton of miscellaneous documents relating to Russian affairs during the years 1700 to 1725, one of which, a 'Mémoire de ce qui s'est passé de plus considerable dans le Nord' (NA, Série K, carton 1352, dossier 1), bears a note saying that it was drawn up 'pour satisfaire la curiosité de Madame la Dauphine'. More conclusively, the NA version is not as complete as that in the FMA. Unlike the latter, it does not contain the several 'Points' ('Punkty' in the original Russian, 'Articles' in the French translation) which on the day of its official opening were raised by the new Ecclesiastical College, for Tsar Peter to resolve, concerning its jurisdiction and formal title. In the first and all subsequent printed editions of the *Ecclesiastical Regulation*, in whatever language, these important 'Points' and Peter's resolutions of them are printed in parallel columns immediately after the *Regulation* proper, as the tsar and his Synod had ordered. It is thus impossible that the FMA translation of the *Regulation*, which includes the 'Points', should have been copied from the NA version, which does not.

The 'Points' are appended to all printed editions of the *Ecclesiastical Regulation*, regardless of language, with one conspicuous exception: the French translation published in 1745, whose anonymous editor admits in his preface that he did not know the identity of the translator, that the text of the 'Ordonnance de Pierre Premier, Czar de Moscovie, pour la Réformation de son clergé' which he was now publishing was 'un présent que m'a fait un de mes amis' (*Anecdotes du règne de Pierre Premier, dit le Grand, Czar de Moscovie*, n.p., 1745; see part 2 for the 'Ordonnance' and the 'Avertissement', pp. vi–viii for the editor's remarks). Tondini identifies the editor of the *Anecdotes* as the Abbé L. C. S. d'Allainval, a dramatist and editor of a collection of Mazarin's letters (Tondini, p. xxvii). Verkhovskoi, whose work includes detailed identifications of editions of the *Regulation* in all languages, repeats Tondini's suggestion, but notes that on the copy of the *Anecdotes* to which he had access there was inscribed the sentence 'par l'abbé Soulas d'Allaival [*sic*]; peut-être par Eléazar Mauvillon, qui vivait en ce temps à Dresde et auquel on attribue l'histoire anonnyme de Pierre I dit le Grand' (Verkhovskoi, i, pp. 217–218). But neither Tondini nor Verkhovskoi was aware of the NA translation, on which the text printed in the *Anecdotes* clearly is based: the latter, like the former, does not contain the 'Points'; and the texts of the two translations are identical, though the latter, compared with the former, has been cut. And so, after it was published in 1745 (the first translation of the *Ecclesiastical Regulation* to be published in French), the NA manuscript ceased, it seems, to circulate, and was forgotten. Today it is not even listed in the NA's catalogue.

Discovery of these two manuscripts has thus helped to clear up the mystery concerning the origin of the first published French translation of the *Ecclesiastical Regulation* and, at the same time, has provided new evidence of the interest aroused among contemporary foreigners, including representatives of the principal Power of Europe, by Peter's church reform.

II. PRINTED SOURCES

A. Primary Sources

(i) Collections of documents

Akty sobrannye v bibliotekakh i arkhivakh rossiiskoi imperii arkheograficheskoyu ekspeditsieyu imp. Akademii Nauk. 4 vols. St. Petersburg, 1836.

Akty istoricheskie sobrannye i izdannye Arkheograficheskoyu Kommissieyu. 4 vols. St. Petersburg, 1841–1842.

Monuments historiques relatifs aux règnes d'Alexis Michaélowitch, Féodor III et Pierre le Grand, Czars de Russie. Extraits des archives du Vatican et de Naples. Edited by A. Theiner. Rome, 1859.

Opisanie dokumentov i del khranyashchikhsya v arkhive Svyateishago Pravitel'stvuyushchago Sinoda. 30 vols. St. Petersburg, 1868–1914.

Pis'ma i bumagi imperatora Petra Velikago. 11 vols. St. Petersburg/Petrograd/Leningrad, 1887–1962.

Pamyatniki russkogo prava. 8 vols. Moscow, 1952–1963.

Polnoe sobranie postanovlenii i rasporyazhenii po vedomstvu pravoslavnago ispovedaniya rossiiskoi imperii. 14 vols. St. Petersburg, 1872–1916.

Polnoe sobranie zakonov rossiiskoi imperii s 1649 goda. 1st Series, 1649–1825. 45 vols. St. Petersburg, 1830.

Sbornik imperatorskago russkago istoricheskago obshchestva. 148 vols. St. Petersburg, 1867–1916.

Zakonodatel'nye akty Petra I. Edited by N. A. Voskresenskii. Vol. i: *Akty o vysshikh gosudarstvennykh ustanovleniyakh.* Moscow/Leningrad, 1945.

(ii) Memoirs, letters, sermons, tracts, etc.

Baron, S. H. (ed.). *The Travels of Olearius in Seventeenth-Century Russia.* Stanford, 1967.

Blomberg, Baron C. J. von. *An Account of Livonia.* London, 1701.

Buddeus, J. F. *Ecclesia Romana cum Ruthenica irreconciliabilis.* Jena, 1719.

Bishop Burnet's History of His Own Time. 2 vols. Edited by G. and T. Burnet. London, 1724–1734.

Burnet, Gilbert. *The Rights of Princes in the Disposing of Ecclesiastical Benefices and Church-lands.* London, 1682.

——. *A Sermon Preached before the King at Whitehall.* London, 1698.

Buvat, J. *Journal de la Régence, 1715–1723.* 2 vols. Edited by E. Campardon. Paris, 1865.

Collins, Samuel. *The Present State of Russia. In a Letter to a Friend at London.* London, 1671.

Consett, Thomas. *The Present State and Regulations of the Church of Russia.* London, 1729. (Includes Consett's translation of the January 1723 edition of the *Ecclesiastical Regulation.*)

Coudrette, Abbé (ed.). *Histoire et analyse du livre 'L'Action de Dieu'. Opuscules de M. Boursier relatifs à cet ouvrage. Mémoire du même auteur sur la divinité des Chinois. Relation des démarches faites par les docteurs de Sorbonne pour la réunion de l'Église de Russie et l'Église Latine. Recueil des pièces qui concernent cette affaire.* 3 vols. Paris, 1753.

Crino, A. M. (ed.). *Fatti e Figure del Seicento Anglo-Toscano: Documenti inediti sui Rapporti litterari, diplomatici, e culturali fra Toscano e Inghilterra.* Florence, 1957.

A Declaration of the Czars of Muscovy against the French King in favour of the poor Protestants distress in this present Persecution. London, 1689.

Demidova, N. F. (ed.). 'Instruktsiya V. N. Tatishcheva o poryadke prepodavaniya v shkolakh pri Ural'skikh kazennykh zavodakh', *Istoricheskii arkhiv*, v (1950).

Eremin, I. P. (ed.). *Feofan Prokopovich: Sochineniya.* Moscow/Leningrad, 1961.

Golubtsov, A. (ed.). 'Chinovniki Kholmogorskago preobrazhenskago sobora', *Chteniya v imperatorskom obshchestve istorii i drevnostei rossiiskikh pri Moskovskom universitete*, 1903 (iv).

Gordon, Patrick. *Passages from the Diary of General Patrick Gordon of Auchlenchries.* Edited by J. Robertson. Aberdeen, 1859.

Gudzii, N. K. (ed.). *Khrestomatiya po drevnei russkoi literature XI–XVII vekov.* 7th edn., Moscow, 1962.

Guerrier, W. (ed.). *Leibniz in seinen Beziehungen zu Russland und Peter dem Grossen.* St. Petersburg/Leipzig, 1873.

Kantemir, Antiokh. *Satiry i drugiya stikhotvorcheskiya sochineniya . . . s istoricheskimi primechaniyami.* St. Petersburg, 1762.

——. *Sobranie stikhotvorenii.* Edited by F. Ya. Priima and Z. I. Gershkovich. Leningrad, 1956.

Kimmel, E. J. (ed.). *Monumenta fidei Ecclesia Orientalis.* 4 vols. Jena, 1850.

Kokorev, A. V. (ed.). *Khrestomatiya po russkoi literature XVIII veka.* Moscow, 1965.

Korb, J. G. *Diary of an Austrian Secretary of Legation at the Court of Czar Peter the Great.* 2 vols. Translated from the original Latin by Count MacDonnell. London, 1863.

——. *Dnevnik puteshestviya v Moskoviyu (1698 i 1699 gg.).* Translated from the Latin by A. I. Maleina. St. Petersburg, 1906.

Kotoshikhin, G. K. *O Rossii v tsarstvovanie Alekseya Mikhailovicha.* 2nd edn., St. Petersburg, 1859.

Krizhanich, Yurii (Jurij Križanić). *Politika.* Edited by V. V. Zelinin and M. N. Tikhomirov. Moscow, 1965.

Kurakin, Prince Boris. *Bumagi, 1676–1727.* In vol. i of M. I. Semevskii (ed.), *Arkhiv Knyaza F. A. Kurakina.* St. Petersburg, 1890.

——. *Gistoriya o tsare Petre Alekseeviche i blizhnikh k nemu lyudyakh, 1682–1694.* In Semevskii (ed.), *Arkhiv Kurakina*, vol. i.

LeClerc, J. *The Life of Dr. Burnet, Late Lord Bishop of Sarum, with an Account of his Writings*. London, 1715.

Malvy, A. and M. Viller (eds.). 'La Confession Orthodoxe de Pierre Moghila: texte latin inédit', *Orientalia Christiana*, x (1927).

Malyshev, V. I. (ed.). 'The *Confession* of Ivan Filippov, 1744', *Oxford Slavonic Papers*, xi (1964).

Manifeste du procez criminel du Czarevitch Alexei Petrovitch, jugé et publié à Saint Petersbourg le 25 juin 1718. Traduit sur l'original Russien et imprimé par ordre de Sa Majesté Czarienne. The Hague, 1718. Also the English translation of the preceding: *The Tryal of the Czarewitz Alexis Petrowitz, Who was condemn'd at Petersbourg on the 25th June 1718 for a Design of Rebellion and Treason against the Life of the Czar his Father*. London, 1725.

Morev, I. (ed.). '*Kamen' Very' Mitropolita Stefana Yavorskago*. St. Petersburg, 1904.

Müller, J. T. (ed.). *Die Symbolischen Bücher der Evangelisch-Lutherischen Kirche*. Gütersloh, 1907.

Myl'nikov, A. S. (ed.). 'Svidetel'stvo inostrannogo nablyudatelya o zhizni Russkogo gosudarstva kontsa XVII veka', *Voprosy istorii*, nos. 1, 3, 4 (1968).

Neuville, Foy de la. *Relation curieuse et nouvelle de Moscovie*. The Hague, 1699.

Overbeck, J. J. (ed.). *The Orthodox Confession of the Catholic and Apostolic Eastern Church from the version of Peter Mogila*. London, 1898.

Paul of Aleppo. *The Travels of Macarius, Patriarch of Antioch; written by his attendant archdeacon, Paul of Aleppo, in Arabic*. 2 vols. Translated by F. C. Belfour. London, 1829–1836.

Pavlov, A. (ed.). *Nomokanon pri Bol'shom Trebnike: ego istoriya i teksty, grecheskii i slavyanskii, s ob''yasnitel'nymi i kritichesimi primechaniyami*. Moscow, 1897.

Perry, John. *The State of Russia under the Present Tsar*. London, 1716.

Philipps, J. T. (trans.). *The Russian Catechism, Composed and Published by Order of the Czar*. 1st edn., London, 1723; 2nd edn., London, 1725.

Podyapol'skaya, E. P. (ed.). *Vosstanie Bulavina, 1707–1709*. Moscow, 1962.

Pogodin, M. P. (ed.). 'Tsarevich Aleksei Petrovich, po svidetel'stvam vnov' otkrytym', *Chteniya v imperatorskom obshchestve istorii i drevnostei rossiiskikh pri Moskovskom universitete*, 1861 (iii).

Prokopovich, Feofan. *Chetyre sochineniya*. Translated from the original Latin by M. Sokolov. Moscow, 1773.

——. *Istoriya imp. Petra Velikago, ot rozhdeniya ego do Poltavskoi batalii*. Edited by M. M. Shcherbatov. St. Petersburg, 1773.

——. *O smerti Petra Velikago, Imperatora Rossiiskago. Kratkaya povest'*. St. Petersburg, 1726.

——. *Panegyricus Petro Primo*. Kiev, 1709.

——. *Pervoe uchenie otrokom. V nemzhe bukvy i slogi. Tazhe: kratkoe tolkovanie zakonnago desyatosloviya, Molitvy Gospodni, Simvola very, i devyati blazhenstv*. Microfilm of the twelfth impression, St. Petersburg, 1724.

Prokopovich, Feofan. *Slovo na pogrebenie Vsepresvetleishago Derzhavneishago Petra Velikago.* St. Petersburg, 1725.

——. *Slovo na pokhvalu Blazhennyya i vechnodostoinyya pamyati Petra Velikago . . . v den' tezoimenitstva ego.* St. Petersburg, 1725.

——. *Sochineniya.* Edited by I. P. Eremin. Moscow/Leningrad, 1961.

Die Reussischen Clerisen Antwort auf das schreiben welches die doctores der Sorbonne, wegen Vereinigung der Reussischen und Franssosischen Kirchen. N.p., 1720.

Robertson, J. (ed.). *Passages from the Diary of General Patrick Gordon of Auchlenchries.* Aberdeen, 1859.

Saint-Simon, Duc de. *Mémoires.* 22 vols. Edited by Chéruel and Regnier. 2nd edn., Paris, 1879–1904.

Shcherbatov, M. (ed.). *Zhurnal ili podennaya zapiska blazhennyya i vechnodostoinyya pamyati Gosudarya imperatora Petra Velikago s 1698 goda dazhe do zaklyucheniya neishtatskago mira.* 2 vols. St. Petersburg, 1770–1772.

Sorbonne (Faculté de Théologie de l'Université de Paris). *Censures et conclusions touchant la souveraineté des rois, la fidelité que leur doivent leurs sujets, la sureté de leurs personnes et la tranquillité de l'Estat.* Paris, 1720.

Staehlin, J. *Original Anecdotes of Peter the Great, collected from the conversation of several persons of distinction at Petersburg.* London, 1787.

Suite de la Clef du Cabinet des Princes de l'Europe, ou Receuil Historique & Politique sur les matières du tems. Issue for August 1717.

Tanner, J. R. (ed.). *Private Correspondence and Miscellaneous Papers of Samuel Pepys.* 2 vols. London, 1926.

Tondini, C. (ed. and trans.). *Règlement Ecclésiastique de Pierre le Grand.* Paris, 1874.

Verkhovskoi, P. V. *Uchrezhdenie Dukhovnoi Kollegii i Dukhovnyi Reglament.* Vol. ii: *Materialy.* Rostov-on-Don, 1916. (Contains the critical edition of the Manifesto of 25 January 1721, of the Synodal oath, of the *Ecclesiastical Regulation* and its Supplement, of several of the lesser works of Feofan Prokopovich, and other important documents.)

Vockerodt, J. G. 'Rossiya pri Petre Velikom (Zapiski Fokeroda)', *Russkii arkhiv*, 1873 (ii).

Weber, F. C. *The Present State of Russia.* 2 vols. London, 1722–1723.

Whitworth, Baron Charles. *An Account of Russia as it was in the Year 1710.* Strawberry Hill, 1758.

Williams, G. (ed.). *The Orthodox Church of the East in the Eighteenth Century: being the Correspondence between the Eastern Patriarchs and the Nonjuring Bishops.* London, 1868.

B. Secondary Sources

(i) Principal authorities

Bogoslovskii, M. M. *Petr I: Materialy dlya biografii.* 5 vols. Moscow, 1940–1948.

Bogoslovskii, M. M. *Oblastnaya reforma Petra Velikago. Provintsiya, 1719–1727*. Moscow, 1902.

Chistovich, I. *Feofan Prokopovich i ego vremya*. St. Petersburg, 1868.

Golikov, I. I. *Deyaniya Petra Velikago, Mudrago Preobrazitelya Rossii*. 15 vols. 2nd edn., Moscow, 1837–1843.

Gorchakov, M. I. *Monastyrskii Prikaz, 1649–1725*. St. Petersburg, 1868.

——. *O zemel'nykh vladeniyakh vserossiiskikh mitropolitov, patriarkhov i sv. sinoda*. St. Petersburg, 1871.

Kafengauz, B. B. and N. I. Pavlenko (eds.). *Rossiya v pervoi chetverti XVIII v*. Moscow, 1954. An unnumbered volume in N. M. Druzhinin and others (gen. eds.), *Ocherki istorii SSSR*. 9 vols. Moscow, 1953–1958.

Kharlampovich, K. V. *Malorossiiskoe vliyanie na velikorusskuyu tserkovnuyu zhizn'*. Kazan', 1914.

Klyuchevskii, V. O. *Sochineniya*. 8 vols. Moscow, 1956–1959.

Milyukov, P. N. *Gosudarstvennoe khozyaistvo Rossii v pervoi chetverti XVIII stoletiya i reforma Petra Velikago*. 2nd edn., St. Petersburg, 1905.

Milyutin, V. 'O nedvizhimykh imushchestvakh dukhovenstva v Rossii', in 4 parts, in *Chteniya v imperatorskom obshchestve istorii i drevnostei rossiiskikh pri Moskovskom universitete*, 1859 (iv), 1860 (iii), 1861 (i), 1861 (ii).

Novosel'skii, A. A. and N. V. Ustyugov (eds.). *Period feodalizma XVII v*. Moscow, 1955. An unnumbered volume in N. M. Druzhinin and others (gen. eds.), *Ocherki istorii SSSR*. 9 vols. Moscow, 1953–1958.

Pascal, Pierre. *Avvakum et les débuts du Raskol*. 2nd edn., Paris, 1963.

Pekarskii, P. *Nauka i literatura v Rossii pri Petre Velikom*. 2 vols. St. Petersburg, 1862.

Runkevich, S. G. *Uchrezhdenie i pervonachal'noe ustroistvo svyateishago pravitel'stvuyushchago sinoda (1721–1725)*. St. Petersburg, 1900.

Smolitsch, I. *Geschichte der Russischen Kirche: 1700–1917*. Leiden, 1964.

Solov'ev, S. M. *Istoriya Rossii s drevneishikh vremen*. 15 vols. Moscow, 1962–1966.

Ustryalov, N. G. *Istoriya tsarstvovaniya Petra Velikago*. 5 vols. St. Petersburg, 1858–1863.

Verkhovskoi, P. V. *Uchrezhdenie Dukhovnoi Kollegii i Dukhovnyi Reglament*. Vol. i: *Issledovanie*. Rostov-on-Don, 1916.

Wittram, Reinhard. *Peter I, Czar und Kaiser: Zur Geschichte Peters des Grossen in seiner Zeit*. 2 vols. Göttingen, 1964.

(ii) Reference works

Bolkhovitinov, Evgenii. *Slovar' istoricheskii o byvshikh v Rossii pisatelyakh dukhovnago china Greko-rossiiskoi tserkvi*. 2 vols. 2nd edn., St. Petersburg, 1827.

Bykova, T. A. and M. M. Gurevich. *Opisanie izdanii grazhdanskoi pechati (1708–1725)*. Moscow/Leningrad, 1955.

——. *Opisanie izdanii napechatannykh kirillitsei (1689–1725)*. Moscow/Leningrad, 1958.

Cross, F. L. (ed.). *The Oxford Dictionary of the Christian Church*. London, 1957.
Kaiser, F. 'Der europäische Anteil an der russischen Rechtsterminologie der petrinischen Zeit', in M. Bernath and others (eds.), *Forschungen zur osteuropäischen Geschichte*, x (Berlin, 1965).
Kondakov, I. P. and others (eds.). *Svodnyi katalog Russkoi knigi grazhdanskoi pechati XVIII veka*. 5 vols. Moscow, 1962–1967.
Opisanie monastyrei v rossiskoi imperii nakhodyashchikhsya. 6th edn., Moscow, 1822.
Pol'nyi pravoslavnyi bogoslovskii entsiklopedicheskii slovar'. 2 vols. St. Petersburg, n.d.
Russkii biograficheskii slovar'. 25 vols. Moscow/St. Petersburg/Petrograd, 1896–1918.
Sopikov, V. S. *Opyt rossiiskoi bibliografii*. 5 parts and an index. Edited by V. N. Rogozhin. St. Petersburg, 1904–1908.
Vacant, A. and others (eds.). *Dictionnaire de théologie catholique*. 15 vols. Paris, 1903–1950.

(iii) Other secondary works

Abercrombie, N. *The Origins of Jansenism*. Oxford, 1936.
Amburger, E. *Geschichte der Behördenorganisation Russlands von Peter dem Grossen bis 1917*. Leiden, 1966.
Ammann, A. M. *Storia della chiesa Russa*. Turin, 1948.
Andreev, A. I. 'Osnovanie akademii nauk v Peterburge', in Andreev (ed.), *Petr Velikii: Sbornik statei*. Moscow/Leningrad, 1947.
——. 'Petr I v Anglii v 1698g.', in Andreev (ed.), *Petr Velikii: Sbornik statei*. Moscow/Leningrad, 1947.
Barsov, T. V. *Svyateishii sinod v ego proshlom*. St. Petersburg, 1896.
Benz, E. *Geist und Leben der Ostkirche*. Hamburg, 1957. English translation by R. and C. Winston, *The Eastern Orthodox Church: Its Thought and Life*. Chicago, 1963.
Berkov, P. N. 'Tomas Konsett, kapellan angliiskoi faktorii v Rossii', in *Problemy mezhdunarodnykh literaturnykh svyazei*. Leningrad, 1962.
Beskrovnyi, L. G. and others (eds.). *Prevrashchenie Rossii v velikuyu derzhavu; narodnye dvizheniya XVII–XVIII vv*. Moscow, 1967. Vol. iii of B. N. Ponomarev and others (gen. eds.), *Istoriya SSSR s drevneishikh vremen do nashikh dnei*. 8 vols. (of projected 12). Moscow, 1966–.
Billington, J. *The Icon and the Axe*. London, 1966.
Birnbaum, H. 'Some Aspects of the Slavonic Renaissance', *Slavonic and East European Review*, xlvii (January 1969).
Bissonnette, G. 'Peter the Great and the Church as an Educational Institution', in J. S. Curtiss (ed.), *Essays in Russian and Soviet History in Honor of G. T. Robinson*. Leiden, 1963.

Bissonnette, G. 'Pufendorf and the Church Reforms of Peter the Great'. Columbia Univ. Ph.D. thesis, 1961.

Blanc, S. 'A propos de la politique économique de Pierre le Grand', *Cahiers du monde russe et soviétique*, iii (January–March 1962).

——. 'L'Église russe à l'aube du "Siècle des Lumières"', *Annales Économies Sociétés Civilisations*, xx (May–June 1965).

——. 'La pratique de l'administration russe dans la première moitié du XVIIIe siècle', *Revue d'histoire moderne et contemporaine*, x (1963), pp. 45–64.

Blum, J. *Lord and Peasant in Russia*. New York, 1964.

Bulgakov, M. *Istoriya Kievskoi akademii*. St. Petersburg, 1843.

Catiforo, A. *Vita di Pietro il Grande, Imperador della Russia*. 3rd edn. revised, Venice, 1748.

Cherniavsky, M. 'The Old Believers and the New Religion', *Slavic Review*, xxv (March 1966).

Chistovich, I. *Feofan Prokopovich i Feofilakt Lopatinskii*. St. Petersburg, 1861.

——. *Istoriya perevoda Biblii na russkii yazyk*. St. Petersburg, 1875.

——. *Istoriya S. Petersburgskoi dukhovnoi akademii*. St. Petersburg, 1857.

Čiževskij, D. *History of Russian Literature from the Eleventh Century to the End of the Baroque*. The Hague, 1960.

Clark, G. N. *The Seventeenth Century*. 2nd edn., Oxford, 1960.

Clarke, T. E. S. and H. C. Foxcroft. *A Life of Gilbert Burnet*. Cambridge, 1907.

Curtiss, J. S. *Church and State in Russia, 1900–1917*. New York, 1940.

Dalton, H. *Beiträge zur Geschichte der evangelischen Kirche in Russland*. 4 vols. Gotha, 1887–1905.

Druzhinin, N. M. and others (eds.). *Absolyutizm v Rossii, XVII–XVIII vv*. Moscow, 1964.

Eaton, H. L. 'Cadasters and Censuses of Muscovy', *Slavic Review*, xxvi (March, 1967).

Eroshkin, N. P. *Istoriya gosudarstvennykh uchrezhdenii dorevolutsionnoi Rossii*. 2nd edn., Moscow, 1968.

Feret, P. *La Faculté de théologie de Paris et ses docteurs les plus célèbres*. Vol. vi: *XVIIIe siècle*. Paris, 1909.

Florinsky, M. T. *Russia: a History and an Interpretation*. 2 vols. New York, 1959–1961.

Florovskii, G. *Puti russkogo bogosloviya*. Paris, 1937.

Florovsky, A. V. 'Russo-Austrian Conflicts in the Early Eighteenth Century', *Slavonic and East European Review*, xlvii (January 1969).

Gallereya Petra Velikago v imperatorskoi publichnoi biblioteke. St. Petersburg, 1903.

Golikova, N. B. *Politicheskie protsessy pri Petre I*. Moscow, 1957.

Gruzdev, B. 'Katikhizisy russkie', in N. N. Glubokovskii (ed.), *Pravoslavnaya bogoslovskaya entsiklopediya*, ix (St. Petersburg, 1908).

Gurvich, G. '*Pravda voli monarshei*' *Feofana Prokopovicha i eya zapadnoevropeiskie istochniki*. Yur'ev, 1915.

Haarlem, Z. de. 'La Mission capucine en Russie à l'époque de Pierre le Grand', in 7 parts, in *Collectanea franciscana*, ix (1941), fasc. 2, 3, 4; xii (1942), fasc. 1, 2, 3, 4.

Hans, N. 'The Moscow School of Mathematics and Navigation (1701)', *Slavonic and East European Review*, xxix (June 1951).

Horak, S. 'The Kiev Academy: A Bridge to Europe in the Seventeenth Century'. Paper read at the 82nd annual meeting of the American Historical Association, December 1967.

Izvekov, D. E. 'Odin iz maloizvestnykh literaturnykh protivnikov Feofana Prokopovicha', in V. Kashpirev (ed.), *Pamyatniki novoi russkoi istorii*, i (St. Petersburg, 1871).

Judge, H. C. 'Church and State under Louis XIV', *History*, xlv (October 1960).

Kahle, W. *Die Begegnung des baltischen Protestantismus mit der russisch orthodoxen Kirche*. Leiden/Cologne, 1959.

Kafengauz, B. B. *I. T. Pososhkov: zhizn' i deyatel'nost'*. Moscow, 1951.

Kaplan, F. I. 'Tatiščev and Kantemir, Two 18th Century Exponents of a Russian Bureaucratic Style of Thought', *Jahrbücher für Geschichte Osteuropas*, xiii (December 1965).

Kapterev, N. F. 'Ierusalimskii Patriarkh Dosithei v ego snosheniyakh s russkim pravitel'stvom (1669–1707)', *Chteniya v imperatorskom obshchestve istorii i drevnostei rossiiskikh pri Moskovskom universitete*, 1891 (ii).

Kartashev, A. V. *Ocherki po istorii russkoi tserkvi*. 2 vols. Paris, 1959.

Klyuchevskii, V. O. *Petr Velikii sredi svoikh sotrudnikov. Ocherk*. St. Petersburg, 1902.

Konstantinov, N. A. and V. Ya. Struminskii (eds.). *Ocherki po istorii nachal'nogo obrazovaniya v Rossii*. Moscow, 1953.

Korolev, A. 'Stefan Yavorskii', *Russkii biograficheskii slovar'*, xix (St. Petersburg, 1909).

Kozlov, O. F. 'Delo Tsarevicha Alekseya', *Voprosy istorii*, no. 9 (1969).

——. 'Reforma tserkvi Petra I i otkliki na nee v russkom obshchestve v pervoi polovine XVIII v.', *Vestnik Moskovskogo universiteta*, no. 5 (1968).

Lappo-Danilevsky, A. S. 'The Development of Science and Learning in Russia', in J. D. Duff (ed.), *Russian Realities and Problems*, Cambridge, 1917.

——. 'L'Idée de l'état et son évolution en Russie depuis les troubles du XVIIe siècle jusqu'aux réformes du XVIIIe', in P. Vinogradoff (ed.), *Essays in Legal History*. London, 1913.

Lewitter, L. R. 'Peter the Great, Poland, and the Westernization of Russia', *Journal of the History of Ideas*, xix (October 1958).

——. 'Poland, Ukraine, and Russia in the Seventeenth Century', in 2 parts, *Slavonic and East European Review*, xxvii (December 1948, May 1949).

Macaire (Metropolitan Makarii). *Théologie dogmatique orthodoxe. Traduite par un Russe*. 2 vols. Paris, 1859.

Martimort, A.-G. *Le gallicanisme de Bossuet*. Paris, 1953.
Mavor, J. *An Economic History of Russia*. 2 vols. 2nd edn., London, 1925.
Melgunov, S. 'Les mouvements religieux et sociaux en Russie aux XVIIe–XVIIIe siècles', *Le monde slave*, xii (December 1926).
Milioukov, P., Ch. Seignobos and L. Eisenmann. *Histoire de Russie*. Vol. i: *Des origines à la mort de Pierre le Grand*. Paris, 1932.
Mintslof, R. *Petr Velikii v inostrannoi literature*. St. Petersburg, 1872.
Morozov, P. 'Feofan Prokopovich kak pisatel'', *Zhurnal ministerstva narodnago prosveshcheniya*, 207–211 (1880).
Moroshkin, I. Ya. 'Feofilakt Lopatinskii', in 2 parts, *Russkaya starina*, nos. 1, 2 (January, February 1886).
——. 'Theodosii Yanovskii, arkhiepiskop novgorodskii', in 3 parts, *Russkaya starina*, nos. 7, 10, 11 (July, October, November 1887).
Ogg, D. *Europe in the Seventeenth Century*. 8th edn., London, 1961.
Panaitescu, P. P. *Dimitrie Cantemir, viata şi opera*. Bucharest, 1958.
——. 'Le Prince Démètre Cantemir et le mouvement intellectuel russe sous Pierre le Grand', *Revue des études slaves*, vi (1926).
Pastor, L. *The History of the Popes*. 40 vols. Edited by R. Kerr, E. Graf, and E. Peeler. London, 1891–1953.
Pierling, P. *La Russie et le Saint-Siège*. 5 vols. Paris, 1896–1906.
——. *La Sorbonne et la Russie, 1717–1747*. Paris, 1882.
Poludenskii, M. 'Petr Velikii v Parizhe', *Russkii arkhiv*, 1865 (iii).
Préclin, E. and E. Jarry. *Les luttes politiques et doctrinales aux XVIIe et XVIIIe siècles*. 2 vols. in one. Paris, 1955–1966.
—— and V.-L. Tapié. *Le dix-septième siècle*. 2nd edn., Paris, 1949.
Rambaud, A. 'La visite de Pierre le Grand à Paris: simples notes', *Revue politique et littéraire* (*Revue bleue*), lii (1896).
Samarin, Yu. F. *Stefan Yavorskii i Feofan Prokopovich*. Moscow, 1880.
Schuyler, E. *Peter the Great, Emperor of Russia*. 2 vols. London, 1884.
Šerech, J. 'On Theofan Prokopovič as Writer and Preacher in his Kiev Period', *Harvard Slavic Studies*, ii (1954).
——. 'Stefan Yavorsky and the Conflict of Ideologies in the Age of Peter I', *Slavonic and East European Review*, xxx (December 1951).
Sheremetevskii, V. 'Gavriil Buzhinskii', *Russkii biograficheskii slovar'*, iv (Moscow, 1914).
Shlyapkin, I. A. *Sv. Dimitrii Rostovskii i ego vremya (1651–1709g.)*. St. Petersburg, 1891.
Shmurlo, E. F. 'Kriticheskie zametki po istorii Petra Velikago. Ob uchastii patriarkha Ioakima v izbranii Petra Velikago na tsarstvo', *Zhurnal ministerstva narodnago prosveshcheniya* (May 1902).
——. *Petr Velikii v otsenke sovremennikov i potomstva*. St. Petersburg, 1912.
Simmons, J. S. G. 'H. W. Ludolf and the Printing of his *Grammatica Russica* at Oxford in 1696', *Oxford Slavonic Papers*, i (1950).

Sinaiskii, A. *Otnoshenie russkoi tserkovnoi vlasti k raskolu staroobryadstva v pervye gody sinodal'nago upravleniya (1721–1725)*. St. Petersburg, 1895.
Smirnov, P. S. *Spory i razdeleniya v russkom raskole v pervoi chetverti XVIII veka.* St. Petersburg, 1909.
Smirnov, S. K. *Istoriya moskovskoi Slavyano-greko-latinskoi akademii.* Moscow, 1855.
——. *Istoriya Troitskoi lavrskoi seminarii.* Moscow, 1867.
Spiridonova, E. V. *Ekonomicheskaya politika i ekonomicheskie vzglyady Petra I.* Moscow, 1952.
Stählin, K. *Geschichte Russlands von den Anfängen bis zur Gegenwart.* 4 vols. Stuttgart, 1923–1939.
Stupperich, R. 'Feofan Prokopoviˇ in Rom', *Zeitschrift für Osteuropäische Geschichte*, v (1931).
——. 'Feofan Prokopovičs Theologische Bestrebungen', *Kyrios*, iv (1936).
——. 'Feofan Prokopovič und Johann F. Buddeus', *Zeitschrift für Osteuropäische Geschichte*, ix (1935).
——. 'Feofan Prokopovič und seine akademische Wirksamkeit in Kiev', *Zeitschrift für Slavische Philologie*, xvii (1941).
——. *Staatsgedanke und Religionspolitik Peters des Grossen.* Berlin, 1936.
Sullivan, J. and C. L. Drage. 'Poems in an Unpublished Manuscript of the *Vinograd rossiiskii*', *Oxford Slavonic Papers*, New Series, i (1968).
Sumner, B. H. *Peter the Great and the Emergence of Russia.* London, 1950.
Syromyatnikov, V. I. *Reguliarnoe gosudarstvo Petra Pervogo i ego ideologiya.* Moscow, 1943.
Tamborra, A. 'Russia e Santa Sede all'epoca di Pietro il Grande', *Archivio Storico Italiano*, cxix (1961).
Tetzner, J. 'Feofan Prokopovič und die russische Frühaufklärung', *Zeitschrift für Slavistik*, iii (1958).
Tikhonravov, N. S. 'Moskovskie vol'nodumtsy nachala XVIII veka i Stefan Yavorskii', in Tikhonravov, *Sochineniya*, ii (Moscow, 1898).
Titlinov, B. 'Feodosii Yanovskii', *Russkii biograficheskii slovar'*, xxv (St. Petersburg, 1913).
——. 'Feofan Prokopovich', *Russkii biograficheskii slovar'*, xxv (St. Petersburg, 1913).
——. 'Feofilakt Lopatinskii', *Russkii biograficheskii slovar'*, xxv (St. Petersburg, 1913).
Tondini, C. *The Popes of Rome and the Popes of the Oriental Orthodox Church.* London, 1871.
Unbegaun, B. 'Russian Grammars before Lomonosov', *Oxford Slavonic Papers*, viii (1958).
Venturi, F. 'Feofan Prokopovič', *Annali delle facoltà di Lettere e Filosofia e di Magistero dell'Università di Cagliari*, xxi (1953).

Voltaire. *Histoire de l'Empire de Russie sous Pierre le Grand.* 2 vols. in one. N.p., 1765.

Vucinich, A. *Science in Russian Culture: a History to 1860.* Stanford, 1963.

Ware, T. *The Orthodox Church.* London, 1963.

Wuyts, A. 'Le Patriarcat russe au concile de Moscou de 1917–1918', *Orientalia Christiana Analecta*, cxxix (1941).

Zenkovsky, S. A. 'The Ideological World of the Denisov Brothers', *Harvard Slavic Studies*, iii (1957).

Index